Central Works of Philosophy

Central Works of Philosophy is a multi-volume set of essays on the core texts of the Western philosophical tradition. From Plato's *Republic* to the present day, the volumes range over 2,500 years of philosophical writing, covering the best, most representative, and most influential work of some of our greatest philosophers. Each essay has been specially commissioned and provides an overview of the work and clear and authoritative exposition of its central ideas. Together these essays introduce the masterpieces of the Western philosophical canon and provide an unrivalled companion for reading and studying philosophy.

T0325299

Central Works of Philosophy
Edited by John Shand

Volume 1: Ancient and Medieval

Volume 2: The Seventeenth and Eighteenth Centuries

Volume 3: The Nineteenth Century

Volume 4: The Twentieth Century: Moore to Popper

Volume 5: The Twentieth Century: Quine and After

Central Works of Philosophy Volume 5

The Twentieth Century: Quine and After

Edited by John Shand

McGill-Queen's University Press

Montreal & Kingston • Ithaca

In memory of my parents, Alexander Hesketh Shand and Muriel Olive Shand

ISBN-13: 978-0-7735-3082-9   ISBN-10: 0-7735-3082-7 (hardcover)
ISBN-13: 978-0-7735-3083-6   ISBN-10: 0-7735-3083-5 (paperback)

Legal deposit third quarter 2006
Bibliothèque nationale du Québec

Published simultaneously outside North America
by Acumen Publishing Limited

McGill-Queen's University Press acknowledges the financial support of the Government of Canada through the Book Publishing Development Program (BPIDP) for its activities.

Library and Archives Canada Cataloguing in Publication

Central works of philosophy / edited by John Shand.

Includes bibliographical references and indexes.
Contents: v. 1. Ancient and medieval -- v. 2. The seventeenth and eighteenth centuries -- v. 3. The nineteenth century -- v. 4. The twentieth century : Moore to Popper -- v. 5. The twentieth century : Quine and after.
ISBN-13: 978-0-7735-3015-7   ISBN-10: 0-7735-3015-0 (v. 1 : bound).
ISBN-13: 978-0-7735-3016-4   ISBN-10: 0-7735-3016-9 (v. 1 : pbk.).
ISBN-13: 978-0-7735-3017-1   ISBN-10: 0-7735-3017-7 (v. 2 : bound).
ISBN-13: 978-0-7735-3018-8   ISBN-10: 0-7735-3018-5 (v. 2 : pbk.).
ISBN-13: 978-0-7735-3052-2   ISBN-10: 0-7735-3052-5 (v. 3 : bound).
ISBN-13: 978-0-7735-3053-9   ISBN-10: 0-7735-3053-3 (v. 3 : pbk.).
ISBN-13: 978-0-7735-3080-5   ISBN-10: 0-7735-3080-0 (v. 4 : bound).
ISBN-13: 978-0-7735-3081-2   ISBN-10: 0-7735-3081-9 (v. 4 : pbk.)
ISBN-13: 978-0-7735-3082-9   ISBN-10: 0-7735-3082-7 (v. 5 : bound)
ISBN-13: 978-0-7735-3083-6   ISBN-10: 0-7735-3083-5 (v. 5 : pbk.)

1. Philosophy--Introductions. I. Shand, John, 1956-

B21.C45 2005   100   C2005-902037-7

Designed and typeset by Kate Williams, Swansea.
Printed and bound in Malta by Gutenberg Press.

Contents

Contributors

Ruth Abbey is Associate Professor of Political Science at the University of Notre Dame. She is the author of *Charles Taylor* (Acumen), editor of *Contemporary Philosophy in Focus: Charles Taylor* and the author of *Nietzsche's Middle Period*.

Anita Avramides is the Southover Manor Trust Fellow in Philosophy at St Hilda's College, Oxford. She works on philosophy of language, philosophy of mind, epistemology and metaphysics. She is the author of *Meaning and Mind: A Gricean Account of Language* and *Other Minds*, and editor of *Women of Ideas*.

Phillip Bricker is Professor and Head of Philosophy at the University of Massachusetts, Amherst. He wrote his doctoral dissertation on possible worlds under the direction of David Lewis. He previously held positions at the University of Notre Dame and Yale University.

John P. Burgess has taught since 1976 at Princeton University, where he is now Professor and Director of Undergraduate Studies. He is the author of *A Subject with No Object* (with Gideon Rosen), *Fixing Frege* and many papers in logic and philosophy of mathematics. His other philosophical interests include metaethics and 'pataphysics.

Peter Clark is Professor of Logic and Philosophy of Science at the University of St Andrews. He works primarily in the philosophy of physical sciences and mathematics and was Editor of the *British Journal for the Philosophy of Science* 1999–2005.

Gary Kemp is Senior Lecturer in Philosophy at the University of Glasgow. He has written on various aspects of the philosophy of logic and language and logic, the history of analytical philosophy, Quine and Davidson.

Anthony Simon Laden is Associate Professor of Philosophy at the University of Illinois, Chicago. He is the author of *Reasonably Radical: Deliberative Liberalism and the Politics of Identity* as well as numerous articles on democracy, deliberation and the work of John Rawls.

Kirk Ludwig is Professor of Philosophy at the University of Florida. He works in epistemology, philosophy of language, and philosophy of mind and action. He is editor of *Donald Davidson*, and co-author with Ernest Lepore of *Donald Davidson: Meaning, Truth, Language and Reality* and *Donald Davidson: Truth-theoretic Semantics*.

Alan Malachowski is Honorary Lecturer in Philosophy at the University of East Anglia. He is the author of *Richard Rorty* (Acumen) and editor of *Reading Rorty*.

A. W. Moore is Professor of Philosophy at the University of Oxford and a Fellow of St Hugh's College, Oxford. His publications include *The Infinite*; *Points of View*; and *Noble in Reason, Infinite in Faculty: Themes and Variations in Kant's Moral and Religious Philosophy* and he is editor of *Philosophy as a Humanistic Discipline*, a collection of essays by Bernard Williams. He is one of Bernard Williams's literary executors.

John Shand studied philosophy at the University of Manchester and King's College, Cambridge. He is an Associate Lecturer in Philosophy at The Open University and is the author of *Arguing Well* and *Philosophy and Philosophers: An Introduction to Western Philosophy* (second edition, Acumen) and editor of *Fundamentals of Philosophy*.

Paul Snowdon is Grote Professor of Mind and Logic at University College London. Before that, until 2001, he was a Fellow of Exeter College, Oxford. He has written mainly about perception and personal identity, but also about issues in the philosophy of P. F. Strawson, who was one of his tutors.

Tim Thornton is Professor of Philosophy and Mental Health at the University of Central Lancashire. His research interests include philosophy of psychiatry and philosophy of thought and language. He is the author of *Wittgenstein on Language and Thought* and *John McDowell* (Acumen) and co-author of the *Oxford Textbook of Philosophy and Psychiatry*.

Peter Vallentyne is Florence G. Kline Professor of Philosophy at the University of Missouri-Columbia. He writes on issues of liberty and equality, and left-libertarianism in particular. He edited *Equality and Justice* and *Contractarianism and Rational Choice* and coedited (with Hillel Steiner) *The Origins of Left Libertarianism* and *Left Libertarianism and Its Critics*.

Bernhard Weiss is Senior Lecturer in Philosophy at the University of Cape Town. He has published a number of papers on anti-realism in the philosophies of language and mathematics and is author of *Michael Dummett* (Acumen).

Preface

The works in the *Central Works of Philosophy* volumes have been chosen because of their fundamental importance in the history of philosophy and for the development of human thought. Other works might have been chosen; however, the underlying idea is that if any works should be chosen, then these certainly should be. In the cases where the work is a philosopher's *magnum opus* the essay on it gives an excellent overview of the philosopher's thought.

Chapter 1 is Gary Kemp on W. V. Quine's *Word and Object*. Quine's position generally might best be called "epistemic holism". This rejects the notion that there is a sharp distinction between necessary *a priori* analytic statements, which are true or false because of the meaning of the terms in the statements, and contingent *a posteriori* synthetic statements, which are true or false because of some fact or state of affairs in the world to which they refer. Rather, our statements as a whole meet the world; the "necessity" of some and the "contingency" of others are matters of degree, and reflect the amount of theoretical and conceptual reorganization and disruption that would be required in giving them up. Quine introduces holism in this book by showing how the meaning of words is inextricably linked to our theories about reality. There is an irremovable indeterminacy of translation between one language and another because there are no ultimate facts that determine the meanings of linguistic expressions uniquely. Empirical inputs are connected to linguistic *responses*, but these can always be variously interpreted; what matters is only that the meaning we ascribe to linguistic expressions works in a satisfactory way in actual empirical situations. He advocates a *naturalized epistemology* in which the theory of knowledge is to be understood not as a distinct *a priori* realm that may only be studied by philosophy, but as a part of a scientific empirical account of the world. A consequence is that metaphysics and ontology cannot be prised apart from science.

Chapter 2 is Paul Snowdon on P. F. Strawson's *Individuals*. Two connected motivations meet collaboratively in this book. One motivation derives from Strawson's view that "ordinary language" philosophy – which seeks to elucidate how our concepts work effectively by looking at how they are actually used, and in the process to dissolve certain philosophical "problems" – while not in itself defective, is philosophically incomplete in not giving an account of why we have the concepts, and thus metaphysical assumptions, that we do. The other motivation, which implies this conclusion about ordinary language philosophy, comes from Strawson's renewed interest in the Kantian transcendental project of showing that our experience as formed by our concepts in general necessarily presupposes certain basic concepts that do not display themselves on the surface of language. Without these basic concepts, we could not have the kind of experience of the world that we do as formed by our less basic concepts. This Strawson calls "descriptive metaphysics". This is unlike "revisionary metaphysics", which aims to show that, despite appearances, reality must essentially be quite other than how it seems to be as presented in our experience. Descriptive metaphysics aims to lay bare the most fundamental conceptual structures we must necessarily possess if our experience of the world is to be of the sort that it is. To do this, "transcendental arguments" must be given that show which elements of our conceptual structure could not be otherwise without our experience being radically altered or lacking altogether. We may lack the concept "red", for example, without any significant consequences for the rest of our conceptually mediated experience. If, however, we lacked the concept of material bodies (entities that are spatially three-dimensional that endure through time) and of persons (entities to which one may ascribe both mental states and bodily characteristics, neither being reducible to the other or eliminable), then our experience of the world would lose its most fundamental presuppositions. Our ability to individuate particular things and reidentify them as the same thing is essential to any imaginable possible experiences, and these depend necessarily on the fundamental presupposition of material bodies and persons encapsulated in the employment of the requisite concepts. Material bodies and persons are thus "basic" particulars. Other particulars, such as events, processes and states, may be located and reidentified only in relation to the basic ontology of material things and persons. Our ability to experience sounds, Strawson seeks to show, is dependent on their being located in a material universe; a purely auditory universe is impossible to imagine. Our ability to ascribe mental states to ourselves depends on our preparedness to ascribe mental states to others considered as persons. The question arises as to what such transcendental arguments show; whether they go beyond the hypothetical in relation to our experiences or whether they establish categorical conclusions about the world; whether they show categorically that the *world* must conform to our most basic conceptual structures, or whether they show merely hypothetically that if we are to have the *experiences* we do, then we must order our experience according to certain basic conceptual structures.

Chapter 3 is Anthony Simon Laden on John Rawls's *A Theory of Justice*. This work, along with that of Robert Nozick, contributed more than any other to shocking back to life the supposed corpse that political philosophy and first-order normative moral theory had become by the middle of the twentieth century. They had been consigned by analytic philosophy to a tomb above whose entrance was the warning that what lay within was the remains of ideas, discussion of which, as far as philosophy is concerned, was futile and illegitimate. The overall aim of *A Theory of Justice* is to present a notion of justice that is fully compatible with the constraints that obtain in liberal democratic societies. Rawls's argument is for justice as fairness. This means balancing the demands of liberty and equality. In liberal societies people are free and so are likely to have diverse life plans, but, it is contended, unlimited liberty leads to the injustices of inequality. The imposition of equality on the basis of utilitarian aggregate calculation ignores the fundamental differences between individuals and treats them as interchangeable units. Rawls aims to give an account that not only determines what would be a just arrangement of society, but also provides a way of its being seen as just by its citizens so as to enhance the society's stability. The basic idea is that of a hypothetical forum where various self-interested rational interest groups decide upon social arrangements behind a "veil of ignorance"; that is, no one knows what social or economic position any individual will occupy in the future society. Such a forum would be prudent and choose as just an arrangement where the worst off are at the highest possible level that is compatible with its being acceptable to all. This tends towards reducing inequality while not eliminating it. Against a background of full and adequate access to rights and liberties, inequality may not be eliminated at all costs, but only if it makes the poor better off and does not make everyone else intolerably worse off.

Chapter 4 is Peter Vallentyne on Robert Nozick's *Anarchy, State, and Utopia*. There are two main aims in Nozick's book: the first is to show that a minimal state (a "night-watchman" that protects only against violence, theft, fraud and breach of contract) could be legitimate even without the consent of all those governed by it (this stands counter to the anarchist); the second is to show that no more than a minimal state could be legitimate unless it had the consent of all. By a "state" Nozick means an organization that claims at least a *de facto* monopoly of the use of coercive force over all those within its territory. Nozick takes *rights* as primary and prior to the existence of the state, and these rights should not be overridden by other moral considerations except in extreme circumstances. Such rights are essential to human beings as rational normative creatures who have the capacity thereby to live or *lead* their lives, and not merely *have* a certain sort of life. Rights, which begin basically with self-ownership, bodily integrity and non-interference, extend to the ownership of objects in the world, and to the just transfer of such objects to others. A state is legitimate if it is typically just in its protection of the rights of all. This legitimacy arises not out of consent, or from the utilitarian benefits arising from the state, but from its emerging as an organization protecting individual rights. Justice is historical and procedural, not an end state of affairs; if initial entitlements are just, and all the steps are just from that beginning (which may involve compensation being given in cases of injustice), then the outcome is just too. Only a minimal state can be justified as legitimate on Nozick's view because of two claims that operate in the same direction: the range of basic rights, the protection of which gives a state legitimacy without consent, is substantial but limited; the attempt to extend that legitimacy beyond the role of rights protection would require universal consent, which is a non-starter.

Chapter 5 is Bernhard Weiss on Michael Dummett's *Truth and Other Enigmas*. This book gathers together in a substantial collection several of Dummett's essays that have made a significant contribution to central and fundamental areas of philosophy. That it contains his ideas on the nature of truth is plainly highlighted in the title; in addition, there is an examination of such enigmatic notions as meaning, time, causation, realism, proof, vagueness and the nature of philosophy itself. As such, the collection conveys well both the depth of Dummett's ideas and the breadth of his concerns. Since the book is a collection of disparate essays written over some considerable period of time, it would be a mistake to look for a unifying theme. This is not to say there are not philosophical theses of broad scope, and a recurrence of certain interconnected philosophical views across the essays. With respect to truth, Dummett questions the viability of realism according to which truth-conditions are determinately either fulfilled or not, independently of our ability to settle the matter; and so he is an anti-realist in this sense. He also questions, in connection with this and other matters, the universal validity of the principle of bivalence, according to which every statement is either true or false. He takes the view that language derives its meaning from its use – that is, by what is done with its different elements by its users – so that for two speakers to agree on their use of a term is for them to agree about its meaning. Many philosophers have held that it is impossible to justify deduction, for if we attempt to justify a rule of deduction, we appear to face a dilemma: either we employ the very rule we are attempting to justify, in which case our justification is circular, or we employ other rules that will then themselves require justification *ad infinitum*. Dummett tackles this enigma by distinguishing between different kinds of circularity and different kinds of justification. On the subject of time, Dummett supports McTaggart's arguments for the unreality of time, providing that what is required for something to be real is that it can have a complete description couched in terms totally independent of any observer.

Chapter 6 is Alan Malachowski on Richard Rorty's *Philosophy and the Mirror of Nature*. Rorty's purpose in this book is to break the hold of a pervasive picture we have of our relation to the world, one that has also bewitched philosophy into having impossible aspirations. The picture we have of this relation is that our minds, or language, can mirror reality; that we have our conception of reality expressed in thought or language, on the one hand, and a world of non-linguistic facts, on the other; the conception is accurate or true when the facts are as the conception claims them to be, that is, when they match. Against this, Rorty is an anti-representationalist and anti-foundationalist. No sense can be given to the dualism of representation/world as required by such a mirroring metaphor; one where we may hold a definitively plain mirror up to reality and reflect it accurately; one where we may be successful or unsuccessful in representing reality in such a manner as to ultimately transcend the totality of the historically located conceptual-belief system we happen to have. We cannot be finally and timelessly right about the world. There is no way to step outside the totality of our conceptual-belief system, take it in one hand, and compare it to the world, raw and unadorned by all concepts and beliefs that render it intelligible to us. This is anti-foundational in that it denies that there are any unrevisable non-theoretical bits of our conceptual-belief system that directly hook on to reality. All we have, and can have, is the conceptual-belief system, which we try to render as coherent as possible according to the sociohistorical standards of our time. Philosophy must therefore give up on its high aim of providing a transcultural common denominator, a transcendental perspective, which might step outside all of the concrete social practices that generate systems indicating what is true and what we are justified in believing. Our beliefs and theories are fallible all the way down, so that our conceptual-belief system is comprehensibly revisable according to what we want from it. In all cases while these revisions are made in a piecemeal manner it is also the case that nothing is immune to change. The new role for philosophy is the edifying one of facilitating conversations between diverse cultures.

Chapter 7 is Kirk Ludwig on Donald Davidson's *Essays on Actions and Events*. This volume collects seminal papers by Davidson in the philosophy of mind and action, many of which revolutionized thinking in these areas. The papers develop Davidson's ideas in three main stages. In the first stage, represented by the papers on the philosophy of action, Davidson proposes that actions are events, specifically bodily movements, which are caused by the agent's reasons for them, and which can be redescribed in terms of their effects. Thus, I move my finger, and this causes another's hurt; I thereby hurt another. Yet this is not a distinct action but the same action described in terms of an effect. Davidson's argument that reasons are causes of actions was first advanced in "Actions, Reasons and Causes", against the prevailing orthodoxy that denied that reasons for actions were their causes, and was so successful as to become the current orthodoxy. The second stage is the development of an account of the nature of events as datable particulars, individuated by their causal relations, and admitting of multiple descriptions, a view implicit in Davidson's philosophy of action. In particular, Davidson argued that understanding adverbial modification in ordinary action sentences requires treating such sentences as committed to events treated as datable particulars, and the adverbs as predicates of them. Thus, if I say that "Lois clapped loudly", then I say in effect, on this account, that there was an event of clapping by Lois and it was loud. In the third stage Davidson argues for a position on the mind–body relation that he calls "anomalous monism" (meaning: "irregular" and "one substance" respectively). According to this position each token mental event is identical with a token physical event, but there are no strict psychophysical laws connecting mental with physical events, which would require type–type correlations. This is a form of non-reductive materialism, an identity theory of particular mental and physical events without an identity theory of mental types with physical types. The picture that emerges treats human beings and their actions as as much a part of the natural world and causal nexus as the planets in their orbits, while still seeing them as something over and above the organized movements of atomic particles.

Chapter 8 is John P. Burgess on Saul Kripke's *Naming and Necessity*. This short, intensely concentrated book contains ideas that make a deep and original contribution to the foundation of philosophy, some of a seemingly quite technical nature, while also being a work remarkably wide-ranging in its implications. In certain areas of philosophy, in particular logic, metaphysics and philosophy of language, the impression of the ideas is indelible. Kripke's thought impinges on such matters as the nature of names, descriptions, essences, identity, the *a priori* and *a posteriori*, the modes of necessity, contingency and possibility, counterfactuals, and natural kinds. In this Kripke undermines some assumptions that had come to be entrenched in analytical philosophy. One such is that that which is necessary can only be known *a priori* and consists of analytic truths, and that that which is contingent can only be known *a posteriori* and consists of synthetic truths. This fits with two intuitions: first, that there is a class of truths, exemplified by mathematics, that appear to be such that they could not have been otherwise, that are true independently of any fact about the world and thus can be known only independently of experience; secondly, that there is a class of truths, such as those of science, that appear to be such that they could have been otherwise, that are true because of some fact about the world and thus can be known only by experience. Thus, there are no necessary *a posteriori* synthetic truths, and no contingent *a priori* analytic truths. For Kripke this neat packaging runs illegitimately across, and pushes together, claims in the realms of metaphysics and epistemology: what is and can be the case on the one hand, and how what is the case may be known on the other. Why should there not be truths that are necessary that may only be known by experience? Why should there not be truths that are contingent that may be known independently of experience? He contends that there is a large class of necessary *a posteriori* synthetic truths: truths that could not have been otherwise, but that can be known only by experience. He claims also that there are contingent *a priori* truths: truths that could have been otherwise, but that can be known independently of experience. The large class of necessary *a posteriori* truths consists of identity statements: things that are thought to be different, but that are in fact the same, and are the same necessarily so. If *a* and *b* are "rigid designators" then they designate (refer to) the same object in all possible worlds. In these cases saying that *a* is identical to *b* (Hesperus [the Evening Star] is Phosphorus [the Morning Star] – that is, Venus) may only be discovered by experience is compatible with saying that *a* is necessarily identical with *b*, for to deny it would be to say that *a* might not have been *a*; but *a* is necessarily identical with itself. Such identities, although necessary, are not a matter of logical analyticity, but are empirical discoveries.

Chapter 9 is Peter Clark on Hilary Putnam's, *Truth, Reason and History*. This book has been highly influential, and contains much-discussed seminal chapters covering a wide area of philosophy: metaphysics, epistemology, meaning, rationality, the mind–body problem and values. The ideas in the book manifest part of the process by which Putnam – to some heretically – moved away from, and became critical of, the analytic–positivist philosophical outlook (a post-analytic path that others have followed) in which he was trained and to which he was initially a contributor. His final destination is quasi-Kantian. At the heart of this is the pervasive denial of metaphysical realism and an assertion that the sort of objectivity it promises to grant is spurious. Far from bolstering the objective authority of natural science and moral values, metaphysical realism weakens it and makes their claims ever open to scepticism by setting up a correspondence relation between our conception of reality and reality itself that is, in principle, impossible to check or give content to. To think about anything at all is to employ concepts; there is no way to take our concepts of reality in one hand and compare them, in the other hand, to unconceptualized reality itself, and thus see if the concepts truly correspond to what is there or to the "furniture of the world". Metaphysical realism is an empty and useless metaphysic. Relativism is also untenable because to endorse it erodes utterly the distinction between something being true and merely seeming to be true, and this in turn does away with making sense of the idea that we are capable of error. Putnam proposes a middle way called "internal realism" that lies between the extremes of metaphysical realism and relativism. Such a position allows us to make sense in a non-empty way, not only of views of reality being true or false, and that there are facts, but also similarly to make sense of the objectivity of values. Values are rendered objective not by metaphysical realism, but by inextricably linking them to the less contentious existence of facts; the fact–value distinction is denied; the description of facts comes laden with values, so there is no problem of justifying our applying values to supposedly value-free facts. In the case of meaning, Putnam holds a position of linguistic externalism according to which meanings are determined not solely by the content of mental states; rather, they depend, in part, on external facts about the world. In all cases, the notion of objectivity here is that of human objectivity defined internally according to our system of concepts and theories considered as a whole, not a notion derived from the possibility of a God's-eye view of reality or of unthought-of-reality as it is in itself.

Chapter 10 is A. W. Moore on Bernard Williams's *Ethics and the Limits of Philosophy*. This book may be seen as a culmination of Williams's substantial contribution to moral philosophy. While Williams's ideas encourage philosophy to assist in a greater understanding of the actuality of lived ethical experience, the limit is that it cannot provide an ethical *theory* that would act as a general test for the correctness of our ethical beliefs. One may set about justifying specific ethical reasoning; but there is no hope of justifying all ethical reasoning in one way, from some "Archimedean point". Nor is there a way of converting the amoralist by argument to take up ethical considerations when deliberating on his actions; the attempts by Aristotle and Kant both fail. Williams thinks it is an arrogant mistake for moral philosophy to attempt to monopolize the answer to the Socratic question "How should one live?" and exclude other relevant considerations, including both practical and aesthetic. Within ethics, no theory, such as utilitarianism, can sort out our ethical intuitions, for there is always the question of what authority the theory has over the intuitions themselves. Williams argues that ethical language is a poor guide to the metaphysics of values, and that value and fact are intricately intertwined. The possibility of ethical knowledge is not rejected by Williams, however. But such knowledge derives from the possession of rich ("thick") ethical concepts and from ethical deliberation being from a point of view. Such a position is neither fully objectivist nor trivially relativist. Controversially, Williams contradicts Socrates' dictum that a worthy life should be reflected on and examined; too much of such reflection can leave one adrift from the ethical concepts that are needed to engage in any ethical thought. The allure of morality is that its most valued qualities are qualities we may possess regardless of any kind of luck, but this too is a deep illusion.

Chapter 11 is Anita Avramides on Thomas Nagel's *The View From Nowhere*. Nagel's book is concerned with the reconciliation of two ways in which we can have a view of the world and our place in it: the subjective (a view from *our* point of view) and the objective (a view from *nowhere*). Together they reveal a remarkable capacity of the human mind: to have our personal perspective, and yet also to be able to step outside it and present a view of the world that is from no particular perspective. The problem that arises is owing to the way in which these two views seem to present us with conflicting judgements about the nature of reality and ourselves. The conflict spills over from metaphysics into matters such as the nature of consciousness, freedom, morality, politics, death and the meaning of life. The subjective may be said to be encapsulated by the world as given in the everyday phenomenology of our experience, while the objective is instantiated in science, which aims for universal validity, stripping away the contingencies of any particular point of view. Nagel aims to juxtapose the two outlooks "at full strength", and to show how the two can be accommodated in such a way that, should this be accomplished, it would give a complete view of the world. This reconciliation rejects the various attempts there have been to reduce one of the perspectives, and the reality revealed by it, to that of the other, as well as attempts to eliminate one horn of the dilemma altogether by showing that its reality is somehow illusory. Nor is Nagel interested in going down the quietist route that aims to show that the duality of the subjective and objective is a misconception that cannot, in truth, arise in the first place. Nagel is guided by a robust realism in holding that there really are two valid perspectives on things: our subjective point of view, where our personal conscious awareness is about the most important thing there can be for us, and the objective point of view, where in the great scheme of the universe we matter for nothing. He aims to show that only by taking both views seriously may we hope to have a proper view of reality.

Chapter 12 is Phillip Bricker on David Lewis's *On the Plurality of Worlds*. This book is a fundamental and systematic work of metaphysics. Philosophers in a wide range of areas within philosophy use modal notions to analyse their subject matter. By modal notions is meant terms such as "possible", "impossible", "necessary" and "contingent", which are used in expressions that claim that something is, for example, possible or that it is necessary. Indeed, such expressions are used extensively in mundane talk. The question is: what is being said when we make a modal claim that something is possible? To what does such a claim ontologically commit us? If we examine a table, we can see that it is actually brown, and we know what we are claiming when we say that it is actually brown: just that it is the case that it is brown. But suppose we claim that the table might possibly be blue. Blue is not a property of the table; if it were, it would actually be blue. But we cannot see the possible blueness of the table; it does not appear as one of its properties along with its actual brownness. One way of making sense of the claim that the table is possibly blue is to say that the table has a counterpart, similar to the actual table, in some *possible world*, and that in that world the table is blue. Lewis systematically defends the view that the best way to make sense of the talk of possibility is to posit the reality of possible worlds in which such possibilities exist. This position is called *modal realism*. There is in fact an array of possible worlds covering the vast number of ways in which things might possibly be, in addition to how they actually are. These parallel possible worlds differ only in their relation to us, and are spatio-temporally and causally isolated from our actual world. Lewis systematically shows that the other ways of construing modal talk that have been proposed, which he calls "ersatz modal realism", are prone to greater problems than modal realism. Lewis's view ushers in a metaphysics that is powerful, wide-ranging and controversial in its implications.

Chapter 13 is Ruth Abbey on Charles Taylor's *Sources of the Self*. In this book Taylor seeks to trace the route by which we have arrived at our modern conception of the self or person, and this is done selectively as a consequence of focusing on how self-understanding is connected to moral values. Selfhood and the good are inextricably intertwined. This is not, however, a critical genealogy – as one may find in Nietzsche – in which discovery of origins in the form of underlying conceptions of the self throw suspicion on the validity of the accompanying values. Rather, the aim is to increase the depth of our understanding of our values by revealing how they have a source in something that could hardly be more basic: our understanding of the self. Indeed, he is in addition, in the balance, positive about the modern notion of selfhood and its values. The attraction of a particular moral outlook is to be traced in the end to its fitting appropriately with our conception of ourselves. In the process of this we may emancipate ourselves from the notion that the modern self is a universal timeless notion, rather than one that has emerged as a result of an historical process; we may also see from this historical perspective that the consequent complexity of the modern self arises from several different strands of selfhood, and this should leave us unafraid when embracing the corresponding plurality of values that such a self leaves open to us. Taylor's conception of the self is primarily a moral one, one formed by "inescapable frameworks"; these are moral frameworks in the broadest sense of beliefs and judgements that give shape, meaning and direction to our lives. No particular moral framework is necessary, but that one has some framework or other is not an optional extra, for they act to place us in the world, defining our sense of who and what we are by relating us to that which matters most to us.

Chapter 14 is Tim Thornton on John McDowell's *Mind and World*. This work aims to show how what may be regarded as the most intractable problem in philosophy may be overcome. The problem is that of giving a satisfactory account of the nature of the relationship between the mind and the world, that is, the relationship between our thought about the world and the world itself. The problem that emerges presents itself as a seemingly intractable dilemma. In order to think about the world, for it to become an object or the content of a thought, and play a part in our having reasons for concluding that the world is a certain way, the world must be intelligible and thus conceptualized. This, however, leaves the worrying predicament that all we have is a free-floating system of conceptual thought. We can never be sure that it reflects the structure of reality because all we can have to check the truthfulness of the picture of reality presented in our concepts is other concepts; there would be no "friction" between our view of the world and the world itself. On the other hand, it is useless to posit unconceptualized elements in our experience of the world, outside the circle of our conceptual thinking, by which we may rationally assess the truth of our picture of the world as presented in our conceptual scheme, since such elements would merely be ineffable brute happenings with no intelligible content that could enter into our reasoning. We cannot "look around" our concepts to view the world stripped of concepts; we cannot take a "sideways on" view and so compare our conceptual scheme and the world. McDowell's strategy is not to solve the problem by showing how one of these alternatives can work, despite appearances, but rather to show how, when properly considered, the supposed dualism of thought and world cannot arise in the first place. The dualism itself – and the concomitant myth of the fully "subjective" and fully "objective" – is a presumptive after-the-fact abstraction that has separated mind and world, but which only makes sense when referred to something more basic. McDowell takes even more seriously than Kant himself the Kantian notion that it makes no sense to talk about our experience of the world without such experience being brought under conceptual thought, and it makes no sense to suggest that our conceptual thought can be cut loose from its being about the world. An intelligible world implies that there is thinker to think about it, and a thinker implies that there is an intelligible world about which the thinker thinks.

John Shand

The Twentieth Century: Quine and After

Introduction

John Shand

It would be a distortion to attribute to philosophy in the latter half of the twentieth century any overall unity of philosophical outlook, and I shall, therefore, not try to impose one. Moreover, the closeness to the present of the works in this period makes it even more difficult than usual to discern a prevailing direction in recent philosophy or identify what value posterity will assign to any particular part of it. If one true observation about late-twentieth-century philosophy may be made, it is perhaps only the trite one of its diversity.[1]

To say, however, that there is no discernible overall unity of philosophical outlook – such as realism, or naturalism, or transcendental idealism – in the period under consideration is not to say there were not at different times within it relative concentrations of interest on particular areas in the subject of philosophy, or that there was not for a limited time the stepping to the fore of certain philosophical methods and approaches.

It might be thought that a unity could be granted negatively to at least some of the philosophers considered here through their common rejection of logical positivism, a philosophical movement that had its heyday in the first half of the twentieth century.[2] But this would be a mistake and far too simple. Partly this is because logical positivism is not the pure unfaceted singular doctrine some suppose it to be. Logical positivism sought, as a generality, on the negative side, to eliminate great swaths of traditional philosophy; rather than attempt to "solve" so-called philosophical "problems", it "dissolved" them by casting them into an outer darkness of literal nonsense where no "solutions" are required.

Propositions are either analytic/*a priori* and trivial (at best the concern of logic and mathematics), or synthetic/*a posteriori* and empirical (and thus the concern of science), leaving no sort of genuine propositions in which to express putative truly philosophical "problems" or "solutions" (such propositions would have to be both *a priori* and not trivially analytic); rather, all that is left is literal nonsense. Logical positivism on the positive side sought to establish that the empirical methods of science delineate the boundaries of legitimate cognitive enquiry about the world. These negative and positive aspects are connected, for a good number of the proffered propositions expressing putative philosophical problems, if not nonsense, turn out when properly analysed to be propositions expressing logical or empirical problems in disguise, their corresponding solutions being matters of logic or science. This connection must be noticed in order to understand one important aspect of the influence of logical positivism on later philosophers. Several pillars of logical positivism certainly came under attack by the philosophers in this volume. W. V. Quine undermines the analytic/synthetic distinction and the corresponding *a priori/a posteriori* distinction on which some of the logical positivist arguments depend; but his differences with the leading logical positivist Rudolf Carnap, for example, even on this matter are less substantial than they appear to be. On a less superficial level there are similarities between Quine's naturalism and logical positivism owing to the common influence of pragmatism.[3] Saul Kripke certainly argued, contrary to the logical positivist view, that the *a priori* and *a posteriori* and the necessary and contingent need not be, respectively, coextensive; but his views may nevertheless be seen as emerging from a critical engagement with insights found in logical positivism. Others questioned the view that moral assertions are non-cognitive emotive affirmations of feelings. Nevertheless many philosophers, following logical positivism's greatest period of influence, took as much from the position as they rejected. Partly this is simply a matter of a perpetuation of logico-linguistic methods and tools of philosophical logic to determine the nature and limits of philosophy, although in essence these predate logical positivism and refer back to the seminal work of Gottlob Frege and Bertrand Russell. Most notably however the belief in science as the ultimate route to knowledge, under the banner of a universal naturalism that rejects the existence of any special autonomous class of philosophical truths, surfaces as strongly in Quine and others as it does in logical positivism, albeit the grounds for it are different. Many philosophers, while critical of some fundamental doctrines of logical positivism, continue to maintain the essential continuity of philosophy and science rather than their discontinuity. Other views, in some ways more traditional ones, that persist in identifying an autonomous class of philosophical problems inaccessible to science are, in a sense, and unlike logical positivism, fundamentally antagonistic to the influential naturalistic strand in recent philosophy. Certainly it is true that metaphysics, impermissible according to logical positivism, revived during the second half of the twentieth century.[4] But even here matters are not straight-forward. Verificationism is a central tenet of logical positivism through which it sought to delineate the bounds of the meaningful, a putative proposition being meaningful if and only if there is some way of verifying it, so that in general the meaning of a proposition is its method of verification. It was rejected because no coherent formulation could be arrived at, but surfaces in a derivative and attenu-ated form as anti-realism, a popular position among recent philosophers such as Michael Dummett. Further, Richard Rorty holds, as does logical positivism, that there are no distinctive philosophical problems and announces the demise of traditional philosophy; his grounds are not that the propositions of philosophy are nonsense, but nevertheless, as with logical positivism, Rorty holds that they do not form any distinct ahistorical concatenation of "problems" and matching "solutions". Hilary Putnam is sometimes characterized as rejecting logical posi-tivism virtually wholesale, but is in fact best seen as one of its most perceptive severe critics, someone who wishes to incorporate its insights in a philosophi-cal outlook that, unlike logical positivism, does justice to the human sciences and avoids physicalist reductionism. One is on safer ground in the area of eth-ics, where any attempt at building a substantive ethical theory was regarded as folly by the logical positivists because putative ethical propositions are merely emotive expressions of taste. Here indeed the core emotivist idea of logical posi-tivism was rejected by many moral philosophers so that they might once again have something valuable to say about ethics. Even so matters are not so simple, because subjectivism, if not pure emotivism, in ethics persisted even as ethical positions were constructed; nor is emotivism itself quite dead, especially in aes-thetics. So the claim that there is no significant unity among the philosophers of the period examined in this volume stands. Indeed, to repeat the earlier trite comment, an ever-greater diversity of views, approaches and styles in philoso-phy seems the most noticeable feature of the period.

A focus of philosophy in the 1950s, at least in the English-speaking world, was so-called Oxford "ordinary language" philosophy. A notable representa-tive was J. L. Austin, who took the analysis of ordinary language to the most intricate and refined level.[5] The movement was based on the view that many entrenched philosophical problems could be solved or eliminated if only one paid careful enough attention to the way language in the minutiae of its opera-tions is actually used. Austin was clear that this attention to words and their meaning is not primarily about language, but rather that it would give an under-standing of the things to which language refers. The position was also marked by its emphasis on the essential separation between the conceptual problems of philosophy and the empirical problems of natural science. A good example of both these characteristics is Gilbert Ryle's *Concept of Mind*, which gives an account of the mind by carefully dispelling endemic confusion among the concepts used in talk about mind, and in so doing makes no reference whatsoever to any scientific literature or research.[6] Indeed, the book is notable for containing no footnotes or formal citations, not even of other works of philosophy. This is not to denigrate the approach; on the contrary, it is a *tour de force* of pure philosophizing.

Many philosophers take the view – a view going far beyond and by no means restricted to ordinary language philosophers – that there is an essential discontinuity between philosophy and science. They maintain that there is an ineradicable core of philosophical problems that no empirical scientific investigations alone can solve. This, it is argued, is because any attempt to solve such problems scientifically either leaves the problems untouched (for example, the problem of free will, issues in ethics, the question of how we should live) or delivers up answers that cannot fail to be question-begging (for example, on the question of whether or not perceptions in general are veridical, how we are to distinguish veridical from non-veridical perception, and the nature of good evidence and knowledge). There are assumptions that are essentially philosophical that undergird natural science and the authority of these assumptions cannot be established by science or "naturalized".[7]

It is with works written at the beginning of the 1960s by P. F. Strawson and W. V. Quine that we begin this volume. After the ordinary language movement, the return to a technical or scientific mode of philosophizing came quickly in the form of Quine's naturalism. His thought may be seen as an amalgam of austere analytic philosophy and robust American pragmatism. A characteristic of analytic philosophy is the promulgation of rigorous formal methods in philosophy and it draws on the logical apparatus provided by Frege, Russell and A. N. Whitehead. A central belief is that philosophical problems may be systematically cleared up analogous to the way in which science solves problems concerning the nature of the natural world.[8] Pragmatism holds that, when treated in a purely abstract manner, philosophical concepts and problems lead to futile irresolvable debates; they should rather, if they are to be given sense and considered fruitfully, be understood in terms of their substantial efficacy, that is, the difference, if any, that their supposition makes to our experience when dealing with the world. In his naturalism, Quine made full use of the logical techniques devised by Frege, Russell and Whitehead at the beginning of the twentieth century. It meshed with a revival of interest in the nineteenth- and early-twentieth-century American pragmatist movement, the best known of its proponents being William James, John Dewey, and C. S. Peirce.[9] Quine's outlook, although tremendously dominant especially in America, was and remains contentious, and is no different in that respect from any other philosophical position. Naturalism had been out of fashion since the middle of the nineteenth century. It stresses the continuity between philosophy and science, not just with respect to methods but also in its content, and holds that seemingly intractable philosophical problems may be solved through scientific investigation; if they cannot, then it is more than likely that the problems are simply poorly framed. There is no special distinct set of philosophical statements or problems; rather, we address the world by way of the court of experience with a single holistic web of interconnected and interdependent statements. The only difference between any two statements is their degree of entrenchment in our total outlook; the difference never amounts to a profound difference in logical kind. No statement is absolutely immune from abandonment; rather, abandonment simply involves the consequence of lesser or greater degrees of adjustment in the rest of the system depending on the statement's place within it. Indeed, changing all the statements making up the system, but not all at the same time, is a possibility.[10] Naturalism is a highly attractive position for many philosophers. One reason may be that it offers hope of bringing philosophy in line with the brilliant success of science, and reassuringly settles the troubling thought that philosophy may be at worst vacuous and fraudulent, or at best embarrassingly unable to show definitive progress, the whole enterprise being based on some deep catastrophic error. Science seems to provide satisfying answers by solving patently genuine puzzles. There is always the contrasting worrying question besetting philosophy: if its puzzles are genuine, why have they not been definitively solved by now? One way out of this dilemma, that does not need to conclude that those philosophical problems that are genuine may be naturalized as scientific problems, is to argue that the function of philosophy is to make explicit, through conceptual analysis, fundamental aspects of thought, action and our relation to the world that are tacitly understood and seemingly simple in each of these spheres but are in fact complex, and to argue that they may not be understood by scientific enquiry because any such enquiry must logically presuppose them.

It was never the case that naturalism was going to get it all its own way and go unchallenged. Virtually simultaneously with Quine's ideas, Strawson outlines a quite different view of philosophy, one that connects conceptual analysis with a neo-Kantian transcendentalism, the latter having been out of fashion since the nineteenth century. In his *The Bounds of Sense*,[11] Strawson makes a connection directly to Kant. In Strawson's view, there is an autonomous realm of philosophical issues out of reach of science, a fundamental part of which he calls "descriptive metaphysics".[12] The difference between descriptive metaphysics and ordinary language philosophy, which also engages in conceptual analysis, is the higher-level ambition and abstraction of the former. Our most basic concepts, those that make any thought at all possible, are not to be discovered through an examination of ordinary language; they are not readily displayed on the surface of language. Less general and less abstract ordinary concepts ("cat") presuppose the application of basic indispensable ones ("material thing"). In order to identify the most basic concepts speculative reflection is required on the general transcendental – one might say logical, rather than empirical – conditions for the possibility of our experience of the world being what it is in its most essential aspects. For example, we may ask what concepts we must employ for it to be possible for us to have any sort of objective experiences. Strawson argues that employing the concept of material bodies is required if we are to think of the world as containing reidentifiable particulars.

Another characteristic of philosophy in the 1950s was a view about ethics, one that for a while became orthodoxy. One finds it in such notable ethicists as C. L. Stevenson, P. H. Nowell-Smith and R. M. Hare.[13] The view was that the proper function of philosophy *per se* with respect to ethics is only the conceptual meta-ethical task of assigning ethical language to its correct logical or linguistic category, and not that of determining what is right or wrong. The job of philosophy is to determine what it is we are doing when we assert that something is ethically right or wrong, and that job may be carried out in isolation from establishing *what* is ethically right or wrong. Few philosophers today would hold either view. Nowell-Smith thinks that metaethics (second-order ethics) can be carried on in complete separation from normative substantive ethics (first-order ethics). Stevenson's form of emotivism too is an influential example of this. He suggested that moral assertions do not state facts (the opposite view being, prima facie, to some at least, a problematic idea), not even facts about a person's feeling towards something, but rather they express approval or disapproval, and so indicate wishes. Moral statements were like requests. Thus, moral language is prescriptive rather than descriptive. Hare agreed with this, but in addition thought the prescriptions at issue were implicitly universal; an intrinsic feature of moral judgements is universalizability; they must apply on all occasions in which the circumstances are the same in relevant respects. One will, however, strive in vain to extract from this much in the way of moral guidance in the form of first-order normative substantive ethical prescriptions. It is more about form and consistency than about content. To assert that if an ethical prescription applies in a certain way to a given situation, then it applies to all situations where the relevant circumstances are the same, does not give any guidance as to which particular ethical prescription applies in any given circumstance. The upshot of this was a decline in the traditional contribution of philosophy to substantive ethical debate. Its function became the formal one of giving the correct logical classification of moral language. This, it was said, is as it should be, for philosophers *qua* philosophers were surely no more obviously morally wise than anyone else.[14] This was to give up one of the ancient roles of philosophy and was an abdication of its responsibility to provide viable rational criteria for ethical choices. It is perhaps no accident that a fashionable intellectual pose of the period was one of nihilistic *Angst*, a position often associated – in a manner that is often inaccurate – with existentialism and the proposal that all ethical choices, and other constraints on how one may live one's life, are ultimately arbitrary.[15] In any event it led many to accuse philosophy of having become etiolated and arid, detached from anything that really matters, a subject whose activity consists of mere pointless wordplay.[16] All this was to change dramatically.

This climate in philosophical ethics, as just outlined, contributed to the moribund state of political philosophy during the 1950s and 1960s, a state that existed despite the political tumult and the violent clash of ideologies of the surrounding times. Many philosophers did not see it as their place *as philosophers* to contribute to the debates thrown up by such events. A few notable exceptions made valuable contributions to political philosophy, such as Isaiah Berlin in his essay "Two Concepts of Liberty"[17] and F. A. Hayek in *The Constitution of Liberty*.[18] Political philosophy was dramatically jolted back to life in the early 1970s with the appearance of two great works in the subject: Robert Nozick's *Anarchy, State, and Utopia* and John Rawls's *A Theory of Justice*.[19] Here were two philosophers who were fully engaged with first-order substantive political matters, with how society should be organized in an ethical sense. Nozick's work was concerned with the justification of political authority and obligation – that others may acquire the legitimate right to coerce us and we are under a duty to obey them – and it led to the conclusion that only a minimal "night watchman" state could be theoretically and morally justified.[20] A key idea here is that for order and prosperity to arise they need not be directly planned for; indeed, planning for them directly undermines them. Rather, order and "the wealth of nations" (as Adam Smith coined it[21]) emerge best spontaneously as an unintended consequence of the enlightened self-interested actions of individuals, guided by the operations of the free market, under the rule of law. This was seized upon by those, sometimes grouped under the name "libertarians", who wished to roll back the extension of the state into the private lives of citizens. John Rawls's ideas are also concerned with the fundamental legitimacy of the laws that we may have an obligation to obey, and the right of coercion when we do not obey. Laws gain such legitimacy through their originating in a process of deliberation that is fair and that can be seen to be fair. The laws are arrived at by a hypothetical process of deliberation that takes place behind a "veil of ignorance" such that individuals and groups of individuals are, while deciding on the laws, blind to the position they might occupy in the consequent society. His conclusions imply a more extensive role for the state than is the case for Nozick, owing to the higher priority Rawls gives to equality as a value, in particular the steps required to ameliorate the injustices of inequality. However, his view is still one consonant with the usual conception of liberal democracy.

There was eventually a general revival in first-order normative substantive ethical theory.[22] Philosophers became again unafraid of tackling issues such as how we should live our lives in the most general sense; indeed, in recent times there has been a veritable flowering of serious work in this area.[23] Many see this as philosophy returning to its roots following a brief aberrant arid period (some might say) in which those roots were denied and the true nature and purpose of philosophy subjugated. A recent trend in philosophy takes this yet further, and may be seen as reattaching philosophy to its roots in an even more profound way. Rather than, at its best, standing apart from the world and pronouncing on how one should live, philosophy – the philosophical stance and philosophical activity – may be seen, under a rich and engaged conception of the subject, as the archetype of an edifying and enlightened way of life, and advocated as such. It is a way of life that is not merely appropriate to the age in which we live, but essential to and necessitated by a true understanding of the human condition.[24]

There was a great interest in philosophy of language in the central part of the period under consideration. Much of this was carried out in a formal or canonical manner, often drawing on the apparatus of philosophical logic, the better to tackle philosophical problems. Quine, Dummett, Donald Davidson, Kripke, Putnam, David Lewis and John McDowell, all, in their different ways, exemplify the idea that philosophical problems may be solved by understanding language. Central to this is a proper understanding of the nature of meaning and reference. This led some to revive essentialism, according to which necessity is not only a property of certain sorts of statements, but may be also attributed metaphysically to some features or objects in the world. However this may be, generally the thought is that the key to tackling problems in philosophy successfully is to be found in a proper understanding and ordering of the language in which such problems are expressed, in particular in giving an analysis of what such expressions mean and in what way, if at all, they refer to the world. This analysis may be applied to issues in epistemology (such as truth and belief), issues in metaphysics (acute attention being given to how we should think about the modalities of necessity and possibility), and issues in the area of values (their place in the world, their objectivity or otherwise). What is at stake often boils down to a core problem, which is perhaps also the core problem of philosophy: the nature of the relation of mind and world. The aim is to give a satisfactory account of the relation between our representations of the world and the world itself, that is, how our conception of the world or thought about the world is to be seen in relation to "the world" considered in itself. One route is to uphold the ultimate duality of mind and world, and explain it; another route is to deny at the outset that a strict duality makes any sense, thus eliminating any need for an explanation based on it. The linguistic approach to this and other issues in philosophy has never really lost its grip on how, generally speaking, philosophy is practised.

Interwoven with the formal linguistic approach throughout the period is the influence, in various ways, of the philosophy of Wittgenstein.[25] Even when his therapeutic, dissolving approach to philosophy is not taken up in its fully fledged form – although it has its wholehearted devotees[26] – his emphasis on the value of understanding the meaning of the concepts we use to think about ourselves and the world when encountering philosophical problems has been significant, and has manifested itself in deep but subtle ways in the ideas of other philosophers.

There has been a huge interest in recent times in problems in the philosophy of mind. This is partly because of the rise of cognitive science, and the sophistication of computers, which for some, at least, hold out the promise of solving age-old problems concerning the nature of sentience and sapience.

The further recent turn in philosophy has been, one might say, a new tolerance and relaxation in the subject that has taken the form of a widening of the subject and a greater acceptance of a plurality of approaches to it. Indications of this are clearly found in Putnam's *Reason, Truth and History*, and yet more graphically in Rorty's *Philosophy and the Mirror of Nature*; both of these philosophers might be described as analytic philosophers who have strayed from the fold. One finds it in others too, for instance in Thomas Nagel and Bernard Williams. Charles Taylor has always stood apart from the analytic mainstream, but his work has also been better considered by those within it in recent years. Rorty goes as far as to portend the end of philosophy. This, however, only seems a valid conclusion on the narrow conception of philosophy as a kind of superscience. There is no reason to accept that philosophy must aspire to such a role, and in a multitude of cases philosophy has not done so. Rorty's work, far from stepping beyond the ambit of philosophy, having supposedly presided over its funeral, has without great difficulty been absorbed into the greater body of philosophy and become a part of it.

One might, again, comment that generally philosophy is returning to its original humanitarian concerns, having been for a while a more esoteric and technical subject; this is not to deny, however, that much of the most rarefied work is of enormous value. Such a picture would be a crude one, but nevertheless it is possessed of more than a grain of truth. Some may argue that this has led to a dangerous embracing of relativism, even of cognitive nihilism, and that this in turn has left us with a lack of clear criteria as to what constitutes good

9

work within philosophy. By and large such fears are unfounded and exaggerated. There is no difficulty in finding rigour and intellectual integrity in recent philosophy, even among those who welcome a broader conception of the subject. The greater extension and pluralism of philosophy have involved a preparedness within philosophy to deal with and regard as respectable matters that were in even recent times pushed to or beyond the periphery of the subject (such as traditional metaphysics, the emotions, the meaning of life) and the use of a variety of methods to tackle such problems. Some of these methods are taken from certain aspects of the continental European tradition, a tradition that was, until relatively recently, ignored or disparaged by the analytic Anglo-American philosophy. There has indeed been an influence the other way, with philosophers in continental Europe increasingly interested in, and indeed exponents of, what might be termed analytic Anglo-American methods and concerns. There has, along with all this, been a vigorous self-reflecting questioning as to just what philosophy is about, what it should and can properly aim to accomplish.

It seems that the perspective produced by the passage of time alone allows us to judge what is valuable in philosophy. Philosophy is far from unique in this respect, of course. Time, like the action of a tide, recedes and leaves some philosophers and philosophical movements standing prominent and permanently valuable in a surrounding amorphous shifting landscape, fixed points around which others do their work. What should be most valued seems clear in retrospect, indeed almost inevitable. Before the tide recedes it is well-nigh impossible to say what will endure, what will still be read and studied in a hundred, or five hundred, years' time. Infrequently the deliverances of the tide of time get it wrong and good things are overlooked – buried, unwarrantedly neglected, requiring a little excavation – but generally, the right things, so to speak, survive. It is hard to understand by what process this occurs, but few would argue that our understanding of what is important in the history of philosophy is fundamentally wrong.

We stand in the midst of the discussion of recent philosophical works, too close to know with certainty which ideas of which philosophers will exercise people's thought many years from now. However, it is clear that the works discussed in this volume are, as well as we can tell from our perspective, the pick of outstanding contributions to the philosophy in recent times.[27]

Notes

1. An excellent overview of English-language philosophy in the period under consideration is found in Thomas Baldwin, *Contemporary Philosophy: Philosophy in English since 1945* (Oxford: Oxford University Press, 2001). Also see John Passmore, *Recent Philosophy* (London: Duckworth, 1988). Those wishing to find out about philosophy in conti-

nental Europe during this period would do well to consult Richard Kearney, *Modern Movements in European Philosophy*, 2nd edn (Manchester: Manchester University Press, 1994).

2. The period in which, among other philosophical movements, logical positivism flourished is covered in the companion volume, John Shand (ed.), *Central Works of Philosophy Volume 4: The Twentieth Century: Moore to Popper* (Chesham: Acumen, 2006). This volume covers canonical works in the first half of the twentieth century. Works given over to understanding logical positivism are Oswald Hanfling, *Logical Positivism* (Oxford: Blackwell, 1981) and Oswald Hanfling (ed.), *Essential Readings in Logical Positivism* (Oxford: Blackwell, 1981). A book that effectively counters certain misconceptions of logical positivism, emphasizing its complexity and its connection to other philosophical positions, is Michael Friedman, *Reconsidering Logical Positivism* (Cambridge: Cambridge University Press, 1999).

3. A. J. Ayer, who gave the most famous expression in English to logical positivism in his book *Language, Truth and Logic* (London: Macmillan, [1936, rev. 1946] 1975), acknowledges a lifelong interest in pragmatism and its influence on him, particularly the work of William James (1842–1910). See A. J. Ayer, *The Origins of Pragmatism* (London: Macmillan, 1968).

4. A significant book of the period in this respect, one noted for engaging wholeheartedly in traditional philosophizing, and metaphysics in particular – tackling issues such as substance, identity, universals and values – propagating throughout a determinedly materialist metaphysics, is Anthony Quinton, *The Nature of Things* (London: Routledge & Kegan Paul, 1973).

5. See J. L. Austin, *Philosophical Papers*, 3rd edn (Oxford: Clarendon Press [1961] 1979); *Sense and Sensibilia* (Oxford: Clarendon Press, 1962); *How to do Things with Words* (Oxford: Clarendon Press, 1962). His writing output was small; indeed the last two published works here are both posthumous reconstructions by others of his lecture notes. Together these works constitute everything of significance.

6. It should be said, however, that Ryle did not share Austin's assumptions about the interest of "ordinary language"; Ryle's approach was characteristically an acutely *a priori* examination of concepts. Ryle was also notably independent-minded and was not one of those philosophers who grouped around Austin.

7. A profound and important discussion supporting this view, in particular the central place that irreducible normative principles and assumptions play in the scientific enterprise, is found in Jean E. Hampton, *The Authority of Reason* (Cambridge: Cambridge University Press, 1998).

8. The analytic Anglo-American philosophical tradition is difficult to define, but it is epitomized, and its flavour is well captured, in a venerable collection of essays by several of its most distinguished exponents: see Herbert Feigel & Wilfrid Sellars (eds), *Readings in Philosophical Analysis* (New York: Appleton-Century-Croft, 1949). The group known as the "Vienna Circle", which flourished between 1907 and 1938, founded logical positivism, and the movement was of central importance in shaping the development of analytic philosophy. A highly influential figure in analytic philosophy in this period, especially in America, was Wilfrid Sellars, his most famous work being *Science, Perception and Reality* (London: Routledge, 1963).

9. An excellent introduction to the pragmatist school is Israel Scheffler, *Four Pragmatists: A Critical Introduction to Peirce, James, Mead and Dewey* (London: Routledge & Kegan

11

JOHN SHAND

Paul, 1974). John P. Murphy, *Pragmatism: From Peirce to Davidson* (Boulder, CO: Westview, 1990) traces pragmatism to modern times. A wide-ranging anthology that follows pragmatism from its inception to the present is Susan Haack & Robert Lane (eds), *Pragmatism, Old and New* (New York: Prometheus, 2005).

10. This alludes to the famous anti-foundationalist metaphor of "Neurath's Boat". Otto Neurath was a member of the Vienna Circle. The point of the metaphor is to imagine a boat whose planks are replaced over time while afloat; one cannot change them all at once for obvious reasons – one needs somewhere to stand, so to speak, while one does it – but eventually one may have a boat that has none of its original constituent planks.

11. P. F. Strawson, *The Bounds of Sense: An Essay on Kant's* Critique of Pure Reason (London: Methuen, 1966).

12. P. F. Strawson, *Individuals: An Essay in Descriptive Metaphysics* (London: Methuen, 1959), 9.

13. See, C. L. Stevenson, *Ethics and Language* (New Haven, CT: Yale University Press, 1944); P. H. Nowell-Smith, *Ethics* (Harmondsworth: Penguin, 1954); R. M. Hare, *The Language of Morals* (Oxford: Clarendon Press, 1952) and *Freedom and Reason* (Oxford: Clarendon Press, 1963).

14. This whole approach is perfectly summed up and surveyed exhaustively in W. D. Hudson, *Modern Moral Philosophy* (London: Macmillan, 1970). The date of publication is not without significance in that it appeared in the period of transition from exclusively second-order moral philosophy to a return to first-order moral philosophy. The title implicitly asserts with confidence that the contents lay out what from now on, properly speaking, moral philosophy should definitively and alone occupy itself with. The opening of Chapter 1 trenchantly sets up the case: "This book is not about what people ought to do. It is about what they are doing when they *talk* about what they ought to do. Moral philosophy, as I understand it, must not be confused with moralizing" (*ibid.*: 1). The change in approach to moral philosophy shows itself in an important work that appeared not long after the one by Hudson, namely, J. L. Mackie, *Ethics: Inventing Right and Wrong* (Harmondsworth: Penguin, 1977). Mackie, by contrast, in his opening Preface, says: "I am concerned in this book with both first and second order topics, with both the content and status of ethics" (*ibid.*: 9).

15. An assemblage of writings under a justifiably broad interpretation of "existentialism" is to be found in Robert C. Solomon, *Existentialism*, 2nd edn (Oxford: Oxford University Press, 2005).

16. An excellent compendium that lays out the state of ethical theory in recent times is James Rachael (ed.), *Ethical Theory* (Oxford: Oxford University Press, 1998).

17. Isaiah Berlin's "Two Concepts of Liberty" appeared in 1958, and is reprinted in a revised version in Isaiah Berlin, *Four Essays on Liberty* (Oxford: Oxford University Press, 1969).

18. See F. A. Hayek, *The Constitution of Liberty* (London: Routledge & Kegan Paul, 1960), and his earlier impassioned *The Road to Serfdom* (Routledge & Kegan Paul, [1944] 1976). Some of this work came on the back of advances in economic theory, economics being a subject that was noticeably more vigorous than political philosophy around this time. The concern for the state of political philosophy during this period, and its neglect by analytic philosophers in particular, is clearly expressed in the introduction of one of the classic Oxford Readings in Philosophy volumes: Anthony Quinton (ed.), *Political Philosophy* (Oxford: Oxford University Press, 1967). Rather imprudently, Quinton

12

notes that amid the general decline, "an occasional magnificent dinosaur stalks on to the scene, such as Hayek's *Constitution of Liberty*, seemingly impervious to the effects of natural selection" (*ibid*.: 2). The work of Hayek, far from falling prey to eventual extinction, exerted a tremendous influence on practical politics and economics world-wide from the 1980s onwards.

19. Among works of comparable stature dealing with proximate issues, these were not quite alone. Philosophy of law, which overlaps political philosophy in many areas, had been kept alive during this period by works such as H. L. A. Hart, *The Concept of Law* (Oxford: Clarendon Press, 1961) and *Punishment and Responsibility* (Oxford: Oxford University Press, 1968, rev. 1970). This vital impetus continued in, for example, the work of Ronald Dworkin, *Taking Rights Seriously* (London: Duckworth, 1978) and in Joseph Raz, *The Morality of Freedom* (Oxford: Oxford University Press, 1988). In addition one should mention the important work of Karl Popper in this area, as found in *The Poverty of Historicism* (London: Routledge & Kegan Paul, 1957), which followed *The Open Society and its Enemies* (London: Routledge & Kegan Paul [1945] 1966 revised).

20. Vital for understanding Nozick properly is an appreciation of the influence of economic theory, or political economy, on his ideas, in particular, that of the "Austrian School" of economics, such as is found in the work of Ludwig von Mises, *Human Action: A Treatise on Economics* (Scholar's Edition) (Auburn, AL: Ludwig von Mises Institute, [1949] 1998); Murray N. Rothbard, *Man, Economy, and State* (Auburn, AL: Ludwig von Mises Institute, [1962] 1993); Milton Friedman, *Capitalism and Freedom* (Chicago, IL: University of Chicago Press, 1962); and of course in the many works of F. A. Hayek. This influence and interest emerge explicitly in Robert Nozick's essay "On Austrian Methodology", *Synthese* **36** (1977), 353–92. A lucid account of the Austrian School of political economy and its implications is to be found in Alexander H. Shand, *The Capitalist Alternative: An Introduction to Neo-Austrian Economics* (Brighton: Harvester-Wheatsheaf, 1984) and *Free Market Morality: The Political Economy of the Austrian School* (London: Routledge, 1990). By contrast with the influence of political economy on Nozick's ideas, John Rawls hails from a legal and, to some extent, religiously informed background.

21. Adam Smith, *The Wealth of Nations* (Harmondsworth: Penguin, [1776] 1986).

22. This continued into the even more concrete area of applied ethics, many examples being found in medical ethics.

23. From among the rich array from which one might choose, a beautifully accomplished recent example is Harry G. Frankfurt, *The Reasons of Love* (Princeton, NJ: Princeton University Press, 2004).

24. See, for example, Robert C. Solomon, *The Joy of Philosophy*: *Thinking Thin versus the Passionate Life* (Oxford: Oxford University Press, 1999).

25. Wittgenstein's philosophy came in two phases. The degree of continuity, or not, between them, is disputed, although the predominant opinion is probably one that emphasizes discontinuity. The first phase is found centrally in the *Tractatus-Logico Philosophicus*, D. F. Pears & B. F. McGuinness (trans.) (London: Routledge, 1961), which first appeared in German in 1921. The second phase is found centrally in his *Philosophical Investigations*, G. E. M. Anscombe (trans.) (Oxford: Blackwell, 1974), which first appeared in German in 1953. Helpful in explaining Wittgenstein's role in twentieth-century philosophy, is P. M. S. Hacker, *Wittgenstein's Place in Twentieth-Century Analytic Philosophy* (Oxford: Blackwell, 1996).

26. See for example P. M. S. Hacker, *Insight and Illusion: Wittgenstein on Philosophy and the Metaphysics of Experience* (Oxford: Oxford University Press, 1972) and Oswald Hanfling, *Wittgenstein's Later Philosophy* (Basingstoke: Macmillan, 1989).

27. I should like to thank Paul Snowdon for his helpful remarks on the Preface and Introduction. Thanks also to Hillel Steiner for valuable consultations on Nozick and Rawls. I appreciate as well remarks made by Peter Clark and Thomas Uebel. On reaching the fifth and final volume of the *Central Works of Philosophy*, thanks both timely and overdue are owed to my wife Judith for her support throughout and the considered meticulous checking of my contribution of the Preface and Introduction to each volume.

1
W. V. Quine
Word and Object

Gary Kemp

Western philosophy since Descartes has been marked by certain seminal books whose concern is the nature and scope of human knowledge. After Descartes's *Meditations*, works by Locke, Berkeley, Hume and Kant are perhaps the most familiar and enduringly influential examples. Quine's *Word and Object* (1960) does not conspicuously announce itself as an intended successor to these, but that is very much what it is. And after Wittgenstein's *Philosophical Investigations*, it is among the most likely of the philosophical fruits of the twentieth century to attain something like the prestige of those earlier works (setting aside the century's great achievements in pure logic and immediately related areas). Yet unlike so many of those earlier works, Quine's book has the rare virtue in philosophy that it is possible, for readers here and now, to entertain seriously the possibility that its principal claims are literally true.

But there are significant barriers to seeing *Word and Object* in this way. First, Quine's way of addressing the signature questions of epistemology and metaphysics may strike one as both indirect and narrow-minded. In fact, one would be forgiven for supposing this to be a book simply about *language*, and a rather surprising one to have issued from a philosopher. For Quine's approach to language is in many ways utterly *empirical*; he discusses the learning of words – including such philosophically unimpressive words as "ouch" – and then most famously the problem of *translation*. The relevance of this to epistemology as usually understood is not immediately evident. The second barrier to properly appreciating the book is that some of the book's central claims are not only iconoclastic but counterintuitive: most notoriously, that translation is *indeterminate*, that is, that there is no fact of the matter as to whether one linguistic expression means the same as another. True, Descartes, Hume and others ask us to swallow even more remarkable things; but even if Quine's pill is easier to swallow, it is not easy.

Our aim will be to explain the shape and content of *Word and Object* in such a way as to see our way round these barriers, and thus to see the book not only as philosophically ambitious and radical, but believable.

Philosophy as Quine found it

Quine often emphasized the influence on him of the Austrian Rudolf Carnap (1891–1970). Appreciating this will provide a way around the first of the two barriers mentioned above: it connects Quine's work directly with the philosophical tradition, and thus with its central concerns and arguments. As we shall see, it also shows the way around the second barrier.

We can begin with Hume, Carnap's avowed inspiration. Hume argued that there is no knowledge that is both *a priori* – independent of experience – yet genuinely about the world. The human mind is limited to what Hume called "impressions" – roughly, sensory input as we subjectively experience it – their traces retained over time as *ideas*, and further ideas constructed from those by logical recombination. On this basis, Hume hoped to account for natural science, but concluded that traditional metaphysics is insupportable. For, whereas the former begins with observation and constructs theories logically on that basis, the latter speculates about the necessarily unperceivable, namely, such things as substance, the Cartesian self, a transcendent God. So much the better, thought Hume, for natural science, and so much the worse for metaphysics.

Hume's philosophy, however, undermined metaphysics much more successfully than it served science. First, Hume argued that since no experience can justify an ascription of causal necessity to an event, the traditional idea of causal necessity has no real application. Secondly, Hume accepted that the very idea of a spatial world containing mind-independent objects cannot be justified on the basis of experience. The best that can be done, in these and related areas, is to explain the habits of the human mind that seem to embody such knowledge. Concerning causation, for example, Hume suggested that an experience of causation so-called is really only an experience of two events accompanied by a subjective expectation that any event relevantly similar to what we call the cause will be followed by what we call the effect. The expectation is itself engendered by "habit", that is, *conditioning*: repeated experience of the pattern disposes us to expect its continuance.

Kant was largely persuaded by Hume's insistence on the empirical basis of knowledge and therefore by his rejection of speculative metaphysics, but could not accept Hume's account of empirical knowledge, especially not his account of scientific principles or laws. To Kant, Hume's system scheme had totally eviscerated what we take natural science to be: we take its concern to be a mind-independent spatial domain of objects in law-governed causal interaction. To explain *why* we believe in such things is not to show that we are *entitled* to. In Kant's eyes, Hume's system forces a retreat either to scepticism or to a radically subjective account of what knowledge is. Kant's initial manoeuvre against Hume was to argue that not all the knowledge that Hume assumes we *do* have can be accounted for in Hume's terms. This is knowledge of mathematics. Hume had assumed mathematics to be both necessary and *a priori*, but had described it rather vaguely as consisting in "relations of ideas" rather than "matters of fact". Kant conceived the crucial question as whether mathematical truths are *analytic* truths, cases such as "Bachelors are unmarried", where the predicate is *contained in the subject*. This is fundamentally a matter of *pure logic*. For example, since the meaning of "bachelor" is "unmarried man", the meaning of "Bachelors are unmarried" is really that *unmarried men are unmarried*, the denial of which – *some unmarried man is married* – is logically contradictory. According to Kant mathematical truths cannot have that status, not even simple ones such as "7 + 5 = 12", let alone more complicated ones. And given the Aristotelian logic of the syllogism that prevailed until a hundred years after Kant, this was correct: there was simply no way to represent truths of arithmetic as purely logical, as "analytic" in Kant's sense.

Kant concluded that mathematics including geometry requires what he called "*a priori* intuition". Arithmetic requires an intuitive grasp of the general idea of a linear succession of objects that has no last member. In geometry, understanding axioms such as "between every two points there is a third" requires a direct apprehension of the structure of pure space that does not depend on observation of actual objects in space. This intuition cannot be *empirical* because, as Hume recognized, truths of mathematics are clearly *necessary* truths; no experience can justify an ascription of necessity. If such truths are necessary but not analytic, then since we do have knowledge of necessary but non-analytic truths, we must recognize a new class of judgements: the synthetic *a priori*. Roughly, Kant held that the truth of such judgements is presupposed by experience as such, that is, experience as we know it, involving thought; they are built into the framework that makes such experience possible. Since they are "conditions of the possibility" of experience, nothing empirical could contradict them; that is why they are necessary.

Kantianism remained deeply influential throughout the 1800s. When Carnap arrived on the scene in the 1920s, however, it had for some decades been under pressure, not so acutely from philosophy, however, as from science itself. First, the advent of non-Euclidean geometries in the first half of the 1800s had shown that other geometries are at least conceptually possible. And by Carnap's time, the success of Einstein's general theory of relativity had suggested that Euclidean geometry does *not* describe actual space. If so, then the whole idea that geometry describes actual space yet is *a priori* could not be correct. Secondly, developments in logic had resurrected the idea that the rest of mathematics – arithmetic, the calculus, and so on – is analytic. Beginning around 1860, some mathematicians had been arguing that pure mathematics could be developed on the basis of elementary arithmetic plus the notion of a *set*, or *collection*. Several figures are important in this story, but the ones that stand out for the philosopher were Gottlob Frege (1848–1925) and Bertrand Russell (1872–1970). Frege's project was based on the decisive advances in logic set out in his *Begriffsschrift* of 1879, which formed the basis of formal logic as it is understood to the present day. Within this more powerful and more rigorous logic, Frege set out to prove not only that mathematics can be developed on the basis of arithmetic with sets, but that arithmetic itself could be developed on the basis of pure *logic* with sets. Moreover, the notion of a set, according to Frege and many others at the time, is really just a notion of logic: it is purely general, having nothing specifically to do with mathematics or any other subject. Frege's programme suffered a serious setback, however. In 1902 Russell pointed out that Frege's system entailed the existence of a *set that contains all sets that do not contain themselves.* If this set contains itself, then it does not; if it does not, then it does. Frege's system was thus inconsistent. Russell's paradox, as it came to be called, showed that the "naive set theory" assumed by Frege and others was untenable. But this did not seem to Russell to derail the programme of basing arithmetic on logic. Russell and Whitehead proposed an alternative logical system in their *Principia Mathematica* (1910); this system was much more complicated, but to Russell and others it sufficed to show that no such thing as Kantian intuition is required for the understanding of mathematics. Kant's starting-point, it seemed, had been completely undermined.[1]

Such was the scene that presented itself to the young Carnap in the 1920s. There is no *a priori* knowledge except pure mathematics, whose basis is logic. This seemed to reopen the door to an empiricism in Hume's style. In his famous work *The Logical Structure of the World* (the *Aufbau*, 1928), Carnap's idea was to use the new logic – including the formal *languages* in terms of which it was developed – to give a completely explicit reformulation of our knowledge as based entirely on sense experience. In particular, all undefined or primitive non-logical expressions would appertain directly to experiences; all sentences that did not directly report experiences would either be (i) logically reducible via definitions to ones that do or (ii) analytic, that is, provable from purely logical rules perhaps together with definitions. Such in outline was Carnap's idea of "reductionism": every significant statement is reducible to some (possibly complex) statement couched in the basic vocabulary of the language that either directly describes experiences or is a matter of logic. Hence Carnap's favoured designation for it: "logical empiricism".

To this project Carnap added three further philosophical ideas, which he saw as implicit in the idea of logical empiricism:

(1) Neither Frege nor Russell possessed a very convincing account of our knowledge of logic *itself*, or of the nature of *logical truth*. Carnap's answer was both simple and radical. Logical truth, and the question of what follows from what, are simply *rules of language*. To speak a language is to be bound by its rules, such as that "bachelor" is interchangeable with "unmarried man", and similarly that an acceptance of *P* and *if P then Q* requires an acceptance of *Q*. Questions of logic are simply questions of the rules of the language one is using: all such matters are *analytic*, in Carnap's sense. Furthermore, the question of what is analytic and what is not is a matter of convention or stipulation. A language is defined by its syntax (vocabulary and grammar) together with further rules that determine what is analytically true in that language and what follows from what. One may choose whatever language one likes, depending on one's purposes. But whichever language one chooses, one thereby chooses a set of rules, and thereby chooses a logic (and a mathematics). Furthermore, all cognitive activity – all theoretically significant thought – must be carried out in terms of a language. Thus, one is always presupposing some set of conventions, hence a logic, which in turn decides what trains of reasoning are valid. It follows that the choice of a language cannot be a theoretically based one, cannot be a "cognitive" one as Carnap puts it. Instead, the choice is a practical matter.

(2) Thus emerges Carnap's *Principle of Tolerance*. If one wishes to make theoretical claims with maximum scientific precision, one must explicitly specify the syntax of the language one is using and the rules that determine its analytic truths and inferential relations. But one cannot be criticized on theoretical grounds for one's choice of language. So even if the basic terms of the language of Carnap's *Aufbau* pertained to sensory experiences, this was not to be construed as a theoretical commitment to the idea that only such a language could serve as a basis of science (he claimed that science could do equally well with a language whose basic terms referred to physical objects). However, it did serve to explore an epistemological

question: could our knowledge be based logically on a foundation of pure sense experience?

Since a language must contain some undefined terms, the Principle of Tolerance extends to ontology: the question of what entities a given theory is committed to. To take a simple example, we can ask existential questions in arithmetic such as "Is there a prime number between 12 and 15?", but we cannot meaningfully ask using the same language "Are there numbers?". Such a question would be what Carnap called an "external question", which can only be answered in terms of the practicality of adopting the language of arithmetic; it is not a theoretical question, all of which are *internal questions*.

(3) Traditional ontology, then, was for Carnap a pseudo-science; questions of what ultimately really exists give way either to practical questions of what language to use, or to straightforward scientific (internal) questions. To this strategy for deflating metaphysics Carnap added another, namely the famous thesis of *verificationism*: the thesis that only verifiable statements are meaningful. This is the strain of Carnap's thinking that links him with logical positivism as popularly known. According to what we have just said, a question has cognitive significance only in so far as it is expressed in a language with clear rules. In a language whose basic terms appertain to sense experience, the cognitive significance of a non-analytic sentence is some combination of possible sense experiences. Thus, certain sorts of claims, such as that the world we experience is not real, or that a transcendent God exists, have no cognitive significance within such a language; their meanings are not reducible to combinations of sense experiences. They are, in a word, unverifiable. Carnap thus agreed entirely with Hume about the nonsensicality of metaphysics, and explicitly referred to Hume as an inspiration.[2]

Quine's first attack on meaning and analyticity

In Carnap's view, the updated concept of analyticity could account for everything legitimately held to be *a priori*. It could account for mathematics and for the dependence of theoretical statements such as laws of nature on observational statements: statements that report sense experience. In his celebrated essay "Two Dogmas of Empiricism",[3] Quine criticized Carnap's reliance on the concept of analyticity, and thus questioned the viability of Carnap's reductionism (in fact, he had shown earlier that the system of Carnap's *Aufbau* does not actually achieve reductionism, but that does not discredit the very idea of reductionism). Briefly, Quine's objection was that analyticity cannot be explained in such a way that (i) it can perform the epistemological function that Carnap had envisaged for it and (ii) it does not presuppose the intelligibility of concepts of exactly the same kind. For example, "*s* is analytic" might be defined as "*s* is true independently of empirical information", "*s* is true by virtue of its meaning" or "*s* is necessarily true". If the concept of analyticity is to explain our knowledge of mathematics and associated matters, then it can do so only if concepts such as meaning, necessity or empirical information can bear such a burden. Quine's point, or one of them, was that a worry about the explanatory value of the concept of analyticity cannot be assuaged by appeal to these other concepts; the worry would simply be transferred to those.

Yet, according to Quine, there is really no need to appeal to such concepts in accounting for human knowledge. It is true that some statements now accepted as true seem to be unrevisable; that is to say, we can scarcely dream of changing our minds about them. We tend to call these "necessary" or "conceptual" truths. However, rather than seeing this property as all-or-nothing, we can see it as a matter of degree. We can see the sum of human knowledge, as Quine famously put it, as a "fabric of sentences", held together by relations of inference. At the periphery stand so-called observation sentences; these are keyed directly to observable events, such as "the mercury is rising". These are closely related to what Quine would later call "observation categoricals", such as "if a sample of water is heated and a thermometer inserted, the mercury rises". This categorical statement together with "this sample of water is heated and a thermometer is inserted" logically implies the observation statement "the mercury is rising". The categorical in turn is logically implied by more general theoretical statements. The most general theoretical statements are the most abstract ones, such as truths of mathematics; their logical relation to particular observation categoricals is very remote, since they tend to figure in all of science, irrespective of subject matter. Thus clearly, for any observation statement, a great many more general statements may be involved in predicting its truth-value. Suppose now that such a prediction is falsified: an observation conflicts with an observation statement that is logically implied by some group of accepted theoretical statements. This tells us that one or more of those statements must be rejected, but it does not tell us which. According to Quine, there is no one uniquely correct response to make in such a situation; perhaps theoretical statement *A* should be rejected; or perhaps *B*, if either would preserve consistency with the observational evidence. It is not the case that a single observation can itself disconfirm a single theoretical sentence. In general, Quine's idea is that it is always a whole body of sentences that are at issue when a theory is tested by observation, and the rational response to an unanticipated observation is not a matter of following an exact rule (for that would just be another statement in the theory); instead, we repair the theory in the most convenient way we can, striving for simplicity and a minimum of change. Yet some sentences – especially those of mathematics – are so thoroughly involved throughout science that it would involve a massive and perhaps wholly impractical overhaul of our "conceptual scheme" to change those. These are the ones at the centre of the fabric or web, the ones we tend to call "necessary truths".

If we look at things this way then there is no reason to think of any statements as analytic in Carnap's sense. They are all in principle revisable, hence not true just by virtue of our speaking the language we do. Still, the holistic web-of-belief idea shows how some might in practice be "immune from revision", or nearly so; this accounts for the feeling that some statements are necessary, without appealing to a special property that some statements have and others lack.

Word and Object: aims and structure

In "Two Dogmas of Empiricism", Quine does not really argue that there is no such thing as analyticity. He merely points out that it seems impossible to explain informatively, and argues that it is not needed for the explanatory task for which it was invoked.

In *Word and Object*, Quine poses some much more challenging questions about the concept of meaning and its role in philosophy, especially epistemology. What sorts of facts are facts about meaning, and how, if at all, are they to be established? Quine announces answers to both in the very first paragraph of *Word and Object*:

> Language is a social art. In acquiring it we have to depend entirely on intersubjectively available cues as to what to say and when. Hence there is no justification for collating meanings, unless in terms of men's dispositions to respond overtly to socially observable stimulations. An effect of recognising this limitation is that the enterprise of translation is found to be involved in a certain systematic indeterminacy … (p. ix)

Quine is first claiming that meaning must be publicly accessible: if it were not, then two speakers could share the same speech dispositions – they would say the same things in all the same situations and so on – yet not mean the same by what they say. This, Quine assumes, is absurd. For one thing, since we only acquire language by learning it from others – copying *their* speech dispositions – there cannot be meanings in one person's words that he or she did not pick up by watching or being taught by others. For another, to suppose that meaning is somehow more determinate or fine-grained than what can be manifested in speech would introduce the gratuitous scepticism that perhaps we never understand each other, despite agreeing in *everything we say* (cf. § "Quine's first attack on meaning and analyticity").

Quine claims next that speech dispositions do not suffice to determine meaning uniquely: for example, a given sentence of one language might be equally well translated by two sentences of another language that do not, in any plausible sense, mean the same as each other. As we shall see, a main reason is that translation is *holistic*. Roughly, this means that only translation schemes for whole languages can be empirically justified, not translations of individual sentences; thus a translation of a given sentence might be correct according to one scheme that is empirically borne out overall, but not correct according to another such scheme. Intuitively the translations may seem utterly unlike, but to suppose that such an unlikeness represents a genuine factual incompatibility is to commit the fallacy of assessing parts out of context, as when we condemn a single act without seeing its necessary role in an overall good. But translation schemes are *not* uniquely fixed by speech-dispositions. Putting this together with the claim that speech dispositions are the only facts there are about meaning, it follows that there simply are no facts about meaning, at least not any of the sort that we might intuitively expect.

Quine's argument for this rather eye-popping thesis – known as the "indeterminacy of translation" – is contained in Chapter 2 of *Word and Object*. In Chapter 1, Quine sets the scene by sketching his own replacement for Carnap's epistemology, one that he would later come to call "naturalized epistemology": in harmony with the web-of-belief metaphor that closed "Two Dogmas of Empiricism", it attempts to explain how knowledge might be conceived in terms of the possession of a language, where, instead of relying on the concept of meaning in describing what it is to have a language, it is described in behavioural and psychological terms. We shall explain the significance of this later. In Chapters 3 and 4, he discusses the features of language involved in *reference*: the connection between language and world, word and object. Subsequent chapters shift to a very different set of questions. Given his rejection of Carnap's outlook on epistemology and ontology – which had seemed to dispose of so many longstanding questions in those areas by appeal to the concept of meaning – what sort of attitude should we take to such questions? How should they be answered? As we shall see, it is here that Quine's philosophy is in many ways at its most radical.

We shall not discuss Chapters 3 and 4 except very selectively and in passing. After discussing the famous argument of Chapter 2, we shall consider Quine's naturalistic picture as described in Chapters 1, 3 and 4, before examining the resulting fresh outlook on philosophical questions exercised in the final three chapters.

Radical translation

At the beginning of Chapter 1, Quine writes:

> One is taught so to associate words with words and other stimulations that there emerges something recognizable as talk of things, and not to be distinguished from truth about the world. The voluminous and intricately structured talk that comes out bears little evident correspondence to the past and present barrage of non-verbal stimulation; yet it is to such stimulation that we must look for whatever empirical content there may be.
>
> (p. 26)

Quine is posing a hard-edged scientific question of a kind that previous philosophers concerned with meaning had rarely considered: since meaning must be in some way identifiable in terms of linguistic dispositions – actual patterns of speech – exactly how do particular linguistic dispositions constitute evidence for ascriptions of meaning (of "empirical content")? Quine speaks of "stimulation" here because he has in mind the following sorts of dispositions: the subject – a speaker of the language being investigated – receives a certain sensory stimulation, for example the kind received when he sees a rabbit, and this causes him to become disposed to assent to a particular sentence. If the subject is an English speaker, this might be "There's a rabbit". Thus if the sentence were posed to the subject upon being so stimulated, he would assent to it. In another kind of case, the stimulation is itself the hearing of a sentence, for example "It's raining"; the subject might, upon hearing this, become disposed to assent to "The river will rise". This is a case of what Quine will often call "sentence-to-sentence" links. The *higher-order* disposition to become disposed to assent to the one sentence on being exposed to an utterance of the other is probably a small piece of the subject's overall theory, embodied in a sentence: "Whenever it rains, the river rises".

In speaking of an English speaker, however, various temptations arise that it is important to avoid. It would seem utterly redundant to ask what our own linguistic dispositions are. As speakers of English we already know, or suppose we know, what expressions of English mean. But this apparent knowledge is no help in answering Quine's question; it drops us right back into the circle that Quine pointed out in "Two Dogmas of Empiricism". Our facility with such terms as *meaning* and *analyticity* is no help at all towards understanding *what they are*, what sorts of facts the facts of meaning consist in, if there are any.

For this reason, Quine proposes his famous thought-experiment of radical translation. If there are objective facts about meaning, then there must be objective facts of the matter as to whether two expressions E and E^* have the same meaning. If they are from different languages, this means there must be a fact of the matter as to whether *E is a correct translation of E*. It therefore must be possible for a "field linguist" to enter a community whose language is totally unknown to him, and, just by applying methods that everyone would recognize as sufficiently objective or scientific, produce a uniquely correct translation manual that matches sentences of the native language to English sentences, or, if more than one such manual may be so generated, the differences must not represent intuitively significant differences in meaning. Crucially, neither the method nor the data can be allowed to use the concept of meaning: if they did, then the field linguist's intuitive judgements of what means what would have infected the operation, and it could not provide the elucidation of the phenomenon of meaning that Quine is after.

Yet this apparent gap between the objective and intuitive viewpoints is not as great as one might suppose. The key is provided by the above points about the *social* nature of language – its learnability by observation – and *linguistic dispositions*. Just as seeing sugar dissolve in water is evidence of a disposition – that sugar dissolves in water – so observed linguistic behaviour is evidence for linguistic dispositions. Thus the objective identification of linguistic dispositions can reasonably be regarded as the self-conscious scientific analogue of the actual learning of language, the acquisition of semantic knowledge. As far as possible, then, the translation manual must seek a matching of linguistic dispositions; ideally, one sentence translates another when native speakers are disposed to assent to them in what for each would be a situation that is suitably congruent with that of the other.

The critical first task for the scientifically self-conscious radical translator, according to Quine, is to discover what he calls the "stimulus meaning of observation sentences" (§§7–10). In particular, we imagine something like the case above involving a rabbit. A rabbit hops past, and the native exclaims "Gavagai!". Perhaps that should be translated as "Rabbit!", the sort of one-word sentence we might utter as short for "There's a rabbit". Another rabbit hops past, and we try saying it ourselves: "Gavagai!" or "Gavagai?". If the native signals assent to this, and dissent when we try it without a rabbit present, this will reinforce the initial conjecture.[4] The *stimulus* meaning of such a sentence is the class of sensory stimulations that would dispose the native to assent to it, together with the class that would dispose him to dissent to it. Intuitively these sentences report what is present *here and now*.[5] Of course the sentences do not *say that* certain sensory stimulations are occurring; the translator translates "Gavagai!" as something like "Rabbit!" on the hypothesis that those two have the same stimulus meaning, which does not resemble the ordinary concept of meaning in any obvious way. The hypothesis is justified because the rabbit causes the same sorts of stimulations in the linguist as in the native. Unlike other sorts of sentences, observation sentences afford an immediately observable correlation between the sentence and what prompts assent to them (compare the case of teaching a small child by pointing and saying words such as "doggy", and so on). Thus Quine would later refer to such sentences as the "entering wedge" for both the infant and linguist first getting to grips with a language. Sentences about the past, about things far away, or that state general facts that never change, cannot be translated directly just by watching the natives talk in their environment (but *some* relevant information is available; see §§11, 14).

Indeterminacy

So far we have been dealing only with observational sentences, translated one-by-one. A translation manual, however, must cope not only with indefinitely many more of those, but also non-observation sentences (in fact, the manual must be able to generate translations for infinitely many sentences; p. 71). To progress further, the translator must divide sentences into parts – words – and translate these. He must, as Quine puts it, formulate "analytical hypotheses" that assign meanings to individual terms on the basis of data about dispositions to assent to sentences (§15). It might seem that the translator has already translated some words – "gavagai", for example, as "rabbit" – but this is really not so. "Gavagai!" has so far been treated as a sentence, possibly used in the way we might exclaim "Rabbit!". To call it a sentence means that it can be assented to or dissented from outright, unlike a mere word (equally, it can be used to perform an assertion, just by itself). And, although the sentence "Gavagai!" can be translated as "Rabbit!" by equation of stimulus meanings, it could just as well have been translated as "Undetached rabbit-part!", or "Temporal stage of a rabbit!", or "Local instantiation of the universal *Rabbithood*!", all understood as sentences rather than terms. These have the same stimulus meaning, since for each pair of these one is present if and only if one of the others is.[6] (An "undetached rabbit part" is, for example, a leg, still attached to the whole rabbit; if we consider a rabbit to be a four-dimensional object occupying the three spatial dimensions plus that of time, a "temporal stage of a rabbit" or rabbit-stage – or a *time-slice of a rabbit* – is a part of a spatially whole rabbit over a particular time interval, that is, the rabbit from time t to time t^*).

To see what is involved in chopping sentences into words, let us consider a simple example. The linguist finds the native disposed to assent to the following in the presence, respectively, of black rabbits and black dogs:

Gavagainirg!
Bavagainirg!

A natural hypothesis is that "gavagai" goes with "rabbit" and "nirg" with "black". Thus begins the reading of *reference* into the native language: thinking not merely of sentences conditioned to stimulation, but of relations between particular words and particular kinds of things. But what about, for example, the hypothesis that the sentence "Gavagai!" means "Temporal stage of a rabbit!"? Why could we not translate the term "gavagai" as "temporal stage of a rabbit"? Rabbits, of course, are not the same things as temporal stages of rabbits. In particular, their identity-conditions differ: two rabbit-stages can be stages of the same rabbit. Thus it might seem we could settle this question by finding out how the natives individuate the things they are talking about: how they count them as one or two. So suppose we query this sentence:

Yo gavagai ipso yo gavagai.

The natives always assent to this when it is queried while pointing to the same rabbit at each utterance of "yo gavagai", and never when pointing at different rabbits. Similar results are obtained for "bavagai" and for other examples. Assuming "yo" is like the demonstrative "this", can we conclude that "gavagai" means rabbits, on the grounds that "ipso" must mean "is the same as"? No we cannot, because the native dispositions are consistent also with translating "gavagai" as *rabbit-stage* and "ipso" as *is a stage of the same animal as* (or *is a stage of the same object as*; §12, §15).

"Rabbit-stage" is just one example of many odd but possible translations. Quine's point, in a word, is this: in order to translate individual terms, the translator makes assumptions about reference. In making such assumptions, however, the translator thereby makes assumptions about what Quine calls the "apparatus of individuation". These are all the linguistic devices involved in counting objects, referring to them on successive occasions as the same, calling the same or different, and so on; in English these include pronouns such as "it" and "he", quantifier words such as "all" and "some", and identity predicates such as "is" or "is the same as". Different hypotheses regarding the terms can be offset by different hypotheses regarding the apparatus of individuation, as illustrated by the example above. Yet there is no more direct way of testing these hypotheses than testing whether they correctly predict native dispositions with respect to whole sentences. Thus *different translations of terms are compatible with all possible relevant data*. This is Quine's thesis of the inscrutability of reference, a facet of the indeterminacy of translation that Quine calls "pressing from below".[7]

It is not, however, the only facet. There is also a more abstract argument called "pressing from above". The whole sum of non-observational sentences accepted by the natives may be taken to constitute their all-inclusive *theory*.[8] Their translations depend almost entirely on analytical hypotheses. The only direct evidence the translator has to go on in this domain is whether or not the natives assent to the sentence; they will always assent to or always dissent from a "standing" sentence such as "Rabbits suckle their young", yielding evidence only for its truth-value. Further, many native terms will have no observational use: what we may call "theoretical terms", especially nouns ("proton", "bank account", "god", etc.) which can be learned only by learning how sentences containing them relate to other sentences. Quine thus makes two points. First, there is no reason to expect that there cannot be sets of analytical hypotheses that deliver incompatible translations of native standing sentences. Their translations can be tested only via translations of terms based on observation sentences along with hypotheses that relate the grammatical structures of the native language to those of the translator's language. The route from data to hypothesis is complex and tenuous (p. 72). Secondly, Quine, along with many other philosophers of science, holds that theory generally is *empirically underdetermined by data* (§16). This means that for any given set of observation sentences, incompatible theories could logically imply that same set. But a translation of native standing sentences is precisely the attribution to them of a theory: if different theories expressed in English imply the English translations of the set of native observation sentences (actually observation *categoricals* of the form "If A then B", where A and B are observation sentences), then, by employing different sets of analytical hypotheses, the natives could be construed as holding either theory.

The interdependence of meaning and theory has smaller-scale manifestations as well. Suppose the natives assent vigorously to a sentence the translation of which, according to hypotheses accepted so far, comes out as "All rabbits are men reincarnate" (p. 69). Should the translator posit a weird native belief, or reconsider previous translations? It depends. If those translations are amply confirmed otherwise, then the translator had better stick with them, especially if alternative schemes would make the native language significantly more complex. But the translator cannot just ascribe weird beliefs whenever convenient; otherwise he could take the native utterance of "Gavagai!" as meaning anything he likes. There is a balance to be struck between simplicity and naturalness of translation and the ascription of intelligible belief. Yet there is no general reason to expect a uniquely correct way of striking the balance, and hard to see what would make such a balance correct, other than the intuitive judgement of the translator.

Exactly what sort of incompatibility between translation manuals is being envisaged? The answer is, no less than *logical* incompatibility (pp. 73–4). This means that two manuals might translate a given sentence of the native language into logically incompatible English sentences S_1 and S_2. Such an outcome need not contravene any data, since the native sentence might be one for which the natives simply do not deliver a verdict: the sentence might be too long to understand, or they might have no opinion; and if we have no opinion as regards S_1 and S_2, then we have no basis for deciding. But even if they do affirm or deny their sentence, or we count either S_1 or S_2 true, these facts would support a translation only proportionally to our confidence in their being right, or in our being right.

The arguments pressing from above and below can both be used to show something very surprising about what is involved in speaking our own language (p. 78; cf. *Pursuit of Truth* (1992): §18). Consider the argument pressing from below: suppose we translate "rabbit" as "gavagai", then that back into English as "rabbit-stage". For the translation back and forth, we perform the transformations of the referential apparatus (pronouns, quantifiers, etc.) needed to make the translations cohere with linguistic dispositions. We now have a translation of "rabbit" as "rabbit-stage". Quine's thesis thus entails that one could construe English in such a way that "rabbit" refers to rabbit-stages, and so on. Thus the thesis of the inscrutability of reference, and of the indeterminacy of translation generally, is by no means simply a theory about the limits of translation between languages: it means that there is no fact of the matter about the meanings of words in English. A similar back-and-forth argument shows that the standing sentences of English could be construed, *in English*, as expressing a different theory.

Large-scale indeterminacies are unlikely to become evident in practice. For one thing, in practice, translation always runs along the rails of convenience, naturalness and so on; "rabbit-stage" is perfectly consistent with data, but no translator would choose it, and there would be no reason to (pp. 70, 74–5). For another, the argument from above depends on a very abstract point: the actual transmutation of our overall theory of the world – built up over aeons – into an empirically equivalent one is well beyond human ingenuity (p. 72). We should also recognize that, however the indeterminacy thesis may seem to violate common sense, there are good explanations why it should seem to. We are apt to take our own facility in speaking for a kind of "knowledge of meaning" that seems quite secure and determinate. Yet this ease and familiarity need not and perhaps cannot, according to Wittgenstein and others, be explained in terms of knowledge of special facts – semantic facts. If we think of it as a practical ability, as *knowing-how*, then Quine's thesis does not undermine it in any way. For similar reasons, we should not think that the indeterminacy thesis can straightforwardly be called into question by considering the case of a bilingual (p. 74). At least for many sentences, the bilingual confidently translates this way rather than that. A fluent bilingual hardly thinks of it as "translation"; he merely speaks two languages rather than one, a matter of practical ability. But the fact that he readily settles on translations that strike him as correct does not rule out other translations that, even if less natural, would be equally justified by objective data. If we think of him as translating self-consciously and so to speak theoretically, then he still has to form analytical hypotheses. Even for observation sentences, he has to consider stimulus meanings; he has the luxury of asking himself what he would say under various stimulations rather than finding an experimental subject, but he is hunting for the same thing, namely equations of stimulus meaning (p. 71).

Finally, it is vital to recognize that the conclusion of Quine's argument is not that translation is impossible, or problematic, or any such thing. On the contrary, it is the opposite view – that there are determinate facts of reference and meaning – that would make translation problematic. For if there were, then the argument would show that they cannot be known, in which case we could never know whether or not we are really communicating. What the argument really shows, then, is that any supposed semantic differences between incompatible but individually satisfactory translation schemes do not matter: as long as the translations are borne out empirically, then there is no sense in which they could be wrong.

The place of reference

For many philosophers, the semantic foundation of language is reference, the relation between word and object. Language acquires its content by virtue of immediate connections between certain terms and certain objects (whether these are physical objects, sense data as for Russell, or momentary whole experiences as in Carnap's *Aufbau*). Quine's outlook departs from this radically. The fundamental relation between language and the world is not reference but the causal relation between sensory stimuli and the disposition to affirm observation *sentences*; that relation is what is suitably stable, public and directly learnable.

Nevertheless, Quine devotes Chapters 4 and 5 to an extended discussion of our "referential apparatus", that is, the various linguistic devices which make it possible to regard particular expressions as referring to particular objects. We shall pass over the detail of these chapters, of which there is a lot, but we should appreciate in general terms what facts about our referential apparatus Quine is attempting to bring out, and why Quine takes this task to be so important, despite having just argued that reference is not determinate, and not the foundation of language.

First comes the question of what linguistic devices are to be seen as referential. At what stage in a child's serial acquisition of English can we justifiably say that the child is using an expression in such a way as to refer to objects? Even if there is no fact of the matter as to what, exactly, "rabbit" refers to, it does not follow that there is no distinction between an expression's *being referential* and its not being so. Thus even if we take reference at "face value", and say as a truism in English that "rabbit" refers to rabbits, we can still ask what linguistic devices a child must master before he can be said to refer to rabbits. At the earliest stages of development, the child learns such observation sentences as "Rabbit!", "Mama!", "Red!", "Wet!" and so on; they are in the same bag, fully explicable in terms of their stimulus meanings. Reference takes hold in stages, with the mastery of further devices. These include: plural endings; articles such as "a" and "the"; the distinction between count nouns and mass terms such as "water"; rudimentary predication as in "red apple", "Mama angry"; demonstratives as in "this apple"; attributives as in "red apple"; and particles such as "every". Briefly, the ascription of full-blooded reference is demanded only when the child acquires competence with questions such as "Is this the same apple as that?": the child must understand questions of *identity*. To understand that is to understand that "apple" refers to distinct objects, and not to do so is to fall short of fully understanding "apple" as a referring term.

Secondly, Quine is concerned in these chapters to set the stage for the rest of the book, devoted largely to questions of ontology. The most general question of ontology is the question "What exists?", a question that cannot be answered independently of having complete knowledge of the universe. We can, however, ask a modest question: what exists *according to our best theories*? In order to answer that question we need to determine which expressions of the language of a theory indicate the theory's existential commitments. Quine's answer is that it is the *referential* expressions in fully meaningful sentences that indicate existence. However, a language such as English has a very complicated range of overlapping devices involved in reference, and it is, as amply displayed by the discussions in these chapters, no small task to discover exactly how they work. Of course, one might wonder how there can be genuine questions of ontology if reference is indeterminate; we shall return to this. At this stage, Quine is concerned rather to show how the apparent disorder of the English referential apparatus can be brought to heel to some extent. For example, despite the baffling variety of ways in which we can speak about an object, every statement "… *a* …" that is genuinely *about* an object *a* can be brought, by means of grammatical transformations permitted by actual English usage, into the form "*a* is an object such that … *it* …" (§23, §29). Further, the use of variables such as "*x*" as is common in mathematics and related fields enables us to write "*a* is an object *x* such that ... *x* ...". This in turn allows us to do the same thing for more than one object, as in "*a*, *b* and *c* are objects *x*, *y* and *z* such that ... *x* ... *y* ... *z* ..."; better than other ways of doing it, this enables us to speak about several objects at once yet keep track of which is which. Even when talking about one object, this seemingly trivial device is maximally clear, and shows its worth (§§30–32) in dealing with especially problematic referential issues, such as those arising from sentences that ascribe propositional attitudes.

For theoretical purposes, however, it may be useful or necessary to seek clarity not merely by restricting ordinary language to certain devices of exemplary clarity, but by changing it, or replacing it. Quine's discussion of this topic is what fully reveals how radical and sweeping his challenge is to previous and even currently orthodox philosophies. We thus turn to it now.

Regimentation in principle and practice

Traditionally, philosophers have asked questions of the form "What is *X*?", where these, for whatever reason, are thought not to be decided empirically (as in the case of "What is water?"). Paradigmatically, analytic philosophers have supposed that such questions are not questions about the *nature of X* to be decided by some kind of *a priori* insight; instead, they are questions about *concepts*, that is, the meaning of "*X*". The aim is to find analytic truths involving "*X*" of the form "Something is *X* if and only if...". Clearly, Quine's account of translation undermines such endeavours; the facts about meaning presupposed by claims to analyticity do not exist.

Quine, unsurprisingly, does not plead for a return to *a priori* insight. What then becomes of philosophical analysis, and what, for that matter, of philosophy? Our purpose in this penultimate section is to articulate Quine's alternative philosophical methodology – especially as regards ontology – and briefly to see how Quine applies the methods it recommends.

We mentioned earlier that Quine's aims are fully continuous with those of previous systematic philosophies. One important strand of this is Quine's question of what would be involved in *clarifying our conceptual scheme* (§33). To achieve such clarity is to achieve a maximally explicit and clear statement of all that "our theory" – our science – actually says about the world, including an explicit specification of the entities that, according to the theory, exist. Clearly, this enterprise will be well served by employing the simplest possible language (§47). That language, as Quine has long argued, is simply the language of the first-order predicate calculus with identity. At its most austere, this includes only: the universal quantifier "$\forall$" (corresponding to "Every" in English); variables x, x', x'', ... (roughly corresponding to English pronouns such as "it", "thing" and the like); one- and two-place predicate-letters F, F', ... R, R' ... (corresponding to English predicates such as "__ is wise", "__ loves __"); identity "$=$"; an adequate set of truth-functions such as negation "$\sim$" and the conditional "$\rightarrow$"; and parentheses (other typical devices including the existential quantifier "$\exists$" can readily be defined in terms of these; see §34). Thus, for example, "Every fool loves someone" might be represented as "$\forall x(Fx \rightarrow \exists y(Rxy))$". This language is *extensional*, in that replacing one expression with another with the same reference or extension never changes the truth-value of any sentence in which the first expression occurs (§47; by contrast, English is normally held to be *non-extensional*; see below). The ontological commitments of a theory expressed in such a language have a univocal form of expression: for anything in the domain of the theory – that is, for anything among the objects the theory is *about* – there will be some assignment of objects to variables such that for some predicate φ of the theory, the open sentence φx is true (in which only x is free). But that, by the definition of the existential quantifier, is what it is for the closed sentence $\exists x \varphi x$ – "There is an object x such that x is φ" – to be true. That is the perfectly straightforward thought behind Quine's oft-cited but oft-misunderstood quip that "to be is to be the value of a variable", and shows why Quine thinks of questions of ontology as being settled in terms of the referential structure of language (§49). In order to determine the ontological commitments of a theory, formulate the theory in terms of the first-order predicate calculus with identity; the ontological commitments of the theory are then expressed by the existential quantifications counted as true by the theory. It is because the referential structure of such a language is so clear – especially by comparison with ordinary English – that it provides an exact univocal way of expressing existence. In English, by contrast, we seem to be able to perform such inferences as "Santa Claus does not exist; therefore some things do not exist"; but how can there be things that do not exist? We also speak in English of such things as *ways of loving* (as in "let me count the ways", etc.). So if she loves me in several ways, then *there are* ways in which she loves me, so *there are ways of loving*. But do we really want to assert, as a serious theoretical claim about what exists, that there are such things as ways of loving? Or, if the foregoing "proof" has violated a rule of English, exactly which rule has it violated? Such questions often simply lack clear answers, and rather than supposing that what is in question is something metaphysically deep, we might then locate the lack of clarity in language itself, that is, ordinary English.

Conspicuous by their absence from such a language are any expressions corresponding to the proper names of ordinary language. If we needed to achieve the effect of a proper name such as "Socrates" in such a language, we are to

33

stipulate some predicate φ as having only Socrates in its extension; we then use Russell's technique whereby "The φ is ψ" is equated with "There is exactly one φ, and it is ψ", which is readily expressed in the basic notation of the predicate calculus (§§37–8; we can think of this as "The Socratizer is ψ"). But are important philosophical problems concerning names not thus simply being evaded (such as how to explain "Pegasus does not exist")? The crucial point here is that Quine regards the employment of logical notation as a matter of *replacement* aimed at clarity and simplicity (§§33, 53). The point is *not* that the adopted linguistic forms duplicate the actual meanings of expressions of ordinary language, for there are no such things. The point is simply that proper names are not needed in language "regimented" for scientific or philosophical purposes; puzzles surrounding their ordinary use may thus be discounted as arising from the practical needs or indiscipline of ordinary language, not from genuine theoretical issues.

This policy is even more striking when Quine turns to the perennially vexing question of the analysis of propositional attitudes. Positions inside a context such as "*A* believes that …" are non-extensional; even where "$a = b$" is true, the truth-values of "*A* believes that *Fa*" and "*A* believes that *Fb*" need not coincide. Further considerations suggest that "believes that" must be explained as indicating a relation between the believer and a proposition, understood not as a sentence but as an abstract object, the meaning of a sentence. Yet Quine insists on an extensional language for science, and rejects the idea of a proposition. That there is a particular proposition expressed by each meaningful sentence implies that there is a fact of the matter about what a sentence means, which Quine has already denied (§42). Quine thus suggests that (what is called *de dicto*) belief be construed in the official language of science simply in terms of certain predicates, such as "__ believes that Cicero denounced Cataline", formed by attaching "believes that" to a sentence to form the predicate (§44).[9] Such predicates are to be understood as syntactical wholes, like "is white", so that the positions *within* them occupied by names such as "Cicero" are not open to substitution by variables or other names. Each will be true of some persons and not of others. This ignores the idea that belief is a relation, but Quine's claim is that it would serve for any serious purposes of the science of psychology, and has the virtues of being extensional and without commitment to either weird entities or the determinacy of meaning (cf. §45). In so far as our talk of propositional attitudes is clear, it does not require such commitments.

Quine sees such proposals not as *a priori* philosophical claims based on conceptual analysis, but as theoretical proposals advanced in the same spirit as any scientific proposal. A physicist, for example, concerned with force is not concerned to elucidate, in abstraction from everything else, the nature of force, still less the meaning of the word "force"; nor is he concerned to preserve everything that common sense might affirm as regards force (see §53). He may employ a term similar to "force" in ordinary English, but his overarching aim is a theory that as a whole successfully predicts certain key data, which dovetail with other accepted theories, and are simple and consistent.

Let us now try to summarize what Quine conceives philosophy to be, in view of his rejection of philosophical appeals to the concept of meaning or analyticity. In rejecting the philosophical appeal to meaning, Quine is rejecting the idea that there is a peculiarly philosophical subject matter or philosophical method. There is no realm of *a priori* truth for the philosopher to call his own. Quine thus rejects the idea of "first philosophy", a theoretical vantage point that stands outside science or ordinary human knowledge and either provides it with foundations or calls it into question (§§4, 56). Instead, as Quine followed the Austrian Philosopher Otto Neurath (1882–1945) in putting it, our "conceptual scheme" is like a ship at sea, which must from time to time be repaired while staying afloat; there is no philosophical dry-dock (§1).[10] Such repairs may include the reformulation of smaller chunks of theory, as in devising theories or linguistic forms in terms of which to ascribe propositional attitudes and the like; also more general structural improvements, such as imposing the language of first-order logic (§33). But no complete overhaul is possible except over a long period of time; just as the ship would sink were it completely taken apart, the philosopher, having presumed to question all knowledge, would have nothing in terms of which to criticize, no accepted statements to guide him in the reconstruction. (Thus Quine explicitly endorses but finds nothing alarming in Hume's claim that the principle of induction is unprovable; it is alarming only if one thinks of the principle's role as that of an *a priori* foundation for science, and not merely as a law that despite its generality is defeasible along with all the others; see the essay "Epistemology Naturalized",[11] pp. 71–6). What is characteristic of philosophy as opposed to the sciences is that it tends to deal with large-scale or abstract issues, such as general questions of ontology or the choice of a language adequate for all science (§33), or parts and features of seeming human knowledge that for very abstract reasons stubbornly resist neat integration into the overall fabric, such as idioms of time (§36), propositional attitude (§§44–5) or counterfactual conditionals (§46). This is often a matter of degree, and some such matters are addressed by both philosophers and scientists: mathematical logic, set theory, the interpretation of quantum mechanics, consciousness and the role of teleology in biological explanation are conspicuous examples.

This understanding of philosophy delivers an especially important consequence for ontology, and indeed for metaphysics generally. Reference, for Quine, is inscrutable. Therefore there is no such thing as standing outside a language and saying: these are the objects the language is really about, and not those. There is no such thing as a science of ontology in that "external" sense. As we explained earlier, however, we may identify those existentially quantified statements in a logically regimented formulation of a theory that, according to the theory, are true. Provided that the theory is true, and suitably streamlined and economical, those statements directly state what there is (§§6, 49). For example since mathematics is essential to virtually all serious science, and it quantifies over numbers (e.g. "There is a number between 2 and 4"), our actual conceptual scheme is resolutely committed to the existence of numbers (§§54–5; although unification and simplicity can be served by construing numbers as certain kinds of *sets*; more generally, set theory can provide all the entities needed for mathematics). What is striking is that for Quine, unlike Carnap, there is a serious subject of ontology, yet, in a way that is not so distant from Carnap's, it tends to deflate the idea that ontology is possessed of a distinctively philosophical kind of *depth*. One can grant that statements of our most austerely regimented theory assert the existence of such entities as numbers, yet wish, all the same, to ask whether such things are *really real*. In denying the possibility of a distinctively philosophical vantage point external to science, Quine denies the intelligibility of such questions; there just is no further question. An ordinary object such as an apple is a *paradigm case* of the real; there is nothing that such a thing could be less real than (§1). This is not to say that ontology cannot be critical or revisionary. Ordinary language may seem to be replete with references to phantom entities such as propositions, fictional objects, the "nearness of you", but Quine's question of ontology is what exists according to the most streamlined formulation in the first-order predicate calculus of scientific knowledge, in which such things will typically find no place.

This brings us finally to statements of metaphysics more generally. Whereas Carnap sought to deflate them or call them nonsense, Quine re-inflates them but only to the fullness of scientific statements generally, and denies that there is any systematic test for whether or not something is nonsense; there is only the rather multi-stranded question of how or whether a given claim can find a place in serious science (§47). Thus for Quine, since it is physics that deals with reality at its most fundamental, it is not too far off the mark to say simply that "physics is metaphysics" (§§48–9, 54). This is the more austere end of what Quine calls "naturalism", the view that the world is simply the natural world, and the methods of knowing it are those diverse ways in which we come to know the natural world. The philosopher takes active part in this at certain trouble spots, but is otherwise related to knowledge much as the actuary is to the corporation: he is the one whose job it is to draw up the accounts, and let the bosses and shareholders know explicitly where they stand.

Word and object

Finally, we can return to the theme announced by the title of the book. To speak of a language, for Quine, is to speak elliptically of a complex structure of *verbal dispositions* such as those discussed above (§ "*Word and Object*: aims and structure"). Understanding or competence in the language consists in possessing such dispositions, and not in knowledge of a special kind of fact, namely semantic facts. Just as the solubility of sugar consists in a certain chemical structure, such dispositions consist in certain states and configurations of the nervous system, but this is unimportant from the point of view of linguistic studies. If the "internal wiring" of two creatures with exactly the same verbal dispositions were drastically different, this would not be a *linguistic* difference between them, since it would clearly be idle to suppose that they might mean different things by their words (p. 8).

Nevertheless, detailed studies of language acquisition and behaviour, including the neural mechanisms that make it possible and their evolutionary pedigree, are not only possible, but contribute to what Quine would later come to call "naturalized epistemology". Thus, for example, our knowledge of middle-sized physical objects has a kind of evolutionary explanation: these are the sorts of things with respect to which it best serves the survival and procreation of the species to be verbally conditioned, that is, to talk about. The relation between evidence and theory can be studied as the complex causal relations between dispositions with respect to observation sentences and other linguistic dispositions (§5). Such general norms of theory construction – simplicity, familiarity and so on – can be explained hypothetically in terms of the biological drive for efficiency (§5). And so on. Epistemology, for Quine, is using science to understand science; it is not the search for a separate foundation for science or knowledge generally, which is an unintelligible endeavour (for more on this theme, see "Epistemology Naturalized" and *From Stimulus to Science* (1995)).

Notes

1. Frege himself persisted in the idea that Euclidean geometry is synthetic *a priori*; he may simply not have known about relativity theory.
2. Of necessity we have passed over many changes of doctrine and emphasis in Carnap's views between the *Aufbau* (1928) and the important essay "Empiricism, Semantics and Ontology" (1950). Perhaps most glaringly, the absolutist character of Carnap's dismissal of traditional metaphysics does not sit well with either the principle of tolerance (announced in *The Logical Syntax of Language* [1934] (1959)) or the distinction between internal and external questions set out in "Empiricism, Semantics and Ontology". Thus it is not quite

fair to regard Quine's attack on reductionism as an attack on the epistemological views actually held by Carnap in 1950, the year of Quine's "Two Dogmas of Empiricism".

3. "Two Dogmas of Empiricism", in *From a Logical Point of View*, 20–46 (Cambridge, MA: Harvard University Press).

4. How can we have identified signs for assent and dissent? Suppose the natives say "Evet" whenever we try repeating their utterances of "Gavagai" in the presence of rabbits, but say "Yok" when we try "Gavagai" in their absence. We can then take "Evet" and "Yok" as "Yes" and "No", respectively (§7).

5. We are passing over the important matter of collateral information, and the relation of observation sentences to the more inclusive class of occasion sentences (§§9–10).

6. Provided that what Quine calls the "modulus" – the duration of the stimulation – is not too long.

7. See Quine's discussion of "Gavagai" in "Ontological Relativity", in *Ontological Relativity and Other Essays* (New York: Columbia University Press, 1969), 30–34.

8. Strictly, we should speak of the sum of *standing sentences*, that is, non-occasion sentences; see note 3.

9. Traditionally, *de dicto* belief is a two-place relation between a believer and a proposition, as in "Plato believes that Socrates is wise". *De re* belief is a three-or-more-place relation between believer, one or more objects, and the meaning of an open sentence such as "*X* is wise". For example, consider "Plato believes, of Socrates, that he is wise". The idea is that given "Socrates = *A*" (for some singular term *A*) together with the *de dicto* form "Plato believes that Socrates is wise", it does not follow that *Plato believes that A is wise*, but from "Socrates = *A*" together with the *de re* form "Plato believes of Socrates that he is wise", it does follow that *Plato believes of A that he is wise*. Quine calls this the distinction between *notional* and *relational* belief.

10. Quine often repeated this point, for the first time in print in his 1950 essay "Identity, Ostension and Hypostasis", reprinted in *From a Logical Point of View*, 65–79 (Cambridge, MA: Harvard University Press, 1953), see 58–9.

11. "Epistemology Naturalized", in *Ontological Relativity and Other Essays*, 69–90 (New York: Columbia University Press, 1969).

Bibliography

Carnap, R. [1928] 1967. *The Logical Structure of the World*, R. George (trans.). Berkeley, CA: University of California Press.

Carnap, R. 1959. *The Logical Syntax of Language*, Countess von Zeppelin (trans.). Paterson, NJ: Littlefield, Adams & Co.

Frege, G. [1879] 1967. *Begriffsschrift: A Formula Language Modelled upon that of Arithmetic, for Pure Thought*, J. van Heijenoort (trans.). Reprinted in *From Frege to Godel: A Source Book in Mathematical Logic*, J. van Heijenoort, 1–82. Cambridge, MA: Harvard University Press.

Hume, D. [1748] 1962. *An Enquiry Concerning Human Understanding*, L. Selby-Brigge (ed.). Oxford: Oxford University Press.

Kant, I. [1787] 1929. *The Critique of Pure Reason*, N. Kemp Smith (ed.). London: Macmillan.

Quine, W. V. 1943. "Notes on Existence and Necessity". *Journal of Philosophy* **40**, 113–27.

Quine, W. V. 1953a. *From a Logical Point of View*. Cambridge, MA: Harvard University Press.

Quine, W. V. 1960. *Word and Object*. Cambridge, MA: Harvard University Press.

Quine, W. V. 1966. *The Ways of Paradox and Other Essays*. Cambridge, MA: Harvard University Press.

Quine, W. V. 1969. *Ontological Relativity and Other Essays*. New York: Columbia University Press.

Quine, W. V. 1981. *Theories and Things*. Cambridge, MA: Harvard University Press.

Quine, W. V. 1992. *Pursuit of Truth*, rev. edn. Cambridge, MA: Harvard University Press.

Quine, W. V. 1995. *From Stimulus to Science*. Cambridge, MA: Harvard University Press.

Whitehead, A. N. & B. Russell, 1910. *Principia Mathematica*. Cambridge: Cambridge University Press.

Further reading

For Russell, Carnap and Quine's relation to Carnap, see Quine's "Truth by Convention", in *The Ways of Paradox and Other Essays* (1966), 77–106, and "Epistemology Naturalized", in *Ontological Relativity and other Essays* (1969), 69–90. Also:

Carnap, R. 1967. *The Logical Structure of the World;* [and] *Pseudoproblems in Philosophy*, R. George (trans.). Berkeley, CA: University of California Press.

Carnap, R. 1959. "The Elimination of Metaphysics through Logical Analysis of Language", A. Pap (trans.). In *Logical Positivism*, A. J. Ayer (ed.), 66–81. London: Macmillan.

Carnap, R. 1956. "Empiricism, Semantics and Ontology". Reprinted in the supplement to *Meaning and Necessity: A Study in Semantics and Modal Logic*, enlarged edn, 205–21. Chicago, IL: University of Chicago Press.

Friedman, M. 1999. *Reconsidering Logical Positivism*. Cambridge: Cambridge University Press.

Hylton, P. 1990. *Russell, Idealism, and the Emergence of Analytic Philosophy*. Oxford: Oxford University Press.

Richardson, A. 1998. *Carnap's Construction of the World*. Cambridge: Cambridge University Press.

Russell, B. 1985. *The Philosophy of Logical Atomism*. La Salle, IL: Open Court .

For further works by Quine, the following are essential: "On What There Is" and "Two Dogmas of Empiricism", in *From a Logical Point of View* (1953), 1–19; 20–46; "Speaking of Objects", "Ontological Relativity" and "Epistemology Naturalized", in *Ontological Relativity and Other Essays* (1969), 69–90; "Things and Their Place in Theories", in *Theories and Things* (1981), 1–23; and finally Quine's last two books: *From Stimulus to Science* (1995) and *Pursuit of Truth* (1992).

For critical studies of Quine, see:

R. Gibson (ed.) 2004. *The Cambridge Companion to Quine*. Cambridge: Cambridge University Press.

Hylton, P. forthcoming. *Quine*. London: Routledge.

2

P. F. Strawson

Individuals

Paul Snowdon

Introduction

Peter Strawson published *Individuals* in 1959. He had been a Fellow at University College, Oxford, since 1948. Later he was appointed as Gilbert Ryle's successor to the Waynflete Professorship in Oxford. Strawson had achieved fame, like Frege earlier and Kripke later, by writing about reference. In "On Referring" (1950a) he criticized Russell's theory of definite descriptions and claimed that at least some uses of expressions of the form "The *F*" are devices for reference rather than a form of general quantification.[1] He moved from this case to consider the question of the general relation between ordinary language and formal logic, in his first book, *Introduction to Logical Theory* (1952). His thesis is that it is not possible to capture the full role of ordinary language in a formal system. Another early article that contributed to Strawson's reputation was "Truth" (1950b), which was part of a debate with J. L. Austin. Austin favoured a version of the correspondence theory, whereas Strawson defended a sophisticated version of F. P. Ramsey's redundancy theory. Strawson also wrote articles about the subject–predicate distinction and Part II of *Individuals* grew from these. In *Individuals* Part I, however, Strawson builds on the approach to reference adumbrated in "On Referring", but asks some more fundamental metaphysical questions about how we refer to objects in the world. Part of the aim is to consider the role of space (and time) as grounds for our thought about objects. He rediscovered or reformulated certain Kantian questions. Later, in

The Bounds of Sense (1966a) he explored head-on the system of Kant's *Critique of Pure Reason*.

Austin was still alive in 1959 and under his influence many philosophers were suspicious of the general questions of traditional philosophy. *Individuals* made the impression it did because, in part, it argued at a level of abstraction far higher than was standard in philosophy at the time, and asked questions that were novel. In calling what he was doing "metaphysics" Strawson was giving expression to this contrast. *Individuals* made an impression also because of the imaginativeness it displayed in pursuing its problems, because of its thoughtful engagement with a range of philosophers, ancient and modern, and because of its intellectual confidence.

Individuals is divided into two parts, both of four chapters. The first part has the general title "Particulars", and discusses what sorts of objects are the ones we basically think and talk about (allegedly material bodies and persons), and what the consequences, conceptual and epistemological, of their centrality are. The second part is entitled "Logical Subjects" and attempts to explain the difference, or part of the difference, between subject expressions and predicates. Both parts are novel and important, but because of its greater influence the first part deserves, and will here receive, a fuller exposition.

Descriptive metaphysics

Strawson describes *Individuals* as "an essay in descriptive metaphysics" (p. 11). He contrasts *descriptive* metaphysics and *revisionary* metaphysics. The topic of metaphysics is, roughly, the *general* structure of our conceptual scheme, but one sort of metaphysician, the describer, aims to describe that general structure, whereas the revisionary metaphysician aims to change and improve that structure. Strawson places, with qualifications, Descartes, Leibniz and Berkeley in the revisionary camp, and Aristotle and Kant in the descriptive camp. Strawson's thesis is that there are central and general aspects of our conceptual scheme that do not change, a "massive central core of human thinking which has no history" (p. 10). Exercises in descriptive metaphysics aim to describe (parts of) that abiding structure.[2] Around that central core, at the more or less specialist peripheries, there are, of course, developments and changes. About descriptive metaphysics Strawson claims, or appears to claim, that it has a priority over revisionary metaphysics, and also that the normal method of philosophical analysis, that is the "close examination of the use of words", is not the best method here, because the basic structure does not "readily display itself on the surface" (p. 10).[3] Strawson is, therefore, hinting at a different and novel method for pursuing descriptive metaphysics, without saying in the introduction what it is. No doubt he has in mind, for one thing, the exploration, in Chapter 2, of the conceptual consequences of imagined forms of experiences radically different to our own.

The revisionary–descriptive contrast is a resonant distinction that has entered into the self-classificatory terminology of philosophy. It deserves some scrutiny. We might ask first what the descriptive metaphysician describes. Strawson says "there is a massive central core of human thinking which has no history …; there are categories and concepts which in their most fundamental character, change not at all" (p. 10). The contrast I am interested in here is between abiding concepts or categories, and abiding thoughts (or types of thoughts). There is a difference because a single set of concepts can be involved in quite different ways of thinking. Thus, the person who thinks that there are no ghosts, and the person who thinks that there are (not no) ghosts, share the same concepts but differ in the thoughts they have with them. It is clear that Strawson is not simply concerned with the concepts but with, as he puts it, our "thinking". Next, an infelicity in Strawson's description of himself as a descriptive metaphysician is that it cannot be said that he is engaged in a *merely* descriptive exercise. Claims are advanced in his discussion about what must be so, what could not be, along with explanations of our thinking, and defences of it against sceptical objections. It is, therefore, quite wrong to think of his strategy as *purely* descriptive. A further problem with the classification is that the two categories (ignoring for the moment precisely what they amount to) are obviously not exhaustive. For example, a metaphysician who describes our basic thoughts and tries to prove they are correct is not simply a descriptive metaphysician, nor is he a revisionary one. Again, someone who gives a profound criticism of a suggested novel system of thought is not in Strawson's sense revisionary, but need not be descriptive either. It would seem then that if we want a comprehensive classification we must select one of Strawson's categories as basic, and define the second as metaphysics that is not of that basic kind. Which should we select? It seems to me that the more useful basic category is that of the revisionary, and the second category should then be the non-revisionary, to which we might assign the term "descriptive". The reason is that if we take as basic the descriptive, meaning "aiming solely at the description of our basic categories" it is dubious that any serious thinker is descriptive in this sense, and, further, the category of the rest would be so heterogeneous as to be unhelpful. We should, then, treat the revisionary category as basic, and in an effort to preserve Strawson's terminology take "descriptive" to mean non-revisionary. Strawson, on that understanding, remains a descriptive metaphysician. What, though, does "revisionary" mean? I think that for Strawson it means this: there are certain fundamental and abiding ways of thinking, which we can regard as the conjunction of propositions $P_1, …, P_N$. To be revisionary a system must claim that some P_i in that group is incorrect. A system would not then count as revisionary if it accepted P_1 and P_2 ... and P_N but wanted to add to our basic ways of thinking a further proposition Q. This, indeed, may be what some idealists, including Kant, think of themselves as advocating. We have here as well a further reason for saying that Strawson's original two categories are not exhaustive. The metaphysician wanting to add Q is neither revisionary nor in the original sense descriptive. In talking of his approach as descriptive metaphysics Strawson intends primarily to convey that his purpose is to describe, and perhaps explain, some aspects of how we do *think and speak*. In his case it is describing how we refer to, and understand reference to, objects.[4]

Chapter 1:"Bodies"

Putting it in a crude way, Strawson's concern in this chapter is to study the way we refer to things when we communicate with others. An example of such reference would be when I use the name "London" in speaking to you to refer to the city. The main question is whether, given that we refer to different kinds of objects, there is a kind that is basic, in the sense that we can refer to them without referring to any other kind, whereas reference to these other kinds depends on reference to the basic kind. Strawson calls reference "identification" and so announces his conclusion in these words; "material bodies are basic to particular-identification" (p. 55). It is natural to ask, as a first question: what besides material bodies, according to Strawson, might be suggested as candidates for being basic? The answer according to the argument is, or seems to be, states, processes and events. Strawson's conclusion, therefore, amounts to the claim that material bodies are more basic in a certain referential *role* than these other sorts of things. In understanding Strawson's thesis it is therefore necessary to understand two things. The first is the theoretical categories in terms of which the conclusion is formulated. These are the role specifiers, which are aspects of or notions related to what Strawson calls particular identification, and those relating to a specification of the candidates for these roles, notably, material bodies (and events). The second is to understand what Strawson's arguments for his conclusion are.

In Section 1 of this chapter, Strawson introduces some role categories. The roles are defined in terms of acts of communication between a speaker and a hearer.[5] When a speaker refers to a particular thing (say, the Eiffel Tower) and the hearer knows which thing is being referred to, then Strawson says that the hearer can identify the referred-to thing. Further, when a speaker refers to a particular thing he or she can be said to make an identifying reference to it.

Strawson's terminology obviously places the notion of identification at the centre of the discussion. Being able to identify *A* amounts roughly to being able to give an informative answer to the question: who or what is *A*?[6]

The final notion that Strawson introduces is that of one type of particular, *A*, being more basic in our conceptual scheme than another type of particular, *B*, if we can identify *A*s without reference to *B*s, but cannot identify *B*s without reference to *A*s. Strawson adds that there may be other significant forms of identification dependence that do not require such a straightforward asymmetry in respect of reference.

Having introduced these concepts, Strawson begins his argument with the question: "When shall we say that a hearer knows what particular is being referred to by a speaker?" (pp. 17–18). Strawson wishes to analyse what it is to know which object *in the world* is being referred to. He distinguishes two cases. The first is where the hearer can pick out the object in question within the group of items he or she currently perceives (or can vividly recall having recently perceived). In this case Strawson says that the hearer can *directly locate* the particular. He also calls it a case of demonstrative identification because it is the kind of identification involved when understanding central cases of demonstrative reference. The second case is where the hearer cannot at the time directly locate the particular. Strawson claims that although a proper name might be employed, ultimately hearer knowledge of reference of this kind must depend on knowledge of a description that applies to the object in question.[7]

Strawson moves the argument on by giving voice to the worry that if the description we rely on is purely general, for example, very tall tower with pointed top and four legs, it seems possible that there might be two such items, and so such a description would not enable one to pick out just one such object.[8] We can call this the reduplication problem. He points out, in reply, that, first, if the descriptions we employ related items to those we can directly locate, for example, "father of that person", there cannot be reduplication. Secondly, there is at least one total system of relative descriptions provided by spatiotemporal relations of things to those in the directly locatable scene, which is universal and guaranteed unique. This we can employ the description "the very tall tower, etc., 25 miles in that direction".

Strawson's attitude to the reduplication worry is that it does not represent a serious problem, but that the availability of a solution to it employing the framework of spatiotemporal relations to directly locatable items supplies a *model* of our thought that is independently plausible. There are two main ideas in Strawson's model. The first is that particular identification ultimately rests on a knowledge of the relation that an item has to the presented scene, and the second that the framework in terms of which the relation is specified is that of space and time. The alternative he considers is that we can employ pure general descriptions, such as, "the first dog born at sea to have saved a monarch". The problems with this are, first, by what right we so much as assume that there is a single thing that satisfies the description, and second, how fixing the item this way we can gain any knowledge of it. Strawson hints that although we, in our situation and with our experiences, employ such a way of thinking in identifying particulars, it remains to determine whether the general capacity to identify particulars of subjects, however situated and whatever the nature of their experiences, requires employment of the spatiotemporal framework.[9]

Strawson next suggests that "operating the scheme of a single unified spatiotemporal system" requires that we are able to make informative identity judgements about some of the particulars we can think of. We should note that when Strawson talks here of identification he is no longer particularly thinking of them as contents of communication between subjects, but rather as contents of information possessed by individual subjects. Strawson's reason for this claim is that we need to employ the same spatiotemporal framework on different occasions and this requires that we can make identity judgements across occasions. Strawson's primary interest in this consequence is, however, epistemological. He claims that it follows that we have, or must have, criteria, or methods, of re-identification. These methods must be consistent with the conditions we find ourselves in, for example, we go to sleep, move and have only a limited range of observation. From this an anti-sceptical conclusion is supposed to follow. Those who are sceptical about our ability to determine such identities do themselves still think in terms of space and time. If Strawson is right, however, it is a condition for operating with those spatiotemporal concepts that we do accept such identities. As Strawson puts it, "He pretends to accept a conceptual scheme, but at the same time quietly rejects one of the conditions of its employment" (p. 35). Strawson is here developing a type of anti-sceptical argument that became known as transcendental arguments.

As well as acceptance of substantive identity claims about *objects*, Strawson argues that it is also necessary to accept identity judgements about *places*. He seems to think that this follows because unless we can re-identify particular places we would be unable to have information about the spatial relations of things that the unified system requires (p. 36). Whether he is right about the necessity, it is clear that in our actual thought we do re-identify places (for example, Trafalgar Square), and without that our ability to track objects would be severely limited. As Strawson points out, however, our ability to identify places turns on our ability to identify objects (for example, Nelson's Column). This means that there is a mutual dependence of our ability to identify places on our ability to identify things.

In the final part of the chapter Strawson returns to the issue of whether there is a category of particulars that are the basic ones to which we identify-ingly refer.[10] When filling out this question Strawson builds "as things are" into the conditions. This seems to mean "given the general character of the particu-lars of different sorts that are in fact around us". If this condition is built into Strawson's conclusion, then his thesis about what is basic cannot be supposed to represent a *necessity* imposed on a speaker *simply* in virtue of the role of the spatiotemporal framework.

Strawson first argues that our ability to identify anything referentially depends on there being a spatiotemporal framework of items or particulars in which we can locate them. He points out that not just any sort of object can constitute such a framework. They must be public three-dimensional objects that endure, to some extent, through time. Of the things we recognize and refer to, only what he calls material bodies amount to such a framework, and so are basic.

Now, Strawson himself calls this argument "general and so vague", and pro-vides a further argument looking in detail at the general categories we have (p. 40). We can point out, however, that there are at least three problems with the general argument. The first is why we must agree that the framework consists of enduring items. Could there not be a framework based on recurring patterns of events? The second issue is whether Strawson is happy to view his claim that only material bodies can yield such a framework as contingent. If there were some suitable structure of recurring enduring public processes, might that have been a satisfactory framework? The third problem is that even if the spatiotem-poral framework must be one specified in terms of material bodies, it does not follow that our ability to refer to them does not itself depend on, or involve, reference to particulars of another kind. We might have two basic mutually dependent categories of reference.

In Section 7, Strawson argues for the same conclusion in a more detailed way. He begins by describing some categories of particulars where it is fairly obvious that our ability to refer to instances of them depends on our ability to refer to other things. One case is that of private particulars, for example, the pain felt by Polonius when stabbed by Hamlet. A second case is that of scientifically postulated unobservable entities, say a particular carbon atom. It can only be referred to via reference to grosser material things. Thirdly, certain large-scale social entities, say the Cabinet of Winston Churchill, can only be referred to via more basic individual material things.

Setting these categories aside, Strawson suggests that the two candidates for being referentially basic are events and processes on the one hand, and material bodies on the other (in the latter Strawson includes chairs but also fields). It is allowed that we refer to some events without reference to bodies, for example, when we pick out an audible explosion, as "that explosion". It is also allowed that we can refer in certain circumstances to non-present events in terms of their relation to present events. Strawson argues, however, first that there are many events where we cannot think of them unless we are thinking of them as body involving. An example would be births, which have to be thought of as the birth of a certain object. So for these events there is dependence of reference on reference to bodies. Secondly, the ability to refer to events without reference to bodies "suffers in general from severe practical limitations" (p. 49). We simply cannot, given the way the world is, pick out all the events we are interested in referring to merely in a series of events. The events do not exhibit the right kind of order and structure. Thirdly, Strawson claims that bodies do provide a sufficiently rich framework so that we can refer to them without having to refer to events and so on. From this complex of considerations it is supposed to follow that material bodies are basic.

Chapter 2: "The Sound World"

Strawson begins Chapter 2 with a question and an assertion. The question is whether there could be a conceptual scheme that acknowledged the existence of objective and identifiable particulars but in which material bodies were not the basic particulars (p. 60). The assertion is that it follows, and has been shown to follow, that material bodies will be basic if objects are thought of as spatial. The question therefore becomes: can there be a non-spatial scheme of concepts that yet involves or permits the idea of objective particulars? Can there be a no-space world in relation to which objective thought is possible? In considering this Strawson drops a restriction that he has so far mainly worked with. The idea of picking out objective particulars does not mean referring to it in conversation with another; rather, it means thinking about it. By "objective"[11] Strawson explains that he means something that is distinguished from both the thinker and his or her experiences and mental states (p. 61). Strawson later introduces a further important clarification of the question that it is useful to set out at this stage. He describes first a conceptual scheme that contains or sustains recognition that the particulars it picks out are mind independent, a way of thinking that requires the presence of psychological concepts and concepts of subjects. Strawson calls this a "non-solipsistic" scheme. In contrast there is a conceptual scheme in which a thing can be picked out as the selfsame thing as earlier encountered, even though it may lack the concepts of experience and subjects. Strawson, quite reasonably, holds that if in the "no-space" world a conceptual scheme describable in the latter way can be constructed it involves recognizably objective notions, even if it does not qualify as non-solipsistic.

How then does Strawson think that this question is to be answered? His first suggestion is that in both sight and touch the experiences have a spatial character, so we need to exclude them. Taste and smell are, he suggests, relatively trivial senses. Hearing, however, does not involve experiences with spatial character and has a richness with which a candidate objective conceptual scheme might engage. So the question now becomes: could a creature with solely non-spatial auditory experiences engage in objective thinking? Can such a creature make re-identificatory judgements?

We are to think of the subject as having complex auditory experiences. The subject might hear the opening five bars of Beethoven's Fifth Symphony, then the opening five bars of the Ninth Symphony, and then the eleventh bar of the Fifth. There is in this nothing that enables the subject to judge that he or she is hearing the selfsame performance of the Fifth, rather than a similar second performance that has reached about the same point. Strawson points out that according to our normal thinking items can be re-encountered on different occasions because they are continuously located in places that we have visited twice. In a "no-space" scheme this understanding is not possible. He suggests that room must be made for an analogue of travel and location, so that the subject has a criterion for distinguishing between the two musical possibilities. The suggestion is that the auditory world contains a master sound that varies in pitch. This is supposed to provide the analogue of location and the analogue of movement is an audible continuous variation in the heard pitch of the master sound. Thus, if the later Fifth Symphony is accompanied by the same pitch of the master sound this entitles the subject to judge that it is the same performance because it is "at the same sound location", but if it had not been so accompanied then it would merely be the same type of performance.

Strawson acknowledges that it is very hard to decide whether this is enough. The imagined experiences exhibit analogies with spatial experience but also, and inevitably, differences. We must simply judge whether they are enough. Strawson's claim about the sound world seems to be that it is enough.

Strawson next asks whether there could be a place within the conceptual scheme based on such experiences for the concept of the self or subject, that is, first-person reference. He allows that something like the distinction between changes of location that merely happen and those in which there is agency can be generated, as can a sound analogue of the experiencer's body. But he suggests that nothing very much is gained by building up these analogies. The next task is, therefore, to investigate in its full richness the character of our actual thought about ourselves.

The question whether objective thinking must be explicitly spatial and Strawson's attempt to answer it by imaginatively constructing a world of complex auditory experiences has inspired many responses, including a substantial essay by Gareth Evans, and so has generated many questions.[12] Of the many observations and questions about the argument I have to restrict myself to three. First, it is important to understand what sort of question is at issue. Although Strawson describes his imagined scenario as a no-space world, there is no licence for that. We are not told what nature the imagined sounds really have, or how they actually relate to space. How, one might ask, could sounds not be spatial entities? The restriction is, rather, that the thinker has experiences that lack spatial content, and is imagined in consequence to lack spatial concepts and understanding. The issue is, then, whether a creature without spatial concepts can have and deploy objective concepts. Even if the correct answer is that it is possible it would not follow that there could be non-spatial objective particulars. Further, if there could be such non-spatial particulars it would not follow that they could be thought of non-spatially. In fact, the idea that there can be such things that have to be conceptualized spatially is a position somewhat in the spirit of Kant. Strawson's reflections then seem non-Kantian in their spirit, although the inspiration for the question is Kant.

Secondly, the central issue is whether the imagined judgements merit the ascription to them of objective content. Why suppose they are objective? The truth is that we have very little idea how to settle or pursue such questions about legitimate content ascription. So despite the fantastic speculative interest in such an issue it is more or less bound to remain undecidable. Opinions will differ as to what that implies.

Thirdly, and related to the previous point, Strawson moves the argument forwards by claiming that objective judgements can be located only if the judger has a criterion for making them. The role of the master sound is to provide such a criterion. It is hard not to feel, however, that it is too rigid to qualify as a criterion. The problem is that on any normal understanding of objective particulars they can move as much as perceivers can move, rapidly or slowly, and, indeed, can swap places. There seems to be no analogue of such a possibility in Strawson's imagined scheme. This lack of slack about the evidence used encourages suspicion that we do not really have here a criterion of objective identity. These two criticisms are not inconsistent. We have little sense of how to resolve such issues, but to the extent that we do the master sound device seems insufficient.

Chapter 3:"Persons"

When discussing the sound world Strawson argues that, despite having such restricted experiences, a subject could think objectively in one sense, in the sense, namely, of recognizing items as numerically the same on different occasions of perceptual encounter; but in another sense of "objective", according to which objective thinking demands distinguishing between oneself and other things, it is not clear that the sound world contains enough to permit or ground objective thinking. In Chapter 3 which is perhaps the most famous in *Individuals*, Strawson drops the experiential restrictions, and poses two related questions: why do we ascribe states of consciousness to something and why to the same thing to which we ascribe physical characteristics?

In response Strawson argues that to these questions no answer is provided in the fact that a subject's states of consciousness causally depend, in a special and complex way, on that object we would call his or her body. This explains, or might explain, the subject's assigning a particular importance to that body, but it does not explain why the subject thinks of himself or herself, or why he or she ascribes physical characteristics to himself or herself.

Strawson's questions presuppose a certain conception of our conceptual practices, and the argument develops by investigating two views that dispute different aspects of those presuppositions. The Cartesian dualist theory holds that the mental characteristics are ascribed to one thing, an ego or self, but that the physical characteristics are ascribed to another entity, the body. What Strawson calls the no-ownership theory, which he tentatively ascribes to Moritz Schlick and middle Wittgenstein, denies that conscious states have a possessor and are, strictly, ascribed to anything.

What might ground the no-ownership picture? It is grounded, according to Strawson, in the principles that only the things whose ownership or possession is in principle transferable can be owned at all. Since the pains that are supposedly mine cannot become another's, they are not really even *mine*. However, the illusion of real private ownership is grounded, according to the no-ownership theorist, in the contingent causal dependence of those experiences that are treated as mine on a particular body. In offering this explanation, according to Strawson, the position descends into incoherence. It does so because there is no way of indicating the class of experiences that are, or are recognized as, causally dependent on my body. It cannot be all experiences because not all experiences are so dependent; nor can the class be picked out simply as those that are so causally dependent because there is nothing contingent in the recognition that all experiences that are causally dependent on this body are causally dependent on this body. The only way to pick out the right class is that it is *my* experiences that are dependent on this body. The position, therefore, requires the inelimina-ble employment of the very notion of possession that it claims is inadmissible. The conclusion is that the no-ownership view is incoherent, and its challenge to one presupposition of Strawson's questions can be set aside.

Having dismissed the no-ownership theory, Strawson advances a principle that is central to the rest of his argument. In Strawson's words "it is a necessary condition of one's ascribing states of consciousness, experiences, to oneself, in the way one does, that one should also ascribe them, or be prepared to ascribe them, to others who are not oneself" (p. 99). Strawson means by this, in part, that when I think of myself as, for example, in pain, I am thinking of myself as fulfilling precisely the same condition as I am supposing another fulfils when I think of them as in pain. Further, my ability to understand the condition apply-ing to myself requires the ability to understand it as applying to others. This claim is supposed to be an application of a completely universal feature of predi-cates. They introduce a general condition not limited to an individual.

This principle has at least two significant implications, according to Strawson. The first is that the Cartesian dualist challenge to the presupposition in Straw-son's questions can be met. The reason is that in order to fulfil the condition of being able to ascribe psychological predicates to others we must at least be able to identify the others, to pick them out in thought. There must, therefore, be a way to pick them out other then as bearers of states of consciousness. This means it must be right to ascribe physical states to them.

It would not be adequate to designate another ego under the description: the ego whose experiences are causally dependent on body B as my experiences are dependent on my body. One reason is that this way of referring to others depends on a prior reference to and thought about oneself. Such thinking can-not, however, be prior.

Strawson summarizes this anti-Cartesian conclusion by saying that we have to acknowledge "the primitiveness of the concept of a person" (p. 101). He means that the concept has to be of a thing that has both psychological and physical characteristics. In this way Strawson also provides an answer to his own second question. Although we cannot analyse our own primary or basic concept of a person into a combination of two distinct entities of different fundamental sorts, we can, according to Strawson, *construct* a *secondary* concept of a pure, non-corporeal consciousness. Nothing in the argument rules out the possibility of application for such a concept.

The second implication that Strawson draws from his principle about psycho-logical predicates is epistemological. To formulate it he defines two categories of predicates. First, there is what he calls M-predicates ("M" is short for mate-rial). These are predicates we apply to ourselves but also to objects to which we would not dream of ascribing states of consciousness. Examples are "weighs 16 stone" and "is in London". The other category is that of P-predicates ("P" is short for "person"). These are the other predicates that we ascribe to ourselves. Examples are "is in pain" and "believes in God". Strawson's thesis is that in order for ascriptions of P-predicates to others to not be secondary or dependent on our first-person ascriptions (a dependence that is ruled out by his basic principle, as he understands it), some of our ways of telling what predicates apply to another must be "logically adequate" (p. 105). This means, or appears to mean, that the best route to judgement must genuinely amount to a way of *knowing*, and its status as such must not depend on, nor must the way involve appeal to, correlations established in the first-person case between the application of P-predicates and other features. The reason is that to establish such correlations if third-person applications depended on them would require that the subject was able to self-ascribe prior to being able to other-ascribe. We simply have to recognize that our central psychological predicates have grounds of ascription that are first-person grounds and other grounds of ascription that are non-first-person grounds. The epistemological consequence is that there is no genuine problem of other minds. To so much as understand the ascription of such predicates to others involves acknowledging that some of our ways of grounding judgements are knowledge-providing. This is Strawson's main anti-sceptical thesis.

Strawson concludes by asking why we have what we might call the concept of a person. "What is it in the natural facts that make it intelligible that we should have this concept?" (p. 111). Strawson singles out for attention bodily action predicates, such as "is going for a walk". He claims that such predicates ascribe features where it seems natural that we have non-observational ways to self-ascribe but also observational ways to other-ascribe the selfsame feature. This is therefore a category of P-predicate where the distinctive status of P-predicates seems wholly unremarkable. Secondly, Strawson notes that the lives of individual people have a degree of independence. We are not creatures devoted solely to continuous integrated social activity (as perhaps some ants are). If our lives had been of such a character then, perhaps, we would not have needed the conceptual structures involved in registering our individual identities.

Some questions about Chapter 3

The argument of the "Persons" chapter is very rich, and I can single out only a few of the issues that might be, or have been, raised. We can initially leave aside Strawson's claims about the epistemological status of (some) P-predicates, and concentrate on his idea that we think of ourselves, persons, as entities that satisfy both P- and M-predicates. We think of ourselves as single two-sided things. This surely *is* how we do think of ourselves. There is, next, the claim that there is nothing wrong in thinking this way. We both think of ourselves this way, and, indeed, *are* this way. Strawson of course subscribes to this claim, which is close to, and certainly committed to, saying that philosophical criticisms of our way of thinking of ourselves, as proposed by, for example, Descartes, are not cogent or persuasive. We should note, however, that holding that there is nothing wrong does not imply that there are not unobvious theoretical truths that can be added to our way of thinking. I have in mind, for example, material- ist ideas about the nature of the states that P-predicates assign or pick out. This possibility grounds a doubt about something that Strawson allows. He allows that within the framework of our basic thinking we can construct the concept of a disembodied consciousness. We can indeed construct such a concept, but its constructability does not imply that there could be such a thing. Maybe it is in the nature of states of consciousness to require complex material conditions for their presence.

If our ordinary way of thinking about ourselves is not wrong then, of course, suggested revisions *are* wrong. Here, though, the question is: what sort of criti- cisms of suggested revisions are cogent? We can distinguish two main attitudes. The first is that the suggested new conception is simply worse as theory. It is, perhaps, unsupported, excessively complicated or generates difficult explana- tory questions. The second attitude is that there is something incoherent about the revisionary suggestion. It can, therefore, be ruled out *a priori*. Now, in con- sidering the alternatives that he does, Strawson emphatically endorses the sec- ond sort of criticism. One of the fundamental questions raised by Strawson's discussion is whether these *a priori* style arguments are cogent. The two alterna- tive conceptions that Strawson highlights are the no-ownership view and Car- tesian dualism. From Strawson's perspective they count as two ways of denying his characterization of how we think about ourselves.

About his discussion of the no-ownership view we can raise two questions. First, what exactly is the view? There is a lack of clarity, in that it is character- ized quite generally as the claim that "experiences are not owned by anything except in the dubious sense of being causally dependent on the state of a par- ticular body" (p. 96). In contrast, Wittgenstein is taken as a possible supporter because he held that in such a sentence as "I have a pain" the word "I" does not denote a possessor (p. 95). This seems to amount to a thesis about the role of "I" and is not about subjects in general. Strawson also characterizes the view as holding that "it is only a linguistic illusion that one ascribes one's states of con- sciousness at all" (p. 94), which again is a remark about self-ascription. Either way, it seems to be a negative claim to the effect that a certain apparent subject expression does not denote or refer to anything in certain psychological sentences. Secondly, does Strawson refute this proposal? Oddly, what he argues is that when a proponent tries to explain what gives rise to "the illusion of the ego" he will have to employ incoherently a designator for himself as subject of, or possessor of, mental states. Even if such an explanation would be incoherent, one might wonder why a proponent of the negative claim must offer any such explanation, or, indeed, this particular explanation? In other words, Strawson's objection seems not to be to the negative claim itself, but to a grafted on explanation for an illusion.

More important by far, however, is the principle that Strawson invokes in discussion of dualism, and also in his epistemological argument. Strawson states the principle thus; "it is a necessary condition of one's ascribing states of consciousness, experiences, to oneself, in the way one does, that one should also ascribe them, or be prepared to ascribe them, to others who are not oneself" (p. 99). Strawson adds that the point is a "purely logical one" (*ibid.*, n.1). Two questions deserve to be raised: is this principle correct, and if it is true what does it imply? The standard answer, which seems correct to me, to the first question, is, I believe, that there is a true principle here, although care needs to be taken over its precise formulation.[13] The second question is, therefore, crucial. Strawson first argues that it follows that the Cartesian conception of subjects cannot be right. To be able to ascribe such predicates to others we must be able to pick them out in other ways, which is to say, under physical descriptions. Two doubts can be voiced. First, does the basic principle about predicates require that one can pick out a range of items? Secondly, since Cartesian egos do have other features besides mental ones, even if they are not physical ones, can they not be picked out using those descriptions? Strawson also draws from the basic principle a significant epistemological conclusion. It is that for some P-predicates our ways of telling that they apply to others must amount to "logically adequate criteria" (p. 105). Strawson says that if they are not logically adequate our ascription of them to others must be based on a correlation between the feature and something physical established in our own case, but this amounts to giving a priority to self-ascriptions. Three questions (out of many) can be voiced. First, what exactly does "logically adequate criteria" mean? Secondly, is it obvious that the only alternative epistemology would be an argument from analogy based on one's own case? This seems to overlook the possibility of an inference to the best explanation.[14] Thirdly, is the epistemological priority of self-ascription built into the argument from analogy ruled out by the purely logical constraint imposed in the basic principle? It is not clear that these must be answered Strawson's way, but nor is it clear that they cannot be.

Chapter 4: "Monads"

In the final chapter of Part I, Strawson chooses to illuminate his earlier conclusions and to continue his argument by considering, in a very abstract way, Leibniz's system, or some aspects of it. There are two fundamental points of contrast. First, Strawson has argued that the ability to pick out or identify objects in general rests ultimately on an ability to relate them to demonstratively discernible objects encountered in experience. Leibniz, in contrast, accepts the principle that any two distinct things are qualitatively different, and that we can in principle single anything out in purely general terms, using the complete notions there are for each individual.[15] Secondly, according to Leibniz, the basic individuals are monads, which are, in some sense, pure minds.[16] Strawson has, however, claimed that the basic mentally endowed entities cannot be purely mental, but must be persons, in his sense. The initial question for Leibniz's theory is what the unique completely general notion corresponding to each individual is. Leibniz talks of the point of view of each individual. However, as Strawson points out, if we understand this talk more or less literally, as a perspective on the world, there is no guarantee of uniqueness. Imagine, for example, a universe consisting of two qualitatively identical objects perceiving each other. In such a universe there is no unique point of view. Leibniz, however, did not believe in viewpoints on a public space. There is for him no public space, nor is there a public time. Viewpoint seems to stand simply for how the object is. Leibniz appears to believe that God must guarantee uniqueness in relation to this. Strawson's response at this point is to suggest that we cannot seriously envisage as a primary conceptual scheme something where uniqueness of reference is based on a theological guarantee. Nor can we envisage a basic scheme in which space and time are, in some sense, purely ideal. Strawson suggests an alternative reading of Leibniz according to which the basic entities are the very notions themselves. With entities such as concepts, according to Strawson, the identity of indiscernibles is guaranteed. Moreover, read this way Leibniz's thought that the basic entities do not causally interact would be vindicated. But this understanding is, as Strawson points out, too remote from our conception of the nature of basic things. Leibniz must think that the basic entities are the instantiators of the general notions. This, however, returns us to the requirement, and problem, that uniqueness is only guaranteed by God. As to the other contrast, Strawson develops a second problem for the idea of individual consciousness as basic entities. What understanding can we have of the difference between there being one such consciousness and there being a thousand such consciousnesses? The problem is soluble for persons because they occupy spaces. But for particular entities that are supposed not to do so, the basis for understanding number seems absent. This is a second problem for dualism.[17] The upshot of the comparison with Leibniz is, then, that both the necessity of thinking in terms of persons and the essential role of demonstrative reference are confirmed.

Subjects and predicates: Chapters 5 and 6

Part I of *Individuals* attempted to say what particulars are the basic subjects of reference, and what explains and follows from that. In Part II, entitled "Logical Subjects", Strawson focuses on the very general ideas of subjects and reference. He starts with the following claim. We have the contrasting notions of subject and predicate. We suppose that putting an instance of a subject expression with a predicate expression gives an assertion or proposition. Now, the claim in question is that although items of any category can be subjects, or the content of subjects, only universals and not particulars can be, or appear as, predicates.[18] Strawson's avowed aim is to "discover the rationale of the traditional view" (p. 138). To consider it he begins, in Chapter 5, by surveying elucidations of the subject–predicate distinction. He divides these elucidations into two broad sorts: first, what he calls grammatical criteria, and secondly, what he calls the category criterion. Under the general name "grammatical criteria" Strawson lists accounts of the subject–predicate distinction in terms of functions that different expressions have. Thus one version, for example, says that in using a subject expression a speaker refers to an individual and in using a predicate the speaker characterizes the individual. Strawson sets out other proposals, by for example, Peter Geach, W. V. Quine and Frege, which are broadly grammatical and functional, and compares them, asking in particular how explanatory they are. By the end he seems to think that we are left with something like the following characterization: subject expressions are nouns that aim to identify something, whereas predicates are the rest of such sentences, including importantly what we might call the verbal element, which contains the assertive or propositional element. He points out interestingly that this does not mean that everything *we* do with verbs or verb phrases, for example, indicating the relation between the time we are speaking of and the time when we ourselves are speaking, has to be indicated by the predicate component.

Strawson also describes what he calls the category criterion. Simplifying considerably, when we make a subject–predicate judgement we can think of its force as affirming a non-relational tie between two terms (or items).[19] The second item has to belong to a *characterizing* or a *sorting* category, which provide a principle for "collecting" objects. An example of characterization is saying that *A* is blue, and an example of a sorting case is saying that *A* is a flower. The category of a flower is one that permits counting, whereas the category of being blue does not. The category criterion proposes that we can define predication thus; y is predicated of x if x is asserted to be non-relationally tied to y either as an instance (the sorting case) or as so characterized. Strawson compares the two criteria and claims there is a correspondence between them, but he asks whether a more basic and explanatory characterization can be found.

In Chapter 6 Strawson reveals his own suggestion. He develops it in two ways, the first of which is the more crucial, but both sides of the theory are extremely ingenious. His first suggestion is that when an ordinary subject expression is used in its role of identifying an empirical particular it is presupposed that the speaker knows the truth of an empirical proposition. Thus, if I successfully refer to an item using the words "That F" I must know that a certain object is the one being demonstrated by me. By contrast, the employment in a sentence of the predicative, or classificatory, part does not presuppose any such empirical knowledge. For example, if I employ the predicate "is triangular" my understanding of the expression does not require empirical knowledge of the existence of anything. Maybe there are no triangles at all. The significance of the predicate does not depend on that. Strawson's proposal is that this fundamental contrast can be applied even where the predicate expressions become complex, and, moreover, the contrast explains certain features that are often themselves appealed to in explanations of the subject–predicate distinction. He proposes that it explains the Fregean intuition that subject expressions are in some sense complete, whereas predicate expressions are not. Further, Strawson suggests that with this contrast established in the central case, analogies can ground the extension of the subject–predicate distinction to other sorts of sentences.

Strawson's account rather brilliantly fits the assumptions about reference and predication that dominated thinking in the middle of the twentieth century. The account looks less plausible now, and I shall voice three reservations. First, there are examples that seem to show that speakers can refer without having identifying knowledge. For example, what identifying knowledge must I have when I use "Gödel" to pick out an individual I have heard talked about by some friends of mine? Secondly, there seem to be predicates that work by picking out sorts via things in the world. Thus, "x is gold" is, perhaps, to be explained as being true of things that are similar in certain ways to these lumps of matter. Such predicates seem to have empirical presuppositions. Needless to say, these two kinds of counter claims are themselves controversial. Finally, what is the justification when explaining a logical distinction for concentrating on empirical discourse?

This was the first part of Strawson's account. He then asks: is there a way to capture in general a type of proposition that is presupposed by the very practice of particular identification? Strawson assumes that if there is such a type of proposition it must not contain reference to particulars, nor must it rest on the classificatory system that applies to those particulars. Strawson's answer is that what is called a *feature-placing language* precisely expresses such claims. An example of a feature-placing claim is "It is raining". In saying this one is not picking out some particular bit of rain. It seems, rather, to amount solely to registering the presence where you are of some rain or other. In registering such a feature the speaker is not recognizing or picking out particular items, with their spatial boundaries and temporal histories. So this type of language, it seems, can count as prior to reference to particulars, and it looks plausible to say that where there are particulars there will, perforce, be truths expressible in a feature-placing language. There is, of course, a significant difference between this general presupposition and the presuppositions of reference supposedly isolated earlier. Strawson is not claiming that actual speakers either go through a phase of employing feature-placing languages or constantly engage in such a level of thinking.

Strawson's proposal is ingenious, but three issues can be raised. First, are there, perhaps, unobvious presuppositions of the feature-placing claims themselves that involve subject–predicate claims? If there are then feature-placing claims would not be properly prior to subject–predicate propositions. Secondly, is it right to regard feature-placing claims as the *unique* presuppositions? It might be thought, for example, that claiming that *b*, a particular item, is *F*, presupposes that *something* is *F*. Could it not be said that such existential claims also amount, in general, to presuppositions of subject introduction? Strawson rejects this because he thinks that the predicates in the general existential claims also figure in the subject–predicate discourse. This is, of course, true, but must that really disallow them? Thirdly, it is not easy to extract a particular type of feature-placing sentence from lots of subject–predicate sentences. For example, if I say "My car is broken", given the manifest variety of cars in respect of shape and material composition, what feature, in the normal sense, is presupposed?

Chapters 7 and 8: "Feature-placing" and "Existence"

In the final two chapters Strawson deepens his consideration of the issues raised by his approach to the subject–predicate distinction. He scrutinizes further the idea of a feature-placing language. He defends the assumption made in Chapter 6 that a feature-placing language is not itself a subject–predicate language. Two ways of so reading it are distinguished. Maybe it is predicating feature instantiations to places, which are the subjects. Strawson counters that there is no real reference to places. Spatial indication is too vague for that. Alternatively, maybe such sentences ascribe instantiation at a (rough) place to a feature taken as subject. As a self-standing language there are no grounds, according to Strawson, to treat it thus. Having prevented the collapse of the feature-placing alternative, Strawson briefly explores the question of how close a feature-placing language could come to saying more or less what we can say employing our subject–predicate language. He sees no way to approach the necessary expressive richness without bringing reference to definite spaces and times. However, with that he allows that the language could approximate to what we can say, but the cost would be a colossal complexity of both its referential and feature-placing expressions.

In the final chapter the main unifying theme is existence. This has, perhaps, two sides. First, Strawson accepts the familiar point that singular nouns in existential sentences (such as "God" in "God exists" or "God does not exist") cannot be counted as subject expressions. Grammar here is misleading. Secondly, he engages, in a mood of tolerant scepticism, with a common philosophical attitude. The attitude is one that claims that abstract objects do not exist, and that this denial places us under an obligation to avoid the employment of nouns in a subject position that appear to stand for such things. As Strawson points out, sentences of the disallowed kinds are very common, and eliminative paraphrases are very hard to find in some cases. Strawson's question is why we should accept that there is a notion of existence that is linked to subject expressions, and not to predicates, and is also such that *in that sense* there is something worrying in supposing that abstract things exist. Strawson fails to unearth any reason for that common opinion.

Conclusion

Strawson links the two parts of his book by pointing out that the supposed basic particulars described in Part I are also, in virtue of being particulars, paradigms of logical subjects. There is, if Strawson is right, such a link. It is, however, hard not to think that there is a considerable degree of independence between the two parts. The metaphysical and epistemological claims of Part I do not depend on or presuppose the logical doctrines developed in Part II, nor is there any dependence the other way. It is, therefore, very much a book of two halves. Of the halves it is the first one that had both an immediate and enduring effect on philosophical discussion.

What has the effect been? *Individuals* strongly influenced discussion of scepticism both about bodies and other minds, without, perhaps, fully persuading people. Its concern with the general conditions of reference has inspired a tradition that has investigated aspects of object-directed thought. The discussion of persons has been central to philosophical debate, because Strawson evidently laid bare some central truths. Finally, it broke the constraining shackles of what seems now a limiting conception of philosophy and reinvigorated the subject.[20]

Notes

1. Russell claimed in his famous theory of definite descriptions that "The F is G" is equivalent to "There is one and only one F and it is G" ("On Denoting", in his *Logic and Knowledge*, 41–36 (London: Allen and Unwin)). This treats "The F" as a disguised quantifier. Strawson proposed that "The F" is sometimes more like "That F", which picks out an item.

2. Of course, if there is constant and deep conceptual change the descriptive metaphysician would simply need to *describe* that.

3. Strawson's remark about method marks one respect in which he is aiming to distinguish between the type of philosophizing he is doing in *Individuals* and the type that had previously gone on (in Oxford).

4. Strawson's project of describing and explaining the fundamental basis of thought and talk about objects has been continued in G. Evans, *Varieties of Reference* (Oxford: Clarendon Press, 1982), D. Wiggins, *Sameness and Substance Renewed* (Cambridge: Cambridge University Press, 2001) and J. Campbell, *Reference and Consciousness* (Oxford: Clarendon Press, 2002). They all count as descriptive metaphysicians.

5. Although Strawson invariably talks of speakers and hearers, it is obvious that no restriction to spoken communication, as opposed to written, is intended.

6. The centrality of the notion of identification in Strawson's model of understanding reference raises the question whether it merits that centrality. That is not a doubt I shall develop here.

7. Strawson's twofold division resembles Russell's famous distinction between knowledge by acquaintance and knowledge by description. The major contrast is that Strawson allows, but Russell does not, that we can be acquainted with public spatial objects.

8. I am, of course, pretending that this might be a general description of the Eiffel tower!

9. In thinking about Strawson's theory it is important to distinguish the general idea that we think of concrete objects as without exception spatiotemporally related, and the further and questionable idea that we must pick them under spatiotemporal descriptions. I can pick out someone as the great-great-grandfather of this man, without having the slightest idea how he was spatially or temporally related to myself.

10. It is not easy to make this question precise. Strawson expresses part of it in these words: "Is there a class or category of particulars such that, as things are, it would not be possible to make all the identifying reference which we do make to particulars of other classes, unless we made identifying references to particulars of that class, whereas it would be possible to make all the identifying references we do make to particulars of that class without making identifying reference to particulars of the other classes?" (1959: 38–9). It is, of

course, Strawson's view that material bodies are basic. It is, however, very doubtful that we could make all the references we do to bodies without referring to other sorts of things. For example, we sometimes refer to people via reference to events, and such reference requires reference to particulars of the event sort. Thus, I might talk of the man injured in that crash. This reference would not occur without reference to events and hence material bodies cannot be counted as basic. In fact, probably nothing is.

11. There is something odd about this use of "objective". On any normal understanding of "objective", the body of the thinking subject, and indeed, the subject, himself or herself, are perfectly objective.

12. See G. Evans, "Things Without the Mind", in *Philosophical Subjects*, Z. Van Straaten (ed.), 76–116 (Oxford: Clarendon Press, 1980). Strawson himself responds to Evans's discussion in "Reply to Evans", in *Philosophical Subjects*, 273–82.

13. It is not a necessary consequence of "*Fx*" being a predicate that one ascribes it to a range of things, nor that one is particularly prepared to do so. It does seem to be a consequence that one understands its ascription across a range.

14. "Inference to the best explanation" is the name given to a pattern of inference in which we conclude something because it is the best explanation for some data. An example would be Robinson Crusoe's inference that he was not alone on seeing what looked like a footprint. The crucial point for us is that if our inferences to other minds are explanatory they do not depend on prior claims about ourselves. For a defence of such a view see H. Putnam, "Other Minds", in *Mind, Language and Reality*, 342–61 (Cambridge: Cambridge University Press, 1975).

15. Leibniz is associated with two principles about identity. The first, called Leibniz's law and generally accepted, can be expressed thus: if *A* is identical to *B* then they must be the same in all respects. The second principle is the identity of indiscernibles. This says that if *A* and *B* are the same in general respects then they are identical. This second principle, when formulated to avoid triviality, is not obviously true, but Leibniz accepted it. If true it guarantees that there is some general difference between every object.

16. Leibniz allows that many monads can be credited with mentality of only a very minimal kind, beneath even proper consciousness.

17. In later writings Strawson developed this anti-dualist point. See "Self, Mind and Body" (1966), reprinted in *Freedom and Resentment and Other Essays*, 169–77 (London: Methuen, 1974).

18. The categories of universal and particular can be explained for our purposes using examples. An individual person or physical object would be a particular; a general type or characteristic, such as bravery or being square, would be a universal. A defining characteristic of universals is that objects can instantiate them. Thus, Winston Churchill instantiates bravery. Particulars are normally divided into concrete and abstract. Thus my pen is a concrete particular, whereas the number two is an abstract particular. Universals are abstract non-particulars. It should not be assumed that this explanation of the terminology commits me to holding that all these different types do really exist. What exists is a philosophical question.

19. The point of calling the tie "non-relational" is to avoid a regress in the analysis. If the affirmed tie were itself to count as some relation then there would have to be another tie involved between the other elements and the tying relation, and then a regress has started. Of course, the device of labelling it "non-relational" does not amount to an explanation as to its nature.

20. I wish to thank John Shand for his advice and encouragement. I should also like to thank Paul Robinson for some very helpful comments.

Bibliography

Writings by Strawson

Strawson P. F. 1950a. "On Referring". Reprinted in *Logico-Linguistic Papers*, 1–27. London: Methuen (1971).

Strawson, P. F. 1950b. "Truth". Reprinted in *Logico-Linguistic Papers*, 190–213. London: Methuen (1971).

Strawson, P. F. 1952. *Introduction to Logical Theory*. London: Methuen.

Strawson, P. F. 1959. *Individuals*. London: Methuen.

Strawson, P. F. 1966a. *The Bounds of Sense*. London: Methuen.

Strawson, P. F. 1966b. "Self, Mind and Body". Reprinted in *Freedom and Resentment and Other Essays*, 169–77. London: Methuen (1974).

Strawson, P. F. 1971. *Logico-Linguistic Papers*. London: Methuen.

Strawson, P. F. 1974a. *Subject and Predicate in Logic and Grammar*. London: Methuen.

Strawson, P. F. 1974b. *Freedom and Resentment and Other Essays*. London: Methuen.

Strawson, P. F. 1980. "Reply to Evans". In *Philosophical Subjects*, Z. Van Straaten (ed.), 273–82. Oxford: Clarendon Press.

Writings by others

Ayer, A. J. 1964a. *The Concept of a Person and Other Essays*. London: Macmillan.

Ayer, A. J. 1964b. "The Concept of a Person". In his *The Concept of a Person and Other Essays*, 82–128. London: Macmillan.

Campbell, J. 1994. *Past, Space and Self*. Cambridge, MA: MIT Press.

Campbell, J. 2002. *Reference and Consciousness*. Oxford: Clarendon Press.

Evans, G. 1980. "Things Without the Mind". In *Philosophical Subjects*, Z. Van Straaten (ed.), 76–116. Oxford: Clarendon Press.

Evans G. 1982. *Varieties of Reference*. Oxford: Clarendon Press.

Evans G. 1985. *Collected Papers*. Oxford: Clarendon Press.

Hacker, P. 2002. "Strawson's Concept of a Person". *Proceedings of the Aristotelian Society* **CII**, 21–40.

Hahn, E. (ed.) 1998. *The Philosophy of P. F. Strawson*. Chicago, IL: Open Court.

Martin, C. B. 1969. "People". In *Contemporary Philosophy in Australia*, R. Brown & C. Rollins (eds), 158–72. London: Allen & Unwin.

Plantinga A. 1967. *God and Other Minds*. Ithaca, NY: Cornell University Press.

Putnam, H. 1975. "Other Minds". In his *Mind, Language and Reality*, 342–61. Cambridge: Cambridge University Press.

Russell, B. 1905. "On Denoting". In his *Logic and Knowledge*. London: Allen and Unwin.

Van Straaten, Z. (ed.) 1980. *Philosophical Subjects*. Oxford: Clarendon Press.

Wiggins, D. 2001. *Sameness and Substance Renewed*. Cambridge: Cambridge University Press.

Williams, B. 1973a. *Problems of the Self*. Cambridge: Cambridge University Press.

Williams, B. 1973b. "Strawson on Individuals". In his *Problems of the Self*, 101–26. Cambridge: Cambridge University Press. Originally published 1961.

Williams, B. 1973c. "Are Persons Bodies?". In his *Problems of the Self*, 64–81. Cambridge: Cambridge University Press. Originally published 1970.

Further reading

Strawson's own engagement with the Kantian themes in Part I is continued in Strawson (1966a). Strawson's discussion in Chapter 1 of reference and space are interestingly considered in Williams (1973b), and Campbell (1994: ch 1). Evans's profound reaction to the sound world is in Evans (1980), with Strawson's further reflections in Strawson (1980). The argument about persons has stimulated massive discussion. Early and interesting criticisms of Strawson are Ayer (1964b), Plantinga (1967), Martin (1969) and Williams (1973c). A sympathetic recent discussion is Hacker (2002). Of most relevance to Part II is Strawson (1974a), in which he develops, with some continuities and some changes, his own ideas about the subject–predicate distinction. Williams (1973b) picks up some issues. Van Straaten (1980) and Hahn (1998) are collections of papers, with responses by Strawson, many of which discuss points raised by *Individuals*.

3

John Rawls

A Theory of Justice

Anthony Simon Laden

In his classes, John Rawls routinely quoted R. G. Collingwood's remark that "the history of political theory is not the history of different answers to one and the same question, but the history of a problem more or less constantly changing, whose solution was changing with it" (Rawls 2000b: xvi). To understand Rawls's own work, we would do well to understand the problem he took himself to be addressing. Fortunately, Rawls tells us what that problem is:

> During much of modern moral philosophy the predominant systematic theory has been some form of utilitarianism. One reason for this is that it has been espoused by a long line of brilliant writers who have built up a body of thought truly impressive in its scope and refinement. ... Those who criticized them often did so on a much narrower front. ... [T]hey failed, I believe, to construct a workable and systematic moral conception to oppose it. The outcome is that we often seem forced to choose between utilitarianism and intuitionism. ...
>
> What I have attempted to do is to generalize and carry to a higher order of abstraction the traditional theory of the social contract. ... [T]his theory seems to offer an alternative to the dominant utilitarianism of the tradition. ... Of the traditional views, it is this conception, I believe, which best approximates our considered judgments of justice and constitutes the most appropriate moral basis for a democratic society. (1999: xviii)

There are two points to take from this passage. First, Rawls aims to provide a systematic alternative to utilitarianism. His argument is thus often comparative rather than deductive, and requires understanding where Rawls thinks utilitarianism goes wrong as well as the contours of his own view.

Secondly, and more importantly, Rawls aims to provide a conception of justice that can serve as an "appropriate moral basis for a democratic society". That is, his arguments show the appropriateness of his theory of justice for a democratic society, rather than how it can be derived from a theory of human nature. Much of Rawls's method, as well as the content of the principles of justice he defends, depends on this point. Democracy places constraints on how and what we argue for, and Rawls's arguments are often shaped by those constraints. Although I shall discuss many of these constraints below, one is worth mentioning at this stage: in a democracy, everyone has equal authority to accept or reject principles of justice. It is thus not the job of professional philosophers or politicians to impose a theory of justice on citizens. They, like all citizens, can only present arguments and reasons for their views, and it is up to each of us to assess those reasons and join in the discussion. As readers of *A Theory of Justice*, our job is not merely to learn its various philosophical moves and positions, but to engage and argue with it. This essay aims to provide a basis for that engagement.

The first section discusses the aspects of Rawls's view that follow from its aim to provide a moral basis for a democratic society. The next three sections then take up the major parts of that argument. The second discusses what Rawls calls "the two principles of justice" as well as some of the institutions and policies that might be necessary to realize them. The third examines the "original position". The fourth looks at Rawls's arguments that a society based on his conception of justice, "justice as fairness", would be stable.

Before beginning the discussion of *A Theory of Justice* in earnest, however, there is a complication that needs noting. There is an important sense in which *A Theory of Justice* is not a single book, but three. Rawls published *A Theory of Justice* in 1971. In preparation for its translation into German in 1975, Rawls revised the original text. All subsequent translations followed the revised text. This text was finally published for the first time in English in 1999, and it is this revised edition to which this essay refers. After 1975, Rawls continued to think about the material in *A Theory of Justice*. In 1993, he published *Political Liberalism*, which takes up the question of democratic legitimacy and sets out the context in which he came to think the arguments for justice as fairness were best made. Situating justice as fairness within political liberalism required some new conceptual machinery and some changes in the presentation of the view, but no serious substantive revisions. In 2000, he published a summary restatement of the arguments in *A Theory of Justice* under the title, *Justice as Fairness: A Restatement.* This book presents the arguments of justice as fairness in a manner consistent with the demands of political liberalism, and with several other changes that Rawls thought improved the arguments.

Space limitations prevent any serious discussion of the relationship between justice as fairness and political liberalism here. In what follows, I shall present the main features of the revised edition of *A Theory of Justice* as if it was the last thing that Rawls wrote, although I shall do so in a way that emphasizes the features of the view that continue to play an important role in light of his later writings.[1]

Justice in a democratic society

What are the special features of a democratic society that would require special features in its conception of justice? Note that a democratic society is more than just a democratic government, or even a society with a democratic government. By calling a society democratic, Rawls means to pick out something about the members of that society and their relationships to one another. First, a democratic society is an association of citizens. Citizens are free and equal, and, collectively, the source of political power and authority within the society. A conception of justice for a democratic society thus must provide fair terms of cooperation among citizens, and do so in a way that those citizens can accept. Fair terms of cooperation among free and equal citizens will have to find a way to balance the claims of liberty and equality (Rawls 2000a: 2). For this balance to be fair, it must specify terms of cooperation that treat individual citizens as distinct: losses to one person cannot be offset by gains to another or even many others (1999: 3). One of the fundamental problems that Rawls sees with utilitarianism is that it allows such trade-offs because it evaluates only the aggregate total utility of a society. As a result, it "does not take seriously the distinction between persons", because it treats citizens as interchangeable vessels of utility (*ibid.*: 25). Justice as fairness, Rawls argues, is a better conception of justice for a democratic society because its principles balance the claims of liberty and equality while not treating citizens as interchangeable.

Secondly, because citizens in a democratic society are free, they are likely to adopt widely different life plans, and endorse different views about what makes life valuable and society good, what Rawls calls "conceptions of the good" (Rawls 1999: 11, 81). An adequate theory of justice cannot ignore these differences. It cannot assume that everyone is a Christian, or interested in making lots of money, or values living in a traditional family. At the same time, a democratic society must at least strive to be "well-ordered" (*ibid.*: 4–5, 397–9). It must aim to have a shared set of rules and principles of justice that govern the interaction of citizens and thus at times constrain their pursuit of their own good. This suggests that an adequate conception of justice for a democratic society will have to give principles of justice (the right) priority over particular conceptions of the good. To insist on the "priority of the right over the good" (*ibid.*: 28) means two things. First, within justice as fairness the principles of justice (the right) are, to the extent possible, articulated and defended without reference to any particular conception of the good. As a result, a society guided by those principles leaves room for different citizens to affirm those principles and yet to have and pursue different conceptions of the good. Secondly, the principles of justice serve to constrain the claims we can make on one another via the state in the name of what we take to be good (*ibid.*: 27–8). So, for instance, since the principles of justice forbid discrimination on the basis of race, the fact that some people's interests and values are served by such discrimination counts as no reason at all to allow such discrimination. Utilitarianism, Rawls claims, can only condemn racism by showing that its harms outweigh its benefits. By making the right prior to the good, justice as fairness maintains that the wrongness of discrimination disqualifies whatever benefits it produces from figuring in our social decisions about whether to allow discrimination.

Democratic institutions and the principles they realize must be freely endorsed by citizens. Citizens will endorse principles of justice if, given their particular commitments and conceptions of the good, they see sufficient value in their continuation and are thus willing to make the necessary sacrifices to maintain them.[2] When citizens endorse principles of justice, Rawls says that the principles are "stable" (*ibid.*: 398). Stability is thus one of the most important criteria for determining whether a particular conception of justice is appropriate for a democratic society.

The aim of offering a conception of justice for a democratic society also shapes Rawls's method. Since citizens are the source of political power, arguments about political principles that shape the terms of social cooperation among citizens must be addressed to them. Rawls describes this requirement as the criterion of "publicity" (*ibid.*: 15). Rawls defines justification as "argument addressed to those who disagree with us, or to ourselves when we are of two minds. … Being designed to reconcile by reason, justification proceeds from what all parties to the discussion hold in common" (*ibid.*: 508). In a democratic society, the parties to the discussion are all citizens, and since citizens do not, by hypothesis, share a full-blown conception of the good, any adequate justification of principles of justice must provide an argument from common premises that can reconcile these differences. Rawls thus aims to provide an argument that can be addressed to our fellow citizens without relying on premises about which we disagree. The systematic nature of utilitarianism gives it an advantage over intuitionism in grounding the kind of public justification that is required in a democracy. If our reasons give out in our intuitions (as intuitionism claims), and those differ, then when we deliberate about the justice of a given law or policy there will be no way to reach a reasoned shared consensus. Democratic politics will, at base, be about majorities and minorities, winners and losers. Rawls holds out the hope that democratic politics can be something more, a means by which we reason together about our common endeavours. At the same time, while a systematic theory will avoid the problem just mentioned, it cannot rely on a full-blown conception of the good that is not shared by all citizens, and so it cannot rest on what Rawls came to call a "comprehensive doctrine", such as utilitarianism (2000a: 32–3). So Rawls's method in *A Theory of Justice* is designed to generate a systematic theory that is nevertheless not comprehensive.

These constraints thus change the aim of political philosophy. Rather than producing a logically sound deduction from self-evident premises, political philosophy should provide arguments that lead us to "reflective equilibrium" (Rawls 1999: 18). We achieve reflective equilibrium when we can bring our considered judgements on a topic at all levels of generality into balance. Achieving reflective equilibrium thus requires that we occasionally revise particular judgements to bring them in line with a theory we find compelling, and sometimes revise the theory when it conflicts with concrete judgements that strike us as particularly well-grounded. We might thus abandon our rejection of same-sex marriage on seeing that such rejection conflicts with our commitments to human equality and toleration. On the other hand, we might reject utilitarianism if it conflicts with our more particular judgements that torture is always wrong. In achieving reflective equilibrium, it is important that the equilibrium we achieve is both general and wide: that it involve a consideration of rival views, and the views and judgements of others (*ibid.*: 42–5).

In order to describe the movement of the argument of justice as fairness from shared premises to particular principles of justice, Rawls distinguishes between "concepts" and "conceptions" (*ibid.*: 5). A concept of justice is a general description of the meaning of the term. A conception of justice, in contrast, provides a more fully worked-out interpretation of the terms in the concept. Rawls claims that while in a democratic society citizens have different conceptions of justice, they nevertheless share a concept of justice: "institutions are just when no arbitrary distinctions are made between persons in the balance between competing claims to the advantages of social life" (*ibid.*: 5). Since we share a concept of justice, we can justify a particular conception of justice to our fellow citizens by showing that it provides the best interpretation of the concept in light of other features of society that our fellow citizens also acknowledge. The argument of *A Theory of Justice* can be seen as developing a particular conception of justice from the concept of justice. It develops a model that captures the essential elements of the concept of justice as it functions in a democratic society, and shows that this model generates the particular conception of justice he calls "justice as fairness". He calls this model the "original position" and this form of argument "constructivist" (1993: 89–99) as it proceeds by constructing a conception out of a concept. The details of this argument will occupy the rest of the essay. Note, however, that achieving wide and general reflective equilibrium requires not only that we make a convincing argument for a set of principles, but also that we show that these principles can be brought into equilibrium with our considered judgements. The bulk of these arguments take place in Parts II and III of *A Theory of Justice*, and I discuss them in §§ "The two principles of justice" and "Moral psychology and stability".

The two principles of justice

Before examining Rawls's constructivist argument, I discuss the content of his conception of justice. At the heart of this conception are the two principles of justice:

> First principle: "Each person is to have an equal right to the most extensive total system of equal basic liberties compatible with a similar system of liberty for all."

> Second Principle: "Social and economic inequalities are to be arranged so that they are both: (a) to the greatest benefit of the least advantaged, consistent with the just savings principle, and (b) attached to offices and positions open to all under conditions of fair equality of opportunity" (Rawls 1999: 266).[3]

These two principles are lexically ordered, meaning that there can be no trade-offs between the first and the second, or between the parts of the second (where (b) is prior to (a)). Thus, a just society does not restrict basic liberties such as the right to vote in order to achieve greater levels of economic equality as doing so would involve violating the first principle to satisfy the second (*ibid.*: 53–4).

These principles provide a basis for assessing the justice of what Rawls calls the "basic structure of society": "the way in which the major social institutions distribute fundamental rights and duties and determine the division of advantages from social cooperation" (*ibid.*: 6). The basic structure includes not only the constitution and agencies of government, but also the major social and economic institutions of a democratic society such as competitive markets, the family and private property.[4] We are to assess the justice of these institutions taken together, by asking whether they work to realize or thwart the two principles of justice.

The two principles aim to capture the basic idea that in a just democratic society citizens are free and equal. Particular inequalities between citizens, whether political, economic or social, are thus only justifiable if they are justifiable to all, and this requires that those inequalities benefit those on the bottom as well as those on the top. This can happen when inequalities serve to provide incentives for arduous work or risky ventures that produce large amounts of social goods. In a society that benefits from these goods, everyone may be better off than anyone in the other, more equal society that does not produce these goods. In addition, the two principles of justice place a special protection on liberty, such that with respect to basic liberties, no inequality is justified.

Although the subject of the first principle is the protection of basic liberties, it has the form of a principle of equality, and has rather important egalitarian implications. The guarantee of basic liberties must be done in a way that is consistent with there being equal liberty for all. Thus, to the extent that my exercise of my liberty would have the effect of curtailing the liberty of someone else whose liberty is already more limited than mine, the first principle of justice would require not the protection, but the regulation, of my liberty. Constitutional protections of individual liberties that constrain the power of majorities work this way, regulating the liberty of political participation of some (those in the majority) in order to protect the liberties, perhaps including the political liberties, of others whose liberties are less extensive or more vulnerable (those in the minority) (Rawls 1999: 200–203).

Secondly, in later writings Rawls adds to the first principle the idea that some basic liberties (namely the political ones such as the right to vote and to participate in politics) need not only be protected but also guaranteed their "fair value": this "ensures that citizens similarly gifted and motivated have roughly an equal chance of influencing the government's policy and of attaining positions of authority irrespective of their economic and social class" (2000a: 46). Since various factors beyond the mere formal guarantee of political rights can undermine the fair value of political liberties, the first principle requires addressing these matters as well. Thus, for example, in the United States today, the campaign finance system gives undue influence to those with greater wealth, thus undermining the fair value of political liberties for those with less wealth. To the extent that this can be remedied by such measures as the public financing of elections, then satisfying the first principle would not require a more egalitarian distribution of wealth. To the degree that such measures are insufficient because those with greater wealth have, for instance, greater access to and control of the public media and thus more influence on the course of public debate, satisfying the first principle may require redistributive measures.

Thirdly, the basic liberties protected by the first principle are specified by a list (this marks a change from the 1971 version). The exact list will depend on various particular features of the society, but it will include such key elements as: "political liberty (the right to vote and to hold public office) and freedom of speech and assembly; liberty of conscience and freedom of thought; freedom of the person, which includes freedom from psychological oppression and physical assault and dismemberment (integrity of the person); the right to hold personal property and freedom from arbitrary arrest and seizure as defined by the concept of the rule of law" (1999: 53).

The second principle consists of three parts: fair equality of opportunity, a just savings principle, and the requirement that social and economic inequalities be to the advantage of the least well-off (the so-called "difference principle"). Fair equality of opportunity is a more stringent requirement than mere formal equality of opportunity or what Rawls refers to as "careers open to talents" (*ibid.*: 73). "Careers open to talents" forbids direct exclusion and discrimination. In a society where there is a great deal of economic inequality, and those with more money can purchase significantly better education, mere formal equality of opportunity will probably result in those from privileged backgrounds occupying most of the positions of power and privilege in the society. Fair equality of opportunity overcomes this perpetuation of advantage, by requiring that "those who are at the same level of talent and ability, and have the same willingness to use them, should have the same prospects of success regardless of their initial place in the social system" (*ibid.*: 63). Fair equality of opportunity thus nullifies the advantages of class from one generation to the next. This can be achieved by placing various limits on the accumulation of wealth, through income and estate taxes, as well as by placing limits on what that wealth can buy, by providing sufficiently high-quality free public education such that wealthy parents cannot buy their children significant educational advantages by sending them to expensive schools. Whatever methods are used to achieve such background conditions, however, must be consistent with the protection of the equal basic liberties afforded by the first principle.

The second part of the second principle requires a just level of savings. No generation is allowed to unfairly use up assets so as to leave future generations at an unfair disadvantage, but at the same time no generation is required to unduly sacrifice its own wellbeing in providing for future generations. Since we do not deserve to be born into a particular generation, we cannot rely on that fact to justify having an unfair level of resources (*ibid.*: 251–8).

The most controversial part of Rawls's second principle is known as the "difference principle". It mandates that beyond achieving fair equality of opportunity, a just society must be organized so that any social and economic inequalities are "to the greatest benefit of the least advantaged" (*ibid.*: 266). Note that this provides a particular interpretation of the general idea that permissible inequalities are those that are to everyone's advantage. The difference principle addresses a shortcoming of the principle of fair equality of opportunity. Fair equality of opportunity offsets advantages in one's social origins, so that being born into a wealthy family (something no one deserves) cannot be a source of social or economic advantage. It does not, however, correct for differences in people's natural talents or levels of motivation. Rawls claims that we no more deserve our natural talents than we deserve to be born into a certain family or class, and so distributing economic and social advantage on the basis of these features would also be "arbitrary from a moral point of view" and thus unfair.[5] Rawls argues that whatever benefits we can derive from our talents and hard work depend so thoroughly on the social system in which we develop and use those talents, that we only have a reasonable claim on those rewards that would be available to us under a fair social system (*ibid.*: 74, 76; 2000a: 72). The difference principle addresses the problem of inequalities due to talents, not by trying to equalize expectations across talent levels directly, but by requiring that whatever benefits accrue to the more talented do so in a manner that maximally benefits the less advantaged. Rawls describes the resultant form of social equality as "democratic equality" and contrasts it with "liberal equality", the title he gives to a conception of justice that includes fair equality of opportunity but no difference principle (Rawls 1999: 65ff.; Cohen 1989).

Rawls calls the moral idea behind the difference principle (and, indeed, the two principles as whole) "reciprocity" (1999: 88). Reciprocity demands that we only exact from a scheme of social cooperation that which we can reasonably expect that others could agree to. It thus lies between a principle of total altruism, whereby everyone sacrifices for the good of others, and total egoism where everyone uses whatever means they have at their disposal to get the best deal possible for themselves. This idea of reciprocity captures the features of the traditional idea of fraternity that are appropriate for a democracy, where citizens recognize one another as free and equal, but are not necessarily bound by stronger ties of affection (*ibid.*: 90–91).

What, exactly, does the difference principle tell us to do? There are four points to keep in mind. First, the general aim is to assess the justice of basic

structures in terms of how those who are worst off in them do. Given two societies that satisfy the first principle of justice, provide fair equality of opportunity
and a just savings principle, the more just of the two societies is the one that
provides the higher standard of living to those at the bottom, regardless of how
those elsewhere in the society fare. Secondly, we are not to look to the individual
who is at the bottom, but to a representative member of the group at the bottom. In defining that group, we may want to use different criteria depending on
what aspect of a social system we are evaluating. Thus, if the question involves
the structure of the economy and the distribution of income and wealth, we
might ask how unskilled workers fare. If we are asking about social institutions
that create and perpetuate unequal systems based on gender or race, then we
should look to members of the gender or race who are disadvantaged (women,
non-whites). In *A Theory of Justice*, Rawls focuses on questions of economic
inequality, and so he focuses on economic criteria to pick out the least favoured
group. Nevertheless, the least favoured group is not definable by anything but
its position in the distribution. Thus, if, in one society, unskilled workers are the
worst off group, and in another society, unskilled workers have a much higher
standard of living, and people with advanced degrees find themselves the worst
off, then the difference principle tells us to compare the plight of the unskilled
workers in the first society with the plight of the people with advanced degrees
in the second society. If the unskilled workers in the first society do better, then
the first society is more just according to the difference principle.

Thirdly, we are to look at people's expectations over a complete life, and not at
a particular time when they are badly off. Fourthly, and most importantly, social
and economic advantages are to be measured in terms of what Rawls calls "primary goods". In *A Theory of Justice*, Rawls describes primary goods as "things
every rational man is presumed to want whatever else he wants" (1999: 79). They
include rights and liberties, income and wealth, and what Rawls calls "the social
bases of self-respect", an idea I discuss more fully in § "Moral psychology and stability" below (*ibid.*: 54, 79).[6] Primary goods are meant to be things that are likely
to be useful to any reasonable and rational plan of life. In addition, they provide
an objective measure of wellbeing that allows for public comparisons of advantage. Since the principles of justice need to be the basis of a public conception
of justice, they must refer to features of persons that are objective and publicly
knowable. This points to another problem with utilitarianism, which measures
wellbeing in terms of happiness or preference satisfaction, not objective or publicly knowable quantities. There may be no publicly agreed upon means of determining a particular group's level of utility in comparison to other groups and so
no agreement about who is worst off in terms of utility, or how their utility is
affected by different basic structures (*ibid.*: 78–80).

What might a just, well-ordered society that realized the two principles of justice look like? Rawls claims that the principles of justice will rule out a socialist command economy because it would violate the first principle. Perhaps more surprisingly, they also rule out welfare state capitalism, because it violates the second principle (*ibid.*: 240–42; 2000a: 137–8). Instead, the two principles of justice support either a liberal socialist society or what he calls a property-owning democracy (1999: xiv–xvi, 242; 2000a: 138–40). Although the difference between property-owning democracy and welfare state capitalism is not stressed in *A Theory of Justice*, Rawls makes a point of differentiating them in his later work, and claims there that the failure to do so was one of the more serious flaws in the earlier work (1999: xiv; 2000a: 132 n.2, 138 n.5). Rawls, unfortunately, does not provide a detailed picture of what a property-owning democracy would look like, although he considers it an "alternative to capitalism" (2000a: 135–6). He does, however, say the following:

> the background institutions of property-owning democracy ... [try] to disperse the ownership of wealth and capital, and thus to prevent a small part of society from controlling the economy and indirectly political life itself. Property-owning democracy avoids this, not by redistributing income to those with less at the end of each period, so to speak, but rather by ensuring the widespread ownership of productive assets and human capital (educated abilities and trained skills) at the beginning of each period; all this against a background of equal basic liberties and fair equality of opportunity. The idea is not simply to assist those who lose out through accident or misfortune (although this must be done), but instead to put all citizens in a position to manage their own affairs and to take part in social cooperation on a footing of mutual respect under appropriately equal conditions.
>
> (1999: xv)

Here we can see a further important feature of the difference principle. By mandating an equitable distribution of social and economic advantages as a matter of justice, institutions that satisfy the difference principle do not treat those who are worst off as charity cases in need of public aid, but as equal citizens, entitled to their fair share:

> The least advantaged are not, if all goes well, the unfortunate and unlucky – objects of our charity and compassion, much less our pity – but those to whom reciprocity is owed as a matter of political justice among those who are free and equal citizens along with everyone

else. Although they control fewer resources, they are doing their full share on terms recognized by all as mutually advantageous and consistent with everyone's self-respect. (2000a: 139)

The original position

Rawls claims that we can see more clearly how the reasons that favour the two principles of justice fit together into a compelling scheme if we can bring our considered judgements to bear through a model of the concept of justice in a democratic society. That model, or "device of representation" as Rawls often calls it, is the "original position". The original position captures the basic insight of social contract theory, by imagining the principles of justice as a kind of agreement among appropriately situated parties (Rawls 1999: 102). Before looking at the details of the original position argument, it is important to be clear about the role it plays within Rawls's overall argument. Finding an appropriate moral basis for a conception of justice for a democratic society requires finding principles that all citizens can agree to, despite their differences. The agreement in the original position is not that agreement, however, as the parties are not, nor are they supposed to resemble, real people. The point of the original position is that it helps to convince actual citizens, such as the readers of *A Theory of Justice*, that reasons they are willing to acknowledge, when combined in a perspicuous manner, favour the two principles of justice over utilitarianism. The argument from the original position has two main parts. First, Rawls argues that the various elements of the original position serve to model features of the concept of justice in a democratic society that we regard as important. Secondly, he argues that the parties thus situated and characterized would choose the two principles of justice discussed in the previous section.

The original position is set up as follows: a number of purely rational, mutually disinterested people come together to choose a set of principles of justice to govern a society. They are purely rational; they are moved only by their own advantage, and not by sympathy for others, moral commitments or, Rawls insists, envy. Each acts to advance the goals of a group of citizens in that society. In the original position, these representatives are symmetrically situated: they have the same knowledge, the same level of influence, the same opportunities to voice their views. Furthermore, the parties are behind what Rawls calls the "veil of ignorance". The veil of ignorance prevents the parties from knowing a number of otherwise relevant facts about the society for which they are choosing principles or the people they represent. They do not know, for example, the level of development of the society, or what place in the society those they represent occupy. They do not know their levels of income, education, status or even their conceptions of the good. All they know are the following: that the circumstances of justice obtain in their society; that those they represent prefer more primary goods to fewer; and various basic laws about human psychology and motivation and economic and social theory. The parties must choose principles of justice from a list that includes, among others, Rawls's two principles and utilitarian principles. They must come to a unanimous and binding agreement about their choice. To do this, they proceed in two steps. First, they select what seem to them the best principles, given what they know, the constraints of their position and their rationality. Since these principles are being chosen as if the choice was final, however, they also need to check whether those for whom they choose will be able to live under them. Thus, in the second step, they try to figure out, on the basis of their general knowledge of human psychology, whether these principles would be stable, whether actual people living under them would come to affirm these principles and willingly guide their conduct in accord with them. The chosen principles are only to be adopted if they would be stable, and so it is only after the two principles of justice are shown to be stable that the argument from the original position is complete (Rawls 1999: 124, 465; 2000a: 89). Showing that the two principles are stable turns out to give us, here and now, further grounds for agreeing to them, and so the discussion of stability completes not only the original position argument but also the argument of the book as a whole.

The various features of the original position capture the elements of the concept of justice for a democratic society. First, justice is "the virtue of practices where there are competing interests and where persons feel entitled to press their rights on each other" (Rawls 1999: 112). We invoke considerations of justice when our interests conflict, and each feels some entitlement to press her case. Rawls models this by making the parties purely rational and mutually disinterested. Furthermore, principles of justice set out fair terms of cooperation. Fairness is ensured because the parties are symmetrically and equally situated. Finally, when deciding on principles of justice, it is not appropriate to favour one principle over another in virtue of what it does for me, even if I can offer more neutral reasons on its behalf. The veil of ignorance prevents the parties from making choices on the basis of such self-regarding reasons. Note that the original position models the rationality of citizens through the characterization of the parties, and the reasonableness of citizens through its structure.[7] Rawls is not attempting to derive moral concepts from non-moral premises.

Since the argument aims to help us reach reflective equilibrium, Rawls points out that the final specification of the original position can be refined to ensure that it produces the desired result (*ibid.*: 122). The force of the overall argument for justice as fairness turns not merely on the step from the specification of the original position to the choice made within it, but rather on helping us to see how the two principles of justice and the institutions they would endorse reflect our ideas of justice. We can thus change parts of the structure in order to bring out those connections more clearly, and the clarity of those connections will have an impact on how we reconcile our particular considered judgements with our more theoretical commitments.

There has been a great deal written on Rawls's argument that the parties in the original position would choose the two principles of justice, and Rawls himself substantially altered his presentation of the argument in his later writings (2000a: 80–134). Nevertheless, the basic ideas have not changed in his various reformulations, and for a basic understanding of *A Theory of Justice* they suffice. Given that the parties are equally and symmetrically situated, we can imagine a natural first proposal being purely egalitarian principles. Since the parties aim to maximize primary goods but do not care about their relative level (they are mutually disinterested and free of envy), they would all also agree to a set of principles that allowed departures from equality when these benefited everyone's share of primary goods.

At this point, however, we can imagine a kind of counterargument wherein one of the parties points out to the others that liberties and opportunity have a special place among the primary goods, and that while an unequal distribution of income and wealth that raised everyone's standard of living might be good for all, it is not so clearly the case that the same would hold for liberty or opportunity. First, it is harder to see how giving some greater liberty than others would have the effect of increasing the liberty of those with less. Secondly, the value of liberty is of a different sort than the value of income and wealth. The parties know that the people they represent have particular conceptions of the good, and that these may very well lead them to have ends that they would consider non-negotiable (Rawls 1999: 180). Think, for instance, of someone with strong religious beliefs, who believes as a result of his faith that he must engage in certain religious practices. Such a person will not regard his ability to worship as he wishes as just another one of his goods that might be traded for something else. The parties thus have a reason to put additional stress on the protection of basic liberties.

Similar arguments can be made for fair equality of opportunity. First, it is hard to see how extending opportunities for only some people on the basis of anything but their talents and willingness to work could serve to increase the opportunities for all. Secondly, having the same opportunities in life as one's fellow citizens is a mark of one's equal standing, and so it plays a role in securing the social bases of self-respect in a way that equality of income does not. Finally, abandoning fair equality of opportunity for mere formal equality of opportunity allows one's opportunity to be in large part determined by one's social background, which one does not deserve. And so we are left with a preliminary argument for the two principles of justice.

In addition, Rawls provides a somewhat more formal argument by way of showing that the two principles would be chosen over utilitarian principles. We can see the force of that argument stemming from a consideration of what Rawls calls the "strains of commitment" (*ibid*.: 153–4). The parties in the original position must choose principles of justice as if they were making an irrevocable choice for all eternity. They must thus consider whether or not the strains of that agreement on those they represent will be bearable or not should, after the veil is lifted, those people turn out to fare poorly in the society. If the strains of commitment will be too great, that is a compelling reason to reject the given principles.

A consideration of the strains of commitment provides strong reasons for the parties to choose the two principles over utilitarianism. First, utilitarianism does not place the same emphasis on the protection of equal basic liberties. Although many utilitarians argue that a system of basic liberties increases overall utility, the protection is secured in an indirect manner, and this leads to the possibility that under utilitarian principles of justice, some individuals could find their liberties curtailed to increase the total utility in the society. Given the potential importance and non-negotiability of the kinds of ends that liberties protect, the parties should reject any conception of justice that provides a less stringent protection of basic liberties than the two principles.

A similar argument can be made about the difference principle over a utilitarian distributive principle. This argument relies on two features of democratic society discussed above. Principles for a democratic society must meet the publicity condition and they must be stable. Rawls argues that principles that embody an idea of reciprocity and mutual respect are more likely to be stable than principles that fail to do so and thus require a greater degree of altruism and sympathetic sacrifice. To see this point, imagine two societies. In the first, the two principles of justice hold. In the second, the first principle holds, there is fair equality of opportunity, but further inequality is governed by a principle of utility: economic inequality is justified to the extent that it raises the total level of wealth in the society. Now imagine that someone in the worst off group in each society asks her fellow citizens why she should accept her lot, and regard the terms of social cooperation as fair. In the first society, the publicly available answer is that the inequalities satisfy the difference principle, and so although she is worse off than others in her society, a different social arrangement would mean that someone, perhaps her, perhaps someone else, would be even worse off than she is now. Such an answer is consistent with her fellow citizens saying to her that she is one of them, and they take her wellbeing seriously. They can thus answer her truthfully in a manner that respects her as a free and equal fellow citizen. Furthermore, she cannot publicly advocate in good faith an alternative arrangement that would improve her lot. By hypothesis, any such alternative would leave some other group even worse off than she is now, and it is not reasonable for her to demand that they accept such an arrangement.

What can be said to the person at the bottom of the utilitarian distribution? By hypothesis, she is worse off than the worst off person in the first society. Why should she accept her status, given that under the two principles of justice she would be better off and no one else would be worse off than she is now? In the utilitarian society, the publicly available answer is that her being badly off makes possible greater total utility in the society. That is, she is poorer than she needs to be in order that people who are already richer than she is can be even richer. Such an answer clearly fails to show her respect as a full equal as it says that society is willing to use her for other people's benefit. As a result, she is not likely to endorse the principles that guide her society; the strains on her commitment will be much greater.

Moral psychology and stability

We now come to the second part of the argument from the original position, which requires that the parties check whether their preferred principles would be stable in an actual well-ordered society. A society will be stable to the extent that those who live in it can affirm its basic principles, not because they are backed by the coercive power of the state, but because citizens value them and the lives they make possible. As Rawls puts the point:

> Best of all, a theory should present a description of an ideally just state of affairs, a conception of a well-ordered society such that the aspiration to realize this state of affairs, and to maintain it in being, answers to our good and is continuous with our natural sentiments. A perfectly just society should be part of an ideal that rational human beings could desire more than anything else once they had full knowledge and experience of what it was.   (1999: 417–18)

The arguments in Part III of *A Theory of Justice*, then, are addressed not only to parties in the original position, but to us as we search for reflective equilibrium. Showing that the two principles can answer to our good cannot be a straightforward exercise, however. First, justice as fairness places the right prior to the good. The principles of justice are not defended on the grounds that they answer to our conception of the good, so there is no initial reason to think that they will. Secondly, we do not share a conception of the good, and so the argument for this claim cannot start from a particular fully developed conception of the good.[8]

Rawls's argument for the goodness of justice as fairness has two parts. First, he shows that doing one's part to uphold and live within just institutions fits into a rational plan of life, and is in this sense good. Secondly, he argues that those who live under justice as fairness will develop a sense of justice that will lead them to act from its principles, and that they will rightly regard this sense of justice as good for them.

Rawls begins the first part of the argument by developing the outline of a theory of the good that he calls "goodness as rationality" (*ibid*.: 347–96). This theory holds that something is good when it has the features that it is rational to want in a thing of that kind (*ibid*.: 350–51). By extension, a life is good when it is lived according to a rational plan of life that the person is able to carry out. Principles of justice are stable, then, if living in a society governed by them can form part of a rational plan of life. This argument proceeds in three steps. First, Rawls introduces what he calls the Aristotelian principle: "other things equal, human beings enjoy the exercise of their realized capacities (their innate or trained abilities), and this enjoyment increases the more the capacity is realized, or the greater its complexity" (*ibid*.: 374). The Aristotelian principle implies that a rational plan of life that includes the realization and exercise of complex capacities will make life more enjoyable than one that does not. This claim is not a moral judgement about the worth of individual lives, nor does it play any role in doling out rewards within justice as fairness. The point is merely that for any given individual, a plan of life that provides these opportunities will lead to a more enjoyable life than one that does not. For most, if not all, people, it is rational to want a life to be more enjoyable, and so, all things being equal, such a life will be good.

Secondly, Rawls claims that the Aristotelian principle has a "companion effect":

> As we witness the exercise of well-trained abilities by others, these displays are enjoyed by us and arouse a desire that we should be able to do the same things ourselves. We want to be like those persons who can exercise the abilities that we find latent in our nature.
>
> (*Ibid*.: 375)

The companion effect acts as a kind of social multiplier on the Aristotelian principle. Our life goes better not only when we develop and exercise our talents, but when those around us do the same.

According to the companion effect, the appreciation of others' skills is a good for us. It turns out, however, that the reverse is also true: other people's appreciation of our activities further contributes to our good. It does so by fostering our self-respect. Recall that the social bases of self-respect count as a primary good. We can now begin to see why. Rawls claims that self-respect involves a person's sense of his own value, and in particular, his "secure conviction that his conception of the good, his plan of life, is worth carrying out" (*ibid.*: 386). In addition, it includes a confidence in one's ability to fulfil one's intentions. Having self-respect is thus a fundamental ingredient in having a good life. As Rawls notes, "When we feel that our plans are of little value, we cannot pursue them with pleasure or take delight in their execution. Nor plagued by failure and self-doubt can we continue in our endeavors" (*ibid.*). Moreover, whether or not we have self-respect is to a great degree dependent on others' recognition of our worth. Thus, among the social bases of self-respect, Rawls includes "finding our persons and deeds appreciated and confirmed by others who are likewise esteemed and their association enjoyed" (*ibid.*).

Putting these three elements together, we find that a rational plan of life can include living in a society where the realization and exercise of complex capacities is not only allowed and encouraged, but appreciated by one's fellows, and where one is in a position to appreciate the similar realization and exercise of their complex capacities. Such a society secures the social bases of our self-respect and according to the Aristotelian principle and its companion effect, our lives go better than in a world that did not afford us such interaction. Note, however, that the kinds of capacities necessary to live with others in a democratic society, to assess particular questions of justice and regulate one's conduct by principles of justice are complex indeed. Furthermore, in a well-ordered society everyone must exercise these capacities even when they are not engaged in politics proper. Finally, in such a society, we can all appreciate and recognize the just activities of each other, and so our exercise of the capacities necessary for justice can be a basis for our self-respect. Thus, no matter what our particular conception of the good is, we can find further good in living in a well-ordered society in which we mutually acknowledge the principles of justice and show one another mutual respect in acting from them (*ibid.*: 388). Since the two principles of justice embody an idea of reciprocity, they provide means by which citizens can show respect to one another. A society that is well ordered by the two principles thereby contributes to the good of its citizens.

The foregoing argument shows that it would be good for citizens to develop what Rawls calls a sense of justice, and that having one in a well-ordered society would contribute to one's good. But this conclusion alone does not show that a society governed by the two principles of justice will be stable; such a society might include elements that serve to prevent the development of a sense of justice despite the advantages of having one. The second argument Rawls develops in Part III addresses this worry.

This second argument shows, first, that citizens growing up in a society that is well ordered by justice as fairness are likely to develop a sense of justice that leads them to affirm and act from the two principles of justice and, secondly, that they are likely to think, on reflection, that it is good that they have such a sense of justice. Rawls describes a sense of justice as "an effective desire to comply with existing rules and to give one another that to which they are entitled" (1999: 274). A particular society generates a sense of justice in its citizens if it moves them to comply with its principles of justice. Rawls claims that a society that is well ordered by the two principles of justice does this more thoroughly than a utilitarian society would.

Rawls lays out a theory of moral development that borrows from the work of Jean Piaget and Lawrence Kohlberg, and which he describes as having roots in Rousseau and Kant (Rawls 1999: 402). It claims that moral education is not a matter of training people to apply essentially external constraints on their natural amoral desires and preferences. Rather, moral learning is:

> The free development of our innate intellectual and emotional capacities according to their natural bent. Once the powers of understanding mature and persons come to recognize their place in society and are able to take up the standpoint of others, they appreciate the mutual benefits of establishing fair terms of social cooperation. We have a natural sympathy with other persons and an innate susceptibility to the pleasures of fellow feeling and self-mastery, and these provide the affective basis for the moral sentiments once we have a clear grasp of our relations to our associates from an appropriately general perspective. (*Ibid.*: 402–3)

Rawls argues that we are prone to respond in kind to shows of affection and respect, and that our moral development is a kind of extended development in the complexity and reciprocity of our relationships to others. We are thus better suited to develop a sense of justice when the principles of justice fit into this pattern, and demand reciprocity of us. As we have seen, this is what the two principles of justice require. In contrast, affirming less egalitarian utilitarian principles would require that we develop a much greater degree of sympathy for others. In a utilitarian society where there is not reciprocity, it will be difficult to maintain the necessary level of sympathy since it will require that those who do not fully benefit from social cooperation find their satisfaction through their sympathetic identification with others who benefit more than they do. Even were they to achieve the level of sympathy required for a sense of utilitarian justice to maintain itself, Rawls argues that such a psychological attitude would have the effect of undermining self-respect. To the extent I find value in my life vicariously through the value of other people's lives, I may lose my grip on the value of my own projects and plans.

Under the two principles of justice, the reciprocity in society fosters my own sense of justice, and this generates a kind of sympathy for others, because I come to see us as involved in a shared enterprise. This sympathy, however, engages with the companion effect of the Aristotelian principle to strengthen rather than erode my self-respect (Rawls 1999: 438).

Finally, Rawls considers the question of what he calls "congruence" between the good and the right. Here he aims to show not only that the institutions that embody the two principles of justice generate a sense of justice in citizens, but that "given the circumstances of a well-ordered society, a person's rational plan of life supports and affirms his sense of justice" (*ibid.*: 450). Rawls begins this argument by distinguishing between "private society" and a "social union" (*ibid.*: 457–61). In a private society, individual participants have their own non-complementary, private ends, and the institutions through which they act are "not thought to have any value in themselves" (*ibid.*: 457). In a private society, institutions serve to coordinate the actions of participants, to minimize conflict and social strife, but no more; participants continue to deal with one another at arm's length, side by side but not together. Neoclassical economics describes the free-market economy as a private society, and many purely economic institutions have these features to a high degree. In a social union, by contrast, participants have at least some shared ends, and see the institutions that help them pursue those ends as good in themselves. That is, the value to individuals of the institutions of a social union goes beyond the institutions' role in fostering the individual's particular ends. A social union can involve participants who have some non-shared ends, even ends that are in conflict. Rawls describes a competitive game as a social union, since all players share the end that there be a good play of the game, and "when this aim is attained, everyone takes pleasure and satisfaction in the very same thing" (1999: 461), even though some win and others lose. In contrast, the commodities trader wants only to maximize his profit and, although he follows the rules of the stock exchange, he does so only instrumentally.

Rawls then claims that our social nature means that we only fully find our good in and through participation in social unions: "persons need one another since it is only in active cooperation with others that one's powers reach fruition. Only in a social union is the individual complete" (*ibid.*: 460 n.4).

Moreover, a well-ordered society is itself a special kind of social union: a social union of social unions (*ibid.*: 462). It is a social union, because in it citizens share the final end of doing justice to one another, and thus value the institutions of the basic structure for their own sake. We have seen some of the reasons for this in the first argument of Part III. In addition, they value the social union of a well-ordered society, because it is a union of social unions. That is, in a just constitutional democracy, there are all sorts of other social unions that citizens participate in, depending on what other ends they share. There are clubs and guilds and professional and political associations and churches and universities and firms. Thus, individual citizens each find social space within a well-ordered society to fully pursue their various rational plans of life. This adds further value to the institutions of the basic structure, because they make it possible for all these other social unions to coexist harmoniously. Once again, the Aristotelian principle and its companion effect help us to see the good of a well-ordered society. Being a citizen in such a society means taking part in a variety of complex tasks that make possible the wide variety of other complex tasks that one may be inclined to perform. In addition, all around one, one's fellow citizens will be doing the same and, as a result of the companion effect, this will further contribute to one's good. So, in so far as our sense of justice inclines us to do what is necessary to maintain the institutions of a well-ordered society, and these institutions contribute to our good by establishing a social union of social unions, we can endorse our sense of justice. The right and the good are congruent, the two principles of justice are stable and the argument is complete.

Notes

1. Readers who wish to further investigate Rawls's later works or the shifts in justice as fairness can look at Rawls, *Justice as Fairness: A Restatement*, E. Kelly (ed.) (Cambridge, MA: Harvard University Press, 2000) and *Political Liberalism* (New York: Columbia University Press, 1993); T. E. Hill Jr, "The Stability Problem in *Political Liberalism*", *Pacific Philosophical Quarterly* 75 (1994), 333–52; D. Estlund, "The Survival of Egalitarian Justice in John Rawls's *Political Liberalism*", *Journal of Political Philosophy* 4 (1996), 68–78; and S. Freeman, "Congruence and the Good of Justice", in *The Cambridge Companion to Rawls*, S. Freeman (ed.), 277–315 (Cambridge: Cambridge University Press, 2003).
2. The value of justice is a particularly tricky and subtle question and one that Rawls wrestled with throughout his career. I return to it in § "Moral psychology and stability". Note, however, that it was the need to provide an argument for the value of justice that was compatible with the diversity of democratic societies that led Rawls to develop political liberalism.
3. As Rawls continued to develop the ideas in *A Theory of Justice*, the second principle remained remarkably unchanged. Rawls did, however, make some significant changes

to the first principle, although not in its basic idea of guaranteeing equal liberties to all. For a discussion of those changes, see Rawls, *Justice as Fairness: A Restatement*, E. Kelly (ed.) (Cambridge, MA: Harvard University Press, 2000), 42–7, and *Political Liberalism* (New York: Columbia University Press, 1993), 289–371.

4. Note that these are meant to be examples of the kinds of institutions that would make up a basic structure, rather than a list of institutions that any just basic structure would have to contain.

5. Note that this does not imply, and Rawls does not hold, that we are not entitled to the rewards a just system of rules offers us for the concerted use of those talents. It merely means that it is not a necessary condition of justice that we are rewarded for our talents.

6. One of Rawls's most significant revisions of his argument concerns the definition of primary goods, and what things count as primary goods. For the fully revised version, see Rawls, *Justice as Fairness*, 57–61.

7. The reasonable is an important concept in Rawls's work. He describes it in his later writings as follows: "reasonable persons are ready to propose, or to acknowledge when proposed by others, the principles needed to specify what can be seen by all as fair terms of cooperation. Reasonable persons also understand that they are to honor these principles, even at the expense of their own interests as circumstances may require, provided others likewise may be expected to honor them" (Rawls, *Justice as Fairness*, 6–7).

8. In fact, as alluded to earlier, Rawls came to think that his argument in *A Theory of Justice* did not fully meet this second criterion, because it relied, one might say, on too robust a theory of human nature. The development of political liberalism was an attempt to recast the argument for justice as fairness to more adequately take heed of this point. Nevertheless, there is much of value in Part III of *A Theory of Justice*. First, it contains a lot of very interesting moral philosophy. Secondly, it ties many strands of Rawls's arguments together, and thus shows most fully the systematic nature of the book as a whole. Finally, to the extent that some readers find the arguments in Part III compelling as stated, they still give those readers grounds for endorsing the two principles.

Bibliography

Cohen, J. 1989. "Democratic Equality". *Ethics* **99**, 727–51.

Estlund, D. 1996. "The Survival of Egalitarian Justice in John Rawls's *Political Liberalism*". *Journal of Political Philosophy* **4**, 68–78.

Freeman, S. 2003. "Congruence and the Good of Justice". In *The Cambridge Companion to Rawls*, S. Freeman (ed.), 277–315. Cambridge: Cambridge University Press.

Hill, Jr, T. E. 1994. "The Stability Problem in *Political Liberalism*". *Pacific Philosophical Quarterly* **75**, 333–52.

Rawls, J. 2000a. *Justice as Fairness: A Restatement*, E. Kelly (ed.). Cambridge, MA: Harvard University Press.

Rawls, J. 2000b. *Lectures on the History of Moral Philosophy*, B. Herman (ed.). Cambridge, MA: Harvard University Press.

Rawls, J. 1999. *A Theory of Justice*, rev. edn. Cambridge, MA: Harvard University Press.

Rawls, J. 1993. *Political Liberalism*. New York: Columbia University Press.

4

Robert Nozick

Anarchy, State, and Utopia

Peter Vallentyne

Robert Nozick's *Anarchy, State, and Utopia* (1974), along with John Rawls's *A Theory of Justice* (1971), radically changed the landscape in analytic political philosophy. For much of the preceding half-century, under the influence of logical positivism's heavy emphasis on empirical verifiability, much of moral philosophy was taken up with metaethics (e.g. the semantics of moral discourse), with little attention given to normative moral theories. Moreover, to the extent that normative theories were considered, utilitarianism was the centre of attention. This all changed with the publication of Rawls's articulation and defence of liberal egalitarianism and Nozick's libertarian challenge to the legitimacy of anything more than the night-watchman state.

At the core of Nozick's book are two arguments. One is that a night-watchman state (which protects only against violence, theft, fraud and breach of contract) could be legitimate, even without the consent of all those to be governed. The other is that nothing more extensive than the night-watchman state is legitimate, except with the consent of all. The argument is complex, and Nozick often inserts long – and very interesting – digressions. Below I shall focus only on his core argument. I shall thus not address his discussions of Rawls's theory of justice (ch. 7, § 2) and other arguments attempting to justify more than the night-watchman state (ch. 8), nor his discussion of utopias (ch. 10).

The anarchist challenge

Nozick attempts to rebut anarchism, which comes in several shapes and forms. The strongest version says that it is *impossible* for any state to be legitimate. Almost everyone finds this view implausible because a state seems perfectly legitimate when, for example, it efficiently and fairly promotes individual wellbeing and all those governed by it have given, under fair conditions, their free and informed consent to it. A weaker version of anarchism – moderate anarchism – holds that a state is morally illegitimate unless all those governed by it have given appropriate consent. Relative to many theories of political morality – such as utilitarianism and (hypothetical) contractarianism – even this moderate version of anarchism is implausible. A version of utilitarianism, for example, can hold that a state is legitimate if it maximizes the total wellbeing in society (compared with other social arrangements). Consent and rights of self-defence play no special role in this theory of political justification. Nozick, however, starts with a libertarian theory of individual rights in which consent and rights of self-defence play very significant roles. In the context of such a theory (which we shall examine below), the moderate anarchist position seems quite compelling. Nozick, however, argues that even here it is mistaken. He argues that the state can be legitimate even without unanimous consent. If his argument is successful, it is a very significant result.

Before considering Nozick's argument, we need to get clearer on what a state is and on his libertarian theory of justice.

The state

Defining statehood is no easy matter, and there is no uncontroversial comprehensive definition. Something like the following, however, seems at least roughly right for our purposes: a *state* is a rule-of-law-based coercive organization that, for a given territory, effectively rules all individuals in it and claims a monopoly on the use of force (e.g. killing, maiming or inflicting pain). This can be unpacked as follows: a state is a *coercive organization* in that it threatens to use force against individuals who do not comply with its dictates (either via prior restraint to prevent non-compliance or via punishment or the extraction of compensation for non-compliance) and it generally implements its threats. A state is *rule-of-law-based* in that in general it uses force only for violation of public and proactive dictates (and not on the whim of its officials). A state *effectively rules* the individuals of a given territory in that those individuals generally obey its dictates. A state *claims a monopoly on the use of force* in that it prohibits the use of force (or credible threat thereof) without its permission.

The rule of law requirement is controversial, and, in any case, Nozick does not invoke it explicitly. He characterizes the state as a coercive organization that has, for a given territory, an effective monopoly on the use of force.[1] This is at least roughly equivalent to the definition given above, if we assume, as we shall, that (i) the rule of law requirement is either met or irrelevant, and (ii) a coercive organization *has an effective monopoly* on the use of force in a given territory (roughly) if and only if it claims a monopoly on the use of the force in that territory and effectively rules that territory.

The (moderate) anarchist claim is thus that no coercive organization that exercises an effective monopoly on the use of force over a given territory is legitimate unless all those governed by it have consented to its rule. It is worth noting here that the claim concerns legitimacy, as opposed to authority. A state is *legitimate* just in case its use of force (and threat thereof) is typically morally permissible. A state has *authority* just in case individuals in its territory typically have at least an all-else-being-equal moral obligation to obey its dictates. Ideally, a state should have both features, but in principle, a state could be legitimate even if it has no political authority (and vice versa). Following Nozick, we shall focus on the legitimacy of the state.

Libertarianism and justice

Nozick argues that a state can be legitimate even without the consent of those governed. He does this on the basis of certain principles of justice. In the philosophical literature, the term "justice" is used in several different ways, but Nozick understands it as the permissible use of force.[2] So understood, justice is not concerned with all of one's moral obligations. It only concerns the moral restrictions on the use of force. The legitimacy of a state is thus a matter of its actions being just.

Nozick holds a kind of libertarian theory of justice, which we shall consider below. We shall start, however, by considering some more general aspects of his theory of justice. First, he holds that normal adult human beings have certain strong natural rights, including the right to bodily integrity (which prohibits killing, torturing or maiming the right-holder). These rights are natural in the sense that they do not depend on any legal or social conventions. All individuals having the requisite features – roughly, the ability to make free and rational choices in accordance with some reflectively chosen conception of the good life – have these rights. The rights are strong in the sense that they are not easily overridden by other moral considerations. Indeed, Nozick believes that these rights are nearly absolute; they may not be infringed except perhaps when necessary and effective in avoiding a great social catastrophe. Positing natural rights is not uncontroversial. Act-consequentialists (such as act-utilitarians) deny that there are any natural rights. Nonetheless, most people would acknowledge that there are some natural rights, and that the right to bodily integrity is among them.

A final general point to note about Nozick's theory of justice is that it is *historical*. What it is just to do depends in part on what happened in the past. It is not normally just to punch another in the face, but it may be if it is part of a consensual boxing match. Likewise, it is not normally just to lock someone in a room, but it may be so if that person murdered several people in the past. Both past consent and past wrongdoings are relevant to what is just at a given time. This aspect of Nozick's theory is highly plausible, and his emphasis on this feature has had a very positive impact on theorizing about justice. It is worth noting, however, that a theory can be historical (i.e. sensitive to the past) without being *purely* historical (i.e. making the future consequences irrelevant).

Nozick's theory of justice is a property-rights-based theory. He claims that individuals have, or can acquire, *full property rights* (or full ownership) over various things, where full property rights over a thing consist (roughly) of:

- the right to *use* and *control use* of the thing by others;[3]
- the right to compensation from those who have violated one's rights in the thing;
- the right to *use force* to stop those who are about to violate one's rights in the thing, to extract compensation from those who have already violated such rights and perhaps to punish such offenders;
- the right to transfer these rights to others; and
- an immunity to losing any of these rights as long as one has not violated, and is not in the process of violating, the rights of others.

Nozick's theory of justice is a libertarian theory, according to which an action is just if and only if it violates no libertarian rights, where the libertarian rights are the following:

- initial *full self-ownership*: each autonomous agent initially has full property rights in himself/herself (paradigmatically rights of bodily integrity, which rule out killing or physically assaulting one without one's permission);[4]
- initial rights of *common use* of the external world: the right to use non-agent things (as long as this violates no one's self-ownership);
- rights of *initial acquisition*: the right to acquire full property rights in unowned things as long as one leaves "enough and as good" for others;

- rights of *acquisition by transfer*: the right to acquire any property right in a thing held by another by voluntary transfer.

This theory of justice is modelled on that of John Locke in *Two Treatises of Government*. Nozick does not systematically defend this theory, but he does provide motivation for its key aspects. The rights of self-ownership, he claims, "reflect the Kantian principle that individuals are ends and not merely means; they may not be sacrificed or used for the achieving of other ends without their consent" (pp. 30–31), "express the inviolability of others" (p. 32) and "reflect the fact of our separate existences" (p. 33). Although the core of full self-ownership – roughly the right, under normal circumstances, to be free of interferences with one's body – seems highly plausible, many would reject some of the other rights included in *full* self-ownership. One could question, for example, whether this right holds even where the harm to the holder is slight and the benefit to others is great (e.g. a small prick to my finger saves the lives of many). One could also question whether one has the right to enslave oneself voluntarily (as full self-ownership asserts).

Nozick does not spend much time discussing initial rights of common use. He simply asserts that the non-agent world is initially unowned, and individuals are free to use any part of it when others are not. He (like Locke) rejects, for example, the view that the world – other than the self-owning agents – is initially owned by some individual or group of individuals. (Such a view was invoked by seventeenth-century proponents of the "divine right of kings", a doctrine that Locke vigorously rejected.)

The right of initial acquisition is the power to acquire private property rights over things that are not already privately owned by others. Locke's version of this right requires that one "mix one's labour" with the thing and that one leave "enough and as good" for others.[5] Nozick notes (pp. 174–5) that the content and significance of the labour-mixing metaphor is not clear: does an astronaut who clears a plot on uninhabited Mars mix his labour with the plot, all of Mars or the entire uninhabited universe? Nozick never resolves this issue, but nothing significant is lost if we replace the labour-mixing requirement with the more general requirement that the individual stake a claim to the object in some appropriate manner (e.g. publicly declare/register that she is claiming ownership of the object). The crucial question concerns the other requirement, that "enough and as good" be left for others. Nozick calls this "the Lockean proviso".

The Lockean proviso can be interpreted in different ways. Nozick interprets it to require that the situation of others not be worsened by the appropriation. More exactly, he interprets it to require that no one be worse off in overall well-being with the appropriation than he or she would be if the appropriation were not to take place (i.e. if the object were to remain in common use). Given that common use is generally inefficient (e.g. because individuals do not have sufficient incentives to preserve the resource), this interpretation of the proviso sets a low baseline and makes it relatively easy for individuals to acquire full private property in unappropriated things.[6]

It is worth noting here that there is disagreement within libertarian theory concerning the right to appropriate unappropriated things. *Extreme right-libertarianism* denies that there is any kind of requirement that enough and as good be left for others. It holds, for example, that the first person to discover, claim or mix labour with an unowned object can thereby fully own it. *Moderate (or Lockean) right-libertarianism* holds that that some kind of Lockean proviso must be satisfied, but interprets the proviso to be a weak requirement (e.g. as Nozick does). *Equal share left-libertarianism* – advocated by Steiner (1994) – holds that the proviso applies and requires that one leave an equally valuable share of unappropriated resources for others (and thus allows one to appropriate only up to one's per capita share of the value of unappropriated resources). *Equal opportunity for wellbeing left-libertarianism* – advocated by Otsuka (2003) – holds that the proviso applies and requires that one leave enough for others so that they each have an opportunity for wellbeing that is at least as valuable as the opportunity for wellbeing that one acquires with the appropriation. This version of the proviso holds that those with less desirable internal endowments (e.g. those who are less smart, strong and handsome) are permitted to appropriate more than those with more desirable internal endowments.[7] Even within libertarian theory, then, Nozick's version of the right to acquired unappropriated things is controversial.

Consider finally the fourth element in Nozick's libertarian theory of justice: the right of acquisition by transfer. The core idea is that if I have full property rights over a car (which includes the right to transfer these rights to others) and you and I each give our free and informed consent for those rights to be transferred to you, then those rights are transferred to you. Nozick emphasizes that justice depends in part on what contractual agreements have been made and thus that no purely end-state (i.e. non-historical) theory of justice can be adequate. He further claims (pp. 155–64) that the relevance of contractual agreements shows that no adequate theory of justice – even if historical – can be *patterned* in the sense of requiring (resources or wellbeing) to be distributed in accordance with some specified pattern of features. The pattern might, for example, be equality (which is not historical) or based on moral desert (which is historical, given that it requires that rewards match desert from past actions). We shall now briefly examine his famous Wilt Chamberlain argument for this claim.

Nozick asks us to consider a hypothetical case in which resources are distributed in accordance with our preferred pattern (e.g. equality or in proportion to moral merit) and Wilt Chamberlain (a famous basketball star in the 1960s and early 1970s) signs a contract with his team according to which he gets 25 cents for each home-game ticket sold. Because he plays so well, the team owner freely agrees to this deal. At the end of the season, Wilt has earned an extra $250,000 and is much richer than everyone else. Nozick claims that such informed and free contractual agreements preserve justice in the sense that, if the original situation was just, then so is the situation that results from such agreements (and no other influences). Consequently, if we stipulate that there were no other relevant influences, the resulting situation must be just, given our assumption that the original one was. Justice, Nozick claims, is procedural: if one starts with a just situation and applies just steps the result must be just. The crucial point here is that given (according to Nozick) that transfers of rights in conformance with free and informed contracts are just steps, the resulting situation will generally not be in accordance with the specified pattern (e.g. equality or proportional to merit). Hence, contractual agreements – and the rights to transfer and to acquire by transfer that make them possible – are incompatible with a patterned theory of justice. Given that individuals surely have the right to engage in contractual agreements, no pattern can be maintained without unjustly restricting people's liberty. Thus, no patterned theory of justice is, he claims, plausible.

This is an important argument, but there are several ways of resisting the conclusion, and I shall mention two. First, if Wilt's initial earning power is significantly greater than that of others, the initial situation might include a very high head tax for him that would equalize opportunities for earnings.[8] Wilt would thus be free to earn a great deal of money playing basketball, but he would also have an enforceable duty to pay high taxes based on his earning power. This would be a kind of historical patterned principle (initial equality opportunity for earnings) in which contractual agreements preserve justice. It is not, however, the kind of patterned theory that Nozick was targeting, since it only imposes the pattern on the initial situation and not on later situations. A second way of resisting Nozick's conclusion is to note that he presupposes that Wilt has *full* rights of acquisition by transfer, which preclude any taxation of transfers. One could, however, endorse less than full rights of acquisition by transfer, and these could make transfers subject to whatever taxation is necessary to preserve the specified pattern. Thus, Wilt would be free to make contracts, but he would know that they may generate a tax bill. Obviously, the issue is complex, and I am here merely flagging aspects of the argument that have been challenged.[9]

In sum, Nozick insightfully articulates and motivates a right-libertarian theory of justice, but does not provide a systematic defence. His discussion does, however, provide a powerful case for thinking that an adequate theory of justice must be historical by being sensitive to what wrongdoings took place in the past and to what agreements were made.

We are now ready, finally, to turn to the central topic of *Anarchy, State, and Utopia*: the possibility of a state being legitimate without the consent of all those governed.

The argument for the legitimacy of the minimal state

A state, recall, is a coercive organization that has, for a given territory, an effective monopoly on the use of force. A state is legitimate just in case its use (via its agents) of force (and threat thereof) is typically morally permissible. There is no puzzle about how, according to certain consequentialist theories, a state could be legitimate without the consent of those governed. It is, however, quite puzzling how a state could be legitimate without the consent of all those governed, if one assumes (as Nozick's libertarianism does) that individuals initially fully own themselves. Such rights protect holders from the use of force by others and give them rights to use force to protect those rights. If individuals do not lose those rights, then any coercive organization that claims a monopoly on the use of force is illegitimate. If Nozick can answer the anarchist challenge and show that – even assuming initial full self-ownership – a state can be legitimate without the consent of all those governed, this will be significant indeed.

Nozick offers an account of how, starting from a state of nature, a legitimate state could arise through an invisible-hand process (i.e. without anyone intending this result) and without violating anyone's rights. In a state of nature, each individual fully owns herself and typically has other rights as well.[10] These rights include the right to enforce these rights by using force to stop others from violating them, to extract compensation when they do and perhaps to punish violators.[11] With the consent of the right-holder, others may assist in this enforcement. It would thus be natural for individuals to form mutual protection associations in which they commit to helping each other enforce their rights. This could lead naturally to individuals hiring private protection agencies to enforce their rights, and this in turn could lead naturally (e.g. because of economic efficiencies) to there being a single dominant protection agency. Nozick argues, as we shall see below, that such a single dominant protection agency can be a state, indeed a legitimate one.

In order for a dominant protection agency to be a state, it must have an effective monopoly on the use of force in its territory. This means that (i) it prohibits everyone in the territory from using force in ways that it has not authorized, and uses force against those who violate this dictate, (ii) it is effective in getting individuals to comply with these prohibitions (e.g. they comply in part because it has so dictated), and (iii) it is the only organization or individual that is effective in this way. The question is whether a dominant protection agency can have these features without violating anyone's rights. It is important to note that not everyone in the given territory need be a (fee-paying) client of the dominant protection agency. Some individuals may be clients of smaller protection agencies and some may not be clients of any protection agency. We must consider both the rights of those who are clients of the dominant protection agency and the rights of those who are not.

There will be no violation of the rights of clients, as long as their contracts with the protection agency require them to transfer *all* their enforcement rights to the agency. Indeed, such an arrangement will typically be efficient, since it will reduce retaliation and counter-retaliation between individuals. Clients, we may thus suppose, voluntarily give up their enforcement rights as part of the contract with their protection agency.[12]

The difficult case concerns the dominant protection agency's enforced prohibition against the use of non-authorized force against its clients *by non-clients*. Given that non-clients have not voluntarily given up their enforcement rights, this appears to be a violation of their rights. There is no problem when the protection agency uses force to stop a non-client from *wrongly* applying his enforcement rights against an innocent client. Here the non-client has no right to use force and is violating the client's rights. The problem arises when a non-client reliably and fairly applies appropriate force against a guilty client (e.g. to prevent a rights violation, to extract compensation or to punish). Nozick claims that in a state of nature each individual has the right to use force to stop others from using unreliable or unfair enforcement mechanisms against herself. For example, I may use force to resist your attempt to extract compensation from me forcibly or punish me for a rights violation that I did not commit. Moreover, I may also, in such a case, use force to resist being tried by a corrupt and biased jury that you hand-picked to assess whether I am guilty. If each client transfers this right to the dominant protection agency, then that agency may use force against anyone – even non-clients – who attempts to use unreliable or unfair enforcement mechanisms against its clients.

The net result is that, although the dominant protection agency does not claim any monopoly on the *right* to use force against those using unfair or unreliable enforcement mechanisms (since non-clients also have the same rights), only the dominant protection agency has the *power* to impose its own views on what is fair and reliable. It claims something close to a *de facto* monopoly on the use of force, even though it does not make any claim to a *de jure* (i.e. as a matter of right) monopoly. It prohibits everyone in the territory – clients and non-clients – from using force against its clients except in accordance with its own rules.[13] Moreover, because the dominant protection agency effectively rules the territory, it has (and not merely claims to have) something close to a *de facto* monopoly on the use of force.

Nozick argues that the dominant protection agency is not yet a state, but it can naturally evolve into one. It is not a state, he claims, because it does not protect everyone in its territory. This is because not everyone need be a client of the dominant protection agency, and those who are not clients are not protected. It is not clear to me that a coercive organization needs to protect all in a given territory in order to be a state. The crucial problem concerns who counts as part of the "all". Many historical "states" have offered minimal protection to slaves and women. Of course, most have offered at least some protection, but, even if they offered no protection, they would still seem to be states (although illegitimate ones). For the sake of argument, however, let us grant this requirement and consider how Nozick believes it will be met.

The crucial issue for Nozick concerns the justness of the dominant protection agency prohibiting – with a threat of force – non-clients from using enforcement procedures, which the agency has not authorized, against clients. There is no problem with prohibiting them from using procedures that will definitely violate the rights of clients. The problem arises when the prohibited enforcement procedure is merely *risky* in the sense that there is a less than certain chance that it will result in injustice. Nozick has an extremely interesting and important discussion of the issues that arise in this case, but we shall have to limit ourselves to the big picture. He argues roughly that it is permissible to prohibit risky activities where those activities would generate a general fear in the population even if it were known that compensation would always be provided to those whose rights were violated. The crucial point here is that he further argues that if a protection agency prohibits non-clients from using risky enforcement procedures, it must compensate them for any disadvantage this imposes. This is what he calls "the principle of compensation" (p. 82). The cheapest and most effective way of providing this compensation is to provide protection services to the non-clients at a reduced price (reduced by the amount of compensation owed). Of course, the non-clients are free to decline those services, but given that those services also protect them against other non-clients, there will be a strong tendency to accept the protective services.[14]

Thus, something approaching universal protection will be achieved by the dominant protection agency. The dominant protection agency will be a state. Moreover, it can, Nozick claims, arise without violating anyone's rights, and thus can be legitimate. We shall now briefly review the key steps in this argument.

One point to note is that Nozick's account of how a state could arise without violating anyone's rights does not establish that any existing state is legitimate. As Nozick emphasizes, justice and legitimacy are historical, and the legitimacy of a state depends at least in part on how it actually arose. The mere fact that a state could be legitimate does little to show that any actual state is legitimate. It would, however, show that anarchism is mistaken to hold that no state can be legitimate without the consent of all those governed. Given that this is Nozick's focus, the hypothetical nature of his account is not a problem. (Admittedly, Nozick sometimes writes, and has been interpreted, as if he claims that his hypothetical account could justify an existing state not having that history. So things are not perfectly clear in this regard; see pp. 292–4.)

A more important issue concerns whether Nozick has indeed established that a state can arise without violating anyone's rights. Clearly, there is no violation of rights when individuals voluntarily contract with a protection agency. They may agree to pay certain fees (taxes) and give up their enforcement rights as part of such agreements. The crucial question concerns non-clients, that is, those who do not contract with the protection agency. After all, even moderate anarchists agree that a state can be legitimate if *everyone* it governs consents to its powers. Nozick argues that the dominant protection agency violates no one's rights when it prohibits non-clients, and uses force to prevent them, from using enforcement procedures that it deems unfair or unreliable (provided that it provides appropriate compensation). I shall now argue that is not so.

Consider two examples:

- Prior restraint: suppose that I am perfectly innocent of violating anyone's rights and that you wrongfully attempt to rob me. Suppose that I use the minimum force necessary to stop you and that this merely involves pushing you to the ground and running away.
- Restitution: suppose that I am perfectly innocent of violating anyone's rights and that you have wrongfully robbed me of my wallet. Later I see you on the street with my wallet and after careful observation confirm that it is mine. I then gently strike your hand, grab my wallet and run away.

In both these cases, I claim, I have a right (at least on the libertarian view) to use these enforcement procedures (of prior restraint and of restitution) and I violate no one's rights in using them. Is Nozick correct that the dominant protection agency does not violate my rights if it prohibits me, as a non-client, from using these procedures, as long as appropriate compensation is paid? I claim that he is mistaken on this issue.

According to Nozick (pp. 102–3), the crucial issue is whether the dominant protection agency has enough information about my enforcement procedure to establish that it is reliable and fair. If it does then, Nozick rightly claims, it may not prohibit my use of it. Nozick further claims, however, that the dominant protection agency may prohibit my enforcement procedure when the agency does not have enough information to establish that it is reliable and fair. This seems mistaken. Suppose that my enforcement procedure is reliable and fair and that I am in fact applying it appropriately against a guilty party (e.g. as in the above examples). The dominant protection agency will not *deem* my enforcement procedure reliable and fair (e.g. because of lack of information), but in this case it is. I am fully within my rights to use them, and the agency violates my rights if it uses force against me in response to my doing so. This remains true even if I am compensated for such interference. Of course, as Nozick emphasizes, the protection agency has to act on the basis of its own judgements, and thus, if it *deems* my enforcement procedures unreliable or unfair, it will *deem* it morally permissible for it to use force in response to it. The crucial point is that the agency may be mistaken and, where it is, it violates the rights of those whose just enforcement procedures it prohibits, even if compensation is paid.

In sum, the crucial question that Nozick addresses is how a state could be legitimate without the consent of all of those it governs. The crucial move that Nozick makes to answer this question is that, prior to any contractual agreements, each individual is permitted (as long as appropriate compensation is paid) to use force to stop others from using enforcement procedures that he or she deems unfair or unreliable. Where there is a single dominant protection agency representing individuals, it is also so permitted on behalf of its clients. I have suggested, however, that Nozick is mistaken that individuals and protection agencies violate no rights when they mistakenly use force to stop someone from using an enforcement procedure that is in fact fair and reliable. If this is so, Nozick's argument for the possibility of a state arising without the consent of all and without violating rights succeeds only if the dominant protection agency approves of all enforcement procedures that are in fact reliable and fair. Given the limitations of human knowledge, this is extremely unlikely. It could happen by chance, but it is not practically possible in the sense that we could reasonably ensure that it is so.

Note, however, that the legitimacy of the state, as I have defined it, requires that the state's use of force be *typically* permissible. This allows that a state can be legitimate without being perfect. It may be enough to meet this test that the state scrupulously (i.e. as carefully as can reasonably be expected of anyone) (i) gather information about what enforcement procedures are reliable and fair, (ii) approve all for which there is strong evidence that they are reliable and fair and (iii) be suitably cautious about using force against non-clients where the evidence is murky. Thus, Nozick's argument may well show that a state can be legitimate without the consent of all those governed, even if he does not show that a state could arise in practice without violating anyone's rights.

The argument for the illegitimacy of more than the night-watchman state

The argument so far has concerned protection agencies, which by definition restrict their activities to protecting their clients against having their rights violated. If Nozick's argument succeeds, it establishes the possibility of the legitimacy of a *minimal state*, which is a state that restricts its activities to protecting the rights of its citizens. A minimal state, however, need not be a *night-watchman state*, which (following Nozick) is a state that restricts its role to protecting its citizens against violence, theft, fraud and breach of contract. Because Nozick holds a right-libertarian theory of justice, he equates the minimal state (which protects all natural rights) with the night-watchman state (which protects only the right-libertarian rights). If, however, individuals have more natural rights than right-libertarianism recognizes (e.g. a right to adequate nutrition or basic healthcare), then his argument, if successful, shows that more than a night-watchman state can be legitimate. The dominant protection agency can permissibly use force (even against non-clients) to ensure that individuals fulfil their duties (e.g. to provide adequate nutrition) to clients.

Nozick argues, however, that nothing more than a night-watchman state can be legitimate. If he is right, then none of the following state activities are legitimate: *promoting impersonal goods* (i.e. goods, such as perhaps great art or cultural artefacts, that are intrinsically valuable for their own sake and not merely good for any individuals); *providing paternalistic protection* (i.e. protecting individuals against themselves; e.g. by prohibiting drug use or requiring retirement savings); *aiding the disadvantaged* (e.g. the poor); and promoting the wellbeing of all by *overcoming market-failures* (i.e. providing goods and services that the market cannot provide in a cost-effective manner).

Nozick argues that nothing more than the night-watchman state is legitimate on the basis of his right-libertarian theory of justice. Given that individuals typically *fully* own themselves and various external things, they have no duty to provide personal services (i.e. labour) or pay taxes (i.e. part with some of their wealth) for the above state activities. Moreover, they have a right against others, including agents of the state, that they not be forced to provide such personal services or pay such taxes. Of course, protection agencies might branch out, provide such services and contractually require their clients to provide such personal services or pay fees for them. This is perfectly legitimate (although few individuals may sign up for such services). The problem concerns non-clients. It would clearly violate the rights of non-clients to impose such requirements.

Nothing more extensive than the night-watchman state is justified on the right-libertarian view.[15] The least controversial component of this view is probably the view that it is illegitimate for the state (or anyone) to coercively require individuals to provide aid for the promotion of impersonal goods (i.e. goods that are good in themselves, as opposed to good for individuals). Although many people think that it is legitimate, for example, for the state to promote the arts, it is usually because they believe the arts are good for at least some of the citizens. It is relatively (but not completely) uncontroversial that coercion is not permissible *merely* to promote impersonal goods.

Somewhat more controversial is the idea that the state may not restrict people's freedom in order to protect them from themselves (i.e. for the state to engage in paternalism). Although many people think that it is legitimate for the state to prohibit recreational drug use and to require people to make payments to a retirement savings plan, this is often at least in part to protect third parties. For example, if drug use leads to crime and poor retired people are typically looked after by others, then such regulations may protect citizens from the costs of other people's choices. Thus, part of the rationale for many seemingly paternalistic laws is the protection of the interests of others. When one considers *purely* paternalistic state restrictions, many people agree with right-libertarianism that such restrictions are illegitimate. The state should leave people free to live their lives as they choose as long as they are not violating the rights (or otherwise harming) others.

Much more controversial is right-libertarianism's claim that it is illegitimate for the state to require individuals to provide aid to the disadvantaged. Of course, the legitimacy of the state requiring citizens to aid others depends on exactly on what is required. The easiest case to defend is one where the state imposes only a small tax on those who are very rich and uses it to ensure merely that everyone has an adequate opportunity to obtain the most basic nutrition, shelter and healthcare. Such aid might, for example, be provided to young orphans and those severely disabled through no fault of their own. Right-libertarianism rejects even such minimal taxation for meeting the very basic needs of others, but most people think that some such taxation is legitimate.

The most controversial right-libertarian claim in this context is the claim that it is illegitimate for the state to provide goods and services that benefit everyone and that the market does not provide efficiently or effectively. Of course, there is much controversy about which goods can be provided effectively by the market and about the role of the state in providing those that are not so provided.

Most people, however, would agree that it is legitimate to provide goods and services that make everyone better off than he or she would be without state provision. Right-libertarianism, however, denies the legitimacy of such a role for the state.

It is important to note that the state can require citizens to provide aid for the above kinds of activities in two distinct ways. One is to require citizens to provide personal services (e.g. serve in the military or serve on a jury). The other is to require citizens to contribute money or other external resources (e.g. to pay for the military or court services). Right-libertarianism is on its firmest ground when it rejects the legitimacy of the state requiring personal services for the above activities and on its weakest ground when it rejects the legitimacy of the state requiring the payment of taxes to fund the above activities. The personal freedom and security of full self-ownership is much easier to defend than the freedom from taxation provided by full property rights in external things.

Putting all this together, we can say that right-libertarianism is on relatively firm ground in its rejection of the legitimacy of (i) any state requirement to provide personal services to promote a purely impersonal good, and (ii) any state prohibition of activities that do not violate the rights or otherwise harm others. Right-libertarianism is, however, on relative weak ground in its rejection of the legitimacy of state taxation to (i) provide for the very basic needs of the most vulnerable members of society (e.g. children and the severely disabled), and (ii) make everyone's life better by providing goods and services that the market does not provide effectively.

In sum, right-libertarianism may be right that individuals fully own themselves and thus that it is illegitimate for the state to limit their freedom by requiring them to provide personal services for the above kinds of state activities. Right-libertarianism's view that individuals can acquire *full* private property in external things, which rules out any taxation, is much more controversial. Almost everyone agrees that individuals can acquire *robust* private property in external things, but most people would reject the view that such rights are so strong that they preclude all forms of taxation. If this view is correct, then more than the minimal night-watchman state is legitimate.

Conclusion

Nozick's defence of the possibility of the legitimacy of the state assumes the rights of full self-ownership (including enforcement rights). This makes Nozick's task particularly difficult, and establishing the possibility of a legitimate state from such a starting-point would be a significant result. Nozick's defence of the impossibility of the legitimacy of any state more extensive than the night-watchman state without the consent of all governed, however, assumes right-libertarianism's commitment to *full* property rights in external things, and this makes Nozick's task particularly easy. It rules out the possibility that individuals have an enforceable duty to pay any taxes to promote any social goals. Given that this view is subject to powerful objections, the significance of the second argument is very limited.[16]

Notes

1. Nozick initially (e.g. p. 23) says that the state claims a monopoly on the use of force, but he later (pp. 117–18) modifies this to it having a *de facto* monopoly on the use of force.
2. Two other uses of "justice" are (i) as distributive fairness, and (ii) as what we owe others. Authors have tended not to keep these three senses distinct.
3. An owner's right to use a thing is, of course, constrained by the rights of others in other things. Thus, for example, my right to use the baseball bat that I fully own does not permit me to smash your car with it.
4. Nozick lays out his theory of justice in Ch. 7, § 1. Unlike most libertarian authors, he does not typically use the term "self-ownership". His invocation and discussion of rights against violence (as well as theft and fraud) makes clear, however, that he invokes full self-ownership. Note also that full ownership of one's self or of a thing includes enforcement (rectification) rights and thus these rights need not be mentioned separately (as Nozick does).
5. Locke also imposes a non-spoilage condition that limits one's property rights to what one can use prior to it spoiling, but Nozick does not invoke this condition.
6. In the text, I interpret Nozick as holding that a particular appropriation is just as long it leaves no one worse off than non-appropriation in that case. Nozick sometimes writes, however, as if the proviso is satisfied as long as the general practice or system of appropriation leaves no one worse off than he or she would be if everything were to remain in the common use. This approach factors in the benefits and costs of the appropriation of other things by other agents. This appeal to a general practice or system, however, does not fit well with Nozick's general libertarian framework, and I ignore it here.
7. For an introduction to left-libertarianism, see Vallentyne and Steiner (2000a, b).
8. A head tax on earning power is, of course, incompatible with full self-ownership. The point here is simply that it can be part of a (historical) patterned principle that respects whatever valid contractual agreements people make.
9. See, for example, B. Fried, "Wilt Chamberlain Revisited: 'Nozick's Justice in Transfer' and the Problem of Market-based Distribution", *Philosophy and Public Affairs* 24 (1995), 226–45 and various essays in G. A. Cohen, *Self-ownership, Freedom and Equality* (Cambridge: Cambridge University Press, 1995).
10. It is important to note that Nozick's argument for the possible legitimacy of the state assumes full self-ownership but does not assume any of the other right-libertarian property rights (in external things). The crucial issue concerns the use of force against a person.

11. Nozick assumes that there is a right to punish, but, following R. Barnett, *The Structure of Liberty: Justice and the Rule of Law* (Oxford: Clarendon Press, 1998), I believe that a plausible version of libertarianism will not include such a right (e.g. because it limits losses of self-ownership to what is necessary to prevent or compensate rights violations). It will instead limit the use of force to prior restraint and compensation extraction. In what follows, I shall therefore typically focus on those two enforcement rights, but the points extend to punishment as well.

12. Nozick notes that protection agencies might not require clients to transfer over all enforcement rights (*Anarchy, State, and Utopia*, 15). They might simply refuse to offer any protection after authorized self-enforcement is used by a client. When he discusses the dominant protection agency, however, he assumes that all enforcement rights have been transferred to the agency. Otherwise, the agency would not claim a monopoly on the use of force.

13. The dominant protection agency does not literally claim a *de facto* monopoly on the use of force, because it does not prohibit the use of force by non-clients against non-clients. Thus Nozick seems to be assuming that the state only needs to claim something close to a *de facto* monopoly on the use of force.

14. It is worth noting that if all non-clients accept the protective services at the reduced rates, then there is a sense in which the legitimacy of the resulting state is grounded in a kind of consent. In this case, it is not entirely clear that the scenario rebuts moderate anarchism. Still, as long as one person rejects the offer of protective services at a reduced rate, moderate anarchism will, if the argument is successful, be rebutted.

15. Nozick does provide an account in Ch. 9 ("Demoktesis") of how something like the extensive modern democratic state could arise and be legitimate. Roughly, the story involves everyone selling shares in themselves and their property so that eventually (e.g. for efficiency reasons) everyone has one share in each person and each thing. As shareholders, they then collectively decide on how the country will be run. This is not a counter-example to Nozick's claim that no state more extensive than the night-watchman state can be legitimate without the consent of all governed, since in this case everyone consents. The critical issue – which Nozick discusses but does not resolve – concerns how those who have not so consented, such as people born later, are to be handled.

16. For helpful comments, I thank Dani Attas, Eric Heidenreich, Brian Kierland, Mike Otsuka, Eric Roark, John Shand, Hillel Steiner, Alan Tomhave, Jon Trerise and Jo Wolff.

Bibliography

Attas, D. 2005. *Liberty, Property, and Markets: A Critique of Libertarianism*. Aldershot: Ashgate.

Barnett, R. 1998. *The Structure of Liberty: Justice and the Rule of Law*. Oxford: Clarendon Press.

Cohen, G. A. 1995. *Self-ownership, Freedom and Equality*. Cambridge: Cambridge University Press.

Fried, B. 1995. "Wilt Chamberlain Revisited: 'Nozick's Justice in Transfer' and the Problem of Market-based Distribution". *Philosophy and Public Affairs* **24**, 226–45.

Hailwood, S. A. 1996. *Exploring Nozick*. Aldershot: Avebury.

Locke, J. [1689] 1963. *Two Treatises of Government*, P. Laslett (ed.). Cambridge: Cambridge University Press.

Machan, T. (ed.) 1982. *The Libertarian Reader*. Totowa, NJ: Rowman & Littlefield.

Miller, D. 2002. "The Justification of Political Authority". In *Robert Nozick*, D. Schmidtz (ed.), 10–33. Cambridge: Cambridge University Press.

Nozick, R. 1974. *Anarchy, State, and Utopia*. New York: Basic Books.

Otsuka, M. 2003. *Libertarianism without Inequality*. Oxford: Clarendon Press.

Paul, J. (ed.) 1982. *Reading Nozick: Essays on* Anarchy, State, and Utopia. Oxford: Blackwell.

Rawls, J. 1971. *A Theory of Justice*. Cambridge, MA: Harvard University Press.

Steiner, H. 1994. *An Essay on Rights*. Oxford: Blackwell.

Vallentyne, P. & H. Steiner (eds) 2000a. *The Origins of Left Libertarianism: An Anthology of Historical Writings*. New York: Palgrave.

Vallentyne, P. & H. Steiner (eds) 2000b. *Left Libertarianism and Its Critics: The Contemporary Debate*. New York: Palgrave.

Wolff, J. 1991. *Robert Nozick*. Stanford, CA: Stanford University Press.

5
Michael Dummett
Truth and Other Enigmas

Bernhard Weiss

Truth and Other Enigmas is a collection of some of Michael Dummett's writings on truth and other enigmas. The other enigmas include: meaning and understanding, time and causation, the past, realism, logic, proof, vagueness and philosophy itself. The writings span a considerable portion of Dummett's career – the years 1959 to 1975 – and reflect his diverse concerns in that period. So it would be a mistake to look for and wrong to impose a single theme that unifies the essays. However, two issues stand out as central, recurring as they do in many of the essays. One issue is the set of debates about realism, that is, those debates that ask whether or not one or another aspect of the world is independent of the way we represent that aspect to ourselves. For example, is there a realm of mathematical entities that exists fully formed independently of our mathematical activity? Are there facts about the past that our use of the past tense aims to capture? The other issue is the view – which Dummett learns primarily from the later Wittgenstein – that the meaning of an expression is fully determined by its use, by the way it is employed by speakers. Much of his work consists in attempts to argue for this thesis, to clarify its content and to work out its consequences. For Dummett one of the most important consequences of the thesis concerns the realism debate and for many other philosophers the prime importance of his work precisely consists in this perception of a link between these two issues. *Truth and Other Enigmas* contains his earliest forays into this nest of issues, forays that are amplified, clarified and modified in later, often more extended works (see, especially, his much more recent collection *The Seas of Language* and his sustained examination in *The*

Logical Basis of Metaphysics). Here I shall begin by looking at the view that meaning is use, then move on to the issue of realism and will round things off with a look at some of the other enigmas.

Meaning as use

The thesis that meaning is use can be thought of as the claim that if two speakers agree in the use they make of an expression then that expression, on each of their lips, means the same. Why should this be the case? Well, if it were possible for two speakers to differ in the meaning they have conferred on an expression, yet for them to use the expression similarly, then that difference of meaning must be one that is not manifested to other speakers. Moreover it would be incapable of being manifested to other speakers, considered purely *as other speakers* (even if expert psycholinguists were able to discern the difference, they would not be capable of so doing purely as speakers). The reason is obvious: the only evidence on which other speakers can base their judgements about the meaning one has conferred on an expression is the evidence of one's use of it. So were meaning to transcend use then the meaning that a speaker confers on an expression would be essentially unavailable to other speakers and, in this sense, would be private to that speaker. Now Dummett takes it that such a conception of meaning is repugnant because "the meaning of a statement consists solely in its rôle as an instrument of communication" (p. 216). If I am to communicate something to you by using a certain sentence then that sentence must have a certain content (meaning) for me and you must be able to *know* that the sentence has that content. But if the content depends on some essentially private state of affairs then there is no way for you to have this knowledge (Dummett says that the audience "would have no means of becoming aware of" (p. 216) the association of sentence with a particular content) and so no way for the sentence to be used in communication. Thus such a conception of meaning is repugnant because it subverts the role of language in communication. Note that what Dummett is saying is that if communication is to occur it must be possible for a hearer to determine a speaker's meaning. It would not suffice for successful communication were the hearer to *happen* to fix on the correct meaning *by chance*; fixing on the correct meaning must, for Dummett, be a non-accidental, indeed a methodical, process. In other words communication does not merely require that speaker and hearer share meanings; rather, it must be possible for them to know or to be aware that they share meanings.

One might indeed wonder whether one should endorse Dummett's strictures on successful communication. But let us not pursue that issue directly. Instead we should consider a slightly different form of what Dummett clearly takes to be another version of essentially the same argument (see pp. 216–17.) To understand an expression is to know its meaning. That is, understanding is a state of knowledge. Ascriptions of knowledge must be justified in terms of capacities that constitute possession of the knowledge. In some cases the relevant capacity will be a capacity to articulate the content of one's knowledge. These are cases where one's knowledge is explicit. Clearly, on pain of vicious circularity or regress, knowledge of language itself cannot always be characterized in this way. For then speakers' ability to use some bits of language would be explained only in terms of their ability to use other bits. So possession of knowledge that amounts to understanding will, on occasion, consist in the ability to display certain capacities: this is implicit knowledge. Now if possession of knowledge is only possible when it can be ascribed by others then Dummett's argument is complete; ascribing implicit knowledge will require exhibition to other speakers of certain capacities in relation to an expression. And what else could these capacities be other than capacities to use the expression appropriately? Our question about whether communication requires knowledge of shared meanings thus becomes the question of whether knowledge of meaning must be ascribable by others. The alternative would clearly be to claim that some states of knowledge are only self-ascribable. *Truth and Other Enigmas* does not discuss this alternative. Rather, in the preface, Dummett "simply records" his conviction that Wittgenstein's private language argument is "incontrovertible" (p. xxxiii). Knowledge that is only self-ascribable is knowledge for which there would be no distinction between seeming to possess it and genuinely possessing it, that is, supposed knowledge that Wittgenstein's private language argument precisely aims to debunk. So Dummett's endorsement of the thesis that meaning is use appears to stem from his acceptance of Wittgenstein's argument.

Let us move on from arguments for the thesis to the nature of the thesis itself since, as Dummett rightly observes, the thesis is little more than a slogan, a guideline for judging the acceptability of an account of meaning but not an account of meaning itself (p. 189). Granted that someone who knows the meaning of an expression knows how to use it, the question remains: how are we to characterize this knowledge? The reason why this is a problem is that an expression will be used in combination with other expressions in grammatical sentences. So to know the use of an expression one would need to know how to use it in all these possible combinations, which, in turn would require an understanding of the expressions with which it is combined. Since the range of these expressions includes every other grammatical expression (simple and complex) in the language, an ability to use the expression would be indistinguishable from an ability to use the language as a whole. Dummett rejects such a position, which he terms holism.

On a holistic view, no model for the individual content of a sentence can be given: we cannot grasp the representative power of any one sentence save by a complete grasp of the linguistic propensities underlying our use of the entire language; and, when we have such a grasp of the whole, there is no way in which this can be systematised so as to give us a clear view of the contribution of any particular part of the apparatus. No sentence can be considered as saying anything on its own: the smallest unit which can be considered as saying something is the totality of sentences believed, at any time, to be true.

(p. 309)

In contrast he thinks that there must be some way of characterizing the particular piece of knowledge that a speaker has when she understands some expression of the language. Views that accept this insistence are called "molecular". How, in general, is a molecular account to be fashioned? Well, if the particular knowledge involved in understanding an expression is knowing its entire use then we are led into holism. So if we are to deny holism we must say that the particular knowledge involved in understanding an expression is knowledge of a restricted set of uses. This privileged set of uses is therefore meaning-determining or canonical. Clearly an account of meaning and understanding of this form does not violate the meaning as use slogan but how do we account for the entire use of the expression? The thought here is that the entire use of the expression flows in some uniform way from its meaning-determining uses. For instance, having characterized the meaning-determining uses of, say, a pair of predicates there will be a uniform procedure applicable to each predicate by means of which we can derive its other uses. So our account of meaning breaks into two parts: the account of meaning-determining uses and the generally applicable account of how other uses flow from these (see pp. 188–9, 302ff.).

This sketch of molecularism clearly raises a number of questions. What are the canonical uses of expressions of various grammatical categories? How are other uses derived from these? But let us set those questions aside and ask why Dummett is attracted by molecularism. The short answer to this question is that he takes it that our task, as philosophers of language, is to construct a theory of meaning where a theory of meaning is a systematic representation of the content of every sentence expressible in the language. That is, we try to show how the meaning of a sentence is determined systematically by the meanings of its parts. Since that is our aim we should not give up on it unless it is proved to be impossible. Holism "is the denial that a theory of meaning is possible" (p. 309) and thus should not be accepted unless molecularism is shown not to be feasible. In other words, molecularism is, as a matter of methodology, our default position.

But the short answer is just a little too pat. Philosophers are apt to prize a systematic theory of meaning (or what is often called a compositional theory of meaning) because it is supposed to *explain* speakers' ability to learn language and their ability to make and understand indefinitely many novel sentences. As Dummett admits in a later work (*The Logical Basis of Metaphysics*) a holistic account of meaning need not be non-compositional since, even on a holistic account, the meaning of a sentence will be a function of the meanings of its parts and the way they are composed. But the meanings of those components will not be characterizable independently of an understanding of the entire language and thus a holistic "theory" of meaning has none of the explanatory power of a molecular theory of meaning; it will not serve the ends for which we attempt to construct a theory of meaning.

Another feature of language that a holistic theory fails to explain or, better, fails to give an adequate account of is change in language. Intuitively, we suppose that there is a genuine distinction between a change in one's beliefs and a change in the meaning possessed by one's sentences. But, since, for a holist, meaning will be a function of the totality of sentences held true (see the quote above), any change in belief is tantamount to a change in meaning. To put the point with a little more subtlety, what we want is an account of the different status of sentences that are held true. Some of these sentences we want to say are true in virtue of meaning – analytic – others are not – these are synthetic. A revision in the truth-value assignments that counts as a change in meaning will involve a change in the truth-value assignment to one or more analytic sentences, one that leaves undisturbed the truth-value assignments to analytic sentences will correspond merely to a change in belief. But for this to be possible we need to make out the distinction between analytic and synthetic sentences, that is, between sentences whose truth-value is a product of our adoption of certain conventions and others that are undetermined by those conventions. Of course it is well known that Quine (pre-eminently in the recent history of the subject) has brought this distinction into question. Quine's point is that there are no sentences that are immune to revision in the following sense: there are no sentences revision in whose truth-value must be construed as a change in meaning. So note that the question is not about whether or not a sentence's truth-value assignment can be revised; it is about whether or not that revision must be seen as a change in meaning. In other words we are asking whether a revision in the truth-value assignment to a sentence constitutes *only* a change in our dispositions to use language. Quine claims that all we have to go on is the way speakers modify their use of language in response to their unfolding experience, but Dummett demurs. He concedes only that the character of our linguistic dispositions may not be immediately transparent to us but this does not mean that we are in Quine's position of observing the way use modifies in response to experience. Rather we are able to reflect on how use would and should alter in hypothetical circumstances. The speaker in Quine's spotlight is alienated from her own use of language; at most, she can offer reliable predictions about her use. In contrast Dummett's speaker senses that her linguistic dispositions confer meanings on her terms by which her use is bound; those linguistic dispositions can be explored and when explored enable her to represent the meanings of her expressions, that is, to represent how fragments of her language function (see pp. 410–14).

Quite clearly the issue of holism versus molecularity raises many questions we shall have to leave untouched. It is an important issue in its own right but is crucially important in understanding Dummett's thought because his views on it are dictated by his fundamental commitments about what sort of activity language use is ("it is *the* rational activity *par excellence*"; Dummett 1993b: 104) and about what sort of account we should therefore aim at. Let us therefore accept the molecularity requirement and move on to question what use-conditions are grasped by speakers in coming to understand a particular sentence.

Our first sally into this area will be entirely negative. Dummett argues that grasp of a sentence's canonical use-conditions cannot amount to grasp of its truth-conditions, at least, as these have been traditionally conceived. Many philosophers (e.g. Frege, the early Wittgenstein, Davidson) have supposed that to understand a sentence is to grasp in what conditions it is true. We can then explain, on this basis, the use of the sentence on its own: it may be asserted just when these conditions obtain; to use the sentence as a command is to command that these conditions be made to obtain, and so on. We can also explain the use of this sentence as a component of other sentences because we explain how the truth-condition of the complex is determined by the truth-condition of its components.

Dummett argues that this traditional conception is flawed. Some sentences are undecidable, that is, there are sentences for which we have no guaranteed means of determining their truth-value. Think of sentences about the past, sentences about remote regions of space, sentences that generalize over totalities that we cannot guarantee to be able to survey, counterfactual and subjunctive conditionals. Traditionally one, nonetheless, thinks that each such sentence is determinately either true or false and, since we cannot guarantee to determine this truth or falsity, each is determinately true or false independently of our knowledge of its truth-value. Now, if the truth-conditional account of meaning is correct then, in understanding undecidable sentences, we grasp truth-conditions that determinately either obtain or fail to obtain independently of our knowledge. We cannot, Dummett argues, grasp such truth-conditions or, better, such an account of understanding violates the slogan that meaning is exhausted by use. If the truth-conditional theorist accepts the requirement that meaning does not transcend use then she must explain how understanding – grasp of truth-conditions – is manifested in the use speakers are able to make of the sentence. As remarked above, understanding cannot always consist in explicit knowledge. So the question is: when the knowledge is implicit what are speakers able to do that demonstrates their grasp of a particular truth-condition? Well, speakers are able to use their capacities to recognize the obtaining of certain states of affairs in the world, states of affairs that confer truth or falsity on sentences or constitute evidence for or against it. Where, but only where, the sentence is decidable can we think of these recognitional capacities as grasp of truth-conditions that determinately either obtain or fail to obtain. For when the sentence is decidable we have a guaranteed way of exercising our recognitional capacities in order to determine the sentence's truth-value. However when the sentence is undecidable we can, at most, exercise our recognitional capacities to determine whether or not we have evidence that tells in favour of or counts against the truth of the sentence. Where we fail to be in the happy circumstance of lighting on a definitive answer we cannot justify the presumption that, nevertheless, there must be some such answer. Or, better, we cannot justify this presumption without, in addition, supposing that there is an ingredient of understanding that goes beyond anything one is able to achieve in relation to the sentence.

Think, if you like, of two speakers. One claims to grasp truth-conditions that determinately either obtain or fail to obtain; the other claims an understanding of the sentence that is exhausted by her ability to be sensitive as to whether recognizable conditions constitute evidence for or against the sentence. (The sentence "J. S. Bach skipped breakfast on the morning before his twenty-fifth birthday" will do to focus one's thinking.) Actually, since the latter set of abilities is clearly part of what it is to understand the sentence, there is a very good question as to how the former ability – the grasp of the truth-condition – delivers the latter set of abilities. But let us set that question aside and suppose it has some answer. The question for us now is: granted that each speaker displays the appropriate sensitivity to evidence, what, in addition, is the first speaker able to do? If silence meets this query then the "extra" ingredient of understanding that delivers knowledge of truth-conditions is an ingredient that transcends use and is thus repugnant to a conception of meaning as use.

Is the truth-conditional theorist condemned to silence? There is comparatively little discussion of possible replies in *Truth and Other Enigmas* (see *Elements of Intuitionism*, concluding philosophical remarks; *The Seas of Language*; *The Logical Basis of Metaphysics*) but one response is touched on. It might seem that a truth-conditional account (of some sort) is bound to be right in the sense that what one grasps must amount to grasp of a truth-condition. This is because truth-conditions relate closely to conditions of correct use:[1] it is correct to assert a sentence when and only when it is true. What really seems to need justifying is the thought that these truth-conditions determinately either obtain or fail to obtain independently of our knowledge, that is, that these truth-conditions are bivalent. How then do we justify bivalence? Well, classical logic accepts the law of excluded middle (LEM) – "*P* or not-*P*" holds for every *P* – and a disjunction is true just in case one of its disjuncts is true. So either "*P*" is true or "*P*" is not true: bivalence holds. Thus what appears to show a speaker's grasp of the bivalent truth-condition is her preparedness to accept LEM. Dummett objects; it cannot be right, he suggests, to attribute to speakers grasp of a certain notion of truth purely on the basis of their preparedness to accept a certain mode of inference or to accept the logical truth of a certain sentence. Rather the way we infer should be justified on the basis of a notion of truth, which we can validly attribute to ourselves on the basis of uses of language that do not implicate that very rule of inference. Dummett's point will then be that there is nothing in our use of language prior to the introduction of LEM that would require attributing to ourselves grasp of bivalent truth-conditions. So, rather than making that attribution purely to legitimate our use of LEM, we should instead face up to the fact that our acceptance of LEM stands in doubt. And many philosophers have found this a startling, if not flatly unacceptable, conclusion. For here we are presented with a philosophical argument to the effect that an aspect of our mundane use of language, namely, inference by LEM, is illegitimate; philosophy, for Dummett, can require revisions in our ordinary first-order practice.

Why do these arguments about the bivalence of truth matter so much? One reason is the connection, which we have briefly noticed, of a notion of truth with a justification of logic. The other reason is Dummett's connection of debates about the notion of truth with debates about realism. And it is to that issue that we now turn.

Truth and realism

For the moment, let us concentrate on metaphysics, and specifically on metaphysical disputes about realism. Such disputes crop up in a number of different areas. One might be a realist about other minds, or about material objects, mathematics, the past, the future or possible worlds. And, of course, realism in each of these areas might be opposed. Dummett is motivated by a sense that there is a commonality to these disputes and his aim is to draw this out. Clearly he is not saying that these disputes are all precisely analogous, only that there is a common form to the commitments assumed by the realists and resisted in various ways by their opponents. He states his aim as follows: "I think it is possible to construct a uniform framework by means of which what may be called the abstract structure of each particular such dispute can be characterised".

Often, one reads that a realist believes that certain entities exist. So a realist about material objects believes that material objects exist; a realist about arithmetic believes that numbers exist. But this cannot be a deep commitment of the realist's for two reasons. First, phenomenalism opposes realism about material objects but does not deny their existence, rather it construes material objects as assemblages of sense data. So the question here is not so much whether such objects exist but whether they are, in some sense, "ultimate" constituents of reality or whether they are reducible to some other entities. Constructivists in mathematics typically do not deny the existence of mathematical entities such as numbers and nor do they construe these as reducible to some other range of entities; rather, they construe mathematical entities as certain sorts of mental constructions or as entities that depend for their existence on our mathematical activity. So in neither of these cases is the existence of a range of entities in question; rather, the status of that existence is questioned either as being, in some sense, ultimate or as being, in some sense, mind independent. A second reason for refusing to make the crux of the debate hinge on the existence of certain entities is that in other cases there is no relevant range of entities. For instance, the realist about the past need not have any view about the existence of a range of entities; rather, she simply maintains that talk of the past aims to represent an objective feature of reality.

Dummett thus suggests that a better way of approaching the commonality of these disputes is to see them not as disputes about a range of entities, but as disputes concerning a certain range of statements (p. 146). What we then need to make sense of in these terms are the notions of being an ultimate constituent of the world; of being a mind-independent entity; and of objectivity. In *Truth and Other Enigmas* Dummett suggests that what we need to focus on is the question of whether "statements of the disputed class possess an objective truth-value, independently of our means of knowing it" (*ibid.*). The realist thus believes that a bivalent notion of truth applies to the statements in question; an anti-realist will deny this. In "Realism" in *Truth and Other Enigmas* Dummett goes on to argue that views about the relevance to the debate of reductionist views – and so views about whether or not an entity is an ultimate constituent of reality – is that they often provide a motivation for rejecting bivalence. But in his later paper of the same title (in *The Seas of Language*) Dummett offers a more nuanced view. There the realist is seen as adopting a bivalent notion of truth based on a notion of reference. The realist is thus seen as adopting a certain sort of semantic theory (a theory about the relation of words to worldly items) and one might plausibly then maintain that the notion of being an ultimate constituent relates to the question of whether the semantic theory attributes a relation of reference to a given set of terms.

Shortly we shall move on to examine Dummett's discussion of traditional disputes about realism, which constitutes the support for his recommended construal of realism. But we are now in a position to link our previous discussion of meaning and truth with debates about realism. What we witnessed there was an argument that seemed to show that we could not legitimate a bivalent notion of truth and that, on the present conception of realism, is just to say that we have a generally applicable argument against realism. But, perhaps more importantly, a general framework suggests itself. The debate about realism concerns what notion of truth is taken as appropriate to a certain range of statements. The notion of truth is tested against the account of meaning and understanding (for instance, what we supposedly discovered is that no acceptable account of meaning and understanding can be reconciled with a bivalent conception of truth). So the arbiter of disputes about realism is the theory of meaning. (There is a deep Fregean assumption here about the relation between understanding and semantic concepts such as truth and reference. We shall find an opportunity to return to this in the next section.)

A nice example is provided by Dummett's take on phenomenalism. The phenomenalist claims that statements about material objects are reducible to statements about (actual and possible) sense data. So for the phenomenalist material objects are not part of the ultimate structure of reality. How is the phenomenalist's reduction supposed to work? As Dummett notes it will, in most cases, consist of two stages:

> ... every material-object statement not asserted as a report of observation must reduce to a subjunctive conditional whose constituents [are] sense-datum statements. E.g., "There is a table in the next room" reduces first to "If I were to go into the next room, I should see a table"; this is in turn to be reduced by translating the antecedent into a statement about kinaesthetic sense-data, and the consequent into one about visual sense-data. (p. 158)

Dummett then reports a complaint that Isaiah Berlin raised against this position. Either there is a table in the next room or there is not. So, on the phenomenalist's interpretation, if I were to go into the next room, I should see a table or if I were to go into the next room, I should not see a table. That entails that one of these subjunctive conditionals must be true (and thus one of the sense-datum reductions of these conditionals must be true). But in that case there would be a subjunctive conditional statement that is true but is not true in virtue of some categorical fact of the world; it is said to be barely true. And this is held to be counterintuitive. But Dummett notes that, if this complaint is apt, we must assume that LEM holds for the original material world statement and *that* assumption might precisely be questioned by the phenomenalist and, indeed, the (first) stage of the reduction might precisely constitute the phenomenalist's motivation for *rejecting* LEM. That is, the phenomenalist might well claim that because a subjunctive conditional cannot be barely true, we cannot assume that either the one subjunctive conditional or its opposite must be true. Thus we cannot assume that either the original material-object statement must be or that its syntactic negation must be true. Thus we cannot justify LEM for that statement in this way. (Note that here I have been a little careful to frame the argument in terms of bivalence of truth rather than simply in terms of the applicability of LEM. This is because Dummett later rues the fact that he had focused too heavily on LEM in this early paper.) So it appears that an essential ingredient of the phenomenalist's rejection of realism will involve a rejection of bivalence and, secondly, that the reduction to sense-datum statements plays no essential role in this, since it is only the *first* stage of the reduction that is implicated. The position, first, rejects the idea that an understanding of material-object statements accrues through an understanding of sense-datum statements. Rather an understanding of a material-object statement would consist in a sensitivity to evidence, provided by observation, for or against its truth. The subjunctive conditional would then spell out how such observational evidence might be garnered but, independently of this evidence, would not be taken as determinately either true or false.

An anti-realist about the past tense cannot base her position on a reductive view about the past. Rather, she sees the past as in some sense mind-dependent. To be more precise, she will claim that there are no matters of fact about the past that are independent of our knowledge. So the anti-realist will refuse to assume that statements about the past have a determinate truth-value unless we have a way of determining that truth-value. In other words, she will reject a bivalent notion of truth. Thus conceiving of the debate as one about the acceptability of a bivalent notion of truth both enables one to conceive of a plausible anti-realism about the past and highlights the similarity of this debate with other debates about realism.

Dummett is sceptical about the application of reductive theories to mathematics. One might arrive at an anti-realist view here because one thinks that the meaning of a mathematical statement depends on what counts as a proof of it: to understand a mathematical statement is to be able to tell whether or not a mathematical construction is or is not a proof of that statement. Since understanding is thus a matter of being sensitive to the status of a construction as a proof, there is no justification of the assumption that mathematical statements are determinately either true or false independently of our ability to furnish a proof; the notion of proof is thus not bivalent. In "The Philosophical Basis of Intuitionistic Logic" Dummett asks himself how one should motivate a change in the logic applicable to mathematics. Since our choice of logic will be influenced crucially by what we take to be the right notion of truth, his question calls for a decision about the acceptability or not of a bivalent notion of truth. We might thus treat this as a discussion about the objectivity of mathematical reality. Another possible treatment of the notion of objectivity might be to take a view of the ontological status of mathematical objects, namely, one might reject their status as objective by holding their existence to depend on our mathematical activity. But Dummett claims that talk of mathematical objects as mental creations is purely metaphorical and so requires that we give such talk some clear content. He then argues that we cannot give such talk any clear content and thus we cannot approach the concept of objectivity through a view about the ontological status of the objects concerned. The argument presented is quite involved but the crux of it is as follows. One way of making sense of the ontological status of mathematical objects as mental creations is to think of mathematical propositions as coming to be true when they are proved. But if by that we mean that a proposition is proved when we *actually* possess a proof of it we shall never have a true universal generalization about numbers, since we shall never prove every instance of a universal generalization. But, if a proposition is true, when we are merely *able* to prove it then we face a choice when we have a procedure that enables us to decide the truth-value of a proposition. We might say that the statement is determinately either true or false in advance of instituting the decision procedure or we might say that the truth-value is indeterminate until the decision procedure is carried out. So according to the first position "$1000000^{1000000}$ is prime" is determinately either true or false; according to the second position it is not. The basis of this difference is that first position endorses the following disjunction, which is denied by the second position:

> If we were to carry out the decision procedure then we would discover that $1000000^{1000000}$ is prime or if we were to carry out the decision procedure then we would discover that $1000000^{1000000}$ is not prime.

However both positions accept the conditional:

> If we were to carry out the decision procedure then we would discover that $1000000^{1000000}$ is prime or that it is not prime.

So the question is: should we, in this sort of case, infer the disjunction of conditionals – the former – from the conditional with disjoined consequent – the latter? And now the problems are as follows:

(i) The choice between these two positions – whether or not we should make the inference – cannot be made purely on the basis of one's view about the ontological status of mathematical objects. Rather, one will need to have a view about whether there is a determinate outcome to carrying out a mathematical calculation.

(ii) If one claims that there is not, then the resulting position involves an extreme and implausible revision of mathematical practice.

(iii) If one claims that there is, then undecidable arithmetic propositions will have determinate truth-values, unless we can provide an *additional* reason for rejecting the idea that generalizations over instances, each of which has a determinate truth-value, also gives rise to statements with determinate truth-values.

Thus the ontological view does not have any clear content independently of other decisions that we would need to make and, arguably, has no content (if one rejects (ii) and endorses (iii)). Note also that Dummett seems to think that the content of a metaphysical position should be seen in terms of the notion of truth it dictates and, consequently, in what revision it imposes in our practice. So he happily embraces the idea that philosophy not only can, but should, be revisionary: it can be revisionary, as we have seen, because we need to justify our practice by providing an acceptable theory of meaning; and now we see that it should be revisionary because the *content* of a metaphysical view is played out in terms of the way it justifies ordinary practice and in terms of which aspects of that practice it succeeds or fails in justifying.

Let us recap our main findings. Realism about a class of statements should be seen as a view about the appropriate notion of truth (more accurately as a view about the form of the correct semantic theory). When conceived in this way the metaphysical position has clear non-metaphorical content, so too does its opposition and more plausible ways of opposing realism come into view. Similarities between the different disputes come to be apparent because analogous semantic claims are at stake in these different areas. Since the acceptability of a semantic theory is judged from the perspective of our overall theory of meaning or, equivalently for Dummett, of understanding, the philosophy of language is the arena in which to arbitrate these metaphysical disputes.

This last point is a crucial element in the Dummettian framework. Its acceptance is extremely controversial and is tantamount to accepting some version of the Fregean claim that sense determines reference. I want to turn next to Dummett's discussion of this issue. But a second point for further discussion should be noted now too. Dummett links our metaphysical/philosophical views with the practices they contemplate by insisting that there must be a justificatory relation between them: the role of philosophy is to provide a justification of various of our practices. In so doing we gain a reflective understanding of those practices that is more systematic but not essentially different from the sort of reflective appreciation of the practice possessed by speakers, gained in the course, perhaps, of teaching, modifying or policing it. A pivotal practice here, because of its supposedly close connection with truth, is deductive inference. So we shall need, in particular, to think about the project of justifying deduction; that will be the topic following the next.

The notion of sense

The most relevant papers to our discussion are "Frege's Distinction Between Sense and Reference" and "The Social Character of Meaning". Included in the first is an argument for the notion of sense and in the second a defence of it from relatively recent attacks. The sense of an expression is an ingredient of understanding it; it is that ingredient which determines its reference. Why suppose that there is such an ingredient, namely, a piece of knowledge, conventionally associated with the expression, that suffices to determine its reference? What we need to make out is two claims: first, that grasp of the meaning of an expression cannot simply consist in knowledge of its reference; and, secondly, that this knowledge must be seen not as merely a concomitant, but as an ingredient of understanding. To begin we need to make a distinction between two sorts of knowledge: predicative and propositional knowledge. Predicative knowledge is knowledge of the form: S knows, of a, that it is F. Examples are: "Wittgenstein knows, of Frege, that he wrote *Grundlagen der Arithmetik*" and "Ludwig van Beethoven knows, of Napoleon, that 'Napoleon' refers to him". Propositional knowledge is knowledge of the form: S knows that p. Examples are: "Wittgenstein knows that Frege wrote *Grundlagen der Arithmetik*" and "Ludwig van Beethoven knows that 'Napoleon' refers to Napoleon".

Now grant the following two premises: (i) predicative knowledge is based on propositional knowledge; and (ii) there is never a single piece of propositional knowledge on which a piece of predicative knowledge needs to be based. Suppose that a speaker is said to know the reference of a term. Then the speaker has a piece of predicative knowledge. In view of (i) this piece of predicative knowledge must be based on a piece of propositional knowledge and, in view of (ii) there is more than one such piece of knowledge that may provide this base. So there is an additional task in specifying that piece of propositional knowledge on which the predictive knowledge is based. So (i) shows that there can be no bare knowledge of reference and (ii) shows that, from the theorist's point of view, one cannot rest at merely characterizing knowledge of reference.

Dummett takes (i) to be certainly true and offers little argument for it. He argues for (ii) on the following grounds. Were (ii) false there would be no need to say any more of a speaker than that S knows, of a, that b refers to it. If we can show that there always is more to say than this then (ii) must be true. Since (i) is true if it is the case that S knows, of a, that b refers to it, then there must be some piece of propositional knowledge on which this is based, say, S knows that b refers to a. But if there is such a piece of propositional knowledge then we must be able to say what possession of this knowledge consists in. Where the knowledge can be articulated by the speaker this is entirely unproblematic. But such knowledge cannot, on pain of circularity in our explanation, be the sort of knowledge on which an ability to speak a language is *based*. So at some point we shall need to account for what a speaker is able to do, which demonstrates that she possesses a piece of propositional knowledge of the above form. We shall need, for instance, to explain her ability to recognize the object as the bearer of the name when it is *appropriately* presented to her. That is, we shall need an account both of how the object is to be presented and of how, given such a presentation, she is able to recognize the object and discriminate it from others. Thus there is always an additional account to be given that takes us beyond the purely predicative account.

Notice that what this shows is that, in understanding an expression, each speaker must have a piece of propositional knowledge. But this is not to say that there is a piece of propositional knowledge that each speaker must have in understanding an expression. For the precise propositional knowledge might vary from one speaker to the next. And unless we can ensure some uniformity here we do not have a strong enough motive to factor the propositional knowledge into understanding (rather than simply allowing that there are pieces of propositional knowledge that are essential concomitants of understanding). To make this point out, Dummett following Frege, considers the content of sentences. The argument is familiar so I will not labour its details. Many identity statements are informative because they convey a particular content. Now were the knowledge involved in understanding to amount to knowledge of reference then identity statements could not be informative; were "$a = b$" true one would know its truth simply on the basis of understanding "a" and "b". So there must be a piece of propositional knowledge possessed by a speaker that is an ingredient of understanding. So the first part of the argument says that there is an additional piece of propositional knowledge and the second part of the argument says that this knowledge must be part of understanding.

But there is a gap in the argument. Sense, recall, is that ingredient of understanding that suffices to determine reference. Nothing that we have so far said has done anything to establish that there is an ingredient of understanding that determines reference. The first part of the argument began from a premise about bare – that is, merely predicative – knowledge of reference and so is impotent to speak to the question about whether or not the content of knowledge does in fact determine reference. The second part of the argument claimed that knowledge involved in understanding simply cannot amount to knowledge of reference and so again cannot tell us whether or not the content of this knowledge *determines* reference.

In essence, the notion of sense plays a dual role: it both explains the cognitive content of sentences – it links language with psychology – and it explains the referential properties of words – it links language with the world. What we need is reason to think that the *same* item plays *both* roles. "The Social Character of Meaning" addresses precisely this question. Dummett's Fregean conception has come under pressure from some sorts of semantic externalists. Externalists of this variety claim that the knowledge one possesses as a speaker does not, in fact, suffice to determine reference, rather reference is determined by further features of the speaker's context such as her causal relations to objects and natural kinds or her community of fellow speakers. Dummett poses the following dilemma to such externalists. Either these further features are precisely those features to which ordinary speakers would appeal, if need be, in order to settle problematic cases of determining a reference, or they are not. In the former case the externalist is not driving a wedge between what speakers know and what determines reference; rather, she is spelling out the character of speakers' knowledge, knowledge that, precisely, suffices to determine reference. In the latter case, the externalist is asking us to imagine a case in which there is a correct means of determining the reference of an expression but of which all speakers of the language might be ignorant. Dummett takes it to be quite absurd to suggest all speakers might be ignorant of the way a term ought to be applied.

Let us put a little more flesh on the bones of this dilemma by considering what Dummett says about Putnam's arguments. Putnam argues that when we introduce a term for a natural kind we do so by means of a stereotype, which is commonly used to apply the term, but we also do so by means of a sample: "Gold is the same stuff as this." One stuff is the same as another when they share an underlying structure, as discerned by some ultimate chemical analysis. So the extension of the term is responsible to the underlying nature of the stuff with which we happen to be surrounded. A doppelgänger of mine on a twin planet might share my understanding of the term "gold" but, if the stuff on his planet has a different composition, then his term will have a different extension: what we understand will fail to determine the term's reference. Dummett demurs from this account. If Putnam is right that the reference of the term "gold" is fixed by the chemist's notion of "same stuff" then Putnam's argument demonstrates the important phenomenon of the division of linguistic labour: some speakers may have an imperfect grasp of a term yet succeed in referring to what those competent with the term refer to because they defer in their use to these more competent speakers. With respect to those competent speakers the account simply spells out the sense of the term. We are on the first horn of Dummett's dilemma. But Putnam goes further, noting that even in communities ignorant of chemistry, such as the ancient Greeks, the reference of their term would be responsible to the stuff's underlying chemical composition. But here Dummett claims that we have no grounds for this attribution and, making the attribution places us on the second horn of his dilemma.

Dummett's argument, in effect, is that it is a feature of our concept of meaning that a single feature must play both roles identified for sense. Pulling apart these roles does violence, at some point, to our conception of meaning because it introduces facts about how an expression ought to be used that are unratified by speakers' actual or potential use.

The justification of deduction

"The Justification of Deduction" is a rich paper in which Dummett addresses a variety of issues to do with the justification of deduction and links these with his views about realism and the theory of meaning. Here I want to isolate just one of these issues, namely, the question of how it is so much as possible to have a justification of deduction. Any justification of a rule of deduction will itself involve deductive reasoning and so will employ either the very rule we are intending to justify or others. In the former case the justification is surely circular, whereas in the latter we face the question of how we are to justify the rules of inference employed in the reasoning. And now either we launch an infinite regress or we develop a circle in which rules of inference are justified by employing rules of inference in whose justification they are already presupposed. Thus a justification of deduction is impossible to achieve.

Dummett's response to this challenge hinges on drawing two distinctions: the distinction between two sorts of circularity and the distinction between two sorts of justification. An argument is blatantly circular when the conclusion appears as one of the premises. But this is not the sort of circularity at stake in deductive justifications of deduction. There the rule of inference in question is not involved in the argument as a premise but is employed, that is, used in drawing the inferences that provide the justification. So it would be worth separating out this quite different sort of circularity and labelling it; let us call it "pragmatic circularity". Now let us introduce another distinction between what Dummett calls explanatory and suasive justifications. A suasive justification is an argument that is put forward in an effort to persuade someone of its conclusion. Although we are often tempted to see all arguments in this vein this would be false to our actual use of arguments. On occasion we put forward an argument for a conclusion that we are thoroughly convinced of; the intention in forming the argument is to explain the truth of the conclusion to ourselves. Such justifications are explanatory. Dummett's claim is the following: in constructing a justification of deduction we are interested in arriving at an explanatory justification and, although the occurrence of a pragmatic circularity is fatal to a suasive justification, it is acceptable in an explanatory justification. In giving ourselves an explanation of the truth of our beliefs we do not need to suspend those beliefs: we may deploy them.

Note, in support of Dummett, that a blatantly circular argument always takes the same form and can be guaranteed to be available. In contrast, pragmatically circular arguments vary in form and need not always be available. If they were always available then Dummett could be accused of crass incoherence, since we could not reconcile this with his logical revisionism. Fortunately, we can easily demonstrate the point with the following example. Consider a classical mathematician who is convinced that truth in mathematics coincides with provability. Now, even if she is willing to reason within mathematics by means of LEM she cannot justify that law. In order for her to accept every instance of "P or not-P" she would have to accept that one or other disjunct is always *true*. Since she thinks of truth as provability, she would have to think that either "P" is provable or "not-P" is provable. But provided she accepts that there are undecidable sentences (namely, sentences that cannot be guaranteed to be either provable or refutable), as we have a right to suppose that she does, she will not be comfortable with the latter thought. So even though she is inclined to accept LEM, she will not be able to justify it to herself once she adopts a conception of truth as provability. Thus it would seem that pragmatically circular justifications do have some value that is not possessed by blatantly circular justifications. The hard question is to be more precise about what this value is, given the fact that we can easily give examples of pragmatically circular arguments for bad rules of inference (see Haack 1982).

The reality of time

Among the other enigmas that Dummett concerns himself with is one that raises another aspect of realism. The issue is the reality of time. I should like to close with a brief look at his short paper on McTaggart ("A Defence of McTaggart's Proof of the Unreality of Time"). McTaggart attempts to prove the unreality of time as follows. Events occurring in time give rise to two sorts of facts: (i) facts about whether an event is past, present or future; and (ii) facts about whether one event occurs before, after or simultaneously with another. Facts of type (i) cannot be reduced to facts of type (ii) since from information about the order of events – facts of type (ii) we cannot make any inference about facts of type (i). Facts of type (i) are essential to time because these involve what is itself essential to time, namely, change; there is no change in facts of type (ii). But now facts of type (i) are contradictory since the predicates "past", "present" and "future" are mutually incompatible yet each applies to every event. Thus time must be unreal.

The obvious reply is that McTaggart has overlooked our use of tense. Take an event that is now past. The predicates that can now correctly be applied to it are: "*is* past", "*was* present" and "*was* future". And these are obviously not incompatible. McTaggart, however, responds that these are only the predicates that correctly apply *now*; it is still true that, for instance, the incompatible predicates "*is* past", "*is* present" and "*is* future" apply to that event. So the move gains us nothing: if there was a problem about the incompatibility of "past", "present" and "future" McTaggart can preserve that problem by focusing purely on the present tense.

What McTaggart is arguing is that we cannot make sense of the phenomenon of time except from the point of view of reports made by observers situated in time. Being situated in time such observers can make reports that involve token-reflexive expressions – expressions such as tense markers that refer to features of the production of a token of that expression – without which we cannot report change. The putative contradictions that emerge are apparent conflicts between such token-reflexive reports made at *different* times. But for that very reason, that is, because the reports are token-reflexive and are made at different times, the conflict is merely apparent.

So is McTaggart wrong to infer that time is unreal? No, claims Dummett, but we do need to import an additional assumption about what it is for something to be real. What McTaggart has shown is that if we are to describe temporal reality we must invoke reports that are token-reflexive, that is, that involve reference to the reporter's perspective in time. And now we can conclude that time is unreal, *if* the reality of a phenomenon requires that there be a complete description of it, a description that is independent of the observer.

Can we accept the conclusion? Arguably not, since what it says is that there are non-temporal relations between events that we apprehend as temporal. But our apprehension of these relations as temporal is an apprehension that itself changes from one time to another. So it appears that there must be a reality to temporal relations at least as these obtain between our apprehensions.

And how do we escape this apparent paradox? Not easily. Apparently we have to deny the assumption of Dummett's reconstructed version of the argument, that is, we have to deny that a real phenomenon need be susceptible to an observer-independent description. We have to make sense of the idea that reality itself, or at least an aspect of it, is dependent on the observer. Dummett leaves his reader pondering this tantalizing suggestion and so shall I.

Note

1. When one uses a sentence correctly one is exempt from a certain sort of criticism. Of course, there may be other criticisms to be made; the assertion of many a true sentence is simply downright rude.

Bibliography

Books by Dummett

[1973] 1981. *Frege: Philosophy of Language*, 2nd edn. London: Duckworth.
[1977] 2000. *Elements of Intuitionism*, 2nd edn. Oxford: Oxford University Press.
1978. *Truth and Other Enigmas*. London: Duckworth.
1981. *The Interpretation of Frege's Philosophy*. London: Duckworth.
1991a. *The Logical Basis of Metaphysics*. London: Duckworth.
1991b. *Frege and Other Philosophers*. Oxford: Oxford University Press.
1991c. *Frege: Philosophy of Mathematics*. London: Duckworth.
1993a. *Origins of Analytical Philosophy*. London: Duckworth.
1993b. *The Seas of Language*. Oxford: Oxford University Press.
2004. *Truth and the Past*. New York: Columbia University Press.

Papers by Dummett

1979. "Reply to Putnam". In *Meaning and Use*, A. Margalit, 125–35. Dordrecht: Reidel.
1987. "Replies". In *Michael Dummett: Contributions to Philosophy*, Barry Taylor (ed.), 219–313. Dordrecht: Nijhoff.
1986. "'A Nice Derangement of Epitaphs': Some Comments on Davidson and Hacking". In *Truth and Interpretation: Perspectives on the Philosophy of Donald Davidson*, E. LePore (ed.), 459–76. Oxford: Blackwell.
1994. "Wittgenstein on Necessity: Some Reflections". In *Reading Putnam*, P. Clark & Bob Hale (eds), 49–65. Oxford: Blackwell.

1995. "Bivalence and Vagueness". *Theoria* **61**, 201–16.

1998. "Truth from the Constructive Standpoint". *Theoria* **64**, 122–38.

Collections of papers on Dummett

Taylor, B. (ed.) 1987. *Michael Dummett: Contributions to Philosophy*. Dordrecht: Nijhoff.

McGuiness, B. & G. Oliveri (eds) 1994. *The Philosophy of Michael Dummett*. Dordrecht: Kluwer.

Heck, R. (ed.) 1997. *Language, Thought and Logic: Essays in Honour of Michael Dummett*. Oxford: Oxford University Press.

Brandl, J. & P. Sullivan (eds) 1998. *New Essays on the Philosophy of Michael Dummett*. Amsterdam: Rodopi.

Auxier, R. E. (ed.) forthcoming. *The Philosophy of Michael Dummett*. Chicago, IL: Open Court.

Works by other authors

Appiah, A. 1986. *For Truth in Semantics*. Oxford: Blackwell.

Brandom, R. 1976. "Truth and Assertibility". *Journal of Philosophy* **83**, 137–49.

Brandom, R. 1994. *Making it Explicit*. Cambridge, MA: Harvard University Press.

Devitt, M. 1983. "Dummett's Anti-realism". *Journal of Philosophy* **80**, 73–99.

Devitt, M. [1984] 1991. *Realism and Truth*, 2nd edn. Oxford: Blackwell.

Edgington, D. 1981. "Meaning, Bivalence and Realism". *Proceedings of the Aristotelian Society* **81**, 153–73.

Evans, G. & J. McDowell (eds) 1976. *Truth and Meaning*. Oxford: Oxford University Press.

George, A. 1988. "The Conveyability of Intuitionism: An Essay on Mathematical Cognition". *Journal of Philosophical Logic* **17**, 133–56.

George, A. 1993. "How not to Refute Realism". *Journal of Philosophy* **2**, 53–72.

Green, K. 2001. *Dummett: Philosophy of Language*. Cambridge: Polity.

Haack, S. 1982. "Dummett's Justification of Deduction". *Mind* **91**, 216–39.

Kripke, S. 1980. *Naming and Necessity*. Oxford: Blackwell.

Luntley, M. 1988. *Language, Logic and Experience: The Case for Anti-realism*. London: Duckworth.

Margalit, A. 1979. *Meaning and Use*. Dordrecht: Reidel.

Matar, A. 1997. *From Dummett's Philosophical Perspective*. Berlin: de Gruyter.

McDowell, J. 1981. "Anti-realism and the Epistemology of Understanding". In *Meaning and Understanding*, H. Parret & B. Bouveresse (eds), 225–48. Berlin: de Gruyter.

McDowell, J. 1982. "Criteria, Defeasibility and Knowledge". *Proceedings of the British Academy* **68**, 455–79.

McGinn, C. 1982. "Realist Semantics and Content-Ascription". *Synthese* **52**, 113–34.

McTaggart, J. E. 1908. "The Unreality in Time". *Mind* **17**, 456–73.

Putnam, H. "The Meaning of 'Meaning'". In his *Mind, Language and Reality: Philosophical Papers Volume 2*, 215–71. Cambridge: Cambridge University Press.

Quine, W. V. O. 1953. "Two Dogmas of Empiricism". In his *From a Logical Point of View*, 20–46. Cambridge, MA: Harvard University Press.

Rosen, G. 1995. "The Shoals of Language". *Mind* **104**(415), 599–609.

Tennant, N. 1987 *Anti-realism and Logic: Truth as Eternal*. Oxford: Clarendon Press.

Tennant, N. 1997. *The Taming of the True*. Oxford: Oxford University Press.

Weiss, B. 2002. *Michael Dummett*. Chesham: Acumen.

Wright, C. 1980. *Wittgenstein on the Foundations of Mathematics*. London: Duckworth.

Wright, C. [1986] 1993. *Realism, Meaning and Truth*, 2nd edn. Oxford: Blackwell.

Wright, C. 1992. *Truth and Objectivity*. Cambridge, MA: Harvard University Press.

6

Richard Rorty

Philosophy and the Mirror of Nature

Alan Malachowski

> When we try to examine the mirror in itself, we discover in the end
> nothing but the things upon it. If we want to grasp the things, we
> finally get hold of nothing but the mirror – This, in the most general
> terms, is the history of knowledge.   (Nietzsche 1995: 127)

Richard Rorty's *Philosophy and the Mirror of Nature* may be viewed as a sustained meditation on the philosophical significance and consequences of these remarks by Nietzsche. It is an iconoclastic book. But it is one that any person seriously interested in what philosophy is, how it came to be what it is and what it might eventually become should want to read, and re-read, whether or not they are disposed to agree with its controversial conclusions. In many ways, it is also a unique text. Certainly, no other book in recent times has launched such a detailed and extensive attack on the presuppositions and preoccupations of the dominant traditions of Western philosophy. Indeed, the closest competitor is probably Ernest Gellner's *Words and Things* (1966), which does not come very close at all. It generated heated controversy for a short time, especially in the Letters section of the London *Times*,[1] but now pales by comparison in terms of depth of argumentation, degree of influence and overall historical scope and ambition.

Philosophy and the Mirror of Nature (henceforth PMN) is also a difficult text, a feature that justifies the present discussion. This difficulty can be deceptive. It is not a stylistic matter. The book is elegantly and, for the most part, clearly written. Furthermore, the author admirably avoids needless jargon and excessive technicality. But, these very qualities can make the prose seem easier to fathom than it is, and this probably helps to explain why so many critics (and even some admirers) have fostered influential misinterpretations of the text.[2]

The difficulties Rorty's accomplished writing partly disguises are at least fourfold. First, in PMN he develops a complex philosophical narrative that takes many twists and turns before its dénouement. The "narrative" is not easy to summarize, although Rorty takes a usefully instructive stab at doing so in his own introduction (PMN: 3–13). This is therefore worth studying closely before tackling the book as a whole. Secondly, and relatedly, the book alludes to and relies on a good deal of historical material. But this is not, so to speak, *plain history*, the kind of history that purports to clearly depict "what actually happened" in the past and draws conclusions accordingly. It is, instead, history written with a particular purpose in mind: to introduce philosophers to the sheer *contingency* of their subject. Rorty aims to undercut their stubborn perception that certain philosophical problems are inevitable, that after human beings began to think and express their various thoughts linguistically they were sooner or later bound to encounter such problems. The third source of difficulty is his use of philosophical argumentation. On the face of things, the book contains a great deal of such argumentation. However, as in the case of history, the arguments deployed serve an unorthodox purpose. Their role is not simply to convince by sheer force of reason, but rather to produce particular desired effects. What matters then, is their "causal", as opposed to "rational", efficacy. And, this means that they are, in the traditional sense, partly "rhetorical". Rorty's suggested shift from reason to rhetoric is very controversial, and threatens to dislodge philosophical argumentation from its special place in the Western tradition. But, it needs to be considered in the wider context of Rorty's views on the nature of intellectual change as a whole, where he also generally downgrades the part played by "reason".

The final difficulty with the text is its complex relationship to philosophy itself. Rorty rightly holds that most progress in philosophy is "parasitic". Individual thinkers make their mark by reacting, whether cooperatively or critically, to the work of their predecessors. PMN, however, seems to do something different. It seeks to dispel the rationale for a whole way of practising philosophy without apparently offering anything constructive in its place, and without attempting to push philosophy forward into some new conceptual space where it can get a fresh start. Consequently it leaves philosophers with no evident motivation to go on doing what they normally do.[3]

PMN thus appears to be trying to bring philosophy to an end. Many commentators have put a more aggressive slant on this. They read PMN as yet another "death of philosophy" text written by a would-be intellectual under-taker. Some take the author sternly to task for selfishly and ungratefully trying to kill off the very tradition that spawned him. Rorty's actual position is more nuanced than this.[4]

It is a particular, attenuated, form of philosophy – epistemology-based phi-losophy – that PMN seeks to dispense with. This kind of philosophy presupposes that it has both the capacity and obligation to assess and, as necessary, shore up or debunk claims to knowledge made in all other areas of intellectual culture. PMN attempts to undermine this conception of philosophy, along with the notion of mind that goes with it (i.e. of mind as a mirror of accurate or inaccurate repre-sentations of the world). Moreover, the book contends that philosophy itself is not the kind of thing that can be brought to a standstill or slaughtered by intel-lectual means alone. Its fate depends, instead, on more general social and cultural considerations such as whether enough people are prepared to read philosophy books, take philosophical arguments seriously and pay the kind of taxes that are required to make philosophy a meaningful part of the education system.

Given the special difficulties we have outlined, perhaps the best way to approach PMN here is to try to show how we should cater for these in tackling the text. That is to say, we should provide some explicit guidance to readers on how best to approach PMN rather than devote our time to the more orthodox tasks of summarizing, explaining and critically evaluating what it says. But in addition to offering such advice, we should do two things. First, we need to preface it with some background material. PMN is important for reasons other than its wider impact on a certain philosophical tradition. It helps us fathom the phenomenon of Rorty himself and the moves he makes later in his career in such works as *Contingency, Irony, and Solidarity* (1988).

Secondly, we also need to examine what Rorty himself considers to be the core chapter of PMN. By exploring the ideas that it contains, by plunging, as it were, into the middle of PMN, we can make it easier for the reader to appreci-ate the significance of the book as a whole. For these ideas spread themselves like tentacles throughout the rest of the pages and influence almost everything else that Rorty has to say. We shall return to discussing this core chapter after presenting the background material and then considering the special difficul-ties posed by PMN.

Some background

Rorty was born in New York City on 4 October 1931. His family circle was highly politicized, and in his reminiscences he frequently refers to a prevailing ambiance of leftist social activism.[5] Nevertheless, after studying at the University of Chicago and Yale University, Rorty favoured an academic career over direct political participation.[6] At Chicago, Rorty's most influential teachers were Rudolf Carnap, Charles Hartshorne and Richard McKeon. And, at Yale his dissertation entitled "The Concept of Potentiality" was supervised by Paul Weiss. It is worth noting, that while Rorty admired the arch "methodological positivist" Carnap, the historical approach of his other teachers made a more lasting impression on him. In 1961, Rorty moved from his first teaching post at Wellesley College to the philosophy department of Princeton University where he remained for some twenty years before taking up the post of Kenan Professor of Humanities at the University of Virginia in 1982. After spending fifteen very fruitful years at Virginia (indeed, his book *Philosophy and Social Hope* (2000a) is dedicated to the university in appreciative recognition of this), Rorty accepted a post in the Department of Comparative Literature at Stanford University, where, still prolific, he currently resides.

On one common, but mistaken, reading of PMN, the book marks an unwelcome turning point in Rorty's otherwise distinguished philosophical career. Prior to its publication in 1980, Rorty had made a significant contribution to analytic philosophy; most notably with his influential work in the philosophy of mind on eliminative materialism,[7] but also with his ingenious treatment of transcendental arguments in his seminal article "Strawson's Objectivity Argument" (1970). On the mistaken reading, Rorty simply throws all this away in PMN, a book that constitutes a sudden, treacherous, mid-life defection from the analytic tradition. However, closer reading of Rorty's earlier writings and of PMN itself reveal that his radical ideas about the nature and direction of philosophy had been brewing much earlier at the time of his engagement in its mainstream debates. Thus, even in writings such as "Mind–Body Identity, Privacy and Categories" (1965), we find some suspicions arising that prepare the ground for the views more robustly expressed in PMN:

> There is simply no such thing as a method of classifying linguistic expressions that has results guaranteed to remain intact despite the results of future empirical inquiry. Thus in this area (*and perhaps in all areas*) there is no method which will have the sort of magisterial neutrality of which linguistic philosophers fondly dream.
>
> (Rorty 1965: 175, emphasis added)

Furthermore, in his substantial introduction to the important collection of articles he gathered together in 1967 under the title *The Linguistic Turn*, Rorty displayed a degree of awareness concerning the importance of historical and meta-philosophical considerations that distanced him from the views and ambitions of most of the authors involved. This "awareness" was already a strong signal that Rorty would be unlikely to ever fit smoothly into the analytic mould.

What PMN represents, on a more considered reading that takes this background into account, is the crystallization of Rorty's long-standing doubts and reservations about the dominant analytic tradition in Western philosophy. It *is* a turning point, but not in the sense of an abrupt turning against that tradition. What PMN does is to allow Rorty to set conclusively to one side many of the key concerns of analytic philosophy, concerns that he has at least partly shared in much of his previous written work, so that he can move on to pursue different kinds of philosophical interests. These involve some explorations of the merits of the alternative to analytic philosophy that pragmatism offers as well as serious consideration of the writings of philosophers outside the analytic fold, such as Heidegger and Derrida. But, they also encourage Rorty to roam further afield into the realms of literature, where he believes the intellectual role of the imagination is given its proper due. Indeed, PMN can be viewed as an attempt to prepare the ground for the emergence of the imagination as a force for good in philosophy.

Narrative and history

> A lack of historical sensibility is the original failing of all philosophers.
> (Nietzsche 1995: 178)

In PMN, Rorty takes Nietzsche's criticisms to heart. And, there are two main ways in which he deploys historical considerations to both deflect them and achieve his own aim of showing that certain traditional philosophical concerns should be set aside because they are both problematic and optional.[8] First, he develops an all-encompassing picture that enables him to throw a cloak of history over his whole venture. Secondly, he constructs various brief historical sketches to illustrate particular points.

Rorty's "big picture" invokes the notion of "philosophy as epistemology" mentioned earlier. It depicts how a number of different thinkers have strived to meet the two main internal requirements of that notion: (i) to define the essential characteristics of knowledge, and (ii) on the basis of (i), to codify history-transcending criteria for separating genuine claims to knowledge from bogus ones.

Rorty contends that the epistemological questions that seem so compelling to his fellow philosophers (e.g. "How can knowledge be defined?" and "How can knowledge be protected from virulent forms of scepticism regarding our ability to obtain it?") emerged from a series of historically motivated projects that began with Plato's insistence that differences in the degree of certainty to which things are known must correspond to differences in those things themselves. This project was modified much later by Descartes's methodological scepticism – his resolve to create certainty from the residue left from doubting whatever could be doubted – and his closely related conception of the mind as something that knows itself far better than it knows anything else. The next step came in the form of the Lockean empirical ambition to determine the limits and scope of human knowledge by mapping out the mind's capacities, a venture that was radically transformed by Kant's notion that the knowable aspects of all objects of empirical knowledge are shaped by the inherent cognitive constitution of the mind. In this big historical picture, it turns out that the mind's role in acquiring knowledge can be studied by non-empirical means. And this apparently puts epistemology – the theory of knowledge – in the driving seat of philosophy while, at the same time, giving philosophy itself a privileged position in culture. Furthermore, nothing that comes afterwards, such as the emphasis on linguistic considerations that is considered "revolutionary" by its adherents (see Ryle 1963), displaces epistemology because no appropriate challenge is issued to the larger preconception that the whole sequence of intellectual events leading to its primacy represents an inevitable unfolding of the workings of rational enquiry; where philosophy is at is where it *has to be* until it resolves its latest crop of problems – its current agenda *cannot* be avoided.

Our description of Rorty's second way of invoking historical concerns needs some careful qualification. Although he does use historical sketches to illustrate particular points and these sketches *do* provide some context for his revisionary accounts of "mind", "knowledge" and "philosophy", they are not, as it were, *evidential*. That is to say, they do not serve as a means of directly confirming the accuracy of the larger picture. To see why, we need to remind ourselves of the function that history serves in Rorty's scheme of things. Rorty's "history-of-philosophy", whether large scale or small, is history that is subservient to his desire to show that the problems traditionally regarded as "perennial", the kind of problems that philosophers contend "arise as soon as one reflects" (PMN: 3), are *optional*, and that engagement with them has by now proved to yield nothing more than a series of obstacles to the pursuit of better things. What this means for the historical material in PMN is that it does not have to be strictly correct. Its purpose is solely to introduce the possibility that things could have been different, that the ideas that fascinate philosophers have not come to exert that fascination solely as a result of previous thinkers reasoning themselves, either collectively or individually, from one explicit intellectual position to another. And this is our cue to say something more about Rorty's general account of intellectual change that we alluded to earlier.

Rorty's views are strongly influenced in this case by Thomas Kuhn, the distinguished, but controversial, philosopher of science.[9] Kuhn challenges the idea that science progresses smoothly *on its own intellectual terms*, that is, according to the direction dictated by its theoretical arguments and their methods of empirical confirmation. Here is Rorty's own instructive take on Kuhn, which, although written some twenty years after its publication, still sheds some light on what is going on in PMN:

> Kuhn's major contribution to remapping culture was to help us see that the natural scientists do not have a special access to reality or truth. He helped dismantle the traditional hierarchy that dates back to Plato's image of the divided line. That line stretched from the messy material world up into a near immaterial world. In the hierarchy Plato proposed, mathematics (which uses pure logic, and no rhetoric at all) is up at the top and literary criticism and political persuasion are down at the bottom. Kuhn fuzzed up the distinction between logic and rhetoric by showing that revolutionary theory-change is not a matter of following our inferences, but of changing the terminology in which truth candidates were formulated and thereby changing the criteria of relevance. (Rorty 2000a: 196)

Much of Rorty's post-PMN career is devoted to developing the implications of the Kuhnian idea that intellectual change is rarely "inference-led". He does this by fleshing out a positive account of the factors that *do* cause such change. Here he contends that phenomena that tend to be neglected in standard reason-based approaches, phenomena such as "images" and "metaphors", play a more important role in fostering, sustaining and ultimately undermining intellectual motivation than "propositions", "theoretical claims" and "formalized arguments".[10] But, it is important to note that this whole process of development begins in PMN when Rorty challenges preconceptions about how *philosophy* undergoes fundamental changes. Rorty's approach is perceptively described by his friend and commentator Richard Bernstein:

> There are moments in history when, because of all sorts of historical accidents – like what is going on in some parts of culture such as science or religion – a new set of metaphors, distinctions, and problems is invented and captures the imagination of followers. For a time, when a particular language game gets entrenched, it sets the direction for "normal" philosophising. After a while, because of some other historical accidents – like the appearance of a new genius or just

plain boredom and sterility – another cluster of metaphors, distinctions and problems usurps the place of what is now a dying tradition. At first the abnormal talk of some new genius may be dismissed as idiosyncratic, as not being "genuine" or "serious" philosophy but sometimes this abnormal talk will set philosophy in new directions. We must resist the Whiggish temptation to rewrite the history of philosophy in our own image – where we see our predecessors as "really" treating what we now take to be fundamental problems. The crucial point for Rorty is to realise that a philosophical paradigm does *not* displace a former one because it can better formulate the legitimate problems of a prior paradigm; rather, because of a set of historical contingencies, it nudges the former paradigm aside.

(Bernstein 1992: 20)

Part of what makes PMN so exciting is the way in which it *lives out its own claims*; Rorty tries to instigate change himself by offering a historically informed alternative picture that is buttressed by images and metaphors rather than straightforward philosophical arguments. He wants to release philosophy from its traditional problematic and from the stranglehold of epistemology – the theory of knowledge – in particular. To try to achieve this, he highlights some of the images and metaphors that lock philosophers into their orthodox concerns, claiming, most importantly, that "the picture which holds traditional philosophy captive is that of the mind as a great mirror, containing various representations – some accurate, some not – and capable of being studied by pure, non-empirical methods" (PMN: 12). Once these "pre-rational" sources of philosophical orthodoxy are shown to involve accidental historical trends and unforeseen circumstances rather than anything of a rationally compelling nature, the veneer of the intellectual inevitability of this orthodoxy is shattered. Then there is no longer any need for thinkers to feel that they *have to* try to discover the answers to questions such as "What are the necessary and sufficient conditions for something to be counted as knowledge?" or "How is it possible for the mind to accurately represent reality?"

Rorty's historical sketches, or vignettes, are deployed as *ad hoc* shock treatments to quickly uncover the historical basis of philosophical concerns that are otherwise thought to be of purely rational interest. So, to take a crucial example, in the first part of PMN where Rorty deals with the philosophy of mind, he uses these sketches to reveal that the so-called intuitions that underpin Cartesian dualism are actually rooted in history. Notice, once again, that the exclusive purpose of Rorty's historical forays is to open the reader up to the *possibility* that philosophy can take different paths through the realm of ideas: that its route is not fixed in advance. Given this expressed purpose, it is not necessary that Rorty deliver anything over and above piecemeal historical plausibility. Complete and detailed historical accuracy is surplus to requirements.[11]

Rorty's use of "narrative" in PMN is all of a piece with his appeal to history. But, there are independent reasons why Rorty regards narrative as an importantly innovative tool. He believes that it can provide an effective means for inducing the Gestalt-like switches of perception that are needed to view philosophical commitments in a fresh light, one that shows them to be "optional", for instance. Narrative can do this because it is able to draw on richer linguistic resources than can normally be found in the arguments and theories philosophers tend to rely on. These resources can be put to work in ways that bypass the theoretical presuppositions and entanglements of the entrenched positions that Rorty feels the need to address. Furthermore, they enable a quick narrative stroke of the pen or quiver of the vocal chords to engage with, subvert or outflank the kinds of metaphors and images that, in Rorty's eyes, do most of the motivational cajoling behind the scenes of philosophical belief acquisition. Rorty also prefers narrative because it is easier to put together without unwittingly incorporating any of the spurious distinctions philosophers introduce to elevate their discourse to positions of repressive, judgemental power over other areas of enquiry.

Some of Rorty's narrative is, as we earlier indicated, interwoven with historical considerations. But he also tells stories that are entirely fictional. These lend imaginative plausibility to the philosophical switches of context that he contrives to free us from orthodox positions. A brilliant example of the latter is his tale of "The Antipodeans", which dominates the second chapter of PMN. It begins in quasi-Nietzschean style: "Far away, on the other side of our galaxy there was a planet on which lived beings like ourselves" (PMN: 70). Then, as it unfolds, the fable challenges preconceptions about the nature of mind, and about how it should be accounted for in philosophy. The challenge comes in the shape of a picture of these beings, the Antipodeans, as creatures who were very much like us except for the fact that they did not believe they had minds. It was not that they *denied* that they had minds, it was simply that issues concerning minds did not, indeed *could not*, surface in their culture because no vocabulary emerged that involved analogues of the word "mind" and various terms *we* associate with it such as "consciousness" or "mental states". These creatures had made breakthroughs in neurology and biochemistry that enabled them to talk very precisely about the details of their "neural states", and this obviated the need for the kind of mind talk we are familiar with. Rorty tells us that when an expedition from Earth arrived on the Antipodeans' planet, the philosophers on board were fascinated by the complete absence of "the concept of mind in their culture". This tale harks back to the time in Rorty's career when he advocated a form of "eliminative materialism" that would itself have dismissed "mind talk" from philosophical discourse. And it has indeed been read by some commentators as an attempt to confirm Rorty's earlier views (Schwartz 1983). However, the story of the Antipodeans should not be taken as one that favours any particular side in disputes *within* the philosophy of mind. For Rorty's own former fascination with materialism is now cast in the same light as the expeditionary philosophers' reluctance to just let go of their belief that the concept of mind they are familiar with is indispensable. The point of the story is to open up that possibility that the whole philosophical problematic traditionally connected with the notion of "mind" is optional.

Conversation

> There are no constraints on inquiry save conversational ones.
> (PMN: 171)[12]

Failure to appreciate the role of history and narrative in PMN has perhaps been exacerbated by a misunderstanding of the central, and most controversial, motif of the book: that of conversation as the main vehicle of enquiry. There is much more to this motif than meets the traditional philosophical eye.

Like all great writers, Rorty knows how to win our attention by encapsulating the essentials of what he wants to say in short, sharp phrases or sentences. But his most memorable aphorisms are self-consciously elliptical. They invariably sparkle against the backcloth of a more considered treatment of the matter in hand that is couched in what Jonathan Rée has aptly called "carefully contrived plain-dealing prose" (Rée 1998: 13). In this sense, Rorty is much more like William James than full-blooded aphorists such as Nietzsche. The comparison is instructive because Rorty is often treated like a latter-day Nietzsche, as if the only philosophical words he ever voices are inflammatory ones.

James, whose reputation has been revived of late, was also treated in much the same way by his early British critics, G. E. Moore and Bertrand Russell.[13] He penned bundles of interesting and insightful qualifications to stiffen his account of truth against the charge of unbridled subjectivism. These were prescient qualifications that later resonated with the "holism" espoused in the less maligned writings of two other eminent American philosophers, W. V. Quine and Donald Davidson. But, they were shrugged off in their own time, and those early critics still made sure that James became known as the philosopher who claimed very strange things such as, "If it pays to believe p then p is true" and "The claim

'X exists' may be true even if X does not exist". It was only when Rorty began to strike out on his own regardless of the damage inflicted on pragmatism in its youth and showed that it could once again make significant contributions to intellectual culture,[14] that more careful, and more sophisticated, readings of James began to supplant those of the analytic rumour-mongers.[15]

Given that Rorty did so much to restore James's standing in the philosophical community, it is ironic that his own writings, and especially PMN, should be abused by critics who, by recklessly skimming off quotations, threaten to make history repeat itself. Perhaps nowhere is their folly in this respect more apparent than in their vitriolic responses to Rorty's pregnant suggestion in PMN that "conversation" should replace "confrontation" as the main determiner of our intellectual beliefs. Such critics tend to overlook the fact that the socially coordinated conversation Rorty is alluding to involves, although it does not *only* involve, the kind of creative and refined communicative exchanges that produce "cultural goods" such as novels, poems and scientific theories. Many react as if he is shamelessly urging us to gorge ourselves on the capricious fruits of inane chatter, thereby casually exposing ourselves to the risk of losing all regard for the noble and more disciplined attempts that thinkers have made to formulate world-constrained beliefs. In short, they take "conversational limits" to mean "coffee shop limits", which sounds, to the philosophical ear, awfully like no limits at all. This shallow interpretation casts the author of PMN into the role of an ill-disciplined relativist, someone who is unwilling to subscribe to any stable conception of belief that stops *truth* running wild.[16]

Rorty's conversational motif derives from Michael Oakeshott's attempt to deflate what he saw as the prevailing philosophical view "that all human utterance is in one mode", that we should "regard all utterances as contributions (of different but comparable merit) to an inquiry, or a debate among inquirers, about ourselves and the world we inhabit" (Oakeshott 1967: 197). Oakeshott's notion of "conversation" as "the appropriate image of human intercourse" has some features we would expect Rorty to find attractive given *his* philosophical predilections. Thus, to take just one evident example, the correlative idea of an ongoing "communicative situation" within which "certainties are shown to be combustible" is bound to seem congenial to someone like Rorty who has heeded the lessons of Quine's famous article "Two Dogmas of Empiricism" (more on this shortly). But, what makes Rorty's adoption of Oakeshott's image so stimulating (and so inflammatory) is the way in which he cuts it free from Oakeshott's primary concerns,[17] and then uses it to capture the radical possibilities opened up by PMN. In Rorty's hands, the notion of "conversation as a dominant mode of enquiry" is shaped into a utopian prospect, a model for a society that aspires to achieve philosophical maturity in the sense of having outgrown what Nietzsche derided as "a craving for metaphysical comfort". Unfortunately many of the critics of PMN fail to recognize what Rorty is trying to do. Obsessed with his supposedly heinous crimes against truth, they ignore the bigger picture and never get round to considering the broader issue as to whether the kind of culture Rorty envisages, one that elevates what Oakeshott calls "unrehearsed intellectual adventure" above the predetermined march of reason, is worth working towards.

Arguments and appropriations

Western philosophy has fostered a self-image according to which it depends essentially on arguments for and against particular claims that can then be marshalled to support definite positions on certain key issues. Here, even when the efficacy of such dependence is questioned, the image remains intact because the thrust of the discussion invariably involves further arguments regarding the possible limitations of arguments. Argumentation seems, then, to be philosophically indispensable. In PMN, Rorty does not deny that arguments can, and often do, play a valuable role in philosophy. Instead, he challenges the idea that their role is ineluctable.

He does this by trying to show that traditional philosophical arguments have no *intrinsic rational merit*, that they can only do the work assigned to them in the context of all sorts of images, metaphors and sociohistorical concerns. Once such a "context" is culturally fixed in place, the conclusion of a suitably embedded argument may well seem to be inescapable. In PMN, Rorty picks away at the contextual threads that have appeared to make traditional philosophical themes unavoidable along with certain conclusions that have evolved out of the consideration of those themes. He is able to do this so effectively because he has appropriated the work of another philosopher who was, ironically, unable to see that his views could be put to such radical use.[18] The philosopher in question is Quine.[19]

One of the important strengths of Rorty's approach in PMN is his ability to draw controversial and far-sighted conclusions from his wide reading of philosophy texts. An excellent example of this is his prescient interpretation of Quine's work. Although Donald Davidson, Quine's natural successor, appears to have exerted a much larger influence on Rorty over the longer term, it was Quine who made the creative breakthrough that pointed him towards the heretical view that in philosophy imagination should take precedence over truth. Quine did this in one fell swoop when, in 1951, he published what would become one of the most influential articles in twentieth-century Anglophone philosophy: "Two Dogmas of Empiricism". In the midst of breaking down the hallowed distinction between statements that are held to be necessary (i.e. those that purportedly concern what *must* be the case, what could not be otherwise) and those deemed to be merely contingent (i.e. those regarding what need not have been the case, what could have been otherwise), Quine constructed a compelling, naturalistic image of the way "truths" function in human societies. Some beliefs are held very firmly in place by a network of other beliefs. This network makes it doubly difficult to overturn such beliefs, first, because it insulates them from worldly matters that might show them to be false, and secondly, because the act of renouncing these beliefs would involve the abandonment of a host of other beliefs, something that, in practical terms, it would be difficult to do. This "social inertia" encourages us to hang on tightly to such beliefs, and at the same time gives them the appearance of being "necessary" (we cannot countenance their falsehood). There are other beliefs that are not so inextricably entangled in networks of other beliefs and not so insulated from the goings on in the world at large. These beliefs are deemed "contingent" because they appear to be easier to give up.

Quine overlooked the wider, socially momentous nature of his contribution because, or so it seems, his imagination, although powerful, did not operate self-reflexively enough in this instance.[20] It failed to imagine the dramatic range of its own powers. Quine's "image of truth" was drawn for a narrow, philosophical audience, but it amounted to a radical revision of the social significance of truth in which some of philosophy's time-honoured concepts fall by the wayside. Instead of the traditional dichotomous portrait, in which the truth-value of statements either fluctuates according to the direction in which the empirical wind blows (i.e. "contingency") or stays fixed regardless to the pillars of language or some deep metaphysical feature of reality (i.e. "necessity"), Quine presents us with a *continuum* wherein sociohistorical forces determine the extent to which truths are dispensable.

In this set up, "truth" does not answer directly to *things*, no matter which. *A fortiori*, it is not determined by appropriate chunks of language-independent reality or appropriate chunks of language itself. Instead, its social status *as truth* is mediated by a myriad of pragmatic connections with a myriad of prevailing convictions. These connections form *webs of belief*, and a particular truth claim will exhibit recalcitrance or otherwise according to its position within such webs: deeply embedded, it will be hard to give up; loosely hemmed in, it can, and when the time is ripe *will*, be let go with relative ease. But, and this was a highly controversial implication that Quine, to his credit, did not overlook or shy away from, *anything* can be held fast or cast adrift as social conditions dictate: "Any statement can be held true come what may, if we make drastic enough adjustments elsewhere in the system … Conversely, by the same token, no statement is immune to revision" (Quine 1953). Rorty benefited twofold from Quine's new "image of truth". By grasping its wider practical upshot, he thereby gained further explanatory insight into how social thought shifts its ground. This enabled him to fashion his own fresh image of the imagination rather than truth as the main motor of intellectual change. But, and this is important, he also acquired Quine's case as useful collateral evidence in favour of this very "image".

The core chapter

Rorty tells us at the outset that "Chapter Four is the central chapter of the book – the one in which the ideas which led to its being written are presented" (PMN: 3). The main aim of the chapter is to undermine the thought that any notion of "privileged representation" can be philosophically useful. And, the ideas Rorty refers to are largely, as he tells us himself, "those of Sellars and Quine" (PMN: 10). They form an important part of what Rorty sees as an ongoing series of internal criticisms levelled by fully paid-up members of the analytic tradition in philosophy, but they gain their potency in this context by being pitted directly against the conception that there are two basic kinds of representations – intuitions and concepts (PMN: 168) – and thus, more generally, against what Rorty terms "the Kantian foundations of analytic philosophy" (PMN: 170).

Earlier, in Chapter 3, Rorty claims that Kant "gave us a history of our subject, fixed its problematic, and professionalised it" (PMN: 149). According to Rorty, Kant did this by incorporating into our conception of a theory of knowledge an alleged insight that C. I. Lewis characterized as follows: "There are in our cognitive experience, two elements; the immediate data, such as those of sense, which are presented or given to the mind, and a form, construction, or interpretation, which represents the activity of thought" (Lewis 1956: 38). Rorty maintains that far from being the product of "bare insight", the partition described here by Lewis is the outcome of a long tradition of philosophizing, a tradition that has been dominated by optional metaphors of epistemological confrontation between the mind and reality. His reading of Heidegger inspired Rorty to put this kind of historical spin on Kant's contribution to "philosophy-as-theory-of-knowledge" and gave him "the idea that the desire for an 'epistemology' is simply the most recent product of an originally chosen set of metaphors" (PMN: 163). In Chapter 4, Rorty uses Wilfrid Sellars and Quine for extra leverage to eject two key distinctions spawned by Kant's intuition–concept division:

(i) The distinction between what is "given" and what is "added by the mind";
(ii) The distinction between the "contingent" (because influenced by what is given) and the "necessary" (because entirely within the mind and under its control) (PMN: 169).

Without some such distinctions, says Rorty, "we will not know what would count as a rational reconstruction of our knowledge" nor will we know "what epistemology's goal or method could be" (*ibid.*). Without them, philosophy-as-theory-of-knowledge ceases to be viable.

Sellars attacks the first of the above distinctions and Quine the second. But Rorty detects two common factors in their demolition jobs: "behaviourism" and "holism". Their approach is "behaviourist" in the sense that they both raise behaviourist issues concerning the epistemic privilege attributed to certain claims on the basis of their being reports of correspondingly privileged representations. Thus Quine poses the question as to whether an anthropologist will ever be able to gather evidence that marks a particular distinction within the actual sentences to which speakers under appropriate scrutiny apparently give their unreserved assent. This is the distinction between contingently empirical and conceptually necessary truths. And Sellars queries whether the weight carried by first-person testimony concerning (say) pains we experience or thoughts we find ourselves thinking is greater than, or somehow significantly different in kind from, that carried by the reports of experts on subjects such as "mental stress" or "the mating behaviour of birds" (PMN: 173). In both cases, the main thrust of the questioning suggests that the distinctions involved outstrip the behavioural evidence for positing their existence. Hence Rorty contends that these issues raised by Quine and Sellars can be subsumed under the following general question: "How do our fellow speakers know when they should take us at our word and when they should seek additional confirmation of what we are saying?" He suggests that the answer to this question need not invoke a philosophically principled way of discriminating modes of confirmation:

> It would seem enough for natives to know which sentences are unquestionably true without knowing which are true "in virtue of language". It would seem enough for our peers to believe there to be no better way of finding out our inner states than from our reports, without their knowing what "lies behind" our making of them. It would seem enough for *us* to know that our peers have this acquiescent attitude. That alone seems sufficient for that inner certainty about our inner states which the tradition has explained by "immediate presence to consciousness" and other expressions of the assump-

tion that reflections in the Mirror of Nature are intrinsically better
known than nature itself.   (PMN: 173–4)

The behaviourist criteria that Rorty alludes to are not themselves supposed to
be philosophically grounded in anything other than empirical evidence. Nor do
they involve "behaviourist analyses" of "knowledge claims" or "mental states"
(PMN: 176). This is because:

> To be a behaviourist in the large sense in which Sellars and Quine are
> behaviourists is not to offer reductionist analyses, but to refuse to
> attempt a certain sort of explanation: the sort of explanation which
> not only interposes such a notion as "acquaintance with meanings"
> or "acquaintance with sensory appearances" between the impact of
> the environment on human beings and their reports about it, but uses
> such notions to explain the reliability of such reports.   (PMN: 176)

This "large behaviourism" constitutes the *holistic* connection between Quine and
Sellars. It holds that epistemic justification or confirmation is "social": that its
lines of support reach out horizontally into the surrounding community of fellow
"knowers" rather than down into "foundations", "reality" or any philosophical
surrogates. In this flattened-out scheme of things: "Nothing counts as justification unless by reference to what we already accept, and … there is no way to get
outside our beliefs and our language so as to find some test other than coherence"
(PMN: 170). Quine and Sellars are thereby committed to the "premise" that "we
understand knowledge when we understand the social justification of belief and
thus have no need to view it as accuracy of representation" (PMN: 170).

Rorty's own gloss on all this invokes his conversational stance towards matters of epistemology: "knowledge" is what members of the appropriate community are inclined or prepared to say in the appropriate practical circumstances,
and justification of their sayings in this regard is "not a matter of a special
relation between ideas (or words) and objects, but of conversation, of social
practice" (PMN: 170). The general moral he draws here is crucial to his overall
project and sums up the main thrust of PMN as a whole:

> Once conversation replaces confrontation, the notion of the Mind as
> Mirror can be discarded. Then the notion of philosophy as the disci-
> pline which looks for privileged representation among those consti-
> tuting the Mirror becomes unintelligible. A thoroughgoing holism has
> no place for the notion of philosophy as "conceptual", as "apodictic",
> as picking out the "foundations" of the rest of culture, as explaining

which representations are "purely given" or "purely conceptual", as presenting a "canonical notation" rather than an empirical discovery, or as isolating "trans-framework heuristic categories".

(PMN: 170–71)

Conclusion

Philosophy and the Mirror of Nature offers the reader who follows its narrative thread a way out of philosophy as it has been traditionally practised in the West. And three philosophical heroes, Heidegger, Wittgenstein and Dewey,[21] are invoked to lend authority to the idea that reflective thought can be released from the epistemological maze first constructed by Plato, then refined down the ages by his philosophical heirs. Their role, however, is largely emblematic. No attempt is made to provide a detailed account of their philosophical positions. Heidegger is presented as a thinker who has distilled the best that can be found in Hegel and Nietzsche, someone who therefore recognizes the historical nature of philosophical ideas. Wittgenstein is portrayed as a satirist who, in his maturity, savagely undercuts the grand ambitions of analytic philosophers, including, most importantly, those of his younger self. And Dewey is hailed for his conception of knowledge wherein "justification" is a "social phenomenon rather than a transaction between the knowing subject and reality" (PMN: 9). However, this apparently casual appropriation of three hugely important, but very different, philosophers has a serious strategic purpose. For Rorty is determined that the path away from the invidious Platonic tradition should not lead straight towards some successor discipline or alternative set of views. Because he is determined to keep the philosophical future open, he deploys Heidegger, Wittgenstein and Dewey as harbingers. Their views are treated as signposts rather than destinations. The same can be said of the "hermeneutics" that figures prominently in the last part of PMN:

> In the interpretation I shall offer "hermeneutics" is not the name for a discipline, nor for achieving the sort of results which epistemology failed to achieve, nor a program of research. On the contrary, hermeneutics is the expression of hope that the cultural space left by the demise of epistemology will not be filled – that our culture should become one in which the demand for constraint and confrontation is no longer felt. (PMN: 315)

As something of a "classic", PMN will be interpreted and reinterpreted over the years in the light of prevailing intellectual circumstances. In a world that it has helped make safe for the work of very radical, counter-traditionalists such as Foucault and Derrida, some readers who have already absorbed PMN's lessons by other intellectual means may find its descriptions of the futile attempts to make mirror imagery work quite poignantly noble and perhaps even enchanting. For them, ironically, PMN may provide a unique way back in to the Platonic problematic.

Notes

1. The controversy concerned Gilbert Ryle's editorial refusal to let the book be reviewed in the distinguished philosophical journal *Mind*. One of the key correspondents, who came out in favour of Gellner, was Bertrand Russell.
2. For more on the nature of these "misinterpretations", see A. Malachowski, *Richard Rorty* (Chesham: Acumen, 2002).
3. And Rorty's critics have often suffered a morbid failure of imagination in response to this. They seem to be unable to conceive of philosophy ever carrying on in anything other than the normal fashion.
4. Even Robert Brandom, an astute and sensitive commentator on Rorty's work, makes this mistake, seeing murderous intentions in PMN that are actually disavowed in the text (R. Brandom (ed.), *Rorty and his Critics* (Oxford: Blackwell, 2000)).
5. For some autobiographical illumination of his background see the first chapter of Rorty's *Philosophy and Social Hope* (Harmondsworth: Penguin, 2000).
6. Rorty has nevertheless taken a keen intellectual interest in politics, as his occasional journalistic pieces on political issues demonstrate. Furthermore in his *Achieving our Country: Leftist Thought in Twentieth Century America* (Cambridge, MA: Harvard University Press, 1998), it becomes clear that political concerns have always been close to his philosophical heart.
7. For an overview, see the first volume of A. Malachowski (ed.), *Richard Rorty* (4 vols) (London: Sage, 2002).
8. When confronted with philosophizing that runs into difficulties and yields little of practical value, Rorty's instinct is to press the question "Do we really need to be doing this?" rather than to simply "press on".
9. The seminal text is T. Kuhn, *The Structure of Scientific Revolutions* (Chicago, IL: University of Chicago Press, 1961).
10. Unfortunately, Rorty's critics tend to claim he is wrong on abstract, *a priori* grounds when they need, instead, to provide concrete examples of important intellectual changes that depend essentially on the reason-centred resources they appeal to in those lofty claims.
11. Many nitpicking criticisms of the historical accuracy of PMN are thus rendered irrelevant. For further development of this point, see Malachowski, *Richard Rorty*, 44–5.
12. For a detailed discussion of this quotation from PMN, see my article "Pragmatism Minus Truth/No Limits", in *Pragmatism* (3 vols), A. Malachowski (ed.) (London: Sage, 2004).
13. For further discussion of these critics, see my "Pragmatism in its Own Right", in *Prag-

matism (3 vols), A. Malachowski (ed.).

14. *Contingency, Irony, and Solidarity* is the text in which Rorty most clearly "strikes out on his own", and, interestingly, he feels little need there to make any appeals to pragmatism.

15. Again, this point is discussed in more detail in Malachowski, "Pragmatism in its Own Right".

16. See Malachowski, "Pragmatism Minus Truth/No Limits".

17. These mainly involved the misapplication of theory to politics.

18. Rorty's "An Imaginative Philosopher: The Legacy of W. V. Quine" (obituary), *Chronicle of Higher Education* (February 2000) adds weight to this assessment of Rorty's approach to Quine.

19. For some terse reservations about Rorty's view of him, see W. V. Quine, "Let Me Accentuate the Positive", in *Reading Rorty*, A. Malachowski (ed.), 117–19 (Oxford: Blackwell, 1990).

20. I first made this suggestion in my editorial introduction to Malachowski (ed.), *Richard Rorty* (4 vols).

21. A quick explanation as to how Rorty is able to harness these seemingly incongruous figures can be found in Malachowski, *Richard Rorty*. For more details, see the appropriately designated essays in Rorty, *Consequences of Pragmatism* (Minneapolis, MN: University of Minnesota Press, 1982).

Bibliography

Bernstein, R. 1992. *The New Constellation: The Ethical-Political Horizons of Modernity/Postmodernity*. Cambridge, MA: MIT Press.

Brandom, R. (ed.) 2000. *Rorty and His Critics*. Oxford: Blackwell.

Devitt, M. 2004. "Rorty's Mirrorless World". In *Pragmatism* (3 vols), A. Malachowski (ed.). London: Sage.

Dickstein, M. (ed.) 1998. *The Revival of Pragmatism: New Essays on Social Thought, Law and Culture*. Durham, NC: Duke University Press.

Festenstein, M. & S. Thompson (eds) 2001. *Richard Rorty: Critical Dialogues*. Cambridge: Polity.

Gadamer, H.-G. 1975. *Truth and Method*. London: Sheed & Ward.

Gellner, E. 1966. *Words and Things*. Harmondsworth: Penguin.

Kuhn, T. 1961. *The Structure of Scientific Revolutions*. Chicago, IL: University of Chicago Press.

Lewis, C. I. 1956. *Mind and the World Order*. New York: Dover.

Malachowski, A. (ed.) 1990. *Reading Rorty*. Oxford: Blackwell.

Malachowski, A. 2002a. *Richard Rorty*. Chesham: Acumen.

Malachowski, A. (ed.) 2002b. *Richard Rorty* (4 vols). London: Sage.

Malachowski, A. (ed.) 2004. *Pragmatism* (3 vols). London: Sage.

Malachowski, A. forthcoming. *The New Pragmatism*. Chesham: Acumen.

Murphy, J. 1990. *Pragmatism: From Pierce to Davidson*. Boulder, CO: Westview.

Nietzsche, F. [1878] 1995. *Human, All Too Human*, G. Handwerk (trans.). Stanford, CA: Stanford University Press.

Oakeshott, M. 1967. *Rationalism in Politics and Other Essays*. Oxford: Oxford University Press.

Putnam, H. 1995. *Pragmatism*. Oxford: Blackwell.

Quine, W. V. 1963. *From a Logical Point of View*. New York: Harper & Row.

Quine, W. V. 1990. "Let Me Accentuate the Positive". In *Reading Rorty*, A. Malachowski (ed.), 117–19. Oxford: Blackwell.

Rée, J. 1998. "Strenuous Unbelief". *London Review of Books*, 15 October.

Rorty, R. 1979. *Philosophy and the Mirror of Nature*. Princeton, NJ: Princeton University Press.

Rorty, R. 1965. "Mind–Body Identity, Privacy, and Categories". *Review of Metaphysics* **18**(24).

Rorty, R. (ed.) 1967. *The Linguistic Turn*. Chicago, IL: University of Chicago Press.

Rorty, R. 1970. "Strawson's Objectivity Argument". *Review of Metaphysics* **24**(36).

Rorty, R. 1982. *Consequences of Pragmatism*. Minneapolis, MN: University of Minnesota Press.

Rorty, R. 1988. *Contingency, Irony, and Solidarity*. Cambridge: Cambridge University Press.

Rorty, R. 1998. *Achieving our Country: Leftist Thought in Twentieth Century America*. Cambridge, MA: Harvard University Press.

Rorty, R. 2000a. *Philosophy and Social Hope*. Harmondsworth: Penguin.

Rorty, R. 2000b. "An Imaginative Philosopher: the Legacy of W. V. Quine" (obituary). *Chronicle of Higher Education*, February.

Ryle, G. 1963. *The Revolution in Philosophy*. London: Macmillan.

Sorell, T. 1990. "The World from Its Own Point of View". In *Reading Rorty*, A. Malachowski (ed.). Oxford: Blackwell.

Schwartz, R. 1983. Review of *Philosophy and the Mirror of Nature*. *Journal of Philosophy* **80**. Reprinted in *Pragmatism* (3 vols), A. Malachowski (ed.) (London: Sage, 2004).

Sellars, W. 1997. *Empiricism and the Philosophy of Mind*. Cambridge, MA: Harvard University Press.

West, C. 1989. *America's Evasion of Philosophy*. Madison, WI: University of Wisconsin Press.

Williams, M. 2000. "Epistemology and the Mirror of Nature". In *Rorty and His Critics*, R. Brandom (ed.). Oxford: Blackwell.

Further reading

Detailed bibliographies of Rorty's own writings can be found in Malachowski (1990) and (2002b), although the latter is now more comprehensive. There is a vast, and rapidly growing, secondary literature on Rorty. The bibliography above concentrates mainly on literature that relates at least in part to *Philosophy and the Mirror of Nature*, or at least helps to place it in context. It also includes the various works referred to in the main text of this article.

7
Donald Davidson
Essays on Actions and Events

Kirk Ludwig

Introduction

Essays on Actions and Events (Davidson 2001a, henceforth EAE) brings together seminal papers by Donald Davidson, one of the most influential philosophers in the analytic tradition in the latter half of the twentieth century, in the areas of the philosophy of action, the metaphysics of events and the philosophy of psychology. Davidson's central contributions to philosophy are presented in EAE and its companion volume *Inquiries into Truth and Interpretation* (Davidson 2001b), which deals with issues in the theory of meaning and philosophy of language.[1] The fifteen essays collected in EAE[2] are divided into three groups: "Intention and Action", "Event and Cause" and "Philosophy of Psychology". The first deals with the nature of agency, action and action explanation. The central theme is that actions are events – bodily movements – caused and explained by reasons, construed as beliefs and desires, which make sense of the action from the point of view of the agent. The second deals with the metaphysics of events, which Davidson argues are dated particulars and part of the metaphysics of ordinary language. The third deals with issues in the philosophy of mind, principally the relation of the mental to the physical, and features Davidson's celebrated thesis of anomalous monism, according to which each mental event is identical to some physical event, although there are no strict laws connecting the mental with the physical. This essay surveys the central contributions of EAE, giving most attention to the work in the philosophy of action, which is connected with and prefigures the work in the latter two parts of EAE.

Philosophy of action

The causal theory of action

The publication of "Actions, Reasons and Causes" (EAE: 3–19) in 1963 brought about a revolution in the philosophy of action. The then orthodoxy, under the influence of Gilbert Ryle's *The Concept of Mind*, and Wittgenstein's *Philosophical Investigations*, was that reasons for actions were not their causes, but related to them in a quite different way, and, hence, that explaining actions by citing the agent's reasons for them was not causal explanation. This was bound up with the Wittgensteinian rejection of mental states or events as inner processes, and the concern not to bring to bear inappropriately on one area of language models drawn from another. In "Actions, Reasons and Causes", Davidson argues, against the prevailing orthodoxy, that reason explanations of actions are causal explanations, and so successfully that this became the new orthodoxy. This shift has obvious connections with larger issues in the philosophy of mind. Our reasons are the beliefs and desires in the light of which we pursue our ends. The sort of explanations we give in citing reasons for actions illuminates reasons and actions, and tells us what constraints have to be met to find a place for them in the natural order. If reason explanations of actions are minimally explanations that cite reasons as their causes, then the most literal forms of behaviourism are fundamentally misguided. For behaviourism treats talk of psychological states as logically equivalent to descriptions of actual and counterfactual behaviour. However, as Hilary Putnam (1968) has put it, a cause is not a logical construction out of its effects.

Davidson calls action explanations that cite an agent's reasons for what he did *rationalizations*. He begins with the observation that: "Whenever someone does something for a reason ... he can be characterized as (a) having some sort of pro attitude toward actions of a certain kind, and (b) believing ... that the action is of that kind" (EAE: 3–4). In Davidson's terminology, reasons are psychological states, beliefs or pro attitudes (i.e. motivational states). He calls a reason for an action that consists in a belief–desire pair of the sort characterized by (a) and (b) a *primary reason* for the action. In terms of the notion of a primary reason, his main thesis can be stated initially as follows:

1. In order to understand how a reason of any kind rationalizes an action it is necessary and sufficient that we see, at least in essential outline, how to construct a primary reason.
2. The primary reason for an action is its cause. (EAE: 4)

Thus, actions are causally explained by citing primary reasons for them.

Actions are what we do for reasons, and so what we do intentionally. (In holding that actions are what we do for reasons, Davidson rejects *purely* causal theories of action, although his own account is a variety of causal theory; see "Agency" (EAE: 43–62) for a detailed discussion of this issue.) The question of the nature of action explanation is then at the same time the question of the nature of actions themselves. Davidson holds that actions are events, and that events are datable particulars, and, hence, that they can be described in a variety of ways. This is central to his defence of the causal theory of action, as well as his later defence of anomalous monism.

Let us say, to take an example of Davidson's, that: "I flip the switch, turn on the light, and illuminate the room. Unbeknownst to me I also alert a prowler to the fact that I am home" (EAE: 4). Davidson holds that I have not performed four actions, but only one, of which four descriptions have been given. What I did in the first instance was to move my finger. On Davidson's view, my moving my finger was my flipping the switch, which was my turning on the light, illuminating the room and, unbeknownst to me, alerting a prowler. Each of these, Davidson holds, is related to the first by way of describing it in terms of something that it caused. For if I am described as doing something that causes the light to turn on, it follows that I turned on the light. If to turn on the light, I must do something else as a causal means, then from my turning on the light it follows that I did something that caused the light to turn on. If it was my flipping the switch that caused the light to turn on, then we can say that I turned on the light *by* flipping the switch. Similarly, I alerted the prowler *by* illuminating the room, which I did *by* turning on the light. I turned on the light in turn *by* flipping the switch. I flipped the switch *by* moving my finger; 'by' here means 'by means of'. The means are usually causal, although there are exceptions. (For example, if I want to colour my drawing, I may do this by colouring it blue. In this case, the relation expressed by 'by' is not causal, but logical.) Action verbs such as 'move' and 'turn on' express both agency and an outcome of its expression that can be described independently. (If 'try' is an action verb, it is an exception.) Often we can state what the outcome is using the intransitive form of the verb. If I moved my finger, then my finger *moved*. If I turned on the light, the light *turned on*. And so on. Some actions we do but not by doing anything else. I do not typically move my finger by doing anything else. Davidson calls these *primitive actions*, and identifies them with bodily movements, in a generous enough sense "to encompass such 'movements' as standing fast, and mental acts like deciding and computing" (EAE: 49). Davidson's thesis then is that all actions are primitive actions, and that primitive actions are identical with bodily movements. As Davidson has put it: "We never do more than move our bodies: the rest is up to nature" (EAE: 59).

If this is correct, reasons relate to actions under descriptions.[3] My reason for flipping the switch was that I wanted to turn on the light and believed that flipping the switch would accomplish that. But that is not my reason for alerting the prowler, for I had no reason to do that. Yet my flipping the switch was my alerting the prowler. Thus, the reason I had for what I did is a reason for it described as a turning on of the light. This requires us to state more carefully what a primary reason for an action is.

> C1. *R* is a primary reason why an agent performed the action *A* under the description *d* only if *R* consists of a pro attitude of the agent towards actions with a certain property, and a belief of the agent that *A*, under the description *d* has that property.
>
> (EAE: 5)

Importantly, the belief is not about actions of a particular type, but rather about the particular action performed; this is required to connect the desire for a type with the particular action concerned.[4]

What we do for reasons we do intentionally. In light of this, in "Actions, Reasons and Causes" Davidson treats '*x* did *A* intentionally' and '*x* acted with the intention of *A*-ing' as ways of indicating something about the reasons *x* had for acting as he did, and the expression 'with the intention of …' as syncategorematic, that is, as understood as a unit. The function of saying that I opened the window *with the intention of letting in some air* is simply to indicate that I had a pro attitude towards letting in some air. Davidson later recognized this as a mistake, and retracted it in "Intention" (see § "Intentions" below).

This sets the stage for the main argument, which has two parts. In the first, Davidson argues that only the causal account can answer the question what makes one of two competing primary reasons for an action the one that explains it when the agent acts on only one of them. In the second part, he defends this answer against objections.

Davidson notes that we can construct a practical syllogism justifying an action from its primary reason. The primary reason for *A*, *x*'s flipping the switch, consists of

> *x*'s desire to turn on the light
> *x*'s belief that *A*, being a flipping of the switch, is a turning on of the light.

The corresponding practical syllogism, where the first premise is taken from the content of the desire, and the others from the belief, is:

> Any action of turning on the light is desirable (has a desirability characteristic)
>
> If A is a flipping of the switch, then A is a turning on of the light.
>
> A is a flipping of the switch.
>
> _____
>
> A is desirable (has a desirability characteristic)

To say A is desirable is not to say it is most desirable, but only desirable in a respect given by the premise. We must therefore understand the conclusion relative to the premises. This shows that every action is in a minimal sense rational, for it is justified in the light of the reasons for it, although this leaves it open that in the light of additional reasons it is not (see § "Weakness of will and the logical character of practical deliberation" below).

That the primary reason for an action justifies it does not show that that is all there is to action explanation, but it may suggest that we need look no further to understand the explanatory force of citing reasons. But crucially this appears not to be enough. For sometimes an agent has more than one primary reason for an action, but acts on only one of them (EAE: 33). Suppose that someone finds that an error has resulted in his having an extra million dollars in his bank account. He believes that he will impugn his reputation if he does not notify the bank immediately of the error; he desires that his *reputation*, which is useful, not be impugned. He also wants to do the right thing, and he decides that the right thing to do is to immediately notify the bank of the error. It seems prima facie possible for him to notify the bank for fear of his reputation being impugned rather than out of the motive to do the right thing, and, alternatively, it seems it is possible for him to do it because it is the right thing rather than to secure his reputation. If so, since both motives give rise to reasons that justify notifying the bank, but only one is, in each case, the reason for the action, there must be more to the relation between reasons for actions and the actions than their justifying those actions. The causal theory of action explanation explains this, while the rivals cannot. Thus, we must add C2 to C1.

> C2. A primary reason for an action is its cause.　　　　　(EAE: 35)

For the argument to be completed, however, the traditional objections to this proposal need to be met. There are five main objections: (i) that causes are events, but reasons are states; (ii) that causes are logically distinct from their effects, but that reasons and actions are not logically independent; (iii) that laws are involved in ordinary causal explanations but not in rationalizations; (iv) that the non-inferential knowledge we have of our reasons is not compatible with their being causes of actions; and (v) that if reasons are causes, then actions are mere happenings and so cannot be free. I discuss only (ii) and (iii), as they link to later themes.

Objection (ii) is based on Hume's observation that causes and effects are distinct occurrences. The thought then is that logical connections are incompatible with this, but reasons and actions are logically connected, so that reasons cannot be causes of actions. Davidson notes that reasons do not entail that an agent acted, for one may have reasons one never acts on. Further, knowing an agent acted does not tell us what his reasons were, but only that he had reasons. Yet the main charge against the objection is that it rests on confusing events and their descriptions. For events, being particulars, do not stand in logical relations to one another. It is rather their descriptions that do. Once we recognize this, we can see that even if there are logical relations between descriptions of events, this does not preclude their being related as cause and effect. This is brought out by noting that if some event B has a cause, one description of the cause is 'The cause of B'. In this case, no one would deny that 'The cause of B caused B' is true, despite there being a logical connection between the descriptions. That an event e is the cause of B entails that B occurs.

The response to the objection that "laws are involved essentially in ordinary causal explanations, but not in rationalizations" (EAE: 38) relies on the observation just made and begins to develop themes that become of great importance in Davidson's later work on the relation of psychology to the hard sciences. Davidson first notes that even if there are not strict laws connecting reasons and actions, there are rough laws that do so. If a friend says she will meet you for lunch at noon, you do not hesitate to show up, expecting confidently that you will find her at the appointed place; at lunch, you are confident that she will not suddenly lunge across the table with her steak knife and stab you to the heart. This might encourage the thought that these rough laws could be improved. Davidson holds that this thought "is delusive ... because generalizations connecting reasons and actions are not – and cannot be sharpened into – the kind of law on the basis of which accurate predications can reliably be made" (EAE: 15). A primary reason is a poor predictor because what results from it depends on the relative weight of the pro attitude among all the others. I want to lose weight; I want another slice of pecan pie. These goals are in conflict. To know what I will do, you need to know the relative weight of the desires. This is shown in action, rather than the action being something predictable from the reasons; when I choose the slice of pecan pie, you know which desire was stronger.

This is, however, not, Davidson maintains, a problem for treating reason explanations as causal explanations. We operate in everyday life for the most part with *ceteris paribus* (other things being equal) laws. An inattentive driver, an icy road: these cause an accident. But what strict law do I know covering these events? These things do not always lead to accidents. Yet we still think we have hold of the cause and effect. The rough *ceteris paribus* law we have points to another stricter law. But we need not know it. When we say that *A* caused *B*, the descriptions we give of *A* and *B* need not be those that subsume them under a strict (causal) law. In the case of reason explanations, Davidson says presciently that the "laws whose existence is required if reasons are causes of actions do not, we may be sure, deal in the concepts in which rationalizations must deal" but may rather "be neurological, chemical, or physical" (EAE: 17).

Weakness of will and the logical character of practical deliberation

Reasons relate to actions under descriptions. Thus, we may have reasons for and against a given action. And we may have reasons for one action and reasons for another action that preclude the first. In these cases, we must adjudicate between the reasons. I may want to buy a house on the Riviera, and to buy an apartment in Paris. My beliefs and desires allow me to construct a practical syllogism in favour of each action. But I have money for only one. I must therefore choose between them. The reasons for one or the other obviously cannot by themselves be sufficient to recommend that all in all it is what I should do. Practical deliberation must take into account and resolve in some way the conflicting motives.

The relation of our judgements about what to do in the light of our reasons, and what we do then on their basis, is the subject "How is Weakness of Will Possible?" (EAE: 21–42). When, through practical deliberation, one decides that one course of action is better than another, but chooses a course of action judged less good, one is subject to weakness of will, or, as Davidson calls it, incontinence. The problem of incontinence provides a foil for articulating the relation between reasons, judgements and action. Incontinent action is characterized officially as follows:

> D. In doing *x* an agent acts incontinently if and only if: (a) the agent does *x* intentionally; (b) the agent believes there is an alternative action *y* open to him; and (c) the agent judges that, all things considered, it would be better to do *y* than to do *x*. [5]
>
> (EAE: 22)

As Davidson lays it out initially, the problem is to reconcile three plausible, but prima facie incompatible principles:

P1.   If an agent wants to do *x* more than he wants to do *y* and he believes himself free to do either *x* or *y*, then he will intentionally do *x* if he does either *x* or *y* intentionally.

P2.   If an agent judges that it would be better to do *x* than to do *y*, then he wants to do *x* more than he wants to do *y*.

P3.   There are incontinent actions.   (EAE: 23)

The prima facie problem is that in incontinent action an agent is said to judge doing *A* to be better all things considered than *B*. Thus, principle P2 appears to tell us that he wanted to do *A* more than *B*. The agent believed both were open to him. P1 therefore tells us that he does *A* intentionally if he does either. But he is incontinent only if he does *B*. Thus, P1–P3 appear to be jointly inconsistent.

The problem is that each of P1–P3 seems plausible. In favour of P1 is that in the end our best guide to what someone wants most is what he actually does, when he is apprised of the facts. In favour of P3 is the fact that people very often seem to do things that even at the time they do not regard as what is best for them. In favour of P2 is the fact that there is a sense in which the commitment that leads to action is itself an expression of a judgement that the action is better than surveyed alternatives.

Rather than deny one of P1–P3, Davidson argues that they are, despite appearances, consistent, and that "a common and important mistake explains our confusion, a mistake about the nature of practical reason" (EAE: 24). The solution Davidson offers to the problem hinges on recognizing a distinction between two different sorts of judgements. In D, the agent is said to judge all things considered that doing one thing is better than doing another. In P2, however, the agent is said to judge doing one thing is better than doing another, without the qualifying phrase 'all things considered'. This marks a difference between the judgement that is the result of practical deliberation, and the judgement that is expressed in action. The key to the distinction is that reasons justify actions only under an aspect. Under some an action may be desirable, and under others undesirable. In so far as this action is an eating of chocolate, it is desirable. In so far as this action is an eating of a poisoned substance, it is undesirable. This shows, as has been noted, that reasons for actions condition the conclusions of the practical syllogisms we construct from them.

Davidson employs a suggestive analogy with probabilistic reasoning.[6] Consider the contrasting predictions in A and B.

A.   If the barometer falls, it almost certainly will rain.
     The barometer is falling.

     It almost certainly will rain.

B.   Red sky at night, it almost certainly will not rain.
     The sky is red tonight.

It almost certainly will not rain.

Both lines of reasoning are correct. But they appear to result in conflicting conclusions. As Davidson says, however, "[t]he crucial blunder is interpreting [the major premises] to allow detachment of the modal conclusion" (EAE: 37). Rather, we understand the conclusion in the light of the premises. The major premise of A, for example, we should read as 'that the barometer falls probabilizes that it will rain'. We can represent this as '$pr(Rx, Fx)$', with 'Rx' standing for 'that it will rain' and 'Fx' standing for 'that the barometer falls'. Then the conclusion will have a similar form in which the two premises are its conditions: $pr(Rx, Fx \& pr(Rx, Fx))$. In common language, the fact *that a falling barometer supports the claim that it will rain*, and *that the barometer is falling*, supports the claim *that it will rain*.

   Davidson suggests that the logic of practical reasoning is similar. The conclusion of a bit of practical reasoning is not detachable from its premises. Suppose our practical syllogism is:

     Buying an apartment in Paris is desirable.
     A is a buying of an apartment in Paris.

     A is desirable.

As in the case of probabilistic reasoning, we do not want to detach the conclusion, for we recognize we can reason by a similar syllogism to an apparently opposite conclusion. Here the major premise must be represented as conditioning the desirability of something to an aspect of it. And the conclusion must be conditioned by both premises. We can say that that an action is a buying of an apartment in Paris *prima facie makes* it good, or, $pf(Gx, Bx)$. Then the conclusion may be represented as $pf(Gx, Bx$ and $pf(Gx, Bx))$.

   In probabilistic reasoning, the judgement we should rely on is the one we make on the basis of all our evidence. This is the requirement of total evidence for inductive reasoning. In practical deliberation, the judgement we should rely on is the one we make on the basis of all the relevant considerations. This is the principle of continence (EAE: 41). In each case, the judgement is conditioned by the evidence and all the relevant reasons we have respectively. Likewise, when we judge on the basis of reasons in practical deliberation that one course of action is better than another, the judgement is a conditional one. The key point then is that in addition to the *conditional* all things considered judgement, in choosing a course of action one makes an *unconditional* judgement about what it is best for one to do. The unconditional judgement can then be a reflection of one's strongest desires as reflected in what one actually does. This allows us to accept both P1 and P2, while at the same time accepting P3, without inconsistency.

Does this solve the puzzle of incontinence? It does not show that incontinent action is reasonable: "in the case of incontinence, the attempt to read reason into behavior is necessarily subject to a degree of frustration" (EAE: 42). But it provides an answer to the question how irrational action is possible: what reasons (desires) justify an action in the light of all our beliefs and desires, and what reasons (desires) are causally strongest can come apart. It is in the distinction between the justificatory function of reasons in light of reflection and their causal power that the possibility of incontinent action is to be found.

There is a further question to put about Davidson's solution, namely, whether the sort of incontinence it makes logical room for is the only sort we find. The reason for doubt is that it seems someone may choose to do something all out, but then be pulled from his course, without losing the commitment, by a stronger desire. If this is possible, then it would seem that P2 is under threat after all.

Intentions

In "Actions, Reasons and Causes", Davidson rejected the view that intentions were psychological states distinct from beliefs and desires. Talk of doing something intentionally or with an intention was taken to be a way of indicating something about the reasons an agent had for what he did. In "Intending" (EAE: 84–102), he revised his view, recognizing the possibility of prior intentions, which one never acts on:

> Someone may intend to build a squirrel house without having decided to do it, deliberated about it, formed an intention to do it, or reasoned about it. And despite his intention, he may never build a squirrel house, try to build a squirrel house, or do anything whatever with the intention of getting a squirrel house built.   (EAE: 83)

Davidson considers and rejects three reductive suggestions about what intentions are, namely, that they are actions, that they are beliefs that one will do a particular thing and that they are desires to do a particular thing. Intentions are clearly states rather than events, so the first suggestion is not plausible. Against the second suggestion, it seems clear both that one can believe one will do something and not intend to do it (perhaps because one thinks one will forget one's intention *not* to do it), and that one can intend to do something one does not believe one will do because it is difficult to bring it off. In addition, it is clear that reasons for believing and reasons for intending are radically different in character, the former involving theoretical reasoning, and the latter involving practical reason. Finally, although intending to do something implies a desire to do it, not every desire to do something could be an intention to do it. Desires do not have the same consistency requirements as intentions. In marking this distinction, Davidson connects the discussion with his earlier discussion of the nature of practical reasoning in "How is Weakness of the Will Possible?" (EAE: 21–24). Corresponding to pro attitudes, Davidson argues, are evaluative judgements.

> There is no short proof that evaluative sentences express desires and other pro attitudes in the way that the sentence 'Snow is white' expresses the belief that snow is white. But the following consideration will perhaps help show what is involved. If someone who knows English says honestly 'snow is white', then he believes snow is white. If my thesis is correct, someone who says honestly 'It is desirable that I stop smoking' has some pro attitude towards his stopping smoking.
>
> (EAE: 86)

Corresponding to wants are prima facie judgements of desirability, for we can have conflicting desires, and we are not inconsistent in having them. The 'all things considered' judgements of practical reasoning are conditioned by the reasons for them, and so also are prima facie judgements of desirability. No prima facie judgement of desirability leads directly to action, for the commitment to action is a commitment to the action being the best thing to do, not just prima facie the best. So a new judgement must arise on the basis of practical reasoning that goes beyond the all things considered judgement, the unconditional or all-out judgement that this action is best. This too, if the above is right, is an expression of a pro attitude. Davidson remarks that practical reasoning can give rise to an action, but also to an intention to act. Thus, he identifies the pro attitude that precedes action with an intention that is expressed by an all-out judgement. Intentions, then, are pro attitudes. But they are not wants or desires, because wants are essentially expressed by prima facie judgements. This is reflected in the fact that having desires for incompatible things is not irrational, but having intentions that cannot be jointly realized in light of one's beliefs is irrational. The identification of the all-out judgement with the intention to act helps to explain why all-out judgements might be thought to be conceptually bound up with the strongest desires one has, as measured by what one does (this is P2 above).

Events

Events in the metaphysics of ordinary language

Davidson's seminal paper "The Logical Form of Action Sentences" (EAE: 105–22) is concerned with the logic of adverbial modification, specifically in sentences that attribute actions to agents. Its central thesis is that understanding the logic of adverbial modification requires us to treat action sentences as involving implicit quantification over events, thus showing that our commitment to the truth of ordinary claims about actions carries with it a commitment to events.

The difficulty that adverbial modification presents for a theory of logical form can be illustrated by considering a sentence such as [1]:

[1]   Brutus stabbed Caesar with a knife on the Ides of March in Rome with his co-conspirators.

Sentence [1] entails, as a matter of its form, each of the sentences obtained from it by removing one or more of the adverbial modifiers, for example, it entails each of [2]–[6]:

[2]   Brutus stabbed Caesar.
[3]   Brutus stabbed Caesar with a knife.
[4]   Brutus stabbed on the Ides of March.
[5]   Brutus stabbed Caesar in Rome.
[6]   Brutus stabbed Caesar with his co-conspirators.

This is a matter of form because we recognize the validity of these entailments independently of the content of the verbs and adverbs involved. The project for a semantic theory is to explain the logico-semantic form of adverbial modification so as to make sense of this.[7]

Davidson's positive proposal, which has been very influential in linguistics, is suggested by the fact that it also follows from [1] that there was a stabbing of Caesar. A stabbing is an event; it occurs at a certain time; it must be done in some way; and so on. This suggests then taking the adverbial modifiers in [1] to be modifiers of an event of stabbing introduced by the main verb. The suggestion, spelled out more precisely, is that the main verb introduces an implicit existential quantifier over events, and that the adverbial modifiers contribute predicates of the event variable bound by the existential quantifier. This is presented informally in [7], and more formally in [8].[8]

[7]   There is an event *e*, such that *e* is a stabbing by Brutus of Caesar, *e* was done with a knife, *e* was done on the Ides of March, *e* was done in Rome, and *e*

was done with Brutus's co-conspirators.

[8] $(\exists e)$ (stabbing(e, Brutus, Caesar) & on(Ides of March, e) & with(e, a knife) & in(e, Rome) & with(e, Brutus's co-conspirators)).

This proposal exhibits the entailment relations that [1] enters into as being a matter of its logical form, as required, and specifically as a matter of conjunction elimination. This provides an argument from semantics both for our commitment to an ontology of events as dated particulars, and for seeing actions as events.

Metaphysics of events

The three essays of EAE "The Individuation of Events" (EAE: 163–80), "Events as Particulars" (EAE: 181–8) and "Eternal versus Ephemeral Events" (EAE: 189–203) provide a defence of the event ontology and metaphysics of events that underlies Davidson's work in the philosophy of action and mind. "Events as Particulars" and "Eternal versus Ephemeral Events" defend the conception of events as particulars against Chisholm's construal of events as facts. I concentrate on "The Individuation of Events", which summarizes the evidence that we are committed to an event ontology, and provides an indirect defence of it by providing a criterion for event individuation, responding to Quine's dictum, "No entity without identity", that is, that we do not understand a kind of entity unless we can say under what conditions identity statements involving things of the kind are true.

To say under what conditions identity statements involving events are true is to provide a "satisfactory filling for the blank in:

If x and y are events, then $x = y$ if and only if _____."   (EAE: 172)

Events are often changes in objects or substances. Davidson accepts that if there were no objects there would be no events, but suggests that this does not show that objects are ontologically more fundamental than events, for the same thing goes in the other direction: we understand what it is for something to be an object in part in terms of the notion of persistence through change.

> Substances owe their special importance in the enterprise of identification to the fact that they survive through time. But the idea of survival is inseparable from the idea of surviving certain sorts of change – of position, size, shape, colour, and so forth. ... Neither the category of substance nor the category of change is conceivable apart from the other.   (EAE: 175)

This means we need a criterion for event individuation independent of that for object identification. The place of an event is not adequate, for different events may occur at the same place at different times. Events if identical occur over the same time intervals, but this is not sufficient for identity either, for they may occur at different places. Davidson considers the suggestion that '___' may be replaced with 'x and y occur in the same place during the same intervals'. Yet, "... if a metal ball becomes warmer during a certain minute, and during the same minute rotates through 35 degrees, must we say these are the same event?" (EAE: 178). The suggestion that Davidson settled on in "The Individuation of Events" is that events are identical if they have the same causes and effects, that is:

If x and y are events, then $x = y$ if and only if $((z)(z$ caused $x \leftrightarrow z$ caused $y)$ and $(z)(x$ caused $z \leftrightarrow y$ caused $z))$.

Davidson suggested also that "the causal nexus provides for events a 'comprehensive and continuously usable framework' for the identification and description of events analogous in many ways to the space-time coordinate system for material objects" (EAE: 180), and that this helps explain why so often we describe events in terms or their causes or effects.

However, subsequent to this essay, Davidson retracted his endorsement of this as an adequate criterion of individuation in the face of Quine's observation that the individuation of any event by appeal to this criterion presupposes the prior individuation of other events, since causes and effects are themselves events (Quine 1985). Instead, he accepts Quine's suggestion that events are identical if and only if they occupy the same region at the same time (EAE: 305–11). This would mean identifying the warming of a metal ball in an interval with its rotation in the same interval. Still, Davidson suggested even in "The Individuation of Events" that there might be something to be said for this, since "it might be maintained that the warming of the ball during m is identical with the sum of the motions of the particles that constitute the ball during m; and so is the rotation" (EAE: 178–9).

Philosophy of psychology

Davidson's most celebrated thesis about the mind–body relation is anomalous monism (etymologically *irregular monism*, where monism (from the Greek 'monos' for single) is the view that there is a single general kind of substance, contrasted with dualism). Anomalous monism holds that each particular (token) mental event is identical with a particular (token) physical event, but that there are no strict psychological or psychophysical laws, so that there are no correlations of types of mental events with types of physical events (type–type correlations). This is a non-reductive version of materialism. It holds that all objects and events are physical, but denies that mental types can be reduced to physical types. This is known as the token–token identity theory, as opposed to the type–type identity theory. This thesis is already signalled obliquely in "Actions, Reasons and Causes", in the discussion of whether there are strict laws connecting reasons with actions, for there Davidson suggests that finding such laws may require shifting to a different vocabulary.

Anomalous monism has been enormously influential. While the possibility of a token–token identity theory had been previously noticed, by many it was assumed that the only way to maintain an identity thesis of the mental with the physical was to adopt a type–type identity theory. Davidson's defence of the token–token identity theory showed that this was not the only way to maintain an identity theory, and is responsible in no small part for current dominance of non-reductive materialism in the philosophy of mind.

The argument for the token–token identity theory is presented as, at the same time a resolution to a prima facie paradox based on three plausible principles, which appear to be jointly inconsistent (EAE: 208).

1. The principle of causal interaction: "at least some mental events interact causally with physical events";
2. The principle of the nomological character of causality: "where there is causality, there must be a law: events related as cause and effect fall under strict deterministic laws";
3. The anomalism of the mental: "there are no strict deterministic laws on the basis of which mental events can be predicted and explained".

Davidson later relaxes the third principle by deleting 'deterministic' (EAE: 224). A strict law may not be deterministic, but it will be a law that "there is no improving in point of precision and comprehensiveness" (EAE: 223).

The three principles look jointly inconsistent because the first two suggest that since mental and physical events causally interact, and thus must be subsumed by strict laws, there must be strict psychophysical laws. But the third principle denies this. By now it will be clear what the response to the puzzle is. It is that the laws under which two events are subsumed may not subsume them under the vocabulary we use initially to pick them out. It is thus compatible with the first and second principles that there are no strict laws connecting the mental with the physical, if there are strict laws connecting each mental event that stands in a causal relation with a physical event under descriptions that are not mental.

The argument from this point to the token–token identity theory requires us to assume that all strict laws are physical laws, and that all mental events interact causally with physical events. If these two further plausible assumptions are correct, then it follows that every mental event has a description under which it is subsumed by a strict physical law, and, hence, is also physical.

The anomalousness of the mental is the most controversial premise. The argument for it is notoriously difficult. Davidson distinguishes between rough or *ceteris paribus* laws of the sort we use to explain things in everyday life, such as that, other things being equal, if a window pane is struck with a rock it breaks, and strict laws that do not require *ceteris paribus* clauses, where all the conditions relevant are filled in and the laws are as precise as it is possible to make them. He also distinguishes between what he calls heteronomic and homonomic laws. Heteronomic laws are laws that draw on vocabulary from different families of concepts. Homonomic laws draw on vocabulary from a single family of concepts. Mental concepts form one family, and physical concepts form another. What constitutes a family of concepts is that the concepts concerned are all responsible to, in the sense that they must conform to, certain constitutive principles governing the application of concepts in the family. An example of such a constitutive principle governing physical concepts is the transitivity of length of rigid objects. If a, b and c are rigid objects, then if a is longer than b and b longer than c, then a is longer than c. This principle is constitutive because if measurement showed that three objects a, b and c violated this principle, that would be conclusive grounds for denying that they were rigid objects. Strict laws, Davidson holds, must be homonomic laws. If this is right, then given that mental and physical concepts belong to different families of concepts, no psychophysical laws could be homonomic and, hence, no psychophysical law could be a strict law.

Mental and physical concepts belong to different families because of the constitutive role that considerations of rationality play in our attributions of the propositional attitudes (beliefs, desires, intentions, etc., so called because they have contents expressible by sentences). Behaviour is interpreted in the light of reasons agents have for what they do. We do not interpret a bodily movement as an action unless it is minimally reasonable from the agent's point of view, that is, unless there is a rationalization of it. But more importantly, even when we allow irrational behaviour, as in the case of weakness of the will, our ability to identify a bit of behaviour as irrational requires us to have already identified very many other attitudes of the agent. For it is only in the light of many other attitudes that we are able to see a particular action as not in line with what the agent thinks it is best to do all things considered. We make sense of the attribution of any given attitude only as a place in a pattern of interlocking attitudes that makes sense of the agent as on the whole reasonably responding to his environment and to his beliefs and desires. Thus, the concepts of the propositional attitudes are subject to defeasible but nonetheless strong constitutive constraints: we do not count anything as an agent with propositional attitudes unless by and large we find it to be rational (EAE: 221–2). This parallels our not treating objects as rigid unless their lengths are transitive. None of our physical concepts could require considerations of rational fit with attribution of other concepts. Hence, physical and mental concepts belong to different families of concepts.

Why cannot concepts that belong to different families figure in strict laws? The argument rests on two considerations, one having to do with the nature of laws, and the other, and more difficult one, having to do with the "disparate commitments" of different families of concepts. Davidson adopts a logical empiricist conception of laws of nature: "Lawlike statements are general statements that support counterfactual and subjunctive claims, and are supported by their instances" (EAE: 217). 'Everyone who sits on this bench is an Irishman' fails the test because it is not supported by positive instances and does not support counterfactuals. Even if we have observed ten people sit on the bench who are Irishmen, this does not give us reason to think the next one will be, or to think that if someone were to sit on the bench, he would be an Irishman. 'Resistance in copper wire increases with temperature', in contrast, is supported by its instances and supports counterfactuals such as, 'If this copper wire were heated, its resistance would increase'. It is support of a lawlike statement by its positive instances that is most relevant to Davidson's argument. The question is not whether psychophysical laws are supported by their instances; it is clear that they are (EAE: 219). The question is rather to what degree they are supported by their instances. Davidson argues that positive instances of general statements linking mental with physical vocabulary at best give us reason to hold rough laws, but can never give us reason to think that the laws will be exceptionless, or could be made exceptionless without a change in the vocabulary used to express them.

> There are no strict psychophysical laws because of the disparate commitments of the mental and the physical schemes. It is a feature of physical reality that physical change can be explained by laws that connect it with other changes and conditions physically described. It is a feature of the mental that the attribution of mental phenomena must be responsible to the background of reasons, beliefs, and intentions of the individual. There cannot be tight connections between the realms if each is to retain allegiance to its proper source of evidence. … The point is … that when we use the concepts of belief, desire, and the rest, we must stand prepared, as the evidence accumulates, to adjust our theory in the light of considerations of overall cogency: the constitutive ideal

of rationality partly controls each phase in the evolution of what must be an evolving theory. ... We must conclude, I think, that nomological slack between the mental and the physical is essential as long as we conceive of man as a rational animal.   (EAE: 222–3)

The basic idea in this passage is that if we have a psychophysical generalization of the form,

For any x, t, if x has M at t, then x has P at $t + \varepsilon$,

while positive instances will give us some reason to think that the next instance of M will be followed by one of P, there is always a risk present that it will not, not because we have not identified all of the background conditions that are required, but because what is relevant to the application of M and P in the first instance is other attributions of mental predicates and physical predicates respectively, governed by distinct constitutive principles, and so what guides us in each case are considerations that are different in kind. This introduces a source of epistemic uncertainty that cannot be removed by a fuller characterization of the background conditions, but only by switching to a vocabulary drawing on a single family of concepts.

If this is right, then there is an obstacle in principle to formulating strict psychophysical laws. This would show that there is a sense in which psychology cannot be modelled on the physical sciences. Strict laws are beyond its reach while it retains the vocabulary that gives it its status as an autonomous science. The conclusion is not forced just by the use of mental vocabulary. It is rather that the physical is a closed comprehensive system of law, while the mental is not, and that every mental event, at least which science could bring within its scope, causally interacts with some physical event. These facts together with the above result show that there cannot be psychological laws that aspire to the status of laws in physics. This extends to all the social sciences since they deal essentially with the actions and attitudes of agents.

Summary

Essays on Actions and Events presents a unified account of human agents and the relation of their reasons and actions to the natural world. Agents are a part of the casual nexus. Their reasons cause and causally explain what they do while at the same time showing what is to be said for them from the agent's point of view. Practical deliberation issues in all things considered judgements about what it is best to do. If all is right in the house of reason, this issues in a corresponding all-out judgement. These evaluative judgements correspond to pro attitudes of different types. The all-out judgement is an intention, a commitment to action. The all things considered judgement is of the nature of an all-in desire, but does not yet express a commitment to action. Irrational behaviour is in one sense surd: there is no accounting for it in light of all an agent's reasons. It is not for that reason impossible. Yet to the extent we can make sense of it we do so against a background of largely rational patterns of thought and action. Actions are events, changes in agent's bodies, which we describe variously in terms of their effects, those intended and unintended, depending on whether the descriptions employed figured in the reasons the agent had for doing what he did. These events are concrete, datable particulars. Ordinary sentences about action involve implicit existential quantification over them, for this provides the best explanation of the systematic entailment relations between sentences about actions. Causal relations hold between events, in virtue of their being subsumed by descriptions that instantiate a strict law connecting events under those descriptions. Yet this, and the fact that attributions of the attitudes that rationalize actions are subject to constitutive constraints of rationality, shows that although reasons and actions are part of the causal net, they are not reducible to the network of physical causes and effects. Each mental event, each reason, is identical to some physical event, or state, but there can be no strict correlation, if Davidson is right, between mental and physical state or event types. For there is no echo of the rational in the physical, and consequently the considerations to which we must be attuned in attributing attitudes and in attributing physical states are not in tune with each other, and this lack of harmony cannot be remedied by filling in *ceteris paribus* clauses in the rough laws we in fact confirm and use. This naturalistic but non-reductive picture of human agency, of rationality, and the relation of the mental to the physical, has had a profound effect on the course of the philosophy of action and mind in contemporary analytic philosophy, and represents one of the major contributions to the subject in the twentieth century.

Notes

1. Since the publication of these two collections, three more have appeared. But it is safe to say that Davidson's most influential work, and the work that is the foundation for his later publications, is represented by the first two volumes of collected papers. Essays discussing Davidson's work in other areas of philosophy can be found in K. Ludwig, *Donald Davidson* (Cambridge: Cambridge University Press, 2003); an extended treatment of his work in the theory of meaning and philosophy of language is provided in Lepore, E. and K. Ludwig, *Donald Davidson's Truth, Meaning, Language and Reality* (Oxford: Oxford University Press, 2006) and *Donald Davidson: Truth-theoretic Semantics* (Oxford: Oxford University Press, 2005).

2. Two additional essays are included in the second edition: "Adverbs of Action" and "Quine on Events".

3. Davidson recurs to the question how to understand the phrase 'under a description' in "Eternal vs. Ephemeral Events" (EAE: 193–6).

4. This meets an objection sometimes levelled against Davidson's theory, namely, that the fact that sometimes we do things for their own sake, and not for the sake of another thing, obviates the need for a means–end belief. But the belief is still required because it is *of* the action to the effect that it is of the desired type.

5. There are some difficulties with the formulation as '*x*' and '*y*' here appear to be doing duty for referring terms, but while we may take '*x*' in this way, we cannot so treat '*y*'; since the agent who acts incontinently does not perform the alternative open to him, the reference to that must be thought of as a reference to a type of action (or quantification over actions of a type) rather than to a particular action. A similar difficulty attends P1 and P2. I pass over it, since it is correctable without damage to the argument.

6. Here Davidson draws on C. G. Hempel, *Aspects of Scientific Explanation, and Other Essays in the Philosophy of Science* (New York: Free Press, 1965).

7. See K. Ludwig & E. Lepore, "What is Logical Form?", in *Logical Form and Language*, G. Preyer & G. Peter (eds), 54–90 (Oxford: Oxford University Press, 2001) for a discussion of logico-semantic form and its relation to logical truth and consequence.

8. One difficulty here is that we have not taken tense into account. Davidson at one point suggests we can make use of the utterance act of a tensed sentence to make sense of tense. There are reasons to think, however, that we need an independent quantifier over times to handle tense adequately. See E. Lepore & K. Ludwig, "Outline of a Truth Conditional Semantics for Tense", in *Tense, Time and Reference*, Q. Smith (ed.) (Cambridge, MA: MIT Press, 2002) for discussion, especially §1.9.

References

Davidson, D. 2001a. *Essays on Actions and Events*. Oxford: Clarendon Press.

Davidson, D. 2001b. *Inquiries into Truth and Interpretation*. Oxford: Clarendon Press.

Hempel, C. G. 1965. *Aspects of Scientific Explanation, and Other Essays in the Philosophy of Science*. New York: Free Press.

Lepore, E. & K. Ludwig 2002. "Outline of a Truth Conditional Semantics for Tense". In *Tense, Time and Reference*, Q. Smith (ed.). Cambridge, MA: MIT Press.

Lepore, E. & K. Ludwig 2005. *Donald Davidson: Truth, Meaning, Language and Reality*. Oxford: Oxford University Press.

Lepore, E. & K. Ludwig 2006. *Donald Davidson's Truth-theoretic Semantics*. Oxford: Oxford University Press.

Ludwig, K. & E. Lepore 2001. "What is Logical Form?" In *Logical Form and Language*, G. Preyer & G. Peter (eds), 54–90. Oxford: Oxford University Press.

Ludwig, K. (ed.) 2003. *Donald Davidson*. Cambridge: Cambridge University Press.

Putnam, H. 1968. "Brains and Behavior". In *Analytic Philosophy II*, J. R. Butler (ed.), 1–19. Oxford: Blackwell.

Quine, W. V. 1985. "Reification and Events". In *Actions and Events: Perspectives on the Philosophy of Donald Davidson*. B. McLaughlin (ed.), 162–71. Oxford: Blackwell.

8
Saul Kripke

Naming and Necessity

John P. Burgess

Chronology

Kripke first became known for technical work on modal logic, the logic of necessity and possibility, much of it done in the late 1950s as a high-school student, and summarized in Kripke (1963). (Among other things this work popularized a revival of the picturesque Leibnizian language according to which necessity is truth in all possible worlds.) Under the influence of Kripke's later work philosophers have come to distinguish several conceptions of necessity and possibility, in a manner to be described below; but Kripke's early technical work was not tied to any special conception. Rather, it provides tools applicable to many conceptions.

It was only in the academic year 1963–64, as the belated publication of his technical work was nearing completion, that Kripke turned to more philosophical questions about the concept of necessity, and was led to raise doubts about the view, widely held among philosophers of the period, that all necessity derives from linguistic convention. At that time Kripke presented his results on that issue, and on issues about reference, which turned out to be connected with it, in seminars at Harvard, where he had been, a year after taking his undergraduate degree, appointed to the Society of Fellows.

There were further seminar presentations elsewhere in the 1960s, and a very condensed account of Kripke's picture of the reference of proper names appeared in Kaplan (1969). But Kripke's views on naming, and especially on necessity, only became generally known after a lecture series at Princeton early in 1970. An incomplete presentation was published the next year (Kripke 1971), and a transcript of the Princeton lectures, plus footnotes and addenda, constituting the first or article version of "Naming and Necessity", appeared the year after (Kripke 1972). The later 1970s brought two related articles (Kripke 1977; 1979). The second or book version of *Naming and Necessity*, with a new preface, appeared the beginning of the next decade (Kripke 1980).

The main trace of this chronology in the work is that writings from before 1963 are treated in some detail in the body of the text, but those from after 1964 – including work having important overlap with Kripke's, especially Keith Donnellan's on proper names and Hilary Putnam's on natural-kind terms – are briefly acknowledged in footnotes but not examined. (But even Kripke's presentation of his own ideas is incomplete, with some topics that had been covered in seminars, such as empty names and negative existentials and essential *versus* necessary properties, barely get a passing mention.)

Even though for philosophers generally it is the material on necessity that is of the greatest interest – especially since Kripke promises an application to the mind–body problem – it will be well to begin with the material on naming, since it is in part presupposed in the material on necessity. And in treating the material on naming, it will be well to begin with the pre-1963 literature just alluded to, since Kripke's positive views gradually emerge from his criticism of his predecessors.

Naming: the Frege–Russell view

For philosophers of language the topic of proper names is fascinating partly because so many greats have tried their hand at it without satisfying their successors. It will be well to begin with one of the greats, Bertrand Russell (and with another, Gottlob Frege, in the background). The puzzle that Russell (following Frege) addresses is this. Given that "Hesperus" and "Phosphorus" denote the same individual, how can the following be true?

(1) It is a substantive astronomical discovery that Hesperus is Phosphorus.

According to Russell, this would be impossible if each of "Hesperus" and "Phosphorus" were a name in the ideal sense of "a simple symbol directly designating an individual which is its meaning". For if the meaning of each name is simply the individual it designates, then since both denote the same object, the two have the same meaning, from which it would seem to follow that "Hesperus is

Phosphorus" has the same meaning as "Hesperus is Hesperus". And *that*, surely, is no substantive astronomical discovery! In the statement of the puzzle one may replace "substantive astronomical discovery" by "not analytic" or "not *a priori*" – or, if George is an astronomical ignoramus, by "not known to George" or "not believed by George".

Russell offered a famous theory of descriptions intended to explain why the puzzle does *not* arise in the case of descriptions as opposed to names. But even without going into Russell's theory it is perhaps obvious that

(2)   It is a substantive astronomical discovery that the brightest celestial object regularly seen near the western horizon after sunset is the same as the brightest celestial object regularly seen near the eastern horizon before sunrise.

can easily be true. (Certainly Frege, who did not have Russell's theory of descriptions, found it so.)

Russell's solution to the puzzle is that "Hesperus" and "Phosphorus", and more generally names in the *ordinary* sense, are not names in his *ideal* sense. Rather, each is associated with some description that constitutes its definition. In the case of "Hesperus" and "Phosphorus" the etymology suggests "the brightest celestial object regularly seen near the western horizon after sunset" and "the brightest celestial object regularly seen near the eastern horizon before sunrise". (And in this solution Russell is again in substantial agreement with Frege, who maintained that, at least in any properly constructed scientific language, any name should have a descriptive definition.)

Naming: post-Russellian, pre-Kripkean views

Although the Frege–Russell *description* theory neatly solves the problem it addresses, it is open to a number of objections. Many were canvassed by philosophers – especially philosophers with Oxford ties – in the late 1950s and early 1960s, including Elizabeth Anscombe, Peter Geach, Paul Grice, William Kneale, Arthur Prior, John Searle and Peter Strawson. Kripke discusses many of these writers, but the following short summary cites only a couple, and concentrates on just two difficulties with the description theory: the epistemological problems of *error* and of *ignorance*.

As to error, consider the name "Socrates". Perhaps the first description that comes to mind as a candidate definition would be: "the philosopher who drank hemlock". Can this be accepted? Suppose a writer in a classics journal claimed to have evidence that the hemlock plant, *Conium maculatum*, was extinct in Attica by the fifth century, and that the philosopher reputed to have drunk hemlock actually drank some other vegetable poison. Would it not be natural to conclude that Socrates did not, after all, drink hemlock? But if Socrates is *by definition* the philosopher who drank hemlock, this conclusion cannot be true regardless of the evidence. Let us try another candidate: "the philosopher who taught Plato". Similar difficulties arise. It would *by definition* be false to conclude that Socrates was not the teacher of Plato, even in advance of considering any evidence that might be produced to the effect that, say, all Plato's knowledge of his reputed teacher comes second-hand from his relatives Critias and Charmides. For similar reasons, none of the major elements of the tradition about Socrates can plausibly be taken to be *definitive* of Socrates.

This sort of observation motivated the rejection of the simple description in favour of the *cluster* theory of Searle (1958). On this view, what is definitive of Socrates is not any one description, but a cluster of them, but not in the sense that "Socrates" is defined by the description "the philosopher who did *all* of the following: drink hemlock, teach Plato, have a snub nose, ...", for that would only exacerbate the problem. Rather, the definition would be something like "the philosopher who did *most* of the following ...". Then the denial of any *one* of the descriptions would never be wrong simply as a matter of definition.

As to ignorance, not everyone has heard all the descriptions of Socrates in the cluster. The trouble is not with people who have heard *nothing* of Socrates, since they do not use the name "Socrates", but with people who have heard *only a little*, but still do use the name. For them the contemplated cluster of descriptions, most of which they have never heard of, cannot be what defines "Socrates". Perhaps Professor *X*, a college history instructor, has lectured her students extensively on Greek philosophers, Socrates included. But perhaps undergraduate *Y* never took in more than that Socrates was some ancient Greek philosopher, which does not distinguish him from any of scores of others whose names may have been dropped. Perhaps *Y* has gone on to teach world history in a middle school, and has mentioned to his students a number of ancient Athenians distinguished in different fields, including Socrates among the philosophers. But perhaps pupil *Z* has not retained more than that Socrates was some famous old guy, which does not distinguish him from dozens of others whose names may have whizzed by.

Hence the *borrowed credentials* supplement to the cluster theory, as in Strawson (1959). It is allowed that for *Z* the definition of Socrates may be "the famous old guy Mister *Y* called 'Socrates'", while for *Y* in turn the definition may be "the Greek philosopher Professor *X* called 'Socrates'". As long as we eventually get back to someone like *X*, who has a definition in terms of a sufficient cluster of descriptions, and so may be credited with a success in referring by "Socrates" to Socrates not dependent on the usage of others, we can credit Y with success on the strength of X's success, and then credit Z with success on the strength of Y's. With this supplement we have arrived at about the furthest point reached before Kripke's intervention.

Naming: epistemological arguments

Kripke's critique of pre-existing views is first of all that the error and ignorance problems go deeper than previously recognized. To begin with borrowed credentials, Y may have been unable to come up with any uniquely identifying description, drawing a blank when trying to recall when he first heard of Socrates. Or the definition Y came up with may be *wrong*. X may have referred to *no one* as Socrates, always calling the philosopher by his Greek name, neither spelled nor pronounced like its Anglicization. Or X may have referred to *several* people as Socrates, including the famous Athenian philosopher and the obscure Bithynian philosopher mentioned by Diogenes Laertius.

Suppose we try a more guarded definition: "whoever it may be that the person (whoever *that* may be) from whom I acquired the name 'Socrates' (however he or she wrote or pronounced it) was speaking of when I acquired the name". But it is one thing to suggest that a speaker of reasonable intelligence should given time be able to come up with such a description, and quite another and much more implausible thing to suggest that one had this carefully guarded definition in mind all along.

Besides, on pain of circularity not *everyone*'s definition of Socrates can be dependent on someone else's. We must eventually come back to the cluster theory. It has been said that the theory allows that it is not by definition false that Socrates did not drink the hemlock, and not by definition false that Socrates did not teach Plato, and so on. But it still follows from the cluster theory that a special issue of a classics journal containing a series of articles claiming one by one of each major element of the tradition about Socrates that it is not quite correct *would* be by definition false. Borges quotes De Quincy as telling us, "Not one thing, but everything tradition attributes to Judas Iscariot is false" ("Three Versions of Judas"). One need not be a fundamentalist to doubt so extreme a statement. But surely neither this claim nor a similar one about Socrates is false merely by *definition*.

Similarly with Kripke's more modern example of Kurt Gödel. All that most of us could come up with by way of description of him would be in terms of his various achievements in logic, proving what are known as the completeness and incompleteness theorems. But suppose someone claimed that Gödel had *not* in fact proved these theorems, but found them among the posthumous papers of one Schmidt and published them under his own name. If by *definition* Gödel is the prover of the theorems, it would follow that when we say "Gödel" we are referring not to the famous professor of the Institute for Advance Studies, but to the unknown Schmidt. Surely this is not reasonable, and if not, then the cluster theory fails.

Naming: the historical chain picture

The real strength of Kripke's critique of earlier views lies in his sketching an alternative picture. This falls into two main parts: a discussion of *baptism*, the first use of a name by the first user of the name; and a discussion of *transmission*, the first use of a name by a later user who acquires it from an earlier one.

According to Kripke, the main application of the description theory is to the case of baptism; generally the object on which a name is to be bestowed is picked out by description or ostension, which latter may be subsumable under the former. What this presumably means is that we may say that the object is picked out by description, provided we understand "description" broadly enough to subsume descriptions involving demonstratives, requiring supplementation by ostension. Thus the baptist may say something like either of the following:

(3) Let the thirteenth brightest star in the sky be called "Alpha Tauri".
(4) Let that bright, orangeish star over there [pointing] be called "Alpha Tauri".

An object that already has a name can be picked out by it, but this is equivalent to picking it out by the description, as in:

(5) Let the star heretofore called "Aldebaran" be called "Alpha Tauri".

There is a complication at this juncture. For as observed by Prior (1963), Donnellan (1966) and elsewhere, a speaker may succeed in using a description to pick out the object he or she *thinks* answers to it, even though it does not. As Kripke interprets this phenomenon, there is a distinction to be made between what the words a speaker uses refer to, and what the speaker succeeds in referring to by using those words. (Compare the well-known analogous distinction in the case of meaning: Mrs Malaprop can succeed in meaning "Comparison is odious" by using the words "Comparison is odorous".) This possibility is illustrated by (3)–(5), which may succeed in picking out Alpha Tauri even though it is not a star, but a system of *two* stars.

Nonetheless, this noted, Kripke concedes that typically at baptism the object baptized is picked out by description (if not as the thing answering to it, then as the thing the baptist thinks answers to it). His claim is that *this description need not remain permanently associated with the name*. Alpha Tauri having been baptized, that celestial object continues to be denoted by that name *even if the description used and every other circumstance of the baptism are forgotten or are misremembered*. Although Kripke does not discuss the point at length, it would seem that an intention to continue using the name for the same object for which one has been using it, even without any recollection or even with a misrecollection of when, where, why and how one began using it, will suffice. And it is not clear that the intention needs to be conscious, or even that it needs to consist in the presence of anything positive, as opposed to the absence of something negative such as the intention to start using the old name for some new object.

Similar remarks apply to uses of the name by a later speaker subsequent to that speaker's *first* use of the name. Nothing need be correctly recalled about from whom, when, where, why and how the name was acquired. As for the *first* use of the name by the new speaker, Kripke concedes that in transmission the object the earlier user is using the name to name *may* be picked out by description, as in baptism. What the new user gets from the old *may* be an explicit statement that the thirteenth brightest star in the sky is named "Alpha Tauri", or that Alpha Tauri is the thirteenth brightest star in the sky. But Kripke insists that *in general* the name is *not* acquired together with any uniquely identifying descriptive information of this kind.

For the new user to acquire the name, it may be enough to see it written or hear it spoken, with enough context to grasp that it is being used *as* name. This is so even if (as with "Socrates" passing from X to Y to Z) insufficient information is obtained to distinguish the object named from others (or none but the rapidly forgettable information that it is the object the previous speaker was using the name for). Indeed, the name may be acquired accompanied with nothing substantial but *mis*information, myths and legends. Such is the case with the children in Kripke's example, who first hear of Newton when someone tells them the apocryphal tale about the apple. What is necessary is that the new user should intend to use the name for the same object the old user was using it for (although if the new user has an erroneous opinion about what object that is, the reference may stray).

Kripke's picture has for obvious reasons been called the "historical chain" picture. It has also sometimes been called the "causal chain" picture, but this label is inappropriate. For (quite apart from any issues about the role of free will in the human decisions involved in transmitting the name from earlier to later users) there need not on Kripke's view be any causal link between the initial baptist and the object baptized. Any object that can be described can be named, and this includes, for instance, causally inert mathematical objects, which figure in a couple of Kripke's examples.

An un-Kripkean view: direct-reference

Kripke has also been said to hold a "direct-reference theory". Now by this label, as by the label "Millian", may be meant merely a theory on which names have no description attached to them as definitions. But the label has come to have another, more specific sense: that of a theory on which *sentences that differ only by the substitution of one name by another name for the same object express the same proposition*, combined with the common assumption that *belief and knowledge are relations between persons and propositions*. (Sometimes "state of affairs" is substituted for "proposition".) But this combination has implausible consequences that Kripke denies.

For example, suppose the student Y encounters the name "Octavian" in one of X's lectures on the late Roman Republic, and the name "Augustus" in one of X's lectures on the early Roman Empire, having skipped the lecture in between in which X told how this individual ended the republic and initiated the empire, and changed his name from "Octavian" to "Augustus". Y then fails a true–false quiz by, among other errors, marking "Octavian = Augustus" as false. Kripke explains how Y can fail to know that "Octavian is Augustus" is true even though the names do not have different descriptive definitions (or any descriptive definitions at all), the explanation being that the two names connect speaker and object through two different historical chains. This also explains why it is not discoverable *a priori* that "Octavian is Augustus" is true. Kripke also takes himself to have explained how Y can fail to know, and why it is not *a priori* discoverable, *that Octavian is Augustus*. And this seems very plausible. X, grading Y's paper, might well mutter, "This student doesn't even know that Octavian is Augustus!"

But the direct reference theorist, while granting that Y doesn't know that "Octavian is Augustus" is true, must hold – since it *is* true, and "Octavian" and "Augustus" refer to the same person – that the proposition that Octavian is Augustus is the same proposition as the proposition that Octavian is Octavian. And since Y surely knows *that*, Y does after all know that Octavian is Augustus (and by similar reasoning could discover *a priori* that Octavian is Augustus). This implausible consequence of direct reference theory is something Kripke rejects. But we have given only a crude summary of direct reference theory. For a sophisticated defence see Soames (2005). The intent here is not to settle the status of direct reference theories but merely to indicate that Kripke's theory is not one.

The modal argument: rigid *versus* flexible designators

Kripke has yet another argument against descriptive theories of names. A passing comet might have dislocated the planets, so that while Venus was still the brightest celestial object regularly seen near the western horizon after sunset, Mars rather than Venus was the brightest celestial object regularly seen near the eastern horizon before sunrise. But even so, Venus, *alias*, Hesperus, *alias* Phosphorus, could not have been anything other than itself, Venus, *alias* Phosphorus, *alias* Hesperus. Thus:

(6) Hesperus is the brightest celestial object regularly seen near the eastern horizon before sunrise.

might have been false, while

(7) Hesperus is Phosphorus.

still would have been true. This is so even if, in the counterfactual situation being contemplated, it was Mars that was *called* "Phosphorus", while it was still Venus that was called "Hesperus". It follows that Phosphorus is not *by definition* the brightest celestial object regularly seen near the eastern horizon before sunrise (and by similar reasoning, Hesperus is not *by definition* the brightest celestial object regularly seen near the western horizon after sunset).

Similarly, although Bill Gates may be the richest person in the world, he is not so *by definition*. He could have given away all his wealth to Ivana Trump, and then *she* would have been the richest person in the world, but she would not have been *Bill Gates*.

Underlying this *modal* argument is the intuition that even when we use the name of a planet or person in discussing a counterfactual astronomical situation, in speaking of how the heavens and earth are not but might have been, we are still using it to designate the planet or person we use it to designate when discussing the actual situation, when speaking of how things are. We are using it to designate that planet or person and not any other – not even another that in the counterfactual situation would have been *called* by the name in question.

This feature of proper names, that of always designating the same individual, even when speaking of counterfactual situations, Kripke calls *rigidity*.

The concept of rigidity is more important than the modal arguments based on it, since there is an evasive manoeuvre a description theorist can take against the latter. The first thing to note is that even when discussing a counterfactual situation in which Bill has given all his wealth to Ivana, it is not unambiguously the case that when we use the description "the richest person in the world" we must be referring to her and not him. For the description contains an implicit verb, made explicit in "the one person to be richer than anyone else in the world". And this verb is subject to inflection for grammatical mood – "to be" may become the indicative "is" or the conditional "would have been" – in a way that creates a flexibility in reference. Thus

(8) If Bill had given all his wealth to Ivana, the richest person in the world would have been female.

is ambiguous as between the truth

(9) If Bill had given all his wealth to Ivana, the one person who would have been richer than anyone else in the world (namely, Ms Trump) would have been female.

and the falsehood

(10) If Bill had given all his wealth to Ivana, the one person who is richer than anyone else in the world (namely, Mr Gates) would have been female.

But now if we take as our description "the one person who *actually* is richer than anyone else in the world", the presence of the adverb "actually" precludes changing the verb from the indicative mood (as "now" would preclude changing the verb from the present tense). The description with "actually" stuck in is inflexible or rigid. It always refers to Bill Gates, even when discussing counterfactual situations in which he gives away or is deprived of his wealth. To be sure, the theory that names are defined by descriptions thus "rigidified" is one no one would have thought of except as an attempt to evade one of Kripke's arguments. But the fact that such evasive action seems feasible makes the error and ignorance arguments more decisive than the modal. The primary importance of the rigidity intuition lies elsewhere.

The necessity of identity: counterfactual *versus* logical necessity

Rigidity implies that the identities linking two names with the same bearer hold *necessarily* in the sense that they *could not have failed to hold*, or *would have held in any counterfactual situation*. For by rigidity, even when speculating counterfactually about hypothetical alternative courses Roman history might have taken, the name "Octavian" continues to denote the same person it does when speaking of the actual course of Roman history, and similarly for "Augustus". But since the persons denoted by "Octavian" and by "Augustus" when speaking of the actual course of Roman history, to wit, Octavian and Augustus, are one and the same, the persons denoted by those names when speculating counterfactually about hypothetical alternative courses of Roman history will also be the same. In other words, even in speaking of the counterfactual situation it will be true to say that Octavian is Augustus. And this is what it means to say that Octavian *could not have failed to be* identical with Augustus. In this sense, the identities of Octavian with Augustus, of Hesperus with Phosphorus, and so on, are *necessary*. But we have already seen that Kripke maintains that such identities are *not* discoverable *a priori*. Such identities are therefore, according to Kripke, examples of *a posteriori* necessities.

Here, however, terminological difficulties arise, since "necessity" has been understood in different senses. Kripke's primary notion of the necessary – what *he* means when he writes of "necessity" *tout court* – is *what is and could not have failed to be*, or *what is and would have been in any counterfactual situation*. Owing to Kripke's having described this kind of necessity as "metaphysical" rather than "epistemological", it has often been called "metaphysical necessity"; but although Kripke did not intend "metaphysical" to have pejorative connotations, it still does for many. Hence it may be better to speak of "counterfactual necessity".

By contrast, the primary notion of necessity in modal logic from the time of C. I. Lewis, the modern founder of the subject, onwards had always been "logical necessity". (Modal logicians had given some consideration to temporal, deontic, physical and other kinds of modalities, but none are relevant here.) This notion admits of a narrower and a broader understanding, and this in two dimensions, depending on whether one adds to pure, elementary logic (the logic of the textbooks) more or less in the way of definitions and/or mathematics. In one dimension, one may understand the "logic" narrowly as what is true by *pure* logic, such as "No unmarried man is married", or more broadly, as what is true by pure logic plus definitions, such as "No bachelor is married". In another dimension, one may understand the "logic" narrowly as what is true by *elementary* logic, such as "If 2 is less than 3 or 4 is less than 3, and 4 is not less than 3, then 2 is less than 3" or, more broadly, as what is true by elementary logic plus mathematics, such as "2 is less than 3, and 4 is not less than 3". It turns out that there are narrower and broader senses of "adding definitions" and of "adding mathematics", so that there are three options in each dimension, or nine combinations in all.

As to adding definitions to logic, Kripke found in some of the post-Russellians canvassed above a distinction between two kinds of definitions, *meaning-giving* and *reference-fixing*, although he equally rejects the claim that names have descriptive definitions whichever definition of "definition" one takes. (Kripke uses "fixing the reference" both for the descriptions that on certain pre-Kripkean theories supposedly remain *permanently* attached to names as non-meaning-giving definitions, and for the descriptions that on his own picture play a *transitory* role in the history of the name, being used to pick out its bearer for initial baptism, and then perhaps forgotten. This potentially confusing double usage has been avoided here.) Kripke's own example to illustrate the distinction is as follows. Before 1960, the *reference* of "metre" was fixed as the distance between two scratches on a standard platinum-iridium alloy bar kept at Sèvres. But according to Kripke even then "metre" did not *mean* "the distance between the two scratches on the standard platinum-iridium alloy bar kept at Sèvres".

Once the distinction is recognized, one may consider only adding meaning-giving definitions, or adding also reference-fixing definitions. Kripke stipulates that for him "analytic" allows definitions only in the narrower, meaning-giving sense, while "*a priori*" allows also definitions in the broader, reference-fixing. Thus he makes room for a very un-Kantian kind of synthetic *a priori*, exemplified by:

(11) The distance between the two scratches on the standard platinum-iridium alloy bar kept at Sèvres is one metre.

(Kripke suggests in passing that this is an example of something *a priori* but counterfactually contingent and not necessary, but this is another issue that he gives barely a passing mention.)

As to adding mathematics to logic, narrowly, one could count in whatever mathematical truths are *provable*; broadly, one could count *all* mathematical truths, whether or not they ever turn out to be provable. There are, for instance, two famous old conjectures of number theory known as Fermat's theorem and Goldbach's conjecture. (Just what they say is not pertinent to the example.) The truth-value of neither was known when Kripke lectured, but the former has since been proved, while the latter is still an open question. On either a narrow or a broad understanding of "adding mathematics", Fermat's theorem will be counted in. On the broad but not the narrow understanding, whichever of Goldbach's conjecture or its negation is true would be counted in, even though there is at present no proof and may never be one. (The Gödel completeness theorem shows that there is no distinction, in pure, elementary logic, between what is logically provable and what is logically true; while the Gödel *incompleteness* theorem suggests that what is mathematically provable must fall short of what is mathematically true.)

Note that adding in mathematics in the broader sense gives a notion going beyond aprioricity. But having mentioned this issue early on, Kripke lets it drop, and thereafter generally says "*a posteriori* (and hence synthetic)" or "not *a priori* (and hence not analytic)" when he could say something slightly stronger: "not *a priori* and not even an *a priori* consequence of mathematical truths (even unprovable ones)". This last is about what "not logically necessary" amounts to if "logically necessary" is taken in the broadest of the various senses just canvassed, counting in both kinds of definitions and both kinds of mathematical truths. Henceforth "logically necessary" or "tautologous" (and therewith "logically impossible" or "contradictory") will be understood in this broad sense.

What Kripke claims is that there are, in his terminology, necessities that are *a posteriori* or, in the terminology just introduced, counterfactual necessities that are not logical necessities. This claim was one of Kripke's most provocative, since it runs counter to the historical tendency, as one passes from Kant to Frege to Carnap, for necessity to dwindle to aprioricity, and aprioricity to analyticity, this last explained as the product of linguistic convention.

The necessity of identity: the Marcus–Quine controversy

As true identities linking names are the most basic example of *a posteriori* necessities, they deserve extended discussion. In this connection, Kripke devotes significant space to recollections of a session of the Boston Colloquium for the Philosophy of Science in 1962, where the speaker was R. B. Marcus, the commentator W. V. Quine, and the member of the audience to participate most notably in the ensuing discussion Kripke himself. (For the published proceedings see Wartofsky (1963); for a fuller history with detailed citations, see Burgess (1997).) The controversy went back to the 1940s, to criticisms by Quine of early, purely formal work by Marcus and related work by Carnap. Marcus's dissertation supervisor, Frederic Fitch, had come to the defence of his student in two papers, with acknowledgments to an earlier review by Arthur Smullyan. Despite subsequent criticism of the Smullyan–Fitch position by Alonzo Church, Marcus had repeated it, with acknowledgments to Fitch, in a paper two years before the colloquium. In the colloquium paper it is repeated again with elaborations but without expected acknowledgments, although the ultimate source in Smullyan was clear to Quine. Kripke, then an undergraduate, was thus coming in on the nth round of an ongoing debate.

The Smullyan–Fitch line followed by Marcus is that if one has names (or, in the Millian language used by Marcus, "tags") then two with the same denotation can be substituted for each other everywhere. It follows that "Phosphorus" can replace the second occurrence of "Hesperus" in "Necessarily Hesperus is Hesperus" to obtain "Necessarily Hesperus is Phosphorus". This is so for *any* sense of necessity, and Marcus explicitly draws the conclusion that identities such as "Hesperus is Phosphorus" are "necessary" in the sense of being *a priori*. Quine objects that they are not. If one tags a planet "Hesperus" one evening, and tags a planet "Phosphorus" one morning, it is a substantive astronomical question whether one has tagged two planets once each or one and the same planet twice, and an *a posteriori* discovery that Hesperus is Phosphorus. In the discussion Marcus ignores the objection until reminded of it by a question from Kripke, to which a reply is given that stuck in his memory.

Marcus first indicates that it is names in an ideal sense that are at issue, and claims that for names in an ideal sense there would presumably be a dictionary, and the operation required to find out that Hesperus is Phosphorus would be like consulting a dictionary, the question being whether this book tells us these words have the same meaning, and in that sense true identities involving names would be analytic. (The claim that a book telling us when two words have the same meaning would tell us when two names in an ideal sense designate the same individual recalls Russell's notion that for a name in the ideal sense the individual designated *is* its meaning.) Quine may want to call the operation of consulting a dictionary "empirical" in some extended or flexible sense, but it is not the empirical operation of scientific observation of the planets; or as Marcus puts it in the edited, published version of the colloquium it is "not like finding out a planet's orbit or its mass". In a paper a few months later this was to become, "One doesn't investigate the planets, but the accompanying lexicon" (Marcus 1963: 132).

Marcus does not explain *why* for "tags" in the ideal sense there would be a dictionary or lexicon; but in the colloquium talk one finds a passage indicating that "tags" are to be applied *only after completing an inventory* of the objects to be tagged. Presumably if one has completed an inventory before tagging, one can keep a record of when one of the inventoried items is given two tags, which record may be called, or likened to, a dictionary or lexicon. But, of course, the contents of the solar system have *not* been inventoried. The Hesperus–Phosphorus case is ancient history, but new asteroids and comets are being discovered all the time, and each time multiple reports come in, it is an *a posteriori*, substantive astronomical question whether they are multiple discoveries of the same object, or discoveries of multiple objects. The operation involved is precisely that required to determine an asteroid's or comet's orbit, since two such bodies are the same precisely when they have the same orbit. This was Quine's objection, and Kripke agrees with it.

Kripke sums up his views about true identities involving names in Kripke (1971) as a trio of assertions: (a) Quine was right that such identities are *a posteriori*; (b) Marcus was right that such identities are necessary; (c) both were wrong in confusing necessity with epistemological notions. This is tidy, but (b) is too generous. It is counterfactually necessary that Hesperus is Phosphorus, while Marcus maintained that it is necessary that Hesperus is Phosphorus in any and every sense in which it is necessary that Hesperus is Hesperus. This only makes Marcus "right" in the sense in which a stopped clock is "right" twice a day. As to (c), *Kripke*, too, just like Marcus and Quine, used "necessary" and "analytic" interchangeably in the 1962 discussion. (By his own account, the bulk of his views on naming and necessity date to 1963–64.)

The necessity of material composition and of origins

According to Kripke, there are more interesting examples of *a posteriori* necessities than true identities linking names. One famous class involves material composition. If a table is made of wood, it could not have been made of glass (let alone ice), even though a table cleverly made of just the right kind of glass (or perhaps even ice) might look so similar to the given table that it could be switched for it without anyone noticing. But examples of this type will not be further discussed here, since Kripke concedes in his addenda that they require more discussion than he has had space to give them. That leaves to be treated briefly below origins, and certain principles pertaining to natural kinds.

Kripke, discussing an example from another writer, is led to consider whether Queen Elizabeth II could have been the daughter of someone other than King George VI; or, to avoid problems with titles, whether Elizabeth Windsor could have been the daughter of someone other than George Windsor, say Harry Truman. Suppose a tabloid runs an article claiming the following: at a crucial conjuncture in the interwar period George Windsor, dismayed by his wife's miscarriage of their first child, and Harry Truman, embarrassed by the pregnancy of a mistress, came to a quick arrangement. The politician's mistress was offered luxurious retirement in Bermuda in exchange for giving up her infant, the princess's miscarriage was hushed up and reports of her continuing pregnancy issued, and the baby once born was hurried to the palace, introduced into the royal bed in a warming pan, and produced as a supposed new child of the reigning family, eventually to ascend the throne – where she sits today!

Doubtless there is no more truth in this article than in anything else one might read in the *National Inquirer, Lingua Franca* or the like. Doubtless the story could be refuted beyond reasonable doubt by DNA testing. But it cannot be refuted by logic alone, however broadly one understands "logic". The story contains no internal self-contradiction, however broadly one understands "contradiction". *It is logically possible that Elizabeth Windsor is the daughter of someone other than George Windsor.*

Kripke maintains, however, that given that she *is* the daughter of George Windsor, *it is not counterfactually possible that Elizabeth Windsor is the daughter of anyone else.* It may be conceded that the story above, although untrue, *could have been* true. And it must be conceded that in that case there would have been a person *called* "Elizabeth Windsor" or "Queen Elizabeth II" who was the daughter of Harry Truman, not George Windsor or King George VI. But Kripke insists that *that* woman, although *called* "Elizabeth Windsor", would not have *been* Elizabeth Windsor. Elizabeth Windsor – the person *we* call by that name – could not have had any other father than the one she did have. If the above story had been true, she would never have been born.

Natural kinds

Kripke maintains that terms for natural kinds, animal and vegetable and mineral, are much like proper names. Using a description, perhaps involving demonstratives and requiring supplementation by ostension, that is true of them or at least that the baptist thinks is true of them, a natural kind of individual may be picked out and given a "common name". This common name or natural-kind term thereafter passes from speaker to speaker, with the original description being perhaps very soon completely forgotten. All this is just as with proper names, and according to Kripke natural-kind terms resemble common names also in giving rise to *a priori* necessities.

Consider, for instance, the evolutionary pedigree of species. In certain areas of the southern hemisphere where there were no placental mammals, marsupials occupied the ecological niches occupied by such mammals elsewhere, and were led by convergent evolution to assume outward forms quite similar to those of some placental mammals. There were "marsupial wolves", for instance, quite similar in appearance to true wolves, though more closely related to kangaroos. Extrapolating somewhat, we can imagine that, some disease having killed off all the larger felines in the warmer areas of the world at some early stage, various species of reptiles evolved cat-like shapes and habits, including reptiles with black and orange stripes that came to be called "tigers". But according to Kripke, these reptiles would not have *been* tigers: not what *we* call tigers. *Those* animals, being cousins of dogs and monkeys, could not have been cousins of turtles and snakes.

The parallel to the Windsor–Truman case should be clear. Besides this kind of example there are a host of others: "gold has atomic number 79", "light is a stream of photons", and famously, "water = H_2O". There is no internal self-contradiction in Dalton's view that water is a compound HO, or even in the ancient view that water is an element. But given the truth of Avogadro's view that water is the compound H_2O, it *could not have been* anything else. A world where a substance of a different chemical formula filled the lakes and rivers would be a world where something other than water filled the lakes and rivers.

The mind–body problem

Then comes the most controversial application: application to the mind–body problem. The random molecular motions that we call "heat" cause certain physiological events – let us call them H-events – in the nerves and ultimately the brain, and therewith cause heat-sensations. Materialists have maintained that the heat-sensations just *are* the H-events. The correlation between H-events and heat-sensations was undeniably an *a posteriori* discovery; but materialists have maintained that this does not tell against the correlation being an identity, since there are many other "contingent identities" in science. For instance, the identity of heat with random molecular motions is one.

Kripke, however, maintains that an identity between natural kinds holds by (counterfactual) necessity if it holds at all. For instance, the identity of heat with random molecular motions is *not* (counterfactually) contingent, although logically contingent and *a posteriori*. There is no internal self-contradiction in the hypothesis – once held by respectable physicists – that heat is a material substance, "caloric fluid". But given that it is not, but rather consists of random molecular motions, it *could not have been* anything else. There might have been a universe where it was a caloric fluid that caused heat-sensations and was *called* "heat". But that would have been a universe where something other than *heat* – other than what causes *our* heat-sensations and what *we* call "heat" – caused heat-sensations and was called "heat".

Kripke, by contrast, maintains that the correlation between H-events and heat-sensations *is* genuinely (counterfactually) contingent. H-events might

182

have been correlated with some non-tactile sensation or with no sensation at all, and hence might not have involved a warm feeling. But *heat-sensations* could not have failed to involve a warm feeling, so if H-events had done so, they would have been non-identical with heat-sensations. But then, the identity of H-events with heat-sensations fails, since an identity between natural kinds holds by (counterfactual) necessity if it holds at all.

Materialism is a deeply entrenched ideology, and materialists did not at once surrender in the face of Kripke's (admittedly rather sketchy) argument. This application of Kripke's framework of semantic and metaphysical ideas, like many others, continues to generate substantial philosophical discussion.

An anti-Kripkean view: two-dimensionalism

It is not just applications of Kripke's framework that remain controversial, but the framework itself. A serious, sustained challenge has been mounted in recent years under the label *two-dimensionalism*. The background is as follows. Philosophers had thought of a (complete) specification of a "possible world" as being given by a (complete) non-contradictory story told in purely qualitative terms, where "qualitative" means at least involving no proper names. Kripke maintains that this is doubly wrong.

On the one hand, a non-contradictory story must bring in proper names before it can be a *complete* description of anything, since proper names cannot be defined by a qualitative (or any) description. That is shown by, among others, the modal argument. The elements of a candidate description one might offer for Socrates (philosopher, hemlock-drinker, teacher of broad-browed dialogue writer, and so on) are all things he need not have been (since he could have followed his father's trade of mason and never become a philosopher).

On the other hand, a non-contradictory story, even (or especially) one involving proper names, need not describe a "world" that is (counterfactually) possible. This is because some features of Socrates, although they may be too obscure to figure in a candidate description, and may be denied without contradiction, are essential to him, so that he could not have existed without them: parentage, for instance, and other features cited in examples of the necessary *a posteriori*.

Two-dimensionalism insists that a (complete) non-contradictory story told in purely qualitative terms *does* constitute a (complete) specification of a possible world w; but there are two different ways of identifying the Socrates (if any) of w. In a primary and absolute sense, the Socrates of w is whoever answers to the relevant cluster of descriptions. In a secondary sense, relative to a given world w_0 that is assumed to be actual, the Socrates of w is the person sharing with the

Socrates of w_0 the parentage and other features in Kripke's examples. The logical necessity of a statement about Socrates is its truth in all possible worlds when the Socrates of each world is picked out in the primary way. The metaphysical necessity of a statement about Socrates can only be assessed relatively. *Given* some world w_0 that is assumed to be actual, metaphysical necessity relative to w_0 is truth in all possible worlds when the Socrates of each world is picked out in the secondary way relative to w_0. This relativity is betrayed in Kripke's examples by such clauses as "*given* that Queen Elizabeth is the daughter of King George" or "*given* that Socrates is the son of Phaenarete and Sophroniscus".

Such is two-dimensionalism, crudely summarized; for a refined exposition see Chalmers (1996) and for a Kripkean critique thereof see Byrne and Pryor (forthcoming). Crudely summarized, the Kripkean criticism is that two-dimensionalism neglects the fact that the modal argument against taking proper names to have descriptive definitions was only one of several and not the most important. Arguments from error and ignorance suggest that it will be very difficult to locate any qualitative description to define "Socrates" or "Elizabeth Windsor", or for that matter "gold" or "water". (For everything said about proper names in this section applies also to natural-kind terms.)

All this is at present a matter of ongoing debate. What is undebatable is that two-dimensionalists, quite as much as direct reference theorists, while they do not agree with Kripke's position in all respects, are heavily indebted to his work.

Is counterfactual necessity "metaphysical"?

As was hinted early on, it was a popular view among philosophers of the twentieth century that all necessary truths derive from linguistic conventions. Naturally, philosophers attracted to this view have been loath to recognize any notion of necessity going beyond the *a priori*, or any notion of apriority going beyond analyticity. Kripke's position, with both the necessary *a posteriori* and the synthetic *a priori*, was therefore doubly unwelcome. But on closer inspection the Kripkean synthetic *a priori* proves to be innocuous, since it derives quite as much as analyticity from linguistic convention: from "definitions" in the reference-fixing rather than meaning-giving sense.

The necessary *a posteriori* may also be innocuous. For one important feature of Kripke's examples, noted in his addenda, is that in every basic example of a P that is necessary but *a posteriori*, it is analytic that if P, then necessarily P, and if not-P, then necessarily not-P. The claim is that it is analytic that *either* Goldbach's conjecture is necessary, *or* its negation is necessary; likewise with other basic examples. (This is not to say that *whenever P* is necessary, it is analytic that *P* is either necessary or impossible. For from *basic* examples with this property one can put together logical compounds without it.)

A crucial consequence is that the "intuitions" Kripke appeals to in determining whether a logically non-contradictory scenario with various stipulations about named individuals is genuinely counterfactually possible or not are arguably *linguistic* intuitions, which of course virtually all analytic philosophers do and must appeal to (these being the intuitions appealed to whenever a philosopher claims that one or another example is or is not analytic). No previously unrecognized mysterious mental faculty of "metaphysical modal intuition" is needed to apprehend counterfactual necessity. Thus, although Kripke calls necessity "metaphysical", it is not *occult*. When this point is appreciated, one source of resistance to Kripke's views disappears.

There do indeed remain some serious objections to regarding even logic in the narrowest sense as true by linguistic convention, notably the problems raised by Quine (1936). Kripke himself has addressed closely related issues, but for his treatment of them one must turn to Kripke (1982).

Bibliography

Burgess, J. 1997. "*Quinus ab Omni Nævo Vindicatus*". *Canadian Journal of Philosophy*, suppl. vol. **23**, 25–66.

Byrne, Alex & J. Pryor forthcoming. "Bad Intensions". In *Two-Dimensional Semantics: Foundations and Applications*, M. Garcia-Carpintero & J. Macia (eds). Oxford: Oxford University Press

Chalmers, D. 1996. *The Conscious Mind: In Search of a Fundamental Theory*. Oxford: Oxford University Press.

Donnellan, K. 1966. "Reference and Definite Descriptions". *Philosophical Review* **75**, 281–304.

Kaplan, D. 1969. "Quantifying In". In *Words and Objections: Essays on the Work of W. V. Quine*, D. Davidson & J. Hintikka (eds), 206–42. Dordrecht: Reidel.

Kripke, S. 1963. "Semantical Considerations on Modal Logic". *Acta Philosophica Fennica* **16**, 83–94.

Kripke, S. 1971. "Identity and Necessity". In *Identity and Individuation*, M. K. Munitz (ed.), 135–64. New York: New York University Press.

Kripke, S. 1972. "Naming and Necessity". In *Semantics of Natural Language*, D. Davidson & G. Harman (eds), 253–355 (Lectures I–III, References), 763–69 (Addenda). Dordrecht: Reidel.

Kripke, S. 1977. "Speaker's Reference and Semantic Reference". *Midwest Studies in Philosophy* **2**, 255–76.

Kripke, S. 1979. "A Puzzle about Belief". In *Meaning and Use*, A. Margalit (ed.), 239–83. Dordrecht: Reidel.

Kripke, S. 1980. *Naming and Necessity*. Oxford: Blackwell.

Kripke, S. 1982. *Wittgenstein on Rules and Private Language*. Oxford: Blackwell.

Marcus, R. B. 1963. "Classes and Attributes in Extended Modal Systems". *Acta Philosophica Fennica* **16**, 123–36.

Prior, A. 1963. "Is the Concept of Referential Opacity Really Necessary?". *Acta Philosophical Fennica* **16**, 189–99.

Quine, W. V. O. 1936. "Truth By Convention". In *Philosophical Essays for A. N. Whitehead*, O. H. Lee (ed.), 90–124. New York: Longman.

Searle, J. R. 1958. "Proper Names". *Mind* **67**, 166–73.

Soames, S. 2005. "Naming and Asserting". In *Semantics vs Pragmatics*, Z. G. Szabó (ed.), 356–82. Oxford: Oxford University Press.

Strawson, P. F. 1959. *Individuals: An Essay in Descriptive Metaphysics*. London: Methuen.

Wartofsky, M. W. (ed.) 1963. *Proceedings of the Boston Colloquium for the Philosophy of Science 1961/1962*. Dordrecht: Reidel.

9
Hilary Putnam
Reason, Truth and History

Peter Clark

In the late 1970s and early 1980s Hilary Putnam produced a major sequence of philosophical works all directed at criticism of a certain view of the relation between language and reality. Two of the most salient of those works were *Reason, Truth and History* (1981; hereafter *RTH*) and *Meaning and the Moral Sciences* (1978). Both works were independently philosophical *tours de force* and both were enormously influential, producing a huge secondary literature. This essay concerns principally the former work, although we shall often have to refer to the latter also. Putnam is unselfconsciously one of those philosophers[1] who is not afraid to change his mind and although he now no longer accepts one of the positive claims of *Reason, Truth and History*, namely internal realism (of which much later), the lasting significance of this work is the nexus of philosophical considerations, particularly concerning the notion of reference, which were raised in the book. These considerations are breathtaking in scope, ranging from a refutation of Cartesian scepticism, through numerous insights in the history of philosophy, to issues concerning the theory of truth and the proper interpretation of well-known limitative theorems in mathematical logic. However, the work should not be thought of as a narrow work in analytic philosophy for not only is it replete in allusions to what is called the "continental tradition" in philosophy but Putnam constantly returns to the notion of the "life-enhancing", to the notion of human flourishing and this book systematically exhibits the enormous humanitarian and social concern that motivates so much of his thought.

Putnam announces in his preface to *RTH* that his major concern is to undermine certain traditional dichotomies both of common sense and traditional philosophy, which he argues are unfounded and deeply misleading. Among these are the mind and the world, the objective and the subjective view of truth and reason, and of fact and value. These dichotomies, he argues, are ill defined and misleading but they are all consequences of a deeply held, very influential, but fundamentally mistaken metaphysical view, that of metaphysical realism. His book is a sustained attempt to show the untenability of this view and to replace it with a radically different thesis, which he calls "internal realism". Once internal realism is accepted the untenable dichotomies no longer follow. The cognitive and moral alienation induced by conceiving the world according to metaphysical realism as existing totally independently of our conceptual apparatus, and thus devoid of value, is replaced by a much superior understanding of our place in nature and of the character of knowledge and truth.

Putnam articulates two contrasting philosophical perspectives: that of the externalist and that of the internalist. He characterizes the externalist perspective as follows:

> On this perspective, the world consists of some fixed totality of mind-independent objects. There is exactly one true and complete description of "the way the world is". Truth involves some sort of correspondence relation between words or thought-signs and external things and sets of things. I shall call this perspective the *externalist* perspective, because its favorite point of view is a God's Eye point of view. (*RTH*: 49)

On the other hand, the view he wishes to defend, the internalist perspective, holds that:

> *what objects does the world consists of?* is a question that it only makes sense to ask *within* a theory or description. Many "internalist" philosophers, though not all, hold further that there is more than one "true" theory or description of the world. "Truth", in an internalist view, is some sort of (idealized) rational acceptability – some sort of ideal coherence of our beliefs with each other and with our experiences *as those experiences are themselves represented in our belief system* – and not correspondence with mind-independent or discourse-independent "states of affairs". There is no God's Eye point of view that we can know or usefully imagine; there are only various points of

view of actual persons reflecting various interests and purposes that
their descriptions and theories subserve.   (*RTH*: 49–50)

He later reiterates the point concerning theory dependence and the role of conceptual schemes from the internalist perspective:

> In an internalist view also, signs do not intrinsically correspond to
> objects, independently of how those signs are employed and by whom.
> But a sign that is actually employed in a particular way by a particu-
> lar community of users can correspond to particular objects *within
> the conceptual scheme of those users*. "Objects" do not exist independ-
> ently of conceptual schemes. We cut up the world into objects when
> we introduce one or another scheme of description. Since the objects
> *and* the signs are alike *internal* to the scheme of description, it is pos-
> sible to say what matches what.   (*RTH*: 52)

Characteristic of the external perspective is the doctrine of metaphysical realism. But what exactly is metaphysical realism? It is not entirely straightforward
to say, as one might expect with so pervasive and deep a view. It might be best
to approach it metaphorically at first and then to try to do better with a specific philosophical claim. We shall follow Putnam's conception that the view is
closely associated with the "God's Eye" perspective.

A little philosophical fantasy

There is a stunning relief etching with watercolour by William Blake completed
in 1794 entitled *Ancient of Days*. It shows God about the design and creation
of the world. God, in the guise of a naked, human male, holds in his hand a pair
of protractors and is bent over, deep in thought, using the protractors to mark
out the geometry of the world. In the watercolour the language of creation is
Euclidean geometry (illustrated by the protractors) and no doubt the laws of
creation are those of Newtonian mechanics and the universal law of gravitation,
all given expression in the language of the differential calculus. It is as if in God's
mind there is a blueprint for the universe and the language of the blueprint is
the differential calculus and Euclidean geometry. The planets are all placed in
their elliptical orbits moving against a background of absolute space and time in
which all the atoms of the universe have been distributed in accordance with this
blueprint. So in effect we can think of the blueprint as a set of four constraints:
a space–time framework, Newtonian absolute space and time; a distribution of

matter and energy within that framework; the specification of the four fundamental laws of nature of mechanics and gravitation; and finally the laws that
govern the combination of atoms (chemistry and biology).

Now let us think of ourselves as observers and scientists in this Newtonian
universe. The first thing to notice is that the language of science, the language
that essentially we do science in, is the differential calculus and Euclidean geometry. That is also the language of the blueprint. So when we are thinking about
the nature of the world there is a pre-established harmony between the way the
world is (as is given in the blueprint) and the language of thought about the
world. Now of course merely because we speak or think in the language in which
the blueprint is written does not mean that what we say is true, but it does mean
that what we say will be true or false, just in case it matches the blueprint or
not. The world has a definite determinate structure given by the blueprint, and
that structure is directly reflected by the language of the blueprint, geometry
and calculus. But the language in which we think, in which we do our science,
is geometry and the calculus, so the language of thought and the "language of
the world" are identical. One, admittedly metaphorical, way of thinking about
the claim of metaphysical realism is that there is a "language of the world" in
the above sense (a privileged language in which the blueprint of the universe is
written) and it is the same as the language of thought or science.

In a sense we might regard the epistemic condition of observers in such a
world as epistemically ideal. Although they may formulate false theories, there
is a notion of closeness to the truth for such theories, namely how closely they
match the design statements in the blueprint, which are formulated in the same
language. (The notion of verisimilitude is notoriously language-dependent.) We
can imagine that their science, as more and more evidence comes in, will converge
towards the statements in the blueprint. Since those statements in the blueprint
constitute the exact truth, there is one true account towards which they are aiming: the "theory of everything" as given by the blueprint. Indeed, we can press this
fortunate state of affairs much further. We have been concentrating on general
claims about the structure of the universe, but we can be much more specific. We
can imagine the language of the blueprint extended in such a way as to contain the
names of the natural kinds that occur in the universe (in our Newtonian model
world this would be a list of the permitted stable combinations of atoms that
might arise chemically and biologically, e.g. gold, radium, mammal, bird etc.). This
would be the list of the real natural kinds. Our thinkers would succeed in referring
to a natural kind using the term X just when the extension of the term X coincides
with the extension of the corresponding natural-kind term in the language of the
blueprint in the actual universe and in all possible worlds. Thus our word "Tree"
refers to the natural kind it does precisely because there is a blueprint language

term ("tree") which has exactly the extension it does in the actual and all possible worlds. Again, of course, thinkers in our Newtonian model world might be mistaken in thinking that they had picked out a natural kind. They might well think that they had succeeded in referring to the kind "phlogiston", but the blueprint contains no kind coextensive with the substance of heat. Rather, what it is for us to succeed in referring to, say, "water" is precisely for there to be a natural kind in the blueprint the extension of which is all the H_2O molecules and it is exactly that collection that we refer to when we use the term "water".

On the face of it then it looks as if thinkers in such a world are in a more or less epistemically ideal situation: they inhabit a world made up of a unique domain of objects and kinds, with a unique structure specified again by the blueprint. They speak a language coincident with the language of the blueprint, so everything they say is either true or false as to whether it corresponds or does not correspond to the unique structure given by the blueprint. That is roughly the claim of metaphysical realism. Our world may be very different from the Newtonian fantasy in fact, but not in the matter of how language and thought match reality. There is a language-independent reality; the structure of that language-independent reality is nevertheless reflected exactly by the structure of our language, such that each sentence of that language is true just in case what it says corresponds with that reality. As we quoted above, that is exactly Putnam's way of characterizing this view.[2]

Let us return to the thought that observers in our Newtonian fantasy universe find themselves in an ideal epistemic situation. It certainly looks as if they might because thought and reality naturally match each other. If they had really taken in all the data, collected all the evidence and made no inductive mistakes, would they not know the whole truth about their world? Put another way, would their final science, their theory of everything at the end of the process of data-gathering, not be identical with the blueprint – they would know the whole truth and nothing but the truth? However, for what we might call local and global reasons, this could not be the case. To make this point we can start with rather local reasons. Recall that our model universe is Newtonian and so observers in that universe will find it impossible to distinguish on the basis of any data as to whether the world they inhabit is at rest with respect to absolute space or moving with respect to it at a constant non-zero velocity. This paradigm example of Quinean underdetermination (see Quine 1960) of theory by data is not generated by the accident that the model world is Newtonian. The point is generic; for if we ask ourselves what our observers might come to believe about their world we can see that a disastrous epistemic possibility has opened up for such thinkers – that of universal scepticism. We have already noted that in virtue of Quinean underdetermination, even their ideal theory, formed when all the data are in, might very well be wrong or seriously incomplete. But the thought must occur to our observers that this possibility once admitted will globalize to include all their theories and representations, and may well infect the adequacy of the concepts they employ.

The sceptical possibility arises that all their thought is mismatched with reality. It may very well appear to them to be internally coherent; further, as far as observable matters are concerned it may well appear true. But how do they know, indeed how could they come to know, that it matches the blueprint? The point is they cannot know, argues Putnam, because of their conception of reference and truth implied by their acceptance of metaphysical realism or the "God's Eye" point of view. For all they know they could be brains in a vat, creatures with a rich cognitive life, that is coherent in itself and satisfied by their world of mental representations, but that corresponds not at all to reality. But, Putnam argues, this possibility that the cognitive life of thinkers might bear no resemblance to reality is self-defeating in much the same way that the thought "I do not exist" is when thought by me. So metaphysical realism entails a proposition (the proposition that: it is a real possibility that our best grasp of the way the world is may bear no relation to the nature of that reality) that is false (because it entails its own negation), so metaphysical realism is false.

The general structure of Putnam's claim has been very well put by Wright (1994). It is worth quoting at length. Wright writes:

> It [metaphysical realism] involves thinking of the world as set over against thought in such a way that it is only by courtesy of a deeply contingent harmony, or felicity, that we succeed, if we do, in forming an overall picture of the world which, at least in its basics, is correct. This is what commits the metaphysical realist to the possibility that even an ideal theory might be false or seriously incomplete. And the same kind of thinking surfaces in the idea that the world comes prejointed, as it were, into real kinds, quite independently of any classificatory activity of ours. Once one thinks of the world in that way, one is presumably committed to the bare possibility of conceptual creatures naturally so constituted as *not* to be prone to form concepts which reflect the real kinds that there are. The real character of the world and its constituents would thus elude both the cognition and the comprehension of such creatures.
>
> Putnam's brains in a vat are exactly such creatures: minds doomed by the character of their interaction with the world they inhabit, and by the nature of that world, not to have the concepts they need in order to be able to capture in thought that world's most fundamental

features and the nature of their relationship with it … Metaphysical realism is committed to the possibility of a certain kind of dislocation, or uncrossable divide between reality and our cognitive activity. If that possibility were realised, there would accordingly, have to be some correct, specific account of the way in which it was realised. And that is just to say that something like the brain in-the-vat story would have to be true.   (Wright 1994: 238)

The brain in the vat story

What is the brain in the vat story and why is it self-refuting? The brain in the vat story is simply an exemplification of the sceptical possibility discussed above: in other words, an account of a possible world in which the sceptical possibility is apparently realized. In this world there are thinkers who have a rich cognitive life, communicate in a language superficially very much like English (call it BIVese) and have pure mental representations much like ours. However, they are in fact disembodied brains in a vat and their thoughts correspond in no way to their real condition. Suppose they try in BIVese to formulate the hypothesis that they are indeed brains in a vat. They will say in BIVese "we are brains in a vat", but the expression of BIVese "brains in a vat" cannot possibly refer to brains in a vat. It cannot do so because, by hypothesis, the very causal relations that must obtain between thinkers using the referring expression "brains in a vat" and actual brains and actual vats do not obtain in the case of the envatted thinkers. So whatever, if anything, "brains in a vat" in BIVese refers to, it is not actual brains and actual vats. So were we to formulate this hypothesis while being brains in a vat, we would not actually be formulating the intended thought at all (we would be formulating what Putnam calls "a thought in a merely bracketed sense" (*RTH*: 28) – a sort of pure mental representation). Hence the claim "We are brains in a vat" formulated in BIVese would be in a certain sense self-refuting, since it cannot under the hypothesis that we are brains in a vat formulate the intended thought. Wright (1994: 224) has provided a short formulation of the argument:

(i)   Our language is disquotational (that is meaningful expressions refer in the standard way, "cat" refers to cat, etc.).

(ii) In BIVese "brain in a vat" does not refer to brains in a vat.

(iii) In our language "brain in a vat" is a meaningful expression.

(iv) In our language "brain in a vat" refers to brains in a vat (using (i) and (ii)).

(v)   So our language is not BIVese (using (iv) and (ii)).

193

(vi) If we are brains in a vat then our language, if any, is BIVese.

(vii) So we are not brains in a vat (using (v) and (vi)).

Clearly (i) and (ii) are crucial premises. Premise (ii) hinges on not the acceptance of a causal theory of reference but rather the minimal claim that in order for there to be successful reference there must be at least some appropriate causal connection between tokens of the referring term and the objects referred to, although this indeed may be very indirect. In the case in question the hypothesis itself, that we are brains in a vat, effectively rules out there being causal connections of the appropriate sort, for if we are brains in a vat then there are no vats of the right sort for us to be in causal connection with.

Such, then, is the core of Putnam's ingenious and intriguing argument. If metaphysical realism is true, then a certain possibility seems naturally to arise, but entertaining the hypothesis that that possibility holds shows in fact that there can be no such coherent possibility, so metaphysical realism is false. As Putnam puts it the argument is very simple: "So, if we *are* Brains in a Vat, we cannot *think* that we are, except in the bracketed sense [we are Brains in a Vat]; and this bracketed thought does not have reference conditions that would make it *true*. So it is not possible after all that we are Brains in a Vat" (*RTH*: 50–51). As we noted above the core of the argument lies in premises (i) and (ii) so there must be something fundamentally inconsistent among these premises and metaphysical realism. What that inconsistency is is brought out by the model-theoretic arguments.

The model-theoretic arguments

There are in fact two kinds of model-theoretic arguments deployed by Putnam. One is based on a "permutation" argument and the other, in a way by far the most profound, is an argument using the Löwenheim–Skolem theorem (Skolem [1920] 1967)). Again, it is how the metaphysical realist sees successful reference as being achieved that will be at the core of the issue. All thought or mental representation is object directed: all thought is about something. To put it another way, thoughts have the property of intentionality; they characteristically refer to something else. How does the language in which our thoughts are formulated achieve this? How is it possible, asks Putnam, that we are capable, where we are, of achieving successful reference? "How is intentionality, reference, possible?" (*RTH*: 2), he argues, is the real problem.

The view that it is something about the thinker's pure mental state that fixes the reference of his terms was decisively refuted by a central argument of Putnam's paper "The Meaning of 'Meaning'" (see § Further reading) and his *Meaning and the Moral Sciences*, the famous "Twin Earth" thesis. A speaker on Earth may use the term water to refer to the liquid H_2O, but on Twin Earth a speaker in the exactly the same mental state may refer to a liquid with all the same observable properties but that is not H_2O by the term "water". Then the term "water" used on Twin Earth refers not to water but to another liquid, yet the mental states of both thinkers are, in all relevant senses, exactly the same.

The suggestion that is Putnam's target in *RTH* is the conception that the reference of terms occurring in sentences can be fixed by the truth of whole sentences containing those terms. The idea is a very natural one. Suppose you are trying to explain to someone, who has never met the notion before, what the term "gene" refers to. You might very well tell him all the key molecular, biological and evolutionary facts that genes are supposed to explain and then say that "gene" refers to exactly those objects that in nature make all of these claims true. Now, whether there are any such objects is a matter for nature to determine. After all, as we have already noted there is no substance phlogiston, but that is because it is in fact impossible to make all of the claims characterizing phlogiston actually true together. It just turns out that the truth-conditions for all the claims characterizing phlogiston are not satisfied in nature. The view under discussion says only that if a term has reference then the reference is fixed by giving the truth-conditions of the sentences containing it. Another way of putting the claim is to go back to the notion that all thought is about something. When we express our thoughts we have an intended interpretation in mind; we mean something; we intend to say something. How can we fix the intended interpretation? According to the view in question we can fix the intended interpretation by laying down the constraint that all that we say is true. Now it might be objected that this is an absurd view because it entirely neglects what Putnam himself was at pains to point out: that there are other constraints on reference. He calls these "theoretical and operational" constraints. An operational constraint would be the requirement that we should get the observational data correct, so all the sentences describing experimental data must come out true. An example of a theoretical constraint might be that we pick the simplest theory that does this. So the operational and theoretical constraints together determine which sentences are true and thus the references of the terms in those sentences. But this objection misses the depth of Putnam's insight. What he noted was that the theoretical and operational constraints amounted in fact just to adding more theory, just more sentences that have to be true on the view in question (Putnam calls it the "received view"). So the objection does not carry weight after all. As he puts it:

> The difficulty with the received view is that it tries to fix the intensions and extensions of individual terms by fixing the truth-conditions

for whole sentences. The idea, as we just saw, is that operational and theoretical constraints (the ones rational inquirers would accept in some sort of ideal limit of inquiry) determine which sentences in the language are *true*. Even if this is right, however, such constraints cannot determine what our terms *refer* to. For there is nothing in the notion of an operational or theoretical constraint to do this directly. And doing it *indirectly*, by putting down constraints which pick out the set of true sentences, and then hoping that by determining the truth-values of whole sentences we can somehow fix what the terms occurring in those sentences refer to, won't work … In fact, it is possible to interpret the entire language in violently different ways, each of them compatible with the requirement that the truth-value of each sentence in each possible world be the one specified. In short, not only does the received view not work; *no view which only fixes the truth-values of whole sentences can fix reference*, even if it specifies truth-values for sentences *in every possible world*.   (*RTH*: 32–3)

Why is this so? It is so because of the permutation argument. Let us revise where we are. We have a language *L* in which is formulated an ideal scientific theory that satisfies all inductive, operational and theoretical constraints. The claim of the "received view" is that the truth of *T* fixes the reference of all the names and terms in *L*. The permutation argument simply says: this cannot be the case because of a (the) basic theorem of model theory that isomorphic interpretations of a language satisfy or make true exactly the same sets of sentences. An interpretation of a language is simply an assignment of objects in a domain to the terms and variables of the language, such that when predicates and relations in the language are interpreted as subsets of the domain, the sentences of the language have a truth-value in that domain. A model of a theory is an interpretation of the language of the theory in which all the sentences of the theory have the truth-value true. The basic theorem says that isomorphic models make the same sentences true. An interpretation *A* of the language *L* is isomorphic to an interpretation *B* if essentially *A* and *B* have the same structure and are equinumerous with each other, that is if one is a "mirror image" of the other. This notion can be made quite precise. A permutation of a domain is simply a mapping of the domain onto itself that is non-trivial (i.e. we will exclude the identity mapping). So if, for example, our domain *A* was the set $\{a, b, c\}$, a permutation of the domain is given by the map f; *A* onto *A* by $f(a) = b, f(b) = c$ and $f(c) = a$. Now f is here a permutation, so the original domain and the permuted domain have exactly the same number of members. Now we can begin to see the force of the permutation argument. Let us take a simple example to make the point.

Go back to our ideal language L. Let us formulate in L the theory T that says of some predicate R of L the following:

Not everything has R.
Something has R.
If anything is identical with u then it does not have R.
If anything is identical with v it does not have R.

(where u and v are names in L). Let us lay down that these sentences be true. If we assign to the name u in L the object a in A, and to the name v the object c, and we assign to the predicate R of L the subset $\{b\}$ of A, then indeed all the sentences of T come out true. Not everything has R because in A, a and c do not. Something has R because b does and since u is assigned a and v is assigned c in A the remaining two sentences are true. Have we then uniquely determined that R refers to $\{b\}$? We have not. Look at the permuted domain $f[A]$. Now assign to the name u of L the object $f(a)$, that is, b and to the name v the object $f(c)$, that is, a. Assign to R the subset $\{f(b)\}$, that is, $\{c\}$. Not everything has R because a and b do not, and so on. Under this permuted interpretation all the sentences of T are again true. But now the reference of R is $\{c\}$. The question "What does R refer to in A?" cannot be uniquely answered.[3] So simply laying down the constraint that the sentences of T must be true (in A) will not fix the references of the terms in the sentences. In general there will always be isomorphic models that satisfy the same sets of sentences.[4] That is the force of the permutation argument. Putnam says of it: "It follows that there are always infinitely many different interpretations of the predicates of a language which assign the 'correct' truth-values to the sentences in all possible worlds, *no matter how these 'correct' truth-values are singled out*" (RTH: 35). But it should be noted that the italicized phrase in this quote holds only if the singling out is done by the addition of more and more sentences that have to be true – more theory as we saw above.

There is also a second argument that shows the depth of Putnam's attack on the received view, which emerges again from model-theoretic considerations in the context of set theory. It might be thought that such an argument would have only very local significance, perhaps for the philosophy of mathematics alone, but this is not so. To see that it is not so one merely has to reflect on the centrality and significance of set theory (the theory of arbitrary collections or aggregates of objects) in our conceptual scheme and how much of mathematics and physics is embedded in, or reconstructed in, the framework of set theory. In a certain sense set theory is the ideal theory for doing mathematics. Further, the argument involves the crucial notions of "admissible" or "intended" interpretation and how such a notion can be made intelligible without the postulation of mysterious cognitive powers possessed by the speakers of a language. Essentially Putnam's argument from the Löwenheim–Skolem theorem encapsulates a dilemma that is quite ubiquitous if one tries to understand how an intended interpretation of a theory can be grasped from a metaphysical realist viewpoint: that dilemma is that there is no stable account that does not either collapse into relativism on the one hand or require the postulation of special very mysterious cognitive powers of intuition on the other (see Putnam 1983).

It is a fundamental result of set theory, perhaps the fundamental result of set theory, that the collection of all subsets of the set of natural numbers, although infinite, cannot be put into one-to-one correspondence with the set of all natural numbers itself.[5] More generally, on a very natural account of size or cardinality[6] the cardinality of a set is strictly less than the cardinality of the set of all the subsets of that set. This is very clear in the finite case. If the set A has two members (say A is the set $\{a, b\}$) then it has four subsets: the empty set $\varnothing$ (which is trivially a subset of every set), $\{a\}$, $\{b\}$, and $\{a, b\}$ (again trivially a set is always a subset of itself). The map that takes member a of A to $\{a\}$ and b of A to $\{b\}$ is a one-to-one correspondence from A into the proper subset $\{\{a\}, \{b\}\}$ of $\{\varnothing, \{a\}, \{b\}, \{a, b\}\}$, but there is no one-to-one correspondence from a four-membered set into a two-membered set. Cantor's beautiful theorem shows how to extend this sort of reasoning to the infinite case. If we say that a set is countable if and only if it can be put into one-to-one correspondence with a subset of the natural numbers then it is a fundamental result of set theory that the power set of the natural numbers (that is the set of all subsets of the natural numbers) is uncountable: there are infinite sets that are uncountable.

Now set *theory* is precisely that: it is a theory expressed as a set of postulates or axioms laying down the existence of certain sets and identity conditions for those sets. In the standard textbook formulation of Zermelo–Fraenkel set theory (the mathematical paradigm formulation of set theory) there are some nine axioms,[7] which assert the existence of certain sets and the identity conditions for sets (e.g. there is an infinite set; given any set, the set of all its subsets exists; any two sets are identical if and only if they have exactly the same members). These axioms can be written down in a first-order language, that is, a language that quantifies only over objects. This is very natural since sets are objects and the axioms taken together characterize our notion of a set. But it is just at this point that a difficulty appears. The axioms of set theory are expressed in a first-order language and it is a central result of the model theory of first-order languages that any set of first-order sentences that has an infinite model has a countably infinite model, that is, if there is an interpretation of the set of sentences that makes all of them true and that is infinite, then there is an interpretation the domain of which forms a collection of objects that can be put into one-to-one correspondence with the natural numbers. This is the downward Löweheim–Skolem theorem (which itself is provable within set theory together with the axiom of choice). But now we appear to have a paradox, a contradiction sometimes called Skolem's paradox. The standard model of set theory (the way we think of the universe of sets) contains the power set of the set of natural numbers as an object. Any model of the axioms must satisfy the theorems of set theory, since they are logical consequences of the axioms. So Cantor's theorem must be true in that model. So in that model the power set of the natural numbers forms an uncountable collection. But by the downward Löwenheim–Skolem theorem, given that set theory has a model, it must have a countable model. But being a model of the theory it must make Cantor's theorem true, so whatever serves in that countable model to represent the power set of the natural numbers must be a countable collection, since the entire domain is countable. But that looks like saying, depending on which interpretation we pick, that the power set of the natural numbers is either countable or uncountable. Which are they?

That this is not a paradox can easily be seen if we deploy what is sometimes called the "outside/inside" account. Although it is true that from the perspective of the standard interpretation of the universe of sets the model provided by the downward Löwenheim–Skolem theorem is countable, and so the object corresponding to the power set of the natural numbers in that model is again countable, there is no object (no function), no set in the domain of that model that counts the object corresponding to the power set of the natural numbers in that model. So it remains entirely true from "inside" the model, so to say, that the power set of the natural numbers is uncountable and so Cantor's theorem is satisfied. Although looked at from the "outside" (the "true" universe of sets) that is a countable model. All sense of contradiction vanishes when the "inside/outside" perspective is understood. As Putnam puts it "What is a 'countable' set from the point of view of one model may be an uncountable set from the point of view of another model" (Putnam 1983: 2).[8]

However, and it was Putnam's insight to see the depth of the matter, a residual issue remains. For it looks as though we are now committed to an ineliminable, perspectival relativism about the notion of set.[9] Ask the question: which is the right perspective? Are we to think of sets in the way given by the standard interpretation or do we think of the universe of sets as provided by the model given by the downward Löwenheim–Skolem theorem? Well, clearly our notion of set is encapsulated by the axioms of set theory, so it might be thought that we could eliminate any relativism by adding more and more axioms, so continually refining the notion of set and thus eliminating non-standard interpretations. But clearly this will not succeed since we will have more and more first-order sentences that will still be subject to the downward Löwenheim–Skolem theorem and so have ineliminable non-standard (non-standard because countable) interpretations at every stage. So adding more axioms will not solve the problem, but then, as Putnam remarked, "But if axioms cannot capture the 'intuitive notion of a set', what possibly could?" (*ibid.*: 3). It looks as if to avoid the relativism about sets we would have to postulate some special faculty of mathematical intuition that allowed us to grasp what we really have in mind when we talk about sets in a way that is not linguistically communicable in its entirety. But this seems a hopeless cause.

As Putnam says, the argument from the downward Löwenheim–Skolem theorem can be extended, just as the permutation argument can, to the whole of our corpus of beliefs. It amounts again to the point that adding further sentences expressing further constraints will not fix reference. It is worth quoting him at length on the point:

> Now the argument that Skolem gave, and that shows that "the intuitive notion of a set" (if there is such a thing) is not "captured" by any formal system, shows that even a *formalization of total science* (if one could construct such a thing), or even a *formalization of all our beliefs* (whether they count as "science" or not), could not rule out denumerable interpretations, and, *a fortiori*, such a formalization could not rule out *unintended* interpretations of this notion.
>
> This shows that "theoretical constraints", whether they come from set theory itself or from "total science", cannot fix the interpretation of the notion *set* in the "intended" way. What of "operational constraints"?
>
> Even if we allow that there might be a *denumerable infinity* of measurable magnitudes, and that each of them might be measured to *arbitrary rational accuracy* … it wouldn't help … In short, there certainly seems to be a *countable* model of our *entire body of belief* which meets all operational constraints.
>
> The philosophical problem appears just at this point. If we are told "axiomatic set theory does not capture the intuitive notion of a set", then it is natural to think that *something else* – our "understanding" – does capture it. But what can our "understanding" come to, at least for a naturalistically minded philosopher, which is more than *the way we use our language*? And the Skolem argument can be extended, as we have just seen, to show that the *total use of language* (operational plus theoretical constraints) does not "fix" a unique "intended interpretation" any more than axiomatic set theory by itself does.   (*Ibid.*: 3–4)

There are two possible objections to Putnam's reasoning that might at first seem devastating. One is that the downward Löwenheim–Skolem theorem applies only to first-order languages, that is, those that quantify only over objects. It fails for second-order and higher-order languages, for example, those that permit quantification over properties and relations. It may thus seem that all Putnam's argument amounts to is a *non sequitur*; since the axioms of set theory can be given a second-order formulation, why then insist on a first-order formulation? Further, models of set theory in its second-order formulation are unique up to isomorphism so the problem of non-isomorphic interpretations that arises with the downward Löwenheim–Skolem theorem would not appear. But this objection will not work for it simply reintroduces the problem in another way. The problem will re-emerge because we now have to understand how to interpret quantification over arbitrary properties and that really means we will have to be presumed to have a prior grasp of the notion of an arbitrary subset of a set and that in the end will be subject to the same relativism as our first-order notion of a set. Non-isomorphic models of set theory will certainly exist if we do not allow quantification over the full power set of the set of all individuals. Thus, the move to second-order languages will not eliminate the fundamental dilemma. A second and rather more telling objection is that the best that the argument can do is to show that even if we add "total science" to the whole of set theory – that is, add every theoretical and operational constraint we may wish to set theory – we will have no *guarantee* that we will thereby have fixed a unique interpretation for the fundamental notion of set. But this is of no help to the metaphysical realist, for as long as unintended interpretations might be available the general enterprise of metaphysical realism – to show how language succeeds in referring, because our understanding determines a unique reference by eliminating all unintended ones – is undermined. It is of no use to say that language fixes a unique interpretation, when it is always possible that unintended interpretations may very well exist at all stages of enquiry, even at the limit stage when everything by way of additional constraints expressed as more claims in the language is in.

Indeed, there are further ways in which set theory and metaphysical realism make very uneasy bedfellows. The metaphysical realist wants to think of the universe and so the universe of sets as a definite *object* with a structure. But what sort of object? It cannot be a set, for if it were we could form the subset of it corresponding to the set of all sets that are not members of themselves; but there is no such set on pain of Russell's paradox.[10] It could be thought of as a special sort of object called a (proper) class, but we do not have the slightest idea as to why some classes cannot be sets except that we get a contradiction if we suppose them to be. Further, since every set has a power set, so the universe of sets is indefinitely extensible, there is nothing that can constitute a natural end to the process of obtaining "new" sets. It is indeed very difficult to think of such a domain as an object that we can grasp in any sense independently of how we understand the axioms of set theory. But that is just what we are required to do by the metaphysical realist. He insists that we are talking about that structure (the universe of sets), but there is no way of saying what that structure is other than by laying down certain sentences (the axioms) as true. But we know that will not fix a unique structure because of the existence of unintended interpretations.

Putnam's diagnosis of the problem was that it stemmed from the fundamental thesis of metaphysical realism that language has to be tied to its intended interpretation by the true reference relation, which really determines what we mean and that comes from thinking of the world as a fixed independently existing structure to be conceived of as entirely independent of our conceptual activity. He believes that this commits us to an insoluble dilemma, inescapable perspectival relativism or the possession of mysterious cognitive powers to grasp what is never articulated. But the dilemma is an illusion driven by a false view of the relation between language and reality. We shall let him have the last word:

> The problem, however, lies with the predicament itself. The predicament only *is* a predicament because we did two things: first, we gave an account of understanding the language in terms of programs and procedures for *using* the language (what else?); and then, secondly, we asked what the possible "models" for the language were, thinking of the models as existing "out there" independent of any description. At this point, something really weird had already happened, had we stopped to notice. On any view, the understanding of the language must determine the reference of the terms, or, rather, must determine the reference given the context of use. If the use, even in a fixed context, doesn't determine reference, then use isn't understanding. The language on the perspective we talked ourselves into, has a full programme of use; but it still lacks an interpretation.
>
> This is the fatal step. To adopt a theory of meaning according to which a language whose whole use is specified still lacks something – namely its "interpretation" – is to accept a problem which *can* only have crazy solutions. To speak as if *this* were my problem, "I know how to use my language, but, now, how shall I single out an interpretation?" is to speak nonsense. Either the use already fixes the 'interpretation' or *nothing* can. (Putnam 1983: 23–4)[11]

Notes

1. Bertrand Russell is another example of a philosopher not afraid to change his mind. Indeed, Putnam bares a strong resemblance as a philosopher to Russell in at least two respects. Russell was a consummate practitioner and contributor to mathematical logic, as is Putnam, and Putnam like Russell is passionately concerned with social and moral issues.

2. It is certainly true that traditional realism has held to at least four assumptions: (i) there is a fixed totality of all objects – of things that there are; (ii) there is a fixed totality of properties and relations; (iii) within that second totality there is an unambiguous partition between properties we project on to the world (say evaluative and moral properties) and properties intrinsic to the world; and (iv) there is a fixed relation of "correspondence" between statements and the world that is sufficient to define the notion of a true statement.

3. More generally the procedure is as follows. Look at the domain of A. Call it $D(A)$. Let the one-place (for simplicity) relation or predicate R, part of the vocabulary of T, be interpreted in A by the relation RA holding among a non-empty proper subset of the objects in $D(A)$. Let f be a (one–one) permutation of $D(A)$. Then we can define a new one-place relation Rf on the permuted domain $f[D(A)]$ as follows: $Rf(f(a))$ if and only if $RA(a)$ for each a in $D(A)$. Now we have a new interpretation of the language L; its domain is the same but it assigns different objects to at least one one-place relation of the language L. Recall that the one-place relation RA is interpreted as a *proper* subset of the domain of A. So we can arrange for the permutation f to assign to a an object not having the property RA. So Rf will be different from our original R; different objects will fall under it; the reference of R (a predicate in the language L) will be different in the original model (where it is RA) and the permuted one (where it is Rf). Finally, if $<a_1, a_2, ..., a_n, ...>$ is any sequence of objects of $D(A)$ that, when assigned to the variables of L, make the sentences of T true, simply assign the sequence of objects $<f(a_1), f(a_2), ..., f(a_n), ...>$. What we can do for one non-trivial relation R occurring in T we can do for all of them together. We can readily see that the two interpretations are isomorphic, essentially because the permutation is one–one, so they will satisfy exactly the same sets of sentences. The new predicate or relation Rf is just what Putnam denotes as the $*$ property. So in his example RA is cat and Rf is cat*. Similarly, if S were another predicate of L, in Putnam's example SA would be mat and Sf would be mat* (see *RTH*: 34–8).

4. The existence of isomorphic models is very important in understanding what our theoretical knowledge can consist in. It is undoubtedly a very awkward phenomenon for various forms of empiricist accounts of our theoretical knowledge. See particularly William Demopoulos, "On the Rational Reconstruction of our Theoretical Knowledge" *British Journal for the Philosophy of Science* **54**(3) (2003), 371–403.

5. A natural number is any member of the unending sequence 0, 1, 2, 3, 4, 5, 6, ...

6. We can say that two sets have the same cardinality (or have the same cardinal number) if and only if there is a one-to-one correspondence among their members; that is, two sets have the same cardinality if and only if they are equinumerous. A set A may be said to have a cardinality strictly less than set B, if there is a one-to-one correspondence from A into a proper subset of B but no one-to-one correspondence exists between B and a subset of A.

7. Strictly speaking this is not correct, for two of the "axioms" are actually axiom *schema*, that is they stand for what is an infinite list of axioms. Thus the Zermelo separation schema – which says that for any set x and any condition F formalizable in the language of set theory there is a subset of x whose members are precisely those members of x that satisfy F – is really an infinite list of axioms each one of that list being an axiom for a specific condition F. A second example is the axiom schema of replacement, which says in effect that if x is a set and F any functional condition then the result of applying F to the members of the set x is also a set. This is really an infinite list of axioms, each axiom corresponding to a specific functional condition F.

8. This is also true of such notions as "is finite" or "is the power set of a given set".

9. This is a conclusion that Skolem himself drew in "Some Remarks on Axiomatised Set Theory", translated and reprinted in *From Frege to Gödel: A Source Book in Mathematical Logic*, J. van Heijenoort (ed.), 290–301 (Cambridge, MA: Harvard University Press, [1922] 1967).

10. Consider the condition formalizable in set theory that holds of a given set x if it is not a member of itself. By the Zermelo separation schema mentioned above, if the universe were a set then the collection of all sets that satisfy the condition would itself be a set. So we would have a set, call it r, the members of which are all and only those sets that are not members of themselves. What about r itself? If r is not a member of r then, by the fact that *all* non-self-membered sets are members of r, r must be a member of r. So r is a member of r. But then since something is a member of r only if it is not self-membered, r cannot be a member of r – which is a contradiction. So the universe cannot be a set; if it were we could apply the Zermelo separation schema for the condition "not being self-membered" and get the contradiction.

11. As Putnam himself says (*RTH*: 6, 66–9) there is a very close connection between these considerations and those of Wittgenstein on rule-following in *Philosophical Investigations*, G. E. M. Anscombe & R. Rhees (eds), G. E. M. Anscombe (trans.) (Oxford: Blackwell, 1953), para. 143–242.

References

Demopoulos, W. 2003. "On the Rational Reconstruction of our Theoretical Knowledge". *British Journal for the Philosophy of Science* 54(3), 371–403.

Putnam, H. 1975. "The Meaning of 'Meaning'". In *Language, Mind and Knowledge*, K. Gunderson (ed.). Minneapolis, MN: University of Minnesota Press.

Putnam, H. 1978. *Meaning and the Moral Sciences*. London: Routledge & Kegan Paul.

Putnam, H. 1981. *Reason, Truth and History*. Cambridge: Cambridge University Press.

Putnam, H. 1983. "Models and Reality". Reprinted in *Realism and Reason: Philosophical Papers, Volume 3*, 1–25. Cambridge: Cambridge University Press

Quine, W. V. 1960. *Word and Object*. Cambridge, MA: MIT Press.

Skolem, T. [1920] 1967. "Logico-combinatorial Investigations in the Satisfiability or Provability of Mathematical Propositions: A Simplified Proof of a Theorem by L. Lowenheim and Generalisations of the Theorem". Translated and reprinted in *From Frege to Gödel: A Source Book in Mathematical Logic*, J. van Heijenoort (ed.), 252–63. Cambridge, MA: Harvard University Press.

Skolem, T. [1922] 1967. "Some Remarks on Axiomatised Set Theory". Translated and reprinted in *From Frege to Gödel: A Source Book in Mathematical Logic*, J. van Heijenoort (ed.), 290–301. Cambridge, MA: Harvard University Press.

Wittgenstein, L. 1953. *Philosophical Investigations*, G. E. M. Anscombe & R. Rhees (eds), G. E. M. Anscombe (trans.). Oxford: Blackwell.

Wright, C. 1994. "On Putnam's Proof that we are not Brains-in-a-Vat". In *Reading Putnam*, P. Clark & B. Hale (eds), 216–41. Oxford: Blackwell.

Further reading

The evolution of Putnam's views on realism makes a fascinating study. Some of his early papers were highly critical of challenges to realism. Particularly notable in this respect are his papers "The Refutation of Conventionalism" and "The Meaning of 'Meaning'", reprinted in Hilary Putnam, *Mind, Language and Reality: Philosophical Papers, Volume 2* (Cambridge: Cambridge University Press, 1975), 153–91, 215–71, respectively, and "What is Mathematical Truth?", reprinted in Hilary Putnam, *Mathematics, Matter and Method: Philosophical Papers, Volume 1* (Cambridge: Cambridge University Press, 1975), 60–78. By the early 1980s, however, he had abandoned metaphysical realism and adopted "internal realism". Two classic papers laying out his arguments are "Models and Reality", reprinted in *Realism and Reason: Philosophical Papers, Volume 3* (Cambridge: Cambridge University Press, 1983), 1–25, and "Why There isn't a Ready Made World", reprinted in *Realism and Reason*, 205–28.

Three of the best critical responses to Putnam's "Models and Reality" are those of David Lewis, "Putnam's Paradox", *Australasian Journal of Philosophy* 62 (1984), 221–36, Timothy Bays, "On Putnam and His Models", *Journal of Philosophy* 98(7) (2001), 331–50, and M. Devitt, *Realism and Truth*, 2nd edn (Oxford: Oxford University Press, 1991), esp. 220–34, 330–38. *Reading Putnam* (Oxford: Blackwell, 1994), the collection of papers edited by Peter Clark and Bob Hale, contains nine papers largely devoted to Putnam's defence of internal realism. The contribution by Michael Hallett, "Putnam and the Skolem Paradox" (*Reading Putnam*, 66–97) is a sustained treatment of the model-theoretic arguments. The background work in logic and set theory to the model-theoretic arguments can be found in Robert R. Stoll, *Set Theory and Logic* (San Francisco, CA: W. H. Freeman, 1961), particularly chapters 5, 7 and 9. Crispin Wright's paper "On Putnam's Proof that we are not Brains-in-a-Vat" (*Reading Putnam*, 216–41) is one of the best treatments in the literature of Putnam's ingenious argument. Two further collections on Putnam's work on realism in general are C. S. Hill (ed.), *The Philosophy of Hilary Putnam*, *Philosophical Topics* 20(1) and James Conant & Urszula M. Zeglen (eds), *Hilary Putnam: Pragmatism and Realism* (London: Routledge, 2002).

The later development of Putnam's views on realism subsequent to the publication of *Reason, Truth and History* can be found in his Paul Carus Lectures, *The Many Faces of Realism* (La Salle, IL: Open Court, 1987), his Gifford Lectures delivered at the University of St Andrews, *Renewing Philosophy* (Cambridge, MA: Harvard University Press, 1992) and "The Dewey Lectures 1994: Sense, Nonsense, and the Senses: An Inquiry into the Powers of the Human Mind", *Journal of Philosophy* 91(9) (September 1994); all three are collected in Putnam's *The Threefold Cord: Mind, Body and World*, (New York: Columbia University Press, 1999). For his current views on some of the themes in *Reason, Truth and History* that have not been treated in this essay see his *The Collapse of the Fact / Value Dichotomy and Other Essays* (Cambridge, MA: Harvard University Press, 2004) and his *Ethics without Ontology* (Cambridge, MA: Harvard University Press, 2004). The twin earth argument and some of the central themes of *Meaning and the Moral Sciences* are explored extensively in Andrew Pressin & Sanford Goldberg (eds), *The Twin Earth Chronicles: Twenty Years of Reflection on Hilary Putnam's the "Meaning of Meaning"* (Armonk, NY: M. E. Sharpe, 1996).

10
Bernard Williams
Ethics and the Limits of Philosophy

A. W. Moore

Introduction

Bernard Williams (1929–2003) was one of the greatest twentieth-century British philosophers, renowned especially for his work in moral philosophy. When *Ethics and the Limits of Philosophy* was published, in 1985, he had already written numerous highly influential articles in the area. He had also written a beautifully concise and widely read introduction to the subject entitled *Morality: An Introduction to Ethics* ([1972] 1993a), and had contributed the second half of a joint publication with J. J. C. Smart entitled *Utilitarianism: For and Against* (Smart & Williams 1973); Williams's contribution, "A Critique of Utilitarianism", provided the case against. A number of significant articles followed. So did *Shame and Necessity* (1993b), in which he pursued a recurrent interest in ancient Greek ethical thought, and *Truth and Truthfulness: An Essay in Genealogy* (2002), in which he provided a Nietzschean account of the virtues of accuracy and sincerity. An earlier publication, *Descartes: The Project of Pure Enquiry* (1978), although not itself a work of moral philosophy, had provided some of the basic tools that Williams subsequently used to contrast ethical thinking with thinking in other areas. But it is *Ethics and the Limits of Philosophy*, by fairly common consent his greatest work, that serves as the *locus classicus* for his ideas in moral philosophy.

Ethics and the Limits of Philosophy may fairly be described as a work in "analytic" philosophy. Not that Williams himself is much concerned about that.

He is more concerned, as he indicates in the preface, about whether his book has the virtue most prized by analytic philosophy: clarity.

It has a kind of clarity. But it does not have the kind of clarity that makes for easy reading. Williams never belabours the obvious; and he rarely makes explicit what he takes to be implicit in something he has already said. His writing is therefore extremely dense. It leaves an enormous amount of work for the reader. Its clarity lies in its content: it is the clarity of understanding by which the reader's work is eventually rewarded. Williams is in my view a superb stylist. But the principal joys of reading him are not the joys, great as they are, of savouring his many witticisms and elegant turns of phrase. They are the joys of honest endeavour: of struggling to come to terms with writing that is rigorous, imaginative, brilliant, deep, and above all thoroughly humane.

When Williams first began to write in moral philosophy, in the early 1960s, the subject had for some time been embroiled in abstract second-order debates about moral language, for instance about whether an act of moral condemnation, such as telling someone "It was reprehensible of you to do that" involved making any genuine assertion. Williams was keen to re-establish contact with the real concerns that animate our ordinary ethical experience. *Ethics and the Limits of Philosophy* is in many respects the culmination of a wonderfully successful crusade to do just that. It shows admirably how much moral philosophy can achieve. There is therefore a profound irony in the fact that one of the main themes of the book, advertised in the second half of its title, is how *little* moral philosophy can achieve. In particular, moral philosophy cannot deliver the very thing that might have been expected of it, a *theory* to guide ethical reasoning. What it can do is to assist the self-understanding of those whose ethical reasoning already has guidance from elsewhere. That is, it can help to provide a critique of lived ethical experience. And that, as alluded to in the first half of the book's title, is precisely what Williams wants it to do in these pages.

In a fascinating postscript to the book, he writes that the hopes expressed in the book "can be compressed into a belief in three things: in truth, in truthfulness, and in the meaning of an individual life" (p. 198). He goes on to explain what he means by this. He hopes, first, that the kind of self-understanding that he seeks to promote may be thoroughly informed by the truth, particularly by the truth about our social and historical bearings; secondly, that our ethical experience may stand up to such self-understanding, even where such self-understanding indicates that it is not what it seems; and thirdly, that if our ethical experience does stand up to such self-understanding, this will leave individuals free to make sense in and of their own lives. In spite of Williams's scepticism about the power of philosophy, his own book is a contribution to the realization of all three hopes.

Chapter 1:"Socrates' Question"

Williams begins with a question that, because it is posed by Socrates in Plato's *Republic* (1961: 352d), he refers to as Socrates' question. As Socrates says, the question is not a trivial one. It is nothing less than the question of *how one should live*.

From the very outset Williams makes clear how little we should expect from philosophy in respect of this question: we certainly should not expect an answer to it. But philosophy may help us to understand the question. A large part of Chapter 1 is accordingly concerned with examining Socrates' question and in particular with determining how much it presupposes. It presupposes little enough, in Williams's view, to be the best starting-point for moral philosophy. But it is not, Williams insists, presuppositionless. One thing that it presupposes is, of course, that issues about how to live can be properly addressed at this high level of generality – if not that there is such a thing as "the right life ... for human beings as such" (p. 20).

One thing that Socrates' question does *not* presuppose, however, is what Williams calls "morality", a particular style of ethical thought to which he returns in the final chapter and which he sees as a pervasive and pernicious feature of the modern world. Whereas "ethics" is just moral philosophy by another name, and is therefore concerned with all manner of approaches to Socrates' question, "morality" – in the helpful contrast that Williams uses these two terms to draw – is one particular approach to Socrates' question that uses certain very distinctive conceptual tools.[1] Two of the most basic of these tools are the idea of a purely voluntary act and the idea of a moral obligation. Morality interprets Socrates' question as a question about which purely voluntary acts there is some moral obligation to perform, and which there is some moral obligation to refrain from performing, and it treats a moral obligation as an inescapable demand that eclipses any other consideration.

Williams challenges both ideas. He thinks that the idea of a "purely" voluntary act, together with all the other ideas in morality's conceptual toolkit that relate to it – responsibility, guilt, blame, and suchlike – are "an illusion" (p. 196). And he resents the importunacy and arrogance that he finds in the idea of a moral obligation. There are, Williams urges, all *sorts* of considerations that can be brought to bear on Socrates' question other than those of obligation. They include ethical considerations of other kinds, such as considerations of general welfare and of virtue. And they include non-ethical considerations, such as aesthetic considerations and indeed considerations of self-interest.

Nor should we think that either ethical considerations or non-ethical considerations can all ultimately be reduced to one basic type. A dominant theme of this chapter is that any realistic answer to Socrates' question must reflect the multi-textured complexity of life itself.

Chapter 2:"The Archimedean Point"

I have talked, as Williams himself does, about "ethical" considerations and "non-ethical" considerations. Williams deliberately holds back from providing an explicit definition of this contrast, which he takes to be both intuitive and vague. What matters, for current purposes, is that ethical considerations – which pertain to our living in society with other people, and which include, for instance, considerations of justice and of mutual respect – sometimes conflict with considerations of shallow self-interest.[2]

This means that if they (ethical considerations) are indeed to be brought to bear on Socrates' question, then there is an issue about how they are to be justified. And it is this issue that structures the next five chapters of the book. Before we address it, however, we must be clear about what we expect of any justification. In particular, Williams says, we must be clear about:

- what the justification is to be given *against*;
- whom it is to be given *to*;
- where it is to be given *from*.

Here Williams is reacting, with characteristic measure, to a kind of alarmism that he finds in much moral philosophy. This alarmism is born of two things. The first of these is the conviction that, if someone is completely amoral, that is to say if someone is completely unmoved by ethical considerations,[3] then it ought to be possible to remedy this by giving the person a suitably compelling *argument*, an argument that it is moral philosophy's very business to supply. The second thing generating the alarmism is despair at the prospect of moral philosophy's supplying anything of the sort. Williams shares the despair, but not the conviction. In other words, he agrees that there is no hope of moral philosophy's supplying any such argument; but he does *not* agree that it is moral philosophy's business to do so. This is yet another example of his scepticism about the kind of force that philosophy can exert. To share the conviction (to think that it *is* moral philosophy's business to supply such an argument) would be, in effect, to think that there ought to be a justification of ethical considerations that can be given: *against* amoralism; *to* the amoralist; *from* some kind of Archimedean point, that is to say from a set of assumptions that the amoralist can himself be expected to share.

Williams's hopes are more modest, or if not more modest then certainly different. He is willing to look for a justification of ethical considerations that can be given *against* amoralism; but not *to* the amoralist; and therefore not necessarily *from* an Archimedean point. The justification that he seeks is one that can be given to those for whom ethical considerations already have some force. In other words, the point is not to *persuade* anyone of anything, but to promote self-understanding, the kind of self-understanding that Williams takes to be the real business of moral philosophy.

Not "necessarily" from an Archimedean point, I said. If the justification is not expected to serve as an instrument of conversion, then of course there is not the same rationale for trying to proceed from assumptions that the amoralist will share. Even so, there is *some* rationale. For the weaker the assumptions on which the justification rests, the deeper the self-understanding it can promote.

Very well; but how weak can these assumptions be? Is proceeding from an Archimedean point possible? Williams does not answer this question in Chapter 2. What he does, at the very end of the chapter, is indicate where the Archimedean point would have to lie if there *were* such a thing: "in the idea of rational action" (p. 28). The next two chapters explore the two best-known attempts, and indeed the two best attempts, to proceed from there: that of Aristotle, whose conception of rational action is relatively rich and determinate; and that of Kant, whose conception of rational action is as thin and as abstract as possible. If neither of those succeeds, then the project of justifying ethical considerations from an Archimedean point, or, as Williams also puts it, "from the ground up" (pp. 28, 202), must be abandoned.

Chapter 3: "Foundations: Well-Being"

I said in the previous section that ethical considerations sometimes conflict with considerations of shallow self-interest. For Aristotle, "shallow" is the operative word. To act in accord with ethical considerations is, on Aristotle's view, to do what is *really*, or most *fundamentally*, in one's self-interest.

There are various reasons why someone might think that ethical considerations and considerations of self-interest ultimately coincide, any one of which they could invoke to show that it was rational to act in accord with the former: in other words, any one of which they could invoke in a justification of ethical considerations from an Archimedean point of the kind described at the end of the previous section. For instance, they might claim that divine retribution awaits those who do not act in accord with ethical considerations. For Aristotle, however, the connection with rationality goes deeper than that. He thinks that acting in accord with ethical considerations, or acting virtuously as he would say, is itself intrinsically rational, in that it gives maximally coherent shape to everything that one is disposed to want or feel or do; and that it is in one's self-interest because what human wellbeing most fundamentally consists in is the life of rationality that quintessentially distinguishes human beings from other animals. (There is a sense, then, in which Aristotle holds that acting virtuously is both rational because it is in one's self-interest and in one's self-interest because it is rational.)

Since Aristotle sees the primary justificatory task of ethics in just the same way as Williams does – to preach, as it were, to the converted – he has nothing to say to those for whom ethical considerations have no force. He has nothing to say *to* them. But he needs to say something *about* them. He needs, as Williams puts it, to provide *"a theory of error*, a substantive account of how people may fail to recognize their real interests" (p. 43, emphasis added). The account that Aristotle provides is in terms of upbringing. For Aristotle, virtuousness cannot be achieved without the right training, any more than other features of the life of rationality can, say literacy or numeracy. Those whose upbringing does not include the right training acquire bad habits of pleasure-seeking that cloud their judgement.

Williams is unimpressed by this account, largely because he is unimpressed by the underlying teleology that makes it appropriate to talk about what human wellbeing most fundamentally consists in. He is also sceptical about whether any modern scientific developments, in, say, evolutionary biology or psychology, can be used to plug this gap. He does think that there are some vital insights afforded by the Aristotelian picture, not least that ethical considerations derive whatever force they have from human nature, as expressed in people's dispositions. But without the underlying teleology, this is not enough to fix what those considerations shall be. Human nature is subject to all sorts of social and historical conditioning, and is expressed in all sorts of dispositions. There are many different ethical outlooks that these dispositions can be used to support, some of which exclude one another. (Williams has more to say about this in the penultimate chapter, on relativism.) There is no such thing, to echo the quotation I gave earlier, as "the right life … for human beings as such".

Chapter 4: "Foundations: Practical Reason"

Having rejected Aristotle's attempt to justify ethical considerations from an Archimedean point, Williams turns to Kant's. Kant likewise wants to show that it is rational to act in accord with ethical considerations, or to act from duty as he would say. But unlike Aristotle, he does not primarily see this in terms of human wellbeing. He takes as his starting-point the very idea of rational action, prescinding altogether from what human beings, either as a species or as individuals, might be disposed to want or feel. Kant argues that it is a precondition of being a rational agent that one be motivated by ethical considerations.

Williams sees *some* hope for an argument along these lines. More specifically, he sees some hope for an argument to the effect that it is a precondition of being a rational agent that one value one's own freedom. But that falls short of what Kant requires. To value one's own freedom is not to be motivated by ethical considerations. (It is not to value the freedom of any other rational agent.)

How does Kant take the extra step? By abstracting from *all* but the rational agent's rational agency. Kant thinks that a rational agent must, if he is to be true to his own essence, act on principles of *pure* rational agency ("pure practical reason"). That is to say, he must act on principles that would be apt to regulate the actions of *all* rational agents. This does require that he value freedom, and indeed rationality; but not his own freedom, nor his own rationality; rather, freedom and rationality *per se*. He must value all rational beings for their own sake. As Kant puts it, "a rational being must always regard himself as lawgiving in a kingdom of ends," where by "a kingdom of ends" he means a law-governed union of rational beings considered as ends in themselves (Kant 1996: 4: 433–4).

Acting, for Kant, is in this respect like thinking. One does not think rationally unless one thinks in accord with principles that would be apt to regulate the thinking of *all* rational thinkers. Thus it would be irrational to think that the real colour of an object was whatever colour one first took it to be. This would leave one vulnerable to the possibility that an object that one first took to be yellow was first taken by someone else, in different lighting conditions perhaps, to be orange. (Its real colour could not be *both* yellow *and* orange. There would have to be some principled way of deciding between these conflicting appearances.)

It is this analogy between acting and thinking in Kant's approach that Williams takes to be precisely what is wrong with the approach. Acting and thinking, for Williams, are *not* alike in this respect. One does not think rationally unless one thinks in a way that is conducive to believing the truth, where what it takes for one to believe the truth is the same as what it takes for anyone else to believe the truth. But one can act rationally by acting in a way that is conducive to satisfying one's desires, where what it takes for one to satisfy one's desires may be quite different from, indeed in tension with, what it takes for someone else to satisfy his or hers. Kant's attempt to justify ethical considerations from an Archimedean point is, in Williams's view, no more successful than Aristotle's.

Chapter 5:"Styles of Ethical Theory"

There may still be some real prospect of justifying ethical considerations from something other than an Archimedean point. For instance, it may be possible, by taking for granted the kind of force that ethical considerations can have, to justify *specific* ethical considerations against their rivals. Moreover, there is no reason why the Aristotelian justification and the Kantian justification, each of which may have failed in its own terms, should not be exploited in providing a justification of this kind. (Thus while there may not be a rational requirement, of the kind that Kant thought there was, to import the same impartiality into one's deliberations about how to act as one does into one's deliberations about what to think, there may be an *ethical* requirement to do so.) The most obvious shape for such a justification to take is that of an *ethical theory*. In pursuing the question whether anything of this kind is available, which Williams does in Chapters 5 and 6, he provides himself with an opportunity to discuss, not only the very idea of an ethical theory, but also some of the ethical theories that have actually been proposed, including one version of utilitarianism, which, along with Aristotelianism and Kantianism, is often reckoned to be the third apex of a dialectical triangle that has dominated moral philosophy.

Williams defines an ethical theory as "a theoretical account of what ethical thought and practice are, which account either implies a general test for the correctness of basic ethical beliefs and principles or else implies that there cannot be such a test" (p. 72). The reason for this rather strange disjunctive definition is that accounts of both kinds purport to tell us, on philosophical grounds, how we should think in ethics. One might suppose that only accounts of the first kind did this. But consider accounts of the second kind (the kind whereby there cannot be a test for the correctness of basic ethical beliefs and principles); and think what would be the limiting case of such an account. It would be the view that "holding an ethical position simply consists of choosing one and sticking to it" (p. 74). Even this view purports to tell us, on philosophical grounds, how we should think in ethics. It does this by telling us "that we cannot really think much at all in ethics" (*ibid.*).

Williams, by contrast, wants to give an account of what ethical thought and practice are whereby we can certainly think in ethics, in all sorts of ways, but "*philosophy* can do little to determine how we should do so" (*ibid.*, emphasis added). He is as sceptical about the prospects of a sound ethical theory as he is about the prospects of a successful foundational project of the kind that we saw Aristotle and Kant undertake.

The two styles of ethical theory on which he turns his sceptical gaze in Chapter 5 are contractualism and utilitarianism. Contractualism is a close cousin of

Kantianism and holds that ethical thought is concerned with what informed, unforced agreements people could reach. Utilitarianism holds that ethical thought is concerned with welfare and its maximization. Each of these leaves considerable room for further refinement (for example, in the case of utilitarianism, by leaving open whether it is individual acts, rules, practices or institutions that are to be assessed in terms of the maximization of welfare, and indeed what counts as welfare). The versions of contractualism and utilitarianism on which Williams focuses are those of John Rawls and Richard Hare respectively, these being particularly clear and powerful versions and, as such, ideal non-straw-man targets at which to direct his disquiet about both styles of theory.

Chapter 6: "Theory and Prejudice"

Let us return to the very idea of an ethical theory. As I have already indicated, this is one of Williams's principal targets in the book.

What kind of authority can such a theory have? To what must it be answerable? In the first instance, it must be answerable to intuitions that we have (for instance, about what it would or would not be acceptable to do in various situations). This is not to deny that an ethical theory can eventually be used to criticize and replace some of our intuitions. Indeed one of the roles that such a theory will be expected to play is precisely that of eliminating conflict between our intuitions, by using some of them to overturn others. The point, however, is that no ethical theory can play this role except by imposing some coherent, manageable structure on to our intuitions that preserves as many of them as possible.

No *ethical theory* can play this role except in this way. There are other, less systematic ways of eliminating conflict between our intuitions. For example, we can simply exercise our judgement about each particular conflict as it arises. Ethical theories can claim no special authority simply by virtue of their capacity to eliminate conflict. From where, then, does their supposed authority derive? In large part, from what Williams calls "a rationalistic conception of rationality" (p. 18). This is an application to personal deliberation of an ideal of public life whereby "in principle every decision … [is] based on grounds that can be discursively explained" (*ibid.*), an ideal that is not realized when we reach a decision by simply exercising our judgement in some particular case. But why should we grant the application of this ideal to personal deliberation? Does it not encourage us to look for an orderliness, a systematicity, and an economy of ideas that are quite unsuited to the complexities of real-life personal deliberation? And anyway, what does the ideal add to the intuitions themselves? As

Williams memorably insists elsewhere, "'You can't kill that, it's a child' is more convincing as a reason than any reason which might be advanced for its being a reason" (1981b: 81; cf. pp. 113–14).

To be sure, it is important for us to reflect on our intuitions. And if we do, we may expose some of them as irrational prejudices; but irrational in as much as they are based on self-deception or social deceit, say, not in as much as they conflict with some ethical theory that we have constructed. It is not a requirement on reflection that it issue in any kind of theory. Nor, for that matter, should we attach special weight, among our ethical views, to those that are the product of reflection.

Utilitarians, notoriously, do attach special weight to those of our ethical views that are the product of reflection; notoriously, because it is both a familiar and an objectionable feature of their theory that it *promotes* disharmony between those of our ethical views that are the product of reflection and those that are not. (In its less objectionable form, the contrast is between different views that we have at different times: in the "cool hour" of reflection and in the heat of the moment. In its more objectionable form, the contrast is between different views that different *groups* among us have: the reflective élite and the rest. The latter is what Williams calls "Government House utilitarianism" (p. 108).) Utilitarianism has this feature because the intuitions in favour of it, which its advocates see as the product of enlightened reflection, themselves provide a reason to preserve and encourage non-utilitarian thinking at the unreflective level: this is because people are more likely to maximize welfare at that level by trying to do something other than maximize welfare.

By the end of Chapter 6, the idea of an ethical theory has more or less withered in the glare of Williams's general scepticism about philosophical ethics, "a scepticism," as he comments dryly, "that is more about philosophy than it is about ethics" (p. 74).

Chapter 7: "The Linguistic Turn"

There are some large issues in moral philosophy concerning the *metaphysics* of value. Is there, for instance, some fundamental distinction between fact and value: between the way things are irrespective of what we think about them and the evaluations that we project on to the way things are? So far, these issues have been in the background. In Chapters 7–9 Williams brings them to the fore. His concern in Chapter 7 is to see what insight can be gained into these issues by using the principal methodological tool of analytic philosophy: the analysis of language.

Many people believe that there is a distinction to be drawn between evaluative words, such as "heinous", "supererogatory", "reprehensible" and "good", and non-evaluative words, such as "sulphuric", "octogenarian", "waterproof" and "blonde"; and that it is impossible to define any word of the former kind using only words of the latter kind. The name "naturalistic fallacy", which was coined by G. E. Moore (1903: §10), is often used for the misguided attempt to do this impossible thing.[4] Provided that there is indeed such a distinction to be drawn, then we might reasonably expect to gain a great deal of insight into the metaphysics of value by attending to the different ways in which words of the two kinds are used.

In fact, however, Williams thinks that this is back to front. He thinks that, in so far as we have any idea what we are supposed to be attending to, indeed in so far as there is any such linguistic distinction to be drawn, this is because of some insight that we are already able to bring to bear on language concerning the metaphysical distinction between fact and value. "In so far as" is in any case the operative phrase. For although Williams himself acknowledges a distinction of sorts between fact and value, it is a very subtle distinction and one that he thinks is not at all well reflected in our language. He thinks that, on the contrary, our language does much to hide it from us, and to foster various illusions about the metaphysics of value (and about the nature of ethics more generally).

What we actually find in language are hundreds upon hundreds of "hybrid" words, such as "chaste", "unfaithful", "brutal" and "proud". These are words that stand for what Williams calls "thick" ethical concepts. The notion of a thick ethical concept is an extremely important one for Williams. It is also one of his most significant legacies. What a thick ethical concept is is a concept that has *both* an evaluative aspect, in that to apply it in a given situation is, in part, to evaluate the situation, *and* a factual aspect, in that to apply it in a given situation is to make a judgement that is subject to correction if the situation turns out not to be a certain way. Thus if I claim that you have been unfaithful, I thereby censure you; but I also say something straightforwardly false if it turns out that you have not in fact gone back on any relevant agreement. Nor is the concept of infidelity just a value-free concept with a flag of disapproval attached. Williams, in opposition to many who have considered these concepts, argues vigorously that fact and value are *inextricably* intertwined in them. This is one reason why the language in which they are couched gives such a poor indication of the underlying metaphysics.

The analysis of language is of very limited use in moral philosophy, then. Nevertheless, it is of some use. It can serve to remind us that our ethical life, just like our ethical language, is a complex multifarious social phenomenon, which varies from one time to another and from one group to another; and that ethical understanding, which needs to account for such variation, also thereby "needs a dimension of social explanation" (p. 131).

Chapter 8: "Knowledge, Science, Convergence"

Chapter 8 is the heart of the book. It is in this chapter that Williams directly confronts these issues about the metaphysics of value (the issue whether there is some fundamental distinction between fact and value and the like).

These issues are also issues, in some sense, about the *objectivity* of our ethical thinking, and it is in these terms that Williams broaches them. He thinks that there is a kind of objectivity that, on any realistic view of the matter, fails to attach to our ethical thinking, even though it does attach to our thinking in other areas. (This connects with my earlier claim that he acknowledges a distinction of sorts between fact and value.) The question is: *what* kind of objectivity?

The word "objectivity" is used in a bewildering variety of ways. But on any construal, objectivity has something to do with agreement. To say that there is a kind of objectivity that does or does not attach to our thinking in a given area is to say something about the prospect of our reaching principled agreement in that area, or, as Williams puts it, of our *converging* in our beliefs in that area. Very well, then, what exactly is it that Williams is prepared to say about the prospect of our converging in some of our beliefs that he is not prepared to say about the prospect of our converging in our ethical beliefs? This turns out to be a surprisingly delicate question.

Williams's position is not that we can reasonably expect to converge in some of our beliefs but cannot reasonably expect to do so in our ethical beliefs. Still less is it that we actually do converge in some of our beliefs but never do so in our ethical beliefs. Nor does it have to do with whether, where there *is* convergence, the beliefs in question merit the title of "knowledge" or not. It has to do with the different ways of *explaining* whatever convergence there is. The fundamental contrast is between science and ethics.

Williams's position is as follows. We do sometimes converge in our ethical beliefs, and those beliefs do sometimes merit the title "knowledge". This can happen when the beliefs in question involve a thick ethical concept. Thus people who use the concept of chastity might have no difficulty in agreeing, and indeed in knowing, whether a certain act is chaste. The crux, however, lies in what is involved in their using the concept of chastity in the first place. Granted the concept's distinctive combination of evaluation and factuality, using it is part of living in a particular social world, a world in which certain things are prized

218

and others abhorred. People need to live in *some* such social world. But, as history amply demonstrates, there is no one such social world in which people need to live. They certainly do not need to live in a world that sustains the concept of chastity. Thus any good reflective explanation for why people converge in their beliefs about what is chaste must include an explanation for why they use the concept of chastity at all; why they live in *that* social world. (This is the "dimension of social explanation" to which Williams refers at the end of Chapter 7.) This explanation cannot itself invoke the concept of chastity, because it must be from a vantage point of reflection outside the social world in question. So it cannot directly vindicate their beliefs. (That is, it cannot conform to the schema: "These people converge in their beliefs about *x* because they are suitably sensitive to truths about *x*." It cannot represent them as agreeing about what is chaste because of insights that they have into what is chaste.) By contrast, a good reflective explanation for why people converge in their beliefs about a particular range of scientific issues, say in their beliefs about what oxygen is like, can invoke the very concepts at work in the beliefs, and hence, provided that the beliefs have been arrived at properly, can vindicate them. (It *can* conform to the schema specified above. It can represent these people as agreeing about what oxygen is like because of insights that they have achieved into what oxygen is like – because of what they have discovered about oxygen.)

One consequence of this position is that whatever ethical knowledge people have they have by unwaveringly and unguardedly exercising their thick ethical concepts. There is no ethical knowledge to be had by reflecting on whether it is "right" to use those concepts or not. This is why Williams presents his argument for the existence of ethical knowledge by invoking the fiction of a "hypertraditional" society, a society that is "maximally homogeneous and minimally given to reflection" (p. 142). It is there, for Williams, that the clearest examples of ethical knowledge are to be found.

But Williams goes further. He argues that, in a society such as our own, where there is plenty of reflection, the reflection can have an unsettling effect. People can come to abandon some of their thick ethical concepts, say because they realize that those concepts are associated with false beliefs, or simply because they become aware of alternatives. That makes it impossible for them to retain whatever knowledge they had by exercising the concepts. It is thus that Williams comes to draw one of the most striking and most controversial conclusions in the book: "the notably un-Socratic conclusion," as he calls it, "that, in ethics, *reflection can destroy knowledge*" (p. 148, original emphasis). This conclusion is "un-Socratic" because Socrates, whose reflective question initiated this whole enquiry and who insisted that a life without reflection – an "unexamined" life – was not worth living, believed that "nothing unreflective could be knowledge

219

in the first place" (p. 168). I shall return to the idea that reflection can destroy knowledge in the final section.

Chapter 9: "Relativism and Reflection"

The contrast between science and ethics that Williams explores in Chapter 8 leads him to say that "science has some chance of being more or less what it seems, a systematized theoretical account of how the world really is, while ethical thought has no chance of being everything it seems" (p. 135). In particular, ethical thought "can never fully manifest the fact that it rests in human dispositions" (pp. 199–200). I have already referred to the hope that Williams expresses in the postscript to the book, that our ethical experience may stand up to any self-understanding that exposes it as other than it seems. In Chapter 9 Williams addresses the question of how, given the onslaught of Chapter 8, it can do this.

What we need, he says, is *confidence*. This is a social phenomenon. Although it is individuals who possess confidence, their confidence is typically fostered and reinforced by such social devices as upbringing, the support of institutions and public discourse. (What does not much help it, Williams insists – developing one of his main themes – is philosophy. On the contrary, philosophy helps to create the need for it.) Confidence enables individuals to abide by their thick ethical concepts despite the unsettling effects of reflection. It is a good thing. But it is not a supremely good thing. Some ways of achieving it, for example by suppressing rational argument, involve undue sacrifice of other things that are good, and they are to be resisted.

Another question that Williams addresses in Chapter 9 is what form of relativism, if any, is implied by his conception: that is, by his conception of different social worlds sustaining different thick ethical concepts, in some cases different to the point of irreconcilability. Not, Williams urges, the crudest form of relativism, whereby we should "be equally well disposed to everyone else's ethical beliefs" (p. 159). There is nothing in his conception to stop us from finding some people's ethical beliefs abhorrent and, where those beliefs impinge on us, trying to combat them. How can there be? It is, as Williams points out, "seriously confused" to think that a relativism about ethical beliefs can issue in "a nonrelativistic morality of universal toleration" (*ibid.*). Even so, Williams's conception, by drawing our attention to the striking differences between our own ethical outlook and the ethical outlooks of other societies, is bound to leave us dissatisfied with the blank thought "We are right, and everyone else is wrong." So does it not imply *some* form of relativism?

Strictly speaking, Williams thinks, it does not. That is, it does not *preclude* the blank thought "We are right, and everyone else is wrong." Nevertheless, having made that blank thought look very unattractive, it does *leave room* for some form of relativism, some way of going beyond the blank thought. It is in this connection that Williams introduces what he calls "the relativism of distance" (p. 162). This is the view that only when a society is sufficiently "close" to ours, which is to say, roughly, only when it is a real option for us to adopt the ethical outlook of that society, is there any question of *appraising* its ethical outlook (as "right", "wrong", "unjust" or whatever). The relativism for which Williams thinks his conception leaves room is a qualified version of this: "qualified" because he does not deny that *some* appraisal of the ethical outlooks of distant societies is allowed and may even, in the specific case of appraisal with respect to justice, be required. Such a qualified relativism of distance may look pretty attenuated. But again there is the contrast with science. A scientific outlook, however distant the society to which it belongs, must always be considered either right or wrong.

Chapter 10: "Morality, the Peculiar Institution"

Chapter 10 is something of an addendum to the rest of the book. In the section on Chapter 1 above, I talked about Williams's antipathy to the particular style of ethical thought that he calls "morality". It is in Chapter 10 that he explains what morality is, "and why we would be better off without it" (p. 174).

I shall not rehearse what I have already said about this. Two points are worth adding briefly. First, despite Williams's opposition to the idea of a moral obligation, he does not oppose *all* ideas of obligation. He readily admits that, in order to live in society with one another, we need to have certain basic and more or less categorical expectations (such as the expectation that we shall not be lied to, and the expectation that we shall not be killed); and that one way in which an ethical life can help here is by instilling in people dispositions to treat the corresponding requirements (in these two cases, the requirement not to lie, and the requirement not to kill) as obligations. Someone under such an obligation may conclude that he or she absolutely *cannot*, or absolutely *must*, do a certain thing. But, Williams insists, this type of conclusion is not, contra morality, peculiar to ethics. Someone may reach the same type of conclusion "for reasons of prudence, self-protection, aesthetic or artistic concern, or sheer self-assertion" (p. 188).

The second point is that Williams gives a very persuasive diagnosis for the appeal of morality. It expresses "the ideal that human existence can be ultimately just" (p. 195). It does this by casting the personal quality that matters more than any other, namely being moral, as beyond all luck, in contrast to being happy or being gifted or being loved, say. But this is precisely where Williams takes greatest exception to morality. "The idea of a value that lies beyond all luck is," he insists, "an illusion" (p. 196). It is the idea of a value that lies "beyond any empirical determination"; a value that lies "not only in trying rather than succeeding, since success depends partly on luck, but in a kind of trying that lies beyond the level at which the capacity to try can itself be a matter of luck" (p. 195). There is, for Williams, no such place for it to lie. In the concluding sentence of the chapter he castigates morality as "a deeply rooted and still powerful misconception of life" (p. 196).

Conclusion

Ethics and the Limits of Philosophy is a wonderful book. To some readers it may appear unduly negative. Too much of it, they may say, consists of attacks on other people's attempts to achieve things in moral philosophy: for instance, on Aristotle's and Kant's attempts to justify ethical considerations from an Archimedean point; on the attempts of those with theoretical aspirations to justify ethical considerations from something other than an Archimedean point; on the attempts of analytic philosophers to gain insights into the metaphysics of value through the analysis of language; and on the attempts of moralists to secure some ultimate justice in our lives. But, even granted that the bulk of the book is negative in this way, there is something positive, indeed courageous, about the very project of coming to terms with all these attacks.[5]

As far as the positive element in the book is concerned, the discussion of confidence in Chapter 9, along with the account of ethical knowledge in which that discussion is embedded, is one of its most significant features, and I shall close by trying briefly to allay some worries about this account. For there are many critics of the book who wonder whether what Williams says about ethical knowledge even makes sense. What has concerned them most is his claim that ethical knowledge can be destroyed by reflection. Williams intends this claim in such a way that those whose knowledge has been destroyed can, in reflecting, *still recognize their former knowledge as knowledge*. This looks incoherent. How can they recognize their former knowledge as knowledge unless they still know what they knew at the time?

In order to make sense of Williams's claim, it helps, I think, to invoke the notion of a point of view. Ethical knowledge is knowledge that involves some thick ethical concept, and is *ipso facto* from some point of view, an ethical point of view defined, in part, by the beliefs and evaluations that give the thick ethical concept its point. (Scientific knowledge, by contrast, is, or at least may be, from no point of view. In as much as it is, it can help to constitute what Williams famously calls an "absolute conception" of reality (p. 111) – an idea that he first developed in his book on Descartes (Williams 1978: 64–8).) Ethical knowledge is by no means the only knowledge that is from some point of view. Tensed knowledge – knowledge about what *was* the case, or about what *is* the case, or about what *will be* the case – is another obvious example. In the case of tensed knowledge, the point of view in question is a temporal one, rather than an ethical one. Now we no longer occupy temporal points of view that we once did. So we are no longer in a position to know some of what we once knew from those points of view. For example, we are no longer in a position to know what we knew when we claimed, pre-1969, "No one has ever walked on the moon." (Admittedly, there are issues here concerning the individuation of knowledge. For of course we are in a position to know that no one *had then* ever walked on the moon. But I think that there are ways of addressing these issues which leave us free to distinguish between what we know now and what we knew then; and which vindicate the claim that what we knew then we are no longer in a position to know.) This does not prevent us from reflecting on our former knowledge and still recognizing it as knowledge. Why, then, should there by any problem in the ethical case, where our no longer occupying an ethical point of view can likewise mean that we are no longer in a position to know what we knew from that point of view?

To be sure, there are further questions concerning what warrant we have for saying that our former knowledge has been *destroyed*. It needs to be impossible for us, in the full light of reflection, to re-adopt the abandoned point of view (just as it is impossible for us, given the passage of time, to re-adopt a temporal point of view). Furthermore, it needs to be impossible in a suitably demanding sense of "impossible". The mere psychological impossibility of our re-adopting the abandoned point of view would not suffice.

In order to see how reflection can indeed create a suitably stringent impossibility here, consider the related case of someone who, after reflection, is afflicted by Cartesian doubts. Such a person may once have known perfectly well that there was a table in front of him but now finds, after reflection, that he has no more than a shaken belief that there is a table in front of him, a belief that no longer counts as knowledge and that cannot, while he is reflecting, be converted back into knowledge. What sense of "cannot" is *this*? Certainly there is a psychological impossibility in this case. But is there not more? Has the reflection not created a demand for justification that is incapable of being met, with the result that no reflective state that he can now get into is properly to *count* as a state of knowledge? If it would not be absurd to say that it has – and I think it would not be – then neither would it be absurd to say that the impossibility in cases of the sort that Williams envisages is similarly constitutive.[6] This would certainly make the impossibility strong enough for his purposes.

Williams himself has much to say on these issues, of course (see especially pp. 167–71). Suffice to conclude that, like everything else in this book, it withstands a good deal of reflection.[7]

Notes

1. Although the contrast is helpful, the terminology is less so, and the reader needs to beware that many standard uses of the word "moral" and its cognates, which Williams himself appropriates, have more to do with what he dubs "ethics" than with what he dubs "morality". The most blatant example of this is in the very phrase "moral philosophy". Another example, which we shall encounter shortly, is the use of "amoral" to describe someone who is completely unmoved by ethical considerations.
2. This phrase is not meant to suggest that considerations of self-interest are *always* shallow: see the beginning of the next section.
3. See above, note 1.
4. But, as Williams says, "it is hard to think of any other widely used phrase in the history of philosophy that is such a spectacular misnomer" (p. 121). For a "fallacy" is normally taken to be a mistake in inference; and a "naturalistic" view is normally taken to be a view "according to which ethics [is] to be understood in worldly terms, without reference to God or any transcendental authority" (p. 121); but neither of these has much to do with the attempt to define evaluative words using only non-evaluative words.
5. This is related to the message conveyed in the poem by Stevens from which Williams quotes at the very beginning of the book. Stevens, in the extract that Williams cites, begins by heralding the "cold … vacancy/when the phantoms are gone and the shaken realist/first sees reality". He then goes on to celebrate "the yes of the realist …, spoken because under every no/lay a passion for yes that has never been broken" ("Ésthetique du Mal", in *The Collected Poems* (London: Faber, 1954)).
6. It is worth considering in this connection Williams's comment about the innocence in certain abandoned points of view: that it "cannot be recreated, since measures would have to be taken to stop people raising questions that are, by now, there to be raised" (p. 164).
7. I am very grateful to Anita Avramides and John Shand for their comments on an earlier version of this essay.

References

Altham, J. E. J. 1995. "Reflection and Confidence". See Altham & Harrison (eds) (1995), 156–69.

Altham, J. E. J. & R. Harrison (eds) 1995. *World, Mind, and Ethics: Essays on the Ethical Philosophy of Bernard Williams*. Cambridge: Cambridge University Press.

Blackburn, S. & B. Williams 1986. "Making Ends Meet: A Discussion of *Ethics and the Limits of Philosophy*". *Philosophical Books* **27**, 193–208.

Fricker, M. 2000. "Confidence and Irony". See Harcourt (ed.) (2000a), 87–112.

Harcourt, E (ed.) 2000a. *Morality, Reflection, and Ideology*. Oxford: Oxford University Press.

Harcourt, E. 2000b. "Introduction". See Harcourt (ed.) (2000a), 1–20.

Hookway, C. 1995. "Fallibilism and Objectivity: Science and Ethics". See Altham & Harrison (eds) (1995), 46–67.

Jardine, N. 1995. "Science, Ethics, and Objectivity". See Altham & Harrison (eds) (1995), 32–45.

Kant, I. 1996. *Groundwork of the Metaphysics of Morals*, M. J. Gregor (trans.). In *Practical Philosophy*, M. J. Gregor (trans. and ed.), 37–108. Cambridge: Cambridge University Press.

McDowell, J. 1986. "Critical Notice of *Ethics and the Limits of Philosophy*". *Mind* **95** (379), 377–86.

McDowell, J. 1995. "Might There Be External Reasons?". See Altham & Harrison (eds) (1995), 68–85.

Moore, A. W. 2003. "Williams on Ethics, Knowledge, and Reflection". *Philosophy* **78**, 337–54.

Moore, G. E. 1903. *Principia Ethica*. Cambridge: Cambridge University Press.

Nussbaum, M. C. 1995. "Aristotle on Human Nature and the Foundations of Ethics". See Altham & Harrison (eds) (1995), 86–131.

Plato 1961. *Republic*, P. Shorey (trans.). In *The Collected Dialogues of Plato*, E. Hamilton & H. Cairns (eds), 575–844. Princeton, NJ: Princeton University Press.

Putnam, H. 1992. *Renewing Philosophy*. Cambridge, MA: Harvard University Press.

Quinn, W. 1993. "Reflection and the Loss of Moral Knowledge: Williams on Objectivity". Reprinted in his *Morality and Action*, 134–48. Cambridge: Cambridge University Press.

Smart, J. J. C. & B. Williams 1973. *Utilitarianism: For and Against*. Cambridge: Cambridge University Press.

Stevens, W. 1954. "Ésthetique du Mal". In *The Collected Poems*. London: Faber.

Taylor, C. 1995. "A Most Peculiar Institution". See Altham & Harrison (eds) (1995), 132–55.

Williams, B. 1973. *Problems of the Self: Philosophical Papers 1956–1972*. Cambridge: Cambridge University Press.

Williams, B. 1978. *Descartes: The Project of Pure Enquiry*. Harmondsworth: Penguin.

Williams, B. 1981a. *Moral Luck: Philosophical Papers 1973–1980*. Cambridge: Cambridge University Press.

Williams, B. 1981b. "Conflicts of Values". Reprinted in *Moral Luck: Philosophical Papers 1973–1980*, 71–82. Cambridge: Cambridge University Press.

Williams, B. [1972] 1993a. *Morality: An Introduction to Ethics*, 2nd edn. Cambridge: Cambridge University Press.

Williams, B. 1993b. *Shame and Necessity*. Berkeley, CA: University of California Press.

Williams, B. 1995a. *Making Sense of Humanity and Other Philosophical Papers 1982–1993*. Cambridge: Cambridge University Press.

Williams, B. 1995b. "Replies". See Altham & Harrison (eds) (1995) 185–224.

Williams, B. 1996. "Truth in Ethics". In *Truth in Ethics*, B. Hooker (ed.), 19–34. Oxford: Blackwell.

Williams, B. 2000. "Naturalism and Genealogy". See Harcourt (ed.) (2000a), 148–61.

Williams, B. 2002. *Truth and Truthfulness: An Essay in Genealogy.*, Princeton, NJ: Princeton University Press.

Williams, B. 2005. *In the Beginning Was the Deed: Realism and Moralism in Political Argument*, G. Hawthorn (ed.). Princeton, NJ: Princeton University Press.

Williams, B. 2006. *Philosophy as a Humanistic Discipline*, A. W. Moore (ed.). Princeton, NJ: Princeton University Press.

Further reading

The works by Williams that are most closely related to *Ethics and the Limits of Philosophy* are those to which I referred in the Introduction. Also relevant are: the last six essays in Williams (1973b); all but the last two essays in Williams (1981a); all the essays in Williams (1995a), especially those in Part I and Part III; Williams (1996; 2005); and all the essays in Part II of Williams (2006).

There are many reviews of the book. The two most outstanding of these are Blackburn's contribution to Blackburn & Williams (1986), to which Williams replies in his contribution to the same; and McDowell (1986).

An excellent collection of essays on Williams's moral philosophy, largely inspired by *Ethics and the Limits of Philosophy*, is Altham & Harrison (eds) (1995). Within this collection, special mention should be made of: Hookway (1995) and Jardine (1995), both of which are concerned with the distinctions that Williams draws between science and ethics; McDowell (1995), which is concerned with the project of founding ethics on pure reason; Nussbaum (1995), which is concerned with Aristotle's foundational project; Taylor (1995), which is concerned with Williams's treatment of "morality"; and Altham (1995), which is concerned with the claim that reflection can destroy knowledge. There are replies to all of these in Williams (1995b).

Another excellent collection that is largely inspired by *Ethics and the Limits of Philosophy* is Harcourt (2000a). Harcourt (2000b), which is Harcourt's own introduction to this collection, and Fricker (2000), which further explores Williams's notion of confidence, are particularly recommended. The collection (Harcourt 2000a) also contains a fine piece by Williams (2000).

For a critical discussion of Williams's conception of science, see "Bernard Williams and the Absolute Conception of the World", in Putnam (1992: ch. 5). For further discussion of the idea that reflection can destroy knowledge, see Moore (2003), in which I develop the argument sketched in the Conclusion, and Quinn (1993).

11
Thomas Nagel
The View From Nowhere

Anita Avramides

Introduction

Persons are subjects of thought and action; they live in a world that science has so successfully managed to understand. As subjects, persons have a very particular perspective on the world and their actions in it: call it the subjective perspective. Persons are also capable of transcending this subjective perspective and of thinking about the world and their behaviour in a detached manner. They are capable of viewing the world not just from *here*, and from the point of view of humanity, but also of viewing it *from nowhere in particular*. *The View From Nowhere* is a philosophical exploration of these perspectives: the subjective and the objective. It is Nagel's firm belief that both perspectives are real and that the truth about our world can only be gained through an understanding of how these two perspectives coexist in all that we think and do. He writes that if we could say how these standpoints or perspectives are related "it would amount to a world view" (p. 3).

Thus Nagel sets his reader up to think about some of the most abiding and difficult problems in philosophy: metaphysical problems about how to think about the mind in relation to the body; epistemological problems concerning a subject's knowledge of the world around her; ethical and political problems concerning how subjects are to conduct themselves in a world inhabited by other subjects; and, finally, some of the oldest of philosophical problems – how I am to think about my birth, my death and the meaning of my life.

Nagel approaches these problems firmly resolved not to give preference to either perspective. What he seeks is a reconciliation, and he wants this reconciliation to be recognizable by each reader of his book. In this sense Nagel aims to be, if not guided by, at least true to, the way things are for each of us. He wants to understand how the objective and subjective vie with one another and to explain how this results in a unified worldview. As Nagel's interest is in reconciliation, he shuns both reduction and elimination: two very powerful drives both in contemporary philosophy and in science. A unified worldview will not be the result of ignoring, downplaying or belittling either the viewpoint of science or that of the individual. Instead, Nagel aims to "juxtapose" these viewpoints "at full strength" (p. 4).

The tension created by the tug of these two perspectives is not limited to philosophy. It pervades human life. In these pages we find discussion of some of the very thoughts and considerations on life that lead many into philosophy in the first place. As Nagel points out in his discussion of freedom, the problem he is addressing is not simply about what we should *say* – at the level of philosophy or even common sense; he is aiming to address an issue that confronts each of us in our lives. In this particular case, it is the question of how we are to view our freedom in the light of the discovery of a determined world order. Here the objective point of view threatens us as human beings, as persons, at our very core; reflection on determinism can leave us feeling impotent and helpless. Thus, philosophical treatment of such an issue deals, as Nagel says, "with such disturbances of the spirit, and not just their verbal expression" (p. 112). This is not philosophy as a sterile activity.

Not only does Nagel practise philosophy in a way that makes clear its connection with problems that confront us in our lives, but he writes in such a way as to engage the reader as a sort of philosophical fellow traveller. He tries to get the reader intellectually to feel the contours of a problem and then explains how one might grope one's way towards a solution. He is careful to locate his own, preferred, solution to a problem in the context of other proposed solutions. Nagel is particularly aware of the danger of obscurity when writing about these issues. In an effort to avoid this, he writes with an admirable clarity and simplicity. He eschews as much as he is able the technical jargon of professional philosophers. In this respect he stands out among philosophers practising today. And he stands out as well for his intellectual honesty. It is not often that one finds a philosopher admitting in his or her writing that they do not know what to say about an issue. But Nagel's writing is peppered with such phrases as "I don't know how to establish this", or "it seems to me that nothing approaching the truth has been written on this subject". And he is honest about the role that, at the end of the day (or argument), gut intuition plays in philosophy. Nagel's intellectual humility is not to be confused with intellectual weakness. Humility is an admission that one may not have all the answers and that the problem is truly difficult. Nagel's work stands, for the student, as one of the best examples of philosophical practice.

Nagel's work is embedded within a philosophical tradition that stretches back to the ancient Greeks. Although his work has overtones that will appeal to the student of phenomenology, it is firmly established within the analytic school of philosophy. One can in places detect the strong influence of other analytic philosophers whose work has dominated philosophy in the twentieth (and twenty-first) centuries, philosophers such as Saul Kripke, Bernard Williams and Derek Parfit. There is a strong emphasis in the book away from a trend within philosophy that gets labelled idealism. What bothers Nagel about idealism is what he takes to be its anthropocentrism. For Nagel, man is not the measure of all things – not even of all things important. Man must realize his place in the universe and adopt a suitable humility with respect to it. What guides Nagel's work is a certain sort of robust realism. Nagel takes his work to be at odds with that of philosophers such as Kant, Wittgenstein and Donald Davidson. In espousing his brand of humility, Nagel is asking philosophers to question certain doctrines that he believes have become deeply entrenched within philosophy. Whichever side is right, what is important is the *debate* that Nagel's work strives – so successfully – to keep alive.

Issues in the philosophy of mind

Nagel begins the book by raising three specific questions to do with the mind: (i) does the mind have an objective character; (ii) what is the relationship of mind to body; and (iii) how can it be that one of the people in the world is *me*?

The last of these questions is somewhat idiosyncratic. It is not clear that it links up directly to what might be called a traditional philosophical concern. Nevertheless, it is a question that fits naturally with the way Nagel is proposing to set things up, as we shall see in a moment. The second of these questions is the most traditional, at least in the history of modern philosophy. That question has its roots in the work of Descartes, and remains one of the most pressing questions in philosophy today. The first of Nagel's questions is very much peculiar to Nagel. It can be seen to grow out of concerns that occupied him in his most famous single article: "What is it Like to be a Bat?" (1979b). What Nagel offers by way of an answer to this question gives him a framework that he uses to structure the discussions of subsequent chapters. Because of the centrality and importance of the answer Nagel gives to the first question, we do well to do our best to understand his answer here in some detail.

If we begin by considering the mind in relationship to the world, we immediately notice that we can identify two very different starting-points. We can begin by taking the mind and its ideas as given, and try to understand how the mind can be in contact with the world. Or we can take the objective world as given and ask how we can accommodate mind within it. Descartes may be held responsible for initiating a tradition in philosophy that adopts the first starting-point. The problems that then arise include some of the most well known in philosophy: scepticism, idealism and solipsism. Nagel rejects this Cartesian starting-point. For Nagel we must begin with objective reality. Notice that Nagel writes of "objective reality". This is not the same as "physical reality". As Nagel sets things up, there is objective reality and there is a physical conception of this objective reality. This point is crucial. By separating out objectivity from its physical conception Nagel leaves room for what he calls "mental objectivity". According to Nagel, there can be different conceptions of objectivity.

Let us begin with the *physical* conception of objectivity. Nagel sees this conception as developing through a series of stages: first we take our perceptions to be caused by bodies that are part of the physical world; next, we recognize that the same physical objects can cause different perceptions in different subjects of perception and can exist without causing any perception; finally, we try to form a conception of the true nature of these bodies in independence of its appearance to us. This physical conception of objectivity has certain important features: it is centreless, and it is featureless (p. 14). It contains "no points of view and nothing that can appear only to a particular point of view" (p. 15).[1] Although Nagel does not elaborate, the physical conception of objectivity he outlines is a conception that he takes to follow the development of science (physics, to be more exact).

One question we can raise for this conception of objectivity is whether it is *complete* (does it account for all that there is?). By definition, the objective conception leaves out specific viewpoints and perceptions. Nagel insists that, as perceptions and viewpoints must be taken to exist, we should conclude that the physical conception of objectivity is incomplete. In saying this Nagel is bucking the trend of reductionism in the philosophy of mind. Nagel rejects this trend in all its guises: behaviourism, functionalism and the identity theory. He also rejects the idea that we can understand the mind on the model of machines or computers. All these proposed ways of accounting for the mind fail for the same reason, according to Nagel: they proceed from an assumption that one particular conception of objective reality is exhaustive of what there is (p. 16). The physical conception of reality leaves something out: it leaves out the mind, the phenomenon of consciousness. We cannot reduce this phenomenon, nor can we eliminate it. Nagel believes that we must incorporate it into our account of what there really is.

This leads Nagel to introduce another conception of objectivity: mental objectivity. Mental objectivity takes seriously the point of view of the subject. We may ask: is the combination of physical and mental objectivity complete (does it account for all that there is)? By its very nature, mental objectivity cannot completely close the gap left open by physical objectivity. This is because the subjective is in essence personal and individual. Nevertheless, Nagel suggests that we can go some way beyond the personal through abstraction, generalization and experiment (p. 19). Where physical objectivity is centreless, mental objectivity is centred. Nagel tends to think of this centre as *we* rather than *I*. Indeed, it is the move from *I* to *we* that is at the heart of the idea of mental *objectivity*. Nagel considers the problem of other minds as a problem the solution of which can help us to appreciate just how mental objectivity can be achieved. Nagel points out that his interest in the problem of other minds is conceptual; it is the problem of how I am to understand the attribution of mental states to others. There seem to be two alternatives: begin with oneself and work one's way out to others; or, begin with a generalized conception of a point of view and think of oneself as one point of view among others. Nagel adopts the second way. What is important here is that Nagel's starting-point is both general *and* perspectival. Nagel suggests we use our imagination to move us beyond our individual subjectivity. But he also holds that our concept of mind is not limited to what we can imagine. According to Nagel our concept of mind stretches to include the subjectively unimaginable mental lives of other species (p. 21). This is rather a radical thing to say, at least within philosophy. It goes against, for example, some of the things philosophers have understood Wittgenstein to have urged. According to this Wittgensteinian way of thinking, there is a real question whether it even makes sense to extend our concept of mind as far as Nagel does. But Nagel quickly rejects this Wittgensteinian way of thinking. He insists that "only a dogmatic verificationism would deny the possibility of forming objective concepts that reach beyond our current capacity to apply them" (p. 24). "Dogmatic verificationism" (which he takes to lead to idealism) is Nagel's term for much of what he takes himself to be arguing against in this book. Nagel reminds us that "the world is not my world, or our world – not even the mental world is" (p. 26).

The very nature of subjectivity puts it at odds with the physical. Nevertheless, unless we are to adopt Descartes's dualism (and Nagel does not want to do that), we need somehow to understand our mind in relation to the physical world. As a way of achieving this, Nagel proposes a dual-aspect theory according to which one thing can have two sets of mutually irreducible essential properties, mental and physical (p. 31). One outstanding problem for such a theory is that the two kinds of property here under discussion seem to be incompatible.

Another outstanding problem is that if we examine our mental concepts we find that they do not entail anything physical. Without a solution to these problems the prospects do not look good for a dual-aspect theory of mind.

Nagel has something to say about the second problem, which he suggests may help us with the first. Nagel's proposal here draws heavily on the work of Kripke (1980).[2] Kripke's work in the philosophy of language has to do with our understanding of proper names. Contrary to Bertrand Russell's famous theory of descriptions, Kripke has argued that proper names should not be thought of as disguised definite descriptions. Rather, proper names should be thought to refer directly to individuals in the world via a (complex) causal link. Kripke has also suggested that this idea be extended to natural-kind terms such as "gold" and "cat". What Nagel takes it we learn from this approach to natural kinds is that the real nature of such things as gold and cats is not fully captured by the subjective conditions for the term's application (p. 39). Thus, while I might think of gold as a yellow malleable substance, these descriptions do not – either individually or collectively – serve to pick out gold. That some stuff is gold is determined by its (empirically discovered) atomic number. Thus, some stuff may be yellow and malleable but not have atomic number 69; it is not gold, but fool's gold. Nagel takes Kripke's idea and extends it yet further, to pain and other mental kinds. The thought is this: like gold, pain (for example) has an empirically discoverable essential nature; and just as the empirical nature of gold is not obvious from the way we talk about gold, so the empirical nature of pain is not obvious from analysis of our concept of pain. But there is a difference here: while gold has a single essential nature, Nagel suggests that pain has *two* natures, both essential. According to Nagel, Descartes's mistake was to think that the nature of mind is given entirely by reflection on our mental concepts. Descartes quite rightly observed that our mental concepts do not entail anything physical, but he was too quick to conclude that mind, therefore, is distinct from body. Nagel suggests that we can avoid Descartes's conclusion if we allow that our mental concepts may have, along with their essential subjective nature, an essential physical nature. This second essential nature is not revealed when we reflect on our mental concepts. What we have to accept is that our mental concepts are open, or contain a gap. If we accept this, we can then allow that what completes the concept (or fills the gap) is something physically objective. This is Nagel's dual-aspect theory. But Nagel does not fully address the question of whether this solution really can help us with the problem to which he offered it as an indirect solution: the incompatibility of mental and physical properties. What Nagel is asking us to accept is that our mental concepts have an essentially subjective nature that they cannot lose and that is available to introspection *and* that they have an essentially physical nature that they cannot lose and is discovered empirically. The problem is that these two natures pull in such different directions that it is hard to see how we can really hold on to both.

Although Nagel does not say enough to overcome all worries, he does make some suggestions about how mental and physical properties are related. It seems unlikely that the relationship here is accidental; indeed, Nagel suggests that these properties may be necessarily related. But he avoids the charge that this just takes us back to the very reduction he earlier rejected by suggesting that both properties may be manifestations of something more fundamental. Just as we must descend to the level of molecular description to understand the connection between increase in temperature and pressure of gas at a constant volume, so we may need to think of our understanding of mental and physical properties as requiring a similar sort of move. He even considers the possibility that we might be intellectually incapable of comprehending such a general understanding of things, a view taken up subsequently and developed by Colin McGinn (1989). The existence of such a (deeper) level leads Nagel to consider the very possibility of panpsychism: everything, when reduced to its simpler parts, has proto-mental properties (Nagel 1979c). There is no doubt that his musings have led him into thinking some bizarre things. In this important, yet enormously difficult, area Nagel is urging us to think the unthinkable. He believes this is going to be necessary, especially once we abandon the pipe dream of a complete physical conception of objectivity. Taking seriously the inescapable but very real properties of mind requires that we think radically about how we can achieve our goal of understanding all that it is possible to understand.

I turn finally, and all too briefly, to the third question raised by Nagel under the heading of issues in the philosophy of mind: how can it be the case that one of the people in the world is *me*?[3] I said earlier that this is not a traditional philosophical concern; indeed some have found it difficult to understand just what Nagel is asking here. Nagel's question may become clearer once we work through his proposed answer to it. Nagel splits his question into two (I shall ask them from *my* – AA's – point of view): (i) How can it be true of a particular person, AA, who is just one of many persons in an objectively centreless world, that she is me?; and (ii) how can I be *merely* a particular person, AA? This second question is designed to capture the curious business of feeling that it is a mere accident that I see the world through AA's eyes, and as a woman who is 5'5" tall. If Nagel had begun from the first-person perspective he would have had the problem of fitting others into the picture. As he chooses to begin with mental and physical objectivity, Nagel's problem is fitting the individual into the picture. Nagel begins with a view from nowhere in particular, but he also allows that mine is a view from here. The view from here can seem a curiosity in light of the view from nowhere. It is this curiosity that Nagel is trying to get at with his two questions here.

Let us start by thinking about the question "How can AA be me?". And let us begin where Nagel begins, with a general, centreless, conception of the world as if from nowhere, and note that "in those oceans of time [AA] is just one person among countless others" (p. 61). How do I get from this detached and rather grand perspective to something so concrete and specific and *small*? Nagel contemplates this and concludes that, although my perspective and position in the world are essential to me, something else is *also* essential to me, something that has nothing to do with my perspective and position in the world (p. 62). What follows from this is that, although I receive my experiences from a very particular point of view, I am capable of treating what I receive in this way as *on an equal footing* with what I learn about more indirectly (*ibid.*). We are now in a position also to look at Nagel's other question, "How can I be AA?". "I" refers to me *qua* subject of the impersonal conception of the world that contains AA. Nagel writes:

> The reference is still essentially indexical, and cannot be eliminated in favor of an objective description, but the thought [I am AA] avoids triviality because it depends on the fact that this impersonal conception of the world, although it accords no special position to [AA], is attached to and developed from the perspective of [AA].   (p. 64)

This, according to Nagel, explains the sense of strangeness I have when I consider that I am this very particular individual. The strangeness results from the fact that I am "both the logical focus of an objective conception of the world and a particular being in that world who occupies no central position whatever" (*ibid.*).

By the end of Chapter 4, Nagel has set the stage for the work in the rest of the book. Nagel takes our subjectivity for granted. He merely asserts that it exists and cannot be ignored, eliminated or reduced. What interests Nagel is that we have different essential natures, and what he wants is to see how we might reconcile these. I would suggest that it is Nagel's idea of mental objectivity, and correlatively his notion of an objective self, that introduces a new and interesting dimension to many old debates in philosophy. In the rest of the book Nagel explores these different natures as they manifest themselves in various domains and looks at how they lead to many fundamental philosophical problems and dilemmas.

Epistemology and metaphysics

In Chapters 5 and 6, Nagel considers questions central to both epistemology and metaphysics. He begins by raising questions concerning the relationship between objectivity and knowledge. He then moves on to look at the issue of realism, and to contrast this realism with the idealism he rejects.

Although Nagel begins with epistemology, his views here are informed by his metaphysics. Metaphysical issues about realism go hand in glove with epistemological issues concerning scepticism. Nagel takes a firm line on both: a realism that holds the world to be independent of my – or any subject's – perception of it goes along with a scepticism that cannot be denied or refuted. As Nagel says, "The extension of power [he means here, knowledge] and the growth of insecurity [he means here, scepticism] go hand in hand" (p. 67). Like Descartes, Nagel takes scepticism seriously; unlike Descartes, Nagel does not believe philosophers can reply to, or dismiss, scepticism. Nagel labels Descartes's attempt to defeat the sceptic "heroic". Heroic theories attempt to *close a gap* that exists between our ordinary and scientific beliefs about the world and the appearance of that world to us. Nagel accepts this gap and insists that it cannot be closed. Nagel acknowledges a very strong tradition in philosophy that tries to show that scepticism is mistaken or misguided in some way. He dismisses it swiftly. His dismissal is founded on the following simple thought: scepticism is self-evidently possible and intelligible. It is important to remember that not all philosophers – whether idealist or realist – would find this simple thought as compelling as Nagel does.

Nagel differs from Descartes in another important respect: Descartes believes, while Nagel does not, that objective knowledge proceeds via a series of steps each of which can be deemed *certain*. This lack of certainty is, for Nagel, part and parcel of a recognition of the gap. Nagel also distances himself from the traditional view of the central problem of epistemology: the "impersonal problem" of saying what conditions we need to add to belief to achieve knowledge. In Nagel's view the central epistemological problem is the "first-person problem" of what to believe and how to justify one's beliefs (p. 69).

The pursuit of knowledge is the pursuit of objective knowledge. This gives us insight into the title Nagel chose for his book: we aim to achieve a view of the world that is not a view from here and now (this is my first-person, feature-full, centred view on the world), but is a *view from nowhere* in particular. This larger and more comprehensive view is intended to take in all our particular points of view. This means that our pursuit of understanding is also a pursuit of self-understanding. The knowledge we seek is both of the world and of our place in it. The comprehensiveness of what we seek leads us to develop what

Nagel calls "double vision": we need both to understand ourselves as part of the natural, fully objective, order and to understand ourselves as individuals whose lives can often seem at odds with that natural order. The impetus to this understanding is, says Nagel "a mystery" (p. 78). In order to understand the basis of this knowledge, Nagel suggests that we consider rationalism. By rationalism he does not mean innate knowledge of truths about the world, but, rather, a capacity, not based on experience, to generate hypotheses about what in general the world may be like (p. 83). In other words, Nagel suggests that the *basis* of our knowledge may be *a priori*.

As we have seen, what Nagel has to say about knowledge is premised on his commitment to realism. Nagel characterizes his realism thus: "the world may be inconceivable to *our* minds" (p. 91). What Nagel aims to oppose with his realism is an idealism that holds that the world could not be inconceivable to our minds. Variations on the theme of idealism are found in the writings of Berkeley, Kant, P. F. Strawson, Davidson and Wittgenstein. Nagel offers swift refutations of the position of each of these great thinkers in turn. Although Nagel nowhere mentions his name, I find Nagel's position on realism remarkably close to that of John Locke. The following is a quotation from Locke's *An Essay on Human Understanding*, and it has many an echo in Nagel's work:

> What other simple Ideas 'tis possible the Creatures in other parts of the Universe may have ... 'tis not for us to determine. But to say, or think there are no such, because we conceive nothing of them, is no better an argument, than if a blind Man should be positive in it, that there was no such thing as Sight and Colour ... Only this, I think, I may confidently say of [our ignorance], that the intellectual and sensible World, are in this perfectly alike; That part, which we see of either of them, holds no proportion with what we see not. And whatsoever we can reach with our Eyes, or our Thoughts of either of them, is but a point, almost nothing, in comparison with the rest.
>
> (Locke [1689] 1975: 553–4)[4]

In accordance with his rationalism, Nagel suggests that we possess a completely general conception of reality, the precise details of which may be (and very likely are) beyond our comprehension. Again in a manner reminiscent of Locke, Nagel writes that we may have an inadequate conception of the existence of much about which we may never form a more adequate conception (p. 93). Nagel is here attempting to fend off one of the hardest questions facing his form of realism. It is not possible to adjudicate this debate here, but we may get a taste for the debate if we consider very briefly the views of one of Nagel's opponents, Donald Davidson. Davidson has suggested that we "see the world through language"; furthermore, Davidson holds that all language is in principle translatable into the one we speak.[5] If Davidson is right, then the world as we think of it apart from ourselves and the world as we think of it are in some rather complex way interdependent. Nagel wants to deny any hint of interdependence. According to Nagel, we are mere blips on the radar of the universe, and the universe is vast in ways that are very likely beyond our ken. There is no doubt that there is much at stake here; there is also no doubt where Nagel wants to position himself in the ongoing debate. In his own words Nagel's position amounts to "a strong form of anti-humanism: the world is not our world, even potentially" (p. 108). Nagel claims that his position is in keeping with a kind of humility and modesty (again compare the views of Locke); although the philosopher who would reject Nagelian realism may also stake out a claim to humility and modesty.

Action and ethics

In Chapters 7–9, Nagel turns to examine issues in and around ethics. He begins with a central problem that confronts us when we consider the issue of objectivity in connection with action: the problem of freedom. The problem arises both in connection with oneself and in connection with others. In connection with oneself it takes this form: when we look at the world objectively – and consider all our actions as causally determined – it is difficult to see how our actions can be free (the classic problem of free will). In connection with others we have the classic problem of free will, but we have an additional problem. If the actions of others are not free, it is difficult to justify our reactive attitudes towards them (to feel angered, for example, by what they did to us) and it looks hard to justify our tendency to hold them responsible for their actions. The problem that objectivity poses for action strikes at the very heart of our sense of ourselves as persons acting together in the world.

Consider the following. Your best friend telephones to say that your boyfriend was seen kissing someone else. Feelings of betrayal, anger and upset will no doubt well up in you. You may have thoughts along the following lines. Your boyfriend had a choice, and he chose to act in a way that was unfaithful. At the very moment that he was tempted to kiss someone else, he could have refrained, he could have remained loyal to you; but he did not, and this is why you are upset with him. You blame him for what he did. You consider that you yourself had the opportunity to kiss someone else just last Saturday night, but you chose not to. You exercised self-control, even though you now think you may have chosen differently if you had known what you now know. But now consider the situation from a more objective point of view. The causal pressures leading up to your boyfriend's action were overwhelming and may be thought to determine his kiss; he was not – and could not be – in control. You do not get upset with an aspirin for dissolving in water. You do not get angry with the clouds that threaten your picnic (at least you recognize that this is irrational). And even your decision not to kiss last Saturday can be viewed as the result of various factors in your background and even the character you inherited from your parents.

P. F. Strawson (1974) famously argued that our feeling of freedom and our reactive attitudes towards others are in some way immune to beliefs concerning the causation and determinism of our actions. We may allow that a particular action could be given a purely causal explanation, and we may hold our feelings in abeyance if we learn, for example, that someone had a particularly tragic upbringing; but what is possible for an act here and there is not possible for our actions as a whole. Nagel disagrees with Strawson. Just as Nagel thinks it is possible – and natural – to be a wholesale sceptic concerning our beliefs about the world, so he thinks that it is possible to generalize the thought that our actions are caused and determined. It is possible to think not just that certain of our acts are determined, but that all of them are. This just *is*, according to Nagel, the philosophical challenge to our freedom. Just as Nagel holds that scepticism is the corollary of realism, so he holds that a challenge to our freedom is the corollary of an objective stance *vis-à-vis* our actions. In both arenas we find a clash between the objective and the subjective point of view. Strawson finds wholesale scepticism implausible and a purely objective stance on our actions impossible; Nagel finds both a very real part of the way things are.

Nagel does not think we have to accept that we are mere helpless observers when confronted with the objective stance. He thinks it should be possible to make the objective standpoint the basis for action, to act while acknowledging a more objective perspective. Nagel labels this the "strategy of objective tolerance" (p. 130). Objective tolerance is supposed to help with the feeling of helplessness that washes over us when we contemplate ourselves objectively. Helplessness results only if we expect objective affirmation of our actions. But Nagel thinks that objective affirmation is too ambitious; toleration is all we can manage. Objective toleration helps us to recognize the possibility of greater objectivity while at the same time allowing us to acknowledge that complete objectivity eludes us; it eludes us because of our subjective nature. At any given time we must act in the light of the most objective view of which we are capable. However, no objective view can, for us, be complete, and the objective view in light of which we act must not be rejected simply because of its incompleteness. Nagel calls this subjective nature a "blind spot" (p. 127); we, as subjects, remain, as it were, behind the lens that surveys the world objectively. And this blind spot affords a space for our autonomy. I can, according to Nagel, be content to make my choices in accordance with my inclinations and view of the world, *while at the same time* acknowledging the possibility of a more objective perspective on my action. The thought seems to be that, even as I contemplate this objective possibility, I can acknowledge that I am still behind the lens. The blind spot is, in effect, our salvation.

Objective tolerance may work when we consider the possibility of looking at our actions *sub specie aeternitatis*, but there are other objectivizing moves for which toleration will not work. What is needed for these is something along the lines of what Nagel calls "objective integration" (p. 132), an important method of which is practical rationality. What Nagel has in mind here is the move, within subjectivity, from basic everyday desires to a higher vantage point with respect to them. From this higher vantage point some of these desires are endorsed, some suppressed and yet others rejected. And there is not one such vantage point, but several. Practical rationality is exercised at several levels. As we move to integrate desires, we encounter prudence. Prudential rationality is exercised from an objective standpoint detached from the present. It is not enmeshed in the present, but can adjudicate between desires past, present and future. Because prudence allows us to gain a perspective on our present desires, Nagel sees it as a moment in the pursuit of our freedom; it is the first stage in the development of an objective will.[6] Nagel suggests that it is the essential activity of such an objective will to recognize values, as opposed to mere preferences (p. 134).

Prudence is one point along the path of objectivity; recognizing oneself as one individual among others is another. Just as the standpoint of prudence is active (prudential motives are produced by this objective standpoint), so the standpoint that involves myself as one among others is also active. Furthermore, just as prudence yields value that is personal, so this impersonal perspective yields value that is impersonal. This impersonal perspective involves objectivity, but not an objectivity that takes us outside the sphere of subjectivity; this perspective is robustly interpersonal. From *this* impersonal perspective – from this place outside our own subjectivity – we enter the world of ethics and politics. Following Kant, Nagel views ethics as increasing the "range of what it is about ourselves that we can will"; this range includes not just our actions but the motives and character traits from which these actions arise (p. 135). As Nagel puts it in one place, what we hope for is to "find ourselves faced with the choices we want to be faced with, in a world that we can want to live in" (p. 136). It is in this way that ethics takes us into politics.

Nagel holds that objectivity is the central problem of ethics (p. 138). And he reminds us constantly of the parallel between belief and value: while in theoretical reasoning we aim to step back from our own individual perspectives, so in practical reasoning we aim to step back from our personal values. We must remember that objectivity in value is still personal – it is interpersonal; objectivity in belief aims to transcend the personal. This point can be obscured by Nagel's generous use of the term "objective". With our beliefs we aim to transcend any perspective; with value we aim to transcend our individual wants and preferences. Accordingly, the question with which ethics begins, is not "What should I do?", but "What should this person do?" (p. 141).

One problem for Nagel's view is that the move to a more objective stance with respect to value may lead to the conclusion that value is an illusion created by our subjective perspective. Nagel identifies this worry as lying behind Humean subjectivism. Nagel hopes to resist Humean subjectivism and the conclusion that "objective value" is an oxymoron. Nagel here stakes out his argumentative strategy: realism with respect to value (like realism with respect to the world around us) operates as a "defeasible presumption" (p. 143). He writes: "in general, there is no way to prove the possibility of realism; one can only refute impossibility arguments, and the more one does this the more confidence one may have in the realist alternative" (p. 144). Nagel then proceeds to consider and attempts to refute Hume's arguments against realism about value, after which he returns to defend his commitment to objective value.

Hume famously claimed that it was not contrary to reason to prefer the destruction of the world to the scratching of one's little finger; Nagel begs to differ. It is Nagel's view that such a preference is objectively wrong, and not to appreciate this is to be in the grip of an overly narrow conception of reasoning (p. 155). On Hume's view, reason is the handmaiden of desire; a person has reason to do what will satisfy her desires at the time of acting. Nagel takes the province of reason to be wider than this. Sometimes, claims Nagel, a desire appears only because I recognize that there is a reason to do or to want something (p. 151). For example, my desire to prevent the destruction of the world may appear as the result of my recognition of the objective value of preserving the world over a scratch to my little finger. But this may be to move too quickly. To help us to see that the anti-Humean position must be right, and to make a case for objective value, Nagel starts by considering the simple case of pain and pleasure. What Nagel wants is to convince us that pain is a bad and pleasure is a good – *no matter who suffers them*. He begins by asking us to acknowledge that having a severe headache gives me a reason to take an aspirin, or that I will experience pain is a reason not to put my hand in the fire. (It is not just the case that I have the rather useful inclination to take an aspirin or not to put my hand in the fire.) If what Nagel says makes sense, then the idea of an objective practical reason makes sense. If Nagel is right, we can say that pain itself is something

I have reason to avoid. But he wants to convince us of more than this. Nagel wants to convince us that pain and pleasure provide more than what he calls "agent-relative" reasons for action: they can provide "agent-neutral" reasons. By this is meant that I have a reason not only to avoid pain to myself, but I also have reason – at least *prima facie* – to relieve the pain of others. The objective value that pain has is a value regardless of who is suffering it. Nagel suggests that the relation between agent-relative and agent-neutral reasons is "probably the central question of ethical theory" (p. 159).

Once impersonal value is admitted, there is a temptation to go the whole hog. This is how Nagel sees traditional forms of consequentialism (especially utilitarianism). According to Nagel, consequentialists take seriously the idea of impersonal value at the expense of personal value. What the consequentialist misses is the way in which personal value limits what may be done in the service of impersonal value. In this connection Nagel discusses deontological constraints. Deontological constraints give reasons not to treat others in certain ways that derive not from impersonal considerations regarding the interests of others, but from personal demands that govern one's relations with others. These constraints involve obligations created by promises, restrictions against lying, prohibitions against the violation of various individual rights and the like. As Nagel points out, "Deontological reasons have their full force against your doing something – not just against its happening" (p. 177). This is why they are not impersonal. Deontological constraints are precisely what utilitarians reject. According to the utilitarian, a death is a death and it matters not how it comes about. Nagel disagrees, although he admits that understanding deontological constraints can be baffling. The important factor here, as Nagel sees it, is intention. According to Nagel, there is something unacceptable about intending to cause someone harm, despite the fact that a greater good may result. What is unacceptable is that intending to cause harm in such cases involves allowing oneself to be guided by evil. If you must kill one person in order to save the life of, say, twenty others, then if your victim does not die after the first wound you must, perforce, administer a second wound. In other words, you must aim to achieve this death. And the problem with doing evil intentionally is that it involves striving against value (p. 182). What deontological constraints point up is the real conflict between subjective and objective points of view. From the objective point of view one is considering the impersonally best alternative; from the subjective point of view one is choosing the best *action*. These two points of view must be balanced against one another, and it is this balance that Nagel thinks will ultimately yield truth in ethics.

There are further complexities here. One of these arises once we notice that not all values are as simple as the ones that are given rise to by the suffering of pain and enjoyment of pleasure. Take, for example, my desire to be a good philosopher, or Ellen MacArthur's desire to sail around the globe. While these desires may give me and Ellen reasons for action, they do not obviously give others reason to help us satisfy our desires. Value in such cases is "essentially perspectival" (p. 168). Nagel struggles to say something that will help us to decide which values are essentially perspectival and which have more objective value. Must we conclude that *only* pains and pleasures yield objective value? Nagel does not think so. He argues that objective value also attaches to liberty, opportunity and the basic resources of life – what Nagel refers to as "very general human goods" (p. 171). And what informs these as agent-neutral values is the idea that no one is more important than anyone else. Once both agent-relative and agent-neutral values are admitted, the question is raised how a life is to be organized so that both can be given their due (p. 174). Nagel sees this as much an issue for political theory as for ethics.

Living right, living well and living a meaningful life

The tension between objective and subjective points of view manifest itself everywhere. Another manifestation of this tension that interests Nagel is between the impersonal demands of morality (living right) and the way each of us leads our lives in accordance with our personal tastes and attachments (living well). Another is an impersonal perspective on our birth, life and death, and a subjective perspective on the same. I shall end by briefly discussing each of these tensions in turn.

The tension between living right and living well that interests Nagel is one he finds discussed in the works of Aristotle (who defines living right in terms of living well), Plato (who argues the reverse of Aristotle's position), Nietzsche (who gives priority to living well), various utilitarian and Kantian writers (who give priority to right living), and those (unidentified) who concede priority to neither. Nagel positions himself closest to utilitarian and Kantian writers, although he wants to allow that we have reason to want both (p. 197). On the side of living well we find considerations of personal interest (I may like to spend my money on an expensive sound system and fine whisky, and to give priority to my friends and family); on the side of living right we find various impersonal demands (such as giving to charity and helping others regardless of their relationship to me). As Nagel sees it, both personal and impersonal considerations give us reasons for action. Impersonal demands weigh very strongly, but they cannot completely block personal ones. Although both considerations may give reasons for action, we may think that *morality* lies on the side of the impersonal and – given the strength of impersonal demands – conclude that living right is incompatible with living well. Nagel hopes to avoid this conclusion by suggesting that a commitment to living well can be impersonally recognized and acknowledged. Interestingly, Nagel here sees a role for politics in helping to ease the tension between living well and living right by arranging the world so that we can all live well without injuring others. One of the aims of politics, according to Nagel, ought to be moral harmony.

This takes us to the last of the tensions between objectivity and subjectivity that Nagel discusses. He writes: "The pursuit of objectivity with respect to value runs the risk of leaving value behind altogether" (p. 209). This can seem particularly true when we consider a human life from an objective perspective. *From the outside* one's birth and death can seem insignificant, and one's life without point. *From the inside*, on the other hand, one's birth, life and death can seem "monstrously important" (*ibid.*). The different perspectives can be seen in the development from a child (engrossed in the personal) to the adult (with the dawning realization of the impersonal). And the problem is not just that I can view my life sometimes from this perspective and sometimes from that, but that I can simultaneously be involved and detached from the life that I lead. A sense of absurdity can result if one overdoes the detachment; life can come to seem meaningless. An inability to act in the world can be an extreme reaction to the detached perspective. Nagel sees this sense of absurdity as a form of scepticism at the level of motivation. Faced with the problem of meaninglessness, Nagel once again reminds us that the engaged and the detached perspectives exist side by side in each of us. But recognition of the two perspectives alone may not be enough. The tension and conflict they produce in us may lead us to try to deny one or another perspective. Thus the religious ascetic may try to deny the subjective perspective by throwing off all worldly ambition and distancing himself from close personal ties. Or the *bon vivant* may try to shake the objective perspective by devoting himself only to his pleasures and interests. Characteristically, Nagel rejects both reactions in favour of a recognition of real conflict. In the place of denial, one must seek to promote harmony between these two very different perspectives on one's life. Indeed, Nagel thinks that the recognition of an objective perspective need not result in absurdity; it can, he suggests, play an important part in human motivation (p. 221). It can do this if we react to the objective stance with a form of humility: "the recognition that you are no more important than you are, and that the fact that something is of importance to you, or that it would be good or bad if you did or suffered something, is a fact of purely local significance" (p. 222). But even with a healthy dose of humility the tension persists; it is, after all, part of the human condition.

The power of the subjective perspective can be felt most strongly, perhaps, when one contemplates one's own birth and one's own death. Consider first one's own birth. Of course, it is an accident that one exists (just think of all the things that had to be in place for your conception to occur); and from a detached perspective one's own birth is not really very important. Nevertheless, it is not very easy to consider one's birth in these terms. There is even a feeling that the world around me could not exist without me. This feeling is not at all compatible with the idea that my life is an accident and my birth unimportant. I may be able to bring myself to think of my birth in these terms, but it is very difficult indeed to shake the feeling that my existence is undeniable. When we turn to contemplate our own death we find a similar difficulty. Even the suicidal can find the contemplation of their own death difficult. As Nagel writes, "Death as an event in the world is easy to think about; the end of my world is not" (p. 225), no matter how awful my world may be. Nagel suggests that the problem here may be deeply embedded. It may be that the subjective point of view simply does not allow for its own annihilation. From the objective point of view things come into existence and then pass away. But the subjective point of view does not contain the possibility of its own non-existence; my life is the actuality on which depend all the possibilities that make up my life. As Nagel writes, "we cannot rise above death by occupying a vantage point that death will destroy" (p. 231). When contemplating one's own death the force of competing perspectives is particularly strong.

As in so many other areas of our lives, we must acknowledge the force of both the subjective and objective standpoint and strive to understand the place of each. Nagel does not deny that there will be real difficulties associated with this acknowledgement. But it his firm belief that the attempt to reconcile these two perspectives gives us the only chance we have to come near to living our lives "in the light of truth" (*ibid.*).

Notes

1. Nagel compares this to the idea of the absolute conception in B. Williams, *Descartes: The Project of Pure Inquiry* (Harmondsworth: Penguin, 1978), 64–8.
2. Compare as well the work of Hilary Putnam, "The Meaning of 'Meaning'", in *Mind, Language and Reality: Philosophical Papers, Vol. 2*, 215–72 (Cambridge: Cambridge University Press, 1975).
3. Nagel pursues issues related to this question in more detail in his paper "The Objective Self", in *Mind and Knowledge*, C. Ginet & S. Shoemaker (eds), 211–32 (Oxford: Oxford University Press, 1983).
4. J. Locke, *An Essay Concerning Human Understanding*, P. H. Niddich (ed.) (Oxford:

Clarendon Press [1689] 1975), Bk IV, ch. iii, 23. Compare Locke's consideration of the blind man with Nagel's (p. 95).

5. See, for example, Davidson's "On the Very Idea of a Conceptual Scheme", reprinted in *Truth and Interpretation*, 183–99 (Oxford: Oxford University Press [1974] 1984) and "Seeing through Language", in *Thought and Language*, J. Preston (ed.), 15–29 (Cambridge: Cambridge University Press).

6. For an extended discussion of this idea see Nagel, *The Possibility of Altruism* (Oxford: Oxford University Press, 1970).

Bibliography

Davidson, D. [1974] 1984. "On the Very Idea of a Conceptual Scheme". Reprinted in his *Truth and Interpretation*, 183–99. Oxford: Oxford University Press.

Davidson, D. 1997. "Seeing through Language". In *Thought and Language*, J. Preston (ed.), 15–29. Cambridge: Cambridge University Press.

Locke, J. [1689] 1975. *An Essay Concerning Human Understanding*, P. H. Niddich (ed.). Oxford: Clarendon Press.

Kripke, S. 1980. *Naming and Necessity*. Cambridge, MA: Harvard University Press.

McGinn, C. 1989. "Can We Solve the Mind–Body Problem?". *Mind* **98**, 349–66.

Nagel, T. 1970. *The Possibility of Altruism*. Oxford: Oxford University Press.

Nagel, T. 1979a. *Mortal Questions*. Cambridge: Cambridge University Press.

Nagel, T. 1979b. "What is it Like to be a Bat?". Reprinted in Nagel (1979a), 165–81.

Nagel, T. 1979c. "Panpsychism". In Nagel (1979a), 181–96.

Nagel, T. 1983. "The Objective Self". In *Mind and Knowledge*, C. Ginet & S. Shoemaker (eds), 211–32. Oxford: Oxford University Press.

Nagel, T. 1986. *The View from Nowhere*. Oxford: Oxford University Press.

Putnam, H. 1975. "The Meaning of 'Meaning'". In *Mind, Language and Reality: Philosophical Papers, Vol. 2*, 215–72. Cambridge: Cambridge University Press.

Strawson, P. F. 1974. "Freedom and Resentment". In *Freedom and Resentment and Other Essays*, 1–26. London: Methuen.

Williams, B. 1978. *Descartes: The Project of Pure Inquiry*. Harmondsworth: Penguin.

12
David Lewis

On the Plurality of Worlds

Phillip Bricker

The notion of a possible world is familiar from Leibniz's philosophy, especially the idea – parodied by Voltaire in *Candide* – that the world we inhabit, the *actual* world, is the best of all possible worlds. But it was primarily in the latter half of the twentieth century that possible worlds became a mainstay of philosophical theorizing. In areas as diverse as philosophy of language, philosophy of science, epistemology, logic, ethics and, of course, metaphysics itself, philosophers helped themselves to possible worlds in order to provide analyses of key concepts from their respective domains. David Lewis contributed analyses in all of these fields, most famously, perhaps, his possible worlds analysis of counterfactual conditionals (Lewis 1973). But these analyses invoking possible worlds cry out for a foundation: how is all this talk about possible worlds to be construed? Do possible worlds exist? If so, what is their nature?

David Lewis responded boldly: this talk of possible worlds is the literal truth. Lewis propounded a thesis of *modal realism*: the world we inhabit – the entire *cosmos* of which we are a part – is but one of a vast plurality of worlds, or *cosmoi*, all causally and spatiotemporally isolated from one another. Whatever *might* have happened in our world *does* happen in one or more of these merely possible worlds: there are worlds in which donkeys talk and pigs fly, donkeys and pigs no less "real" or "concrete" than actual donkeys and pigs. Moreover, whatever you *might* have done but did not do *is* done in another possible world by a *counterpart* of you, someone just like you up until shortly before the time in question, but whose life diverges from yours thereafter. According to modal realism, the

246

actual and the merely possible do not differ in their ontological status. They differ only in their relation to us: merely possible worlds are spatiotemporally and causally inaccessible; we cannot get there from here.

When David Lewis first endorsed modal realism in the late 1960s and early 1970s, it elicited "incredulous stares" from other philosophers, even from other practitioners of possible worlds analyses (as reported in Lewis 1973: 86). But by the early 1980s, a spate of papers had been published in which those incredulous stares were backed by argument, and in which seemingly "more sensible" approaches to possible worlds were presented, approaches, for example, taking possible worlds to be "abstract objects" of some sort. *On the Plurality of Worlds* is Lewis's response: an extended elaboration and defence of modal realism. The greatness of this work lies not so much in its power to persuade – Lewis himself did not think the case for modal realism was, or could be, decisive – but in the masterful presentation of positions and arguments in the metaphysics of modality, and in the many problems in outlying areas of metaphysics that are clarified along the way. It is systematic philosophy at its finest.

Ontological commitment to possible worlds

Why, according to Lewis, should one believe in a plurality of worlds? In an earlier work, Lewis based his argument on a Quinean criterion of ontological commitment applied to ordinary language (Lewis 1973: 84). We say, for example, "There are many ways things could have been besides the way they actually are." Taken at face value, this commits us to entities called "ways things could have been", which Lewis identifies with possible worlds. But it was soon pointed out that the phrase 'ways things could have been' seems to refer, if at all, to abstract entities – perhaps uninstantiated properties – not to Lewis's concrete worlds (Stalnaker 1976). In *On the Plurality of Worlds*, Lewis abandons any attempt to defend possible worlds by way of ordinary language, and turns instead to systematic philosophy. The chief concern of systematic philosophy is *total theory*, the whole of what we take to be true. Possible worlds, if accepted, provide the means to reduce the diversity of notions that must be taken as primitive, thereby improving the unity and economy of our total theory. Moreover, possible worlds, Lewis claims, provide a "paradise for philosophers" analogous to the way that *sets* have been said to provide a paradise for mathematicians (because, given the realm of sets, one has the wherewithal to provide true and adequate interpretations for all mathematical theories). So, when asked "Why believe in a plurality of worlds?", Lewis responds, "because the hypothesis is serviceable, and that is a reason to think that it is true" (p. 3).

Lewis does not claim, of course, that usefulness, by itself, is a decisive reason: there may be hidden costs to accepting possible worlds; there may be alternatives to possible worlds that provide the same benefits without the costs. Lewis's defence of modal realism, therefore, involves an extensive cost-benefit analysis. His conclusion is that, on balance, modal realism defeats its rivals: rival theories that can provide the same benefits all have more serious costs. A controversial underlying assumption of Lewis's argument, that a theory that better satisfies the pragmatic virtues such as simplicity and unity is *more likely* to be true, is noted by Lewis, but never called into question.

Analysing modality

On the Plurality of Worlds consists of four lengthy chapters each divided into multiple sections. Lewis devotes four sections of the first chapter, "A Philosopher's Paradise", to an extensive survey of the uses to which possible worlds have been put. This provides him with an opportunity to present, and sometimes clarify, his view on such diverse topics as supervenience, counterfactuals, the analysis of belief, semantics for natural language and theories of properties and relations.[1] But the survey begins with the most famous application of possible worlds: the analysis of the alethic modal notions, *necessity* and *possibility*. That will be my focus here.

Consider the modal statement: necessarily, all swans are birds. This statement can be analysed in terms of possible worlds as: at every possible world, all swans are birds.[2] The necessity operator becomes a *universal* quantifier over possible worlds. Moreover, quantifiers in the embedded proposition are restricted to the domain of the world of evaluation: *all swans are birds* is true at a world just in case all swans *inhabiting the world* are birds. (Since possible worlds, for the modal realist, are like places, truth at a world is analogous to truth in some place: *all swans are black* is true in Australia just in case all swans *inhabiting Australia* are black.) Now consider the modal statement: possibly, there are blue swans. That statement is analysed as: at some possible world, there are blue swans. The possibility operator becomes an *existential* quantifier over possible worlds. The embedded proposition, *there are blue swans*, holds at a world just in case some swan *inhabiting the world* is blue. These analyses of necessity and possibility have genuine explanatory power: they elucidate the logical relations between the modal notions. For example, if a proposition is not possible, it necessarily is not so; and if a proposition is not necessary, it possibly is not so. The quantificational analysis allows these modal inferences to be explained in terms of familiar logical inferences involving 'every', 'some' and 'not'.

Thus far, I have considered only the analysis of modality *de dicto*: the modal operators, *necessarily* and *possibly*, were applied to entire propositions. What about the analysis of modality *de re*, the application of modal properties to things? Consider, for example, the modal property, *being necessarily human*, which is formed by applying the modal operator, *necessarily*, to the property, *being human*. One might think that to say that George W. Bush is necessarily human is just to say: Bush is human at every world he inhabits, at every world containing him as one of its parts. But on Lewis's conception of possible worlds as non-overlapping concrete universes, that will not do: since Bush inhabits the actual world, he fails to inhabit any other possible world. The proposed analysis, then, would wrongly make all of Bush's actual properties necessary. Lewis's solution is to analyse modality *de re* in terms of what properties one's *counterparts* have at other possible worlds. He writes: "Your counterparts resemble you closely in content and context in important respects. They resemble you more closely than do other things at their worlds. But they are not really you. … [They are who] you *would have been*, had the world been otherwise" (Lewis 1968: 114–15). Then, *Bush is necessarily human* is analysed by quantifying both over possible worlds and counterparts: at every possible world, every counterpart of Bush is human. Similarly, *Bush might have been a plumber* can be analysed by existentially quantifying over possible worlds and counterparts: at some possible world, some counterpart of Bush is a plumber. On Lewis's account, modality *de dicto* is the central notion, depending only on what possible worlds there are. Modality *de re* is derivative, and more fluid: it depends also on a counterpart relation that, being a relation of similarity, is open to subjective and contextual factors.

That modal realism allows one to analyse modality *de dicto* and *de re* is for Lewis one of its chief selling points. Over and over, Lewis objects to alternative accounts of possible worlds on the grounds that they must accept primitive modality in one form or another. But is the modal realist not also committed to primitive modality by taking the notion of *possible* world (or *possible* individual) as basic? No, for Lewis the 'possible' is redundant: there are no *im*possible worlds (or individuals). Thus, Lewis has no need of primitive modality to divide the worlds (or individuals) into two classes: possible and impossible. (Henceforth I will often drop the 'possible', and speak simply of "worlds".)

What is wrong with primitive modality? Two things. First of all, Lewis thinks that an important factor in the evaluation of metaphysical theories is *economy*, both ontological and ideological. To accept primitive modality is to take on a serious ideological commitment and thereby offend against economy. Lewis concedes, however, that this reason is not decisive: in this case, as in many others, there is a trade-off between primitive ideology and extravagant ontology, and philosophers may disagree as to where the greater cost lies. Secondly, primitive notions, even though unanalysed, should nonetheless be understood. A theory that invokes primitives that are mysterious fails this test. But modality *is* mysterious. Modal properties do not fit easily into an empiricist worldview: one can observe that Bush is human, but not that he is necessarily human. Modal properties do not seem to stand alongside fundamental qualitative properties as part of the furniture of the world. Thus, modality cries out for explanation in non-modal terms. Theories that take modality as primitive, then, will sacrifice much or all of the explanatory power of modal realism.

Isolation

In the last four sections of Chapter 1, Lewis presents some of the tenets of modal realism in more detail under the headings "Isolation", "Concreteness", "Plenitude" and "Actuality". I shall say something about each of these in turn.

According to modal realism, worlds (in general) are large composite objects. In the section "Isolation", Lewis provides demarcation criteria for worlds in terms of the relations between their parts. He asks the question, "What are the necessary and sufficient conditions for two individuals to be *worldmates*, to be part of one and the same world?" His answer is this: individuals are worldmates if and only if they are spatiotemporally related, that is, if and only if every part of one stands in some distance relation – be it spatial or temporal, great or small – to every part of the other. A world is *unified*, then, by the spatiotemporal relations among its parts.

One direction of the analysis of the worldmate relation (sufficiency) is uncontroversial. Whatever stands at some spatial or temporal distance to us is part of our world; contrapositively, non-actual individuals stand at no spatial or temporal distance to us, or to anything actual. In general, every world is *spatiotemporally isolated* from every other world. (The worlds are also for Lewis *causally* isolated from one another, as follows from Lewis's counterfactual analysis of causation.) According to the other direction of the analysis (necessity), worlds are unified *only* by spatiotemporal relations; every part of a world is spatiotemporally related to every other part of that world. This direction is more problematic, for at least two reasons. First, could there not be worlds that are unified by relations that are not spatiotemporal? Indeed, it is controversial, even with respect to the actual world, whether entities in the quantum domain stand in anything like spatiotemporal relations to one another; the classic account of spacetime may simply break down.[3] Secondly, could a single world not be composed of disconnected spacetimes, so-called "island universes"? Indeed, could there not be a part of actuality spatiotemporally and causally isolated from the part we inhabit? Lewis must answer "no". When Lewis's analysis of the world-mate relation is combined with the standard analysis of possibility as truth at some world, island universes turn out to be impossible: at no world are there two disconnected spacetimes. This is potentially a problem for Lewis, because other fundamental metaphysical principles that Lewis accepts seem to entail that island universes are possible after all (see Bricker 2001: 35–7).

In any case, the analysis of the worldmate relation in terms of spatiotemporal relations allows Lewis to then provide an analysis of the notion of world: a *world* is any maximal spatiotemporally interrelated individual – an individual all of whose parts are spatiotemporally related to one another, and not to anything else. If one assumes with Lewis that being spatiotemporally related is an equivalence relation (reflexive, symmetric and transitive), it follows that each individual (that belongs to a world) belongs to exactly one world: the sum (or aggregate) of all those individuals that are spatiotemporally related to it. Note that the notion of world has been analysed in non-modal terms – spatiotemporal relations, mereology and logic – thus vindicating the modal realist's claim to eschew primitive modality.

Concreteness

It is natural to characterize modal realism – as Lewis himself sometimes does – as the acceptance of a plurality of *concrete* worlds. This captures the idea that the merely possible worlds do not differ in ontological kind from the actual world, the concrete universe of which we are a part. But Lewis is hesitant to say out-right that worlds are concrete because the distinction between concrete and abstract, as used by contemporary philosophers, is ambiguous and lacking in clarity. In the section "Concreteness", Lewis distinguishes four different ways of drawing the abstract–concrete distinction, and then queries how each applies to his notion of world. It turns out that, on all four ways (with some minor qualifications), worlds do indeed come out as "concrete" for Lewis:

- *The way of example.* Worlds (typically) have parts that are paradigmatically concrete, such as donkeys, and protons, and stars.
- *The way of conflation.* Worlds are particulars, not universals; they are individuals, not sets.
- *The negative way.* Worlds (typically) have parts that stand in spatiotemporal and causal relations to one another.
- *The way of abstraction.* Worlds are fully determinate in all qualitative respects; they are not abstractions from anything else.

But even if "worlds are concrete" comes out true on all ways of drawing the distinction, to say simply "worlds are concrete" is to say something very ambiguous. Perhaps, Lewis suggests, it would be better to drop the abstract–concrete terminology altogether, and to list directly, as above, the fundamental features of worlds.

Plenitude

If possible worlds are to serve in an analysis of modality, there will have to be enough of them: for any way a world could possibly be, there will have to be a world that is that way. Otherwise, there will be "gaps in logical space", the space whose "points" are all and only the worlds; there will be possibilities that lack worlds to represent them. In the section "Plenitude", Lewis asks what general principles would be sufficient to guarantee that there exists an appropriate abundance of worlds. His discussion focuses on a *principle of recombination*, roughly: anything can coexist, or fail to coexist, with anything else. The principle naturally divides into two halves. According to the first half, any two (or more) things, possibly from different worlds, can be patched together in a single world in any arrangement permitted by shape and size. To illustrate, if there could be a unicorn, and there could be a dragon, then there could be a unicorn and a dragon side by side. How will this be interpreted in terms of worlds? Since worlds do not overlap, a unicorn from one world and a dragon from another cannot *themselves* exist side by side. The principle is to be interpreted in terms of *intrinsic duplicates*: at some world, a duplicate of the unicorn and a duplicate of the dragon exist side by side.

According to the second half of the principle of recombination, whenever two distinct things coexist at a world, there is another world at which one of them exists without the other. This half of the principle embodies the Humean denial of necessary connections between distinct existents. ('Distinct', in this context, means non-overlapping, rather than non-identical.) To illustrate, since a talking head exists contiguous to a living human body, there could exist an unattached talking head, separate from any living body. More precisely, there is a world at which a duplicate of the talking head exists but at which no duplicate of the rest of the living body exists.

The principle of recombination allows one to infer, given the existence of *some* possible worlds, the existence of whatever *other* possible worlds can be obtained by "cutting and splicing". The principle is clear in theory, but somewhat murky in application. For example, the principle presumably is behind our belief that talking donkeys and flying pigs are possible, but it is hard to see how applying the principle to macroscopic objects will give this result: a flying pig is not just a pig with wings stuck on. The relevant recombination presumably takes place at the genetic, or even the atomic, level. But then our confidence that the principle yields flying pigs is hostage to our confidence that what it is to be a pig can be analysed in terms of DNA sequences, or fundamental particles; and that seems wrong, since the question of analysis does not appear to play a role in the modal belief.

In any case, it is clear that the principle of recombination, when applied to the actual world and its parts, is sufficient to guarantee the existence of a vast plurality of worlds. Might the principle by itself provide for an appropriate plenitude of worlds, sufficient to ensure that there are no "gaps in logical space"? No, a great many worlds will still be left out. Two sorts of additional principles of plenitude will be needed to guarantee their existence. First, if one starts with a world of three-dimensional objects and applies the principle of recombination, any world that results is still (at most) three-dimensional. But it seems possible that there be a world with four or more spatial dimensions. An additional principle will be needed, then, to guarantee that a plenitude of spatial (and spatio-temporal) structures is represented among the worlds.[4] Secondly, if one applies the principle of recombination to *actual* objects instantiating *actual* properties, one never arrives at an object instantiating *alien* fundamental properties, fundamental properties nowhere instantiated at the actual world. But it seems possible for there to be more or different fundamental properties than there actually are. An additional principle will be needed, it seems, to guarantee a sufficient plenitude of fundamental properties and relations. Although at the end of the section on plenitude Lewis gestures towards the need for additional principles of these two sorts, he does not attempt to provide formulations.

Actuality

In the final section of Chapter 1, "Actuality", Lewis asks how the notion of actuality should be understood by a modal realist. Is actuality a fundamental, absolute property that I (and my worldmates) have but that my counterparts in other worlds lack? If so, it would have to be a rather special sort of property: it could not be an (intrinsic) *qualitative* property because actual individuals have non-actual qualitative duplicates. (Moreover, if actuality were a qualitative property always shared by duplicates, then the principle of recombination would require that there be worlds at which actual and non-actual things coexist, which is absurd.) But, even if we put to one side the mysterious nature of such an absolute property of actuality, a more serious problem looms: how, if actuality is absolute, could I know that I am actual? I have counterparts in other worlds that are epistemically situated exactly as I am; whatever evidence I have for believing that *I* am actual, they have exactly similar evidence for believing that *they* are actual. But if no evidence distinguishes my predicament from theirs, then I do not really *know* that I am not in their predicament: for all I know, I am a merely possible person falsely believing myself to be actual. Thus, Lewis concludes, modal realism together with absolute actuality leads to scepticism about whether I am actual. Such scepticism, however, is absurd. A modal realist, then, should reject absolute actuality.

Lewis proposes instead that actuality is an indexical notion: when I say of something that it is actual, I am saying that it is a part of *this* world, the world that *I* (the speaker) inhabit. In other words, given Lewis's analysis of world, when I say of something that it is actual, I am saying simply that it is spatio-temporally related to me. On the indexical account, I know that I am actual as a trivial matter of meaning: I know, trivially, that I am part of the world I am part of. Knowing I am actual, then, is analogous to knowing I am here, which also is trivial, analytic knowledge: I know, trivially, that I am located where I am (the speaker is) located. In neither case do I need to examine myself to discover that I have some special property – *being actual*, *being here*. Nor is my counterpart off in some other world deceived when he thinks to himself that he is actual. For although in my mouth, 'actual' applies to me and not to him, in his mouth, 'actual' applies to him and not to me (if he speaks English, and so means by 'actual' what I do). My counterpart is not deceived when he thinks to himself "I am actual", any more than someone off in another country (or planet) is deceived when he thinks to himself "I am here".

On the indexical theory of actuality, actuality becomes a relative matter: no world is absolutely actual; every world is actual relative to itself (and its inhabitants), and non-actual relative to any other world (and its inhabitants). Someone might object: taking actuality to be relative in this way fails to take actuality with metaphysical seriousness. With that Lewis happily agrees: a deflationary account of actuality goes hand in hand with the modal realist assertion that the merely possible worlds do not differ from the actual world in ontological status. And only a deflationary account can explain how we know that we are actual.

Everything is actual?

In the eight sections of Chapter 2, "Paradox in Paradise?", Lewis considers eight objections to modal realism and provides a reply to each. I shall discuss four of these objections, the four that are most familiar, and most fundamental.

The first objection, in the section "Everything is Actual?", is that what Lewis calls "possible worlds" are not properly called possible worlds at all: Lewisian worlds, if they exist, would be parts of actuality, not alternatives to it. Modal realism, then, correctly interpreted, posits a massively bloated actuality, not a realm of *possibilia* existing separate and distinct from the realm of the actual. But if this is the correct interpretation of what the modal realist believes, then the analysis of modality in terms of quantification over these so-called "possible worlds" cannot be correct: modal statements have to do with alternatives to actuality, not parts of it.

Lewis concedes that "if the other worlds would be just parts of actuality, modal realism is kaput" (p. 112). But, on his indexical analysis of 'actuality', the other worlds, being spatiotemporally isolated from our world, are not properly called "actual". So, the objection, if it is good, must be that the indexical analysis is incorrect. There are two ways that the objection might be pressed. One might hold that 'actual', like 'entity', is a so-called "blanket term": it is analytic that 'actual' applies to whatever exists, to anything in the realm of being. Lewis argues, however, that even if it is part of our common-sense view that whatever exists is actual, it is not plausibly taken to be analytic: it is coherent to posit non-actual, merely possible objects. But there is a second, more powerful way to press the objection that the modal realist believes in a plurality of actual worlds, a way that Lewis does not consider. Plausibly, it is analytic that 'actual' is a *categorial* term: anything ontologically of the same basic kind as something actual is itself actual. In other words: a merely possible object and an actual object, even if qualitative duplicates of one another, belong to distinct ontological kinds. If this is accepted, then Lewis's claim that there are non-actual worlds ontologically on a par with the actual world would indeed be incoherent. The only way to believe in a plurality of non-actual possible worlds, then, would be to combine it with absolute actuality, to hold that there is an absolute distinction between the actual and the merely possible – in which case the daunting problem of scepticism about actuality would have to be faced anew.[5]

How can we know?

A second, powerful objection to modal realism is epistemic. Modal realism holds that we have substantial modal knowledge, both specific, such as that talking donkeys are possible, and general, such as is embodied in the principle of recombination. On analysis, that knowledge turns out to be knowledge of the goings on at other possible worlds. But, the objection goes, we cannot have such knowledge because the other worlds are causally isolated from us, and knowledge of any subject matter requires that there be some sort of causal connection.

Lewis's response is twofold. First, he rejects the premise that causal acquaintance is necessary for knowledge of a subject matter. Here he invokes mathematics as a precedent: we have knowledge of mathematical entities – numbers, sets and so on – even though such entities are "abstract", and stand in no causal relations to anything. Lewis's response appears to presuppose Platonism, the view that a realist interpretation of mathematics is correct; no doubt those who object to modal realism on epistemological grounds would object no less to Platonism. But Lewis's goal is not to refute the objector; achieving a stand-off will do. He is content to argue that modal realism is no worse off epistemologically than realism about mathematical entities.

However, achieving even a stand-off requires a subsidiary argument to the effect that the mathematical and modal cases really are analogous. Is that so? Mathematical entities are abstract; Lewis's worlds are concrete. Is that not a relevant difference with respect to how these entities can be known? "No", says Lewis. The distinction that matters for epistemology is that between the contingent and the necessary: knowledge of contingent truth requires causal contact with what is known; knowledge of necessary truth does not. Mathematics and modality may differ with respect to the "concreteness" of their subject matter; but with respect to what matters for epistemology, they are the same.

A road to indifference?

A third objection is that modal realism leads to moral indifference. If modal realism were true, one could have no moral reason to choose an act that leads to good over an act that leads to evil because, whatever one chooses to do, the same total of good and evil will occur throughout all the worlds. Thus, Robert Adams asks, "What is wrong with actualizing evils since they will occur in other possible worlds anyway?" (Adams 1974: 216). If one chooses the act with the good outcome, one has a counterpart no less real who chooses the act with the evil outcome; if one chooses the act with the evil outcome, one has a counterpart who chooses the act that leads to good. This objection, unlike the two previously considered, does not claim that modal realism is incoherent; the modal realist has the option to simply embrace the demise of morality. But Lewis is conservatively inclined: if modal realism would require that we revise in fundamental ways our conception of ourselves as moral agents, that would, Lewis agrees, provide strong reason to reject it.

Lewis concedes that modal realism makes trouble for at least one ethical theory: universalistic utilitarianism, the view that that act is morally best which maximizes the sum total of utility (happiness, welfare, etc.) for *everyone, everywhere*, with the 'every' unrestricted. But such an ethical theory is implausible on independent grounds: it conflicts with common-sense attitudes towards morality in at least two ways. First, the good and evil that we care about is the good and evil that occurs to those who stand in some special relation to us: our family, our friends, perhaps our countryman, or our fellow Earthlings. Common-sense morality is *agent centred*, not *agent neutral*. Morality, as commonly understood, does not prohibit us from restricting our moral concern to our worldmates, or some portion thereof. Secondly, even if one allowed that, contrary to common-sense morality, good and evil everywhere should count equally in our calculations, there would still be an adequate answer to Adams's question "What is wrong with actualizing evils since they will occur in other possible worlds anyway?". To actualize evils, Lewis responds, is to be an evil-doer, a causal source of evil. Thus, even if one's acts cannot change the total sum of good or evil throughout the worlds, there may still be a moral reason to choose one act over another. One ought to choose an act that makes one a causal source of good rather than evil; and this is in no way undermined by the existence of counterparts who choose instead to actualize evil. What *I* ought to do depends not only on the range of possible outcomes, but on my causal relation to the outcome that results in my world. In conclusion, then, if a modal realist accepts that morality is agent centred in one or both of these ways, modal realism will not threaten morality by leading to moral indifference.

The incredulous stare

The final objection to modal realism is what Lewis calls "the incredulous stare". Simply put, it is that modal realism, with its talking donkeys and flying pigs no less "real" or "concrete" than actual donkeys and pigs, is too incredible to be believed. No matter how great the theoretical benefits of modal realism, no matter how successful it is in systematically unifying and simplifying our total theory, the cost of believing such an incredible theory will always be too great. Lewis accepts that modal realism disagrees severely with common sense, and he accepts that this is a serious cost to the theory. But it is not a prohibitive cost, not unless there are alternative theories of possible worlds that can achieve most or all of the benefits of modal realism without incurring serious costs of their own. This leads Lewis to the third chapter of the book: an examination of alternative theories of possible worlds.

Ersatz modal realism

Lewis's third chapter, "Paradise on the Cheap?", is devoted to an elaboration and criticism of the various views he calls *ersatz modal realism*, views that provide abstract surrogates to play the role of Lewis's concrete possible worlds and individuals. According to ersatz modal realism ("ersatzism" for short), there is only one concrete world. But there are countless abstract entities – the ersatz worlds – that represent ways the one concrete world might have been. (Calling them "ersatz", of course, is to take the modal realist perspective; those who do not believe in Lewis's concrete worlds may think of the abstract entities as the real thing – perhaps properly called "possible worlds" – not as sham substitutes.) One of the ersatz worlds correctly represents the concrete world in complete detail: it is the *actualized* ersatz world. The other ersatz worlds all misrepresent the concrete world in some respect; they are all therefore *unactualized*. Similarly, ersatzism posits ersatz possible individuals that are actualized or unactualized depending on whether or not they accurately represent any concrete individual. On the ersatzist account – unlike modal realism – there is a distinction between being *actualized* and being *actual*. Typically, ersatzists are self-proclaimed *actualists*, and so they hold that the ersatz *possibilia*, actualized or not, are all actual. Perhaps they are "metaphysical actualists", holding that ersatz *possibilia* are actual because they are abstract entities, and abstract entities are actual by nature; or perhaps they are "analytic actualists", holding that ersatz *possibilia* are actual because it is analytic that *everything* is actual. Either way, the ersatzist seems to have an advantage over the modal realist in agreeing with common sense that whatever exists is actual.

More importantly, the ersatzist has an advantage over the modal realist in agreeing with common sense about the extent of concrete reality: there are no more concrete donkeys, for example, than we ordinarily think there are. True, the ersatzist believes in countless infinities of abstract representations of donkeys; but common sense does not have a firm opinion as to the extent of abstract reality, and so the positing of abstract *possibilia* does not offend common-sense beliefs. At any rate, so says the ersatzist.

Now, if the ersatzist can supply a sufficient plenitude of ersatz worlds and individuals, then she can take over the analyses proffered by the modal realist. For example, she can say that it is possible that a donkey talk just in case some ersatz world represents that a donkey talks. And where the modal realist constructs entities out of concrete *possibilia* to play various theoretical roles – for example, to serve as meanings or properties – the ersatz modal realist can mimic that construction using ersatz worlds and individuals. It seems, then, that the ersatzist can have the benefits of Lewis's *possibilia* without bearing the costs. But, Lewis argues, appearances here are deceptive.

Lewis believes there are severe costs to ersatz modal realism, but different versions have different costs. So he divides the various versions into three sorts depending on how the ersatz worlds *represent* (or *misrepresent*) the one concrete world. According to *linguistic ersatzism*, ersatz worlds are like stories or theories, they are constructed from the words or sentences of some language (called the "worldmaking language") and they represent by virtue of the stipulated meanings of these words and sentences. According to *pictorial ersatzism*, ersatz worlds are like pictures or scale models, and they represent by isomorphism, by being as structurally and qualitatively similar to a concrete world as is compatible with their being abstract. According to *magical ersatzism*, the ersatz worlds represent in a primitive and inexplicable way; they represent what they do simply because it is their nature to do so. Lewis's exposition and criticism of these three views is lengthy and involved. In what follows, I provide a brief account of his arguments against linguistic and magical ersatzism. (I shall not discuss pictorial ersatzism. Lewis's chief argument against it is that, when properly and fully developed, it collapses into a version of modal realism, and so cannot really provide the benefits sought by the ersatzist programme.)

Linguistic ersatzism

Linguistic ersatzism is based on the following natural idea: although concrete, non-actual worlds are hard to believe in, there is no problem believing in *sentences* purporting to describe such non-actual worlds. Perhaps, instead of concrete worlds with flying pigs as parts, we can make do with ersatz worlds constructed from sentences such as the sentence 'Pigs fly'. There will be no mystery as to how such ersatz worlds represent that pigs fly: the representational properties of the ersatz worlds derive directly from the meanings of the sentences they contain.

Here is one way of carrying out the idea.[6] Collect together into a set all the sentences that would be true if some Lewisian world were actualized; this gives an abstract surrogate for that world. Since any Lewisian world possibly exists, the set of sentences that would be true at the world is *consistent*, implies no contradiction. And since any Lewisian world is fully determinate, the set of sentences that would be true at the world is *maximal* consistent, containing for any sentence, either that sentence or its negation. Conversely, any maximal consistent set of sentences is an appropriate surrogate for some Lewisian concrete world, the world at which all its sentences are true. So, the linguistic ersatzist holds that the ersatz worlds are just the maximal consistent sets of sentences of an appropriate worldmaking language.

259

What language should be used to construct the ersatz worlds? A natural language, such as English, will not quite do because its words and sentences are often vague, ambiguous and context-dependent. So, let us suppose that these unlovely features have been purged from the worldmaking language: every sentence of the language is determinately true or false at any possible world. A more serious problem is that English, so purged, may be descriptively impoverished even with respect to its power to describe individuals and properties at the actual world. A simple solution is to enrich the language by letting actual things be *names* of themselves, and properties be *predicates* that express themselves – what Lewis calls a *Lagadonian language*. (Of course, a Lagadonian language is rather inconvenient for its users; one has to display an object in order to talk about it. But what matters for the purposes of ersatzism is just that the sentences of the worldmaking language have clearly defined meanings in virtue of which the ersatz worlds represent.) Finally, we do not want the worldmaking language to be *logically* impoverished; so let us suppose that there are no logical limitations on the language's expressive powers, even if that means adding infinitary logical connectives to the language. Now, the ersatz worlds will be the maximal consistent sentences of this descriptively and logically enriched worldmaking language.

Lewis has two main objections. The first is that the linguistic ersatzist needs primitive modality; for the notion of consistency used in the construction is a modal notion, not reducible to any non-modal notion of (formal) logical consistency, whether syntactically or model-theoretically defined. (For example, although 'some bachelors are married' is consistent in formal logic, it is not consistent in the sense relevant to the construction of ersatz worlds: there should not be any worlds at which some bachelors are married.) Lewis is aware, however, that many ersatzists will gladly help themselves to this much primitive modality if that is the full cost of a ticket to paradise.

The second objection is not so easily discounted by the ersatzist. It is that, even after the worldmaking language has been enriched in the ways discussed above, it will still lack the descriptive resources to provide enough worlds to match the worlds of the modal realist. The problem arises when one considers the possibility of alien individuals instantiating alien fundamental properties. It seems hard to deny that the world could have satisfied different physical laws involving different fundamental properties; otherwise many physical theories that turned out false would be wrongly classified as metaphysically impossible. Now, alien fundamental properties present no problem for the modal realist because the alien worlds at which they are instantiated do not need to be reduced to anything else: the modal realist simply posits that, since it is possible that there be alien fundamental properties, there are worlds at which such properties are instantiated. But the linguistic ersatzist has to construct these alien worlds out of his worldmaking language, a language that lacks any predicates for alien fundamental properties. The Lagadonian strategy is of no avail here, because the ersatzist does not believe there exist any alien properties to serve as predicates expressing themselves: there is only the one concrete world, with its actual properties. And to simply stipulate that the worldmaking language contains predicates expressing alien properties, without there being any account of how a predicate manages to express one such property rather than another, is to move away from linguistic ersatzism, and allow that representation is primitive and irreducible – the view called magical ersatzism, to be discussed shortly.

The problem is not that the linguistic ersatzist cannot construct an ersatz world at which it is true that alien fundamental properties are instantiated. For, if the worldmaking language has the resources to quantify over properties, the sentence 'there exists a fundamental property not identical to … [here list all actually instantiated fundamental properties]', will be a consistent sentence of the worldmaking language, and so will belong to some maximal consistent set of sentences, some ersatz world. But there will not be enough such ersatz worlds to match the alien worlds of the modal realist. That is because the modal realist will hold (on the basis of the principle of recombination) that for each description of an alien world that the ersatzist can supply, there are many concrete alien worlds differing from one another either by containing different alien properties, or by permuting the alien properties they contain. Linguistic ersatzism, then, conflates distinct alien possibilities; it provides only one ersatz world to substitute for many Lewisian alien worlds. And this will have a detrimental effect on the truth-conditions for modal statements. For example, the ersatzist cannot provide worlds to validate the (intuitively) correct modal inference: it is possible in many ways that p; therefore, there are many possibilities in which p. In short, the linguistic ersatz worlds cannot provide all the theoretical benefits of the modal realist's concrete worlds.

Magical ersatzism

Linguistic ersatzism runs into trouble with alien possibilities because it attempts to construct its ersatz worlds out of entities confined to the one concrete world. Magical ersatzism avoids this problem by positing, rather than constructing, its ersatz worlds: they are primitive entities with primitive powers of representing the ways the concrete world might have been. Magical ersatzism, then, is a form of realism about possible worlds, but one in which the worlds are abstract – perhaps properties, or states of affairs – rather than concrete.[7] Since the magical ersatz worlds represent in a primitive way, their internal structure is irrelevant. So we might as well suppose that they have no internal structure; they are mereological simples. One of these simples – the actualized ersatz world – bears the relation *represents (in complete detail)* to the concrete world; the other ersatz worlds misrepresent the concrete world in some way, and so do not bear this relation to the concrete world. The representation relation is fundamental and primitive, not reducible to anything else.

Lewis's chief objection to magical ersatzism is that such primitive representation involves an odious form of primitive modality; it requires that there be necessary connections that violate the principle of recombination. Recall that, according to that principle, distinct existents can coexist in any arrangement permitted by shape and size. Lewis primarily had in mind *spatiotemporal* arrangements, since, for Lewis, spatiotemporal relations are the clearest example of fundamental external relations. But the principle should apply no less to whatever other fundamental external relations there may be. For the case at hand, we are concerned with how the concrete world and the ersatz worlds are "arranged" *vis-à-vis* the relation of representation. Consider the ersatz world that correctly represents the concrete world, and some other ersatz world that does not. Lewis asks: why could it not go the other way, with the second ersatz world standing in the representation relation to the concrete world, rather than the first? Should it not be possible for the concrete world and the ersatz worlds to be differently "arranged"? If one holds, as the ersatzist must, that there is one way they are "arranged", and that that arrangement is absolutely necessary, then one will be saddled with necessary connections between distinct existents: the ersatz worlds and the one concrete world. These connections are "magical", in that it is beyond our ability to understand how or why they should occur. Moreover, this sort of primitive modality, according to Lewis, is somehow worse than the sort of primitive modality needed by the linguistic ersatzist: the distinction between those linguistic representations that are possible and those that are not.

Lewis's argument against the magical ersatz worlds is sweeping in its scope. Primitive intensional entities, such as propositions, properties and relations, will likewise be swept away, because all such entities stand in fundamental external relations – truth, instantiation – to concrete entities, relations that violate Lewis's generalized principle of recombination. But perhaps the argument is too sweeping to be credible. For it seems that sets, too, with their relation of membership to concrete entities, will violate Lewis's constraints. And Lewis does not suggest doing without sets in his ontology, lest mathematics lack a foundation. Whether Lewis's argument can be restricted in some way so as to apply to magical ersatz worlds and primitive intensional entities, but not to sets, remains an open question.[8]

Counterpart theory: an objection

The fourth and final chapter, "Counterparts or Double Lives?", is devoted to the infamous "problem of transworld identity" and related matters.[9] The chapter includes a thorough defence and elaboration of Lewis's counterpart theoretic solution: the idea, introduced above, that modality *de re* is to be analysed in terms of a counterpart relation based on qualitative similarity.

Is there a problem of transworld identity? In one sense, the answer is "no": modal realists and ersatzists alike agree that one and the same concrete individual can truly be said to *exist at* more than one possible world, where an individual exists at a world just if the world represents *de re* that that individual exists. But the modal realist and the ersatzist will give different accounts of representation *de re*. For the modal realist, there are two ways for a (concrete) individual to exist at a world: one way is to be a part of the world; another way is to have a counterpart as a part of the world. Thus, a (concrete) individual can exist at more than one world without being a part of more than one world, without allowing that worlds overlap. Ersatzists, too, will need to give an account of representation *de re*. Although different ersatzists will give different accounts, on no ersatzist account will the concrete individual exist at an abstract ersatz world by being a part of it. So the ersatzist, no less than the modal realist, rejects transworld identity in the literal sense of being a part of more than one world.

An ersatzist could choose to be a counterpart theorist, taking abstract ersatz *possibilia* to be counterparts of actual, concrete individuals. But most prominent ersatzists have argued that counterpart theory provides unacceptable truth-conditions for *de re* modal statements. For example, Saul Kripke famously complained that, according to counterpart theory:

> if we say "Humphrey might have won the election (if only he had done such-and-such)", we are not talking about something that might have happened to *Humphrey*, but to someone else, a "counterpart". Probably, however, Humphrey could not care less whether someone *else*, no matter how much resembling him, would have been victorious in another possible world. (Kripke 1980: 45)

Kripke's objection naturally falls into two parts. The first part is that, on the analysis of modality *de re* provided by counterpart theory, the modal property, *might have won the election*, is attributed to Humphrey's *counterpart* rather than to Humphrey himself. But surely, the objection continues, when we say that "Humphrey might have won", we mean to say something about *Humphrey*. This part of the objection, however, is easily answered. According to counterpart theory, Humphrey himself has the modal property, *might have won the election*, in virtue of his counterpart having the (non-modal) property, *won the election*. Moreover, that Humphrey has a winning counterpart is a matter of the qualitative character of Humphrey and his surroundings; so on the counterpart theoretic analysis, the modal statement is indeed a claim about Humphrey.

The second part of Kripke's objection is more troublesome. We have a strong intuition, not only that the modal statement "Humphrey might have won the election" is about Humphrey, but that it is *only* about Humphrey (and his surroundings). On counterpart theory, however, the modal statement is also about a merely possible person in some merely possible world; and that, Kripke might say, is simply not what we take the modal statement to mean. The first thing to say in response is that the charge of unintuitiveness would apply equally to the ersatzist's use of abstract ersatz worlds to provide truth-conditions for modal statements; for our intuitive understanding of modal statements such as "Humphrey might have won the election" does not *seem* to invoke abstract worlds any more than counterparts of Humphrey. The objection, then, if it is good, would seem to cut equally against modal realism and ersatzism, and favour an anti-realist view that rejected worlds, real or ersatz. But is the objection good? Should our pre-theoretic intuitions as to what our statements are and are not *about* carry much, or even any, weight? I think not. A philosophical analysis of our ordinary modal statements must assign the right truth-values and validate the right inferences; but requiring more would fatally hamper philosophical attempts to attain theoretical systematization.

Representation *de re*: four questions

The four remaining sections of Chapter 4 address four important questions about how representation *de re* works. I have space here only to state the questions and indicate the gist of Lewis's responses. The first two questions pertain just to modal realism. The first is: if the modal realist were to allow overlapping worlds, were to allow a concrete individual to be part of more than one concrete world, could counterpart theory be avoided? Could a modal realist say that the properties an individual has at any world are just the properties it has *simpliciter*, rather than the properties had by a counterpart inhabiting that world? (If so, representation *de re* would work by transworld identity in the literal sense.) "No", replies Lewis. An individual's intrinsic properties are sometimes accidental, in which case it has different intrinsic properties at different worlds. And that is impossible if representation *de re* works by literal transworld identity.

The second question is: could the concrete individuals we ordinarily refer to – people, and puddles, and protons – be *transworld sums*, partly in one world, partly in another? Then, the modal realist could say that an individual has a property at a world just if the part of it that is wholly contained in the world has the property *simpliciter*. Lewis rejects such transworld sums, not because he thinks they do not exist – he puts no restriction on mereological composition – but because he thinks on semantic grounds that our ordinary names and descriptions do not refer to them. And, in any case, taking ordinary objects to be transworld sums would do nothing to satisfy the intuitions that seem to support transworld identity over counterpart theory.

The final two questions are for modal realists and ersatzists alike. The third question is whether representation *de re* is determined entirely by the qualitative nature of worlds, or whether instead there could be two worlds qualitatively alike that nonetheless differed as to what they represented *de re* of some individual? The *haecceitist* holds that representation *de re* is not qualitatively determined, and seems to have strong intuitions on her side. But Lewis argues that these haecceitist intuitions are better accommodated in another way: by allowing that distinct possibilities may sometimes be realized within a single possible world.

Finally, Lewis asks: is representation *de re* a constant matter, fixed once and for all? Or does it vary with context, and sometimes have no determinate answer at all? Lewis argues for the latter approach according to which questions of essence and accident do not have the absolute metaphysical significance often attributed to them, but instead often shift with the wind.

Conclusion

Since the publication of *On the Plurality of Worlds* in 1986, scores of articles have been published in philosophical journals responding to Lewis's arguments. I think it is safe to say that modal realism is viewed today as more defensible, and ersatz modal realism as more problematic, than previously had been the case.[10] Still, only a small minority of philosophers are willing to give modal realism (or one of its close variations) unqualified support. Indeed, most philosophers, if driven away from ersatzism by Lewis's arguments, find themselves pushed not towards modal realism, but towards some anti-realist approach, an approach that rejects both concrete and abstract *possibilia*.[11] Perhaps Lewis's "paradise for philosophers" is simply not to be had, a will-o'-the-wisp. Perhaps belief in a plurality of concrete worlds is just too far-fetched, supporting arguments notwithstanding. Perhaps. I invite the reader to engage with Lewis's compelling book in order to judge for herself.[12]

Notes

1. For a discussion of Lewis's views on these and other topics with modal underpinnings, see Daniel Nolan, *David Lewis* (Chesham: Acumen, 2005).
2. Here and below, I follow Lewis in speaking of what is the case *at* a possible world, rather than *in* a possible world. This usage grew out of "indexical semantics", where possible worlds and times are treated analogously at the formal level.
3. Perhaps Lewis's introduction of analogical spatiotemporal relations (pp. 75–6) goes part way to answering this objection; but it does not seem to go far enough. For discussion, see Phillip Bricker, "Isolation and Unification: The Realist Analysis of Possible Worlds", *Philosophical Studies* **84** (1996), 225–38.
4. See Phillip Bricker, "Plenitude of Possible Structures", *Journal of Philosophy* **88** (1991), 607–19, for a comparison of various formulations of such a principle.
5. In Phillip Bricker, "Absolute Actuality and the Plurality of Worlds", in *Philosophical Perspectives 20: Metaphysics*, J. Hawthorne (ed.) (Oxford: Blackwell, forthcoming), I argue that a believer in (concrete) possible worlds can combine indexicality of the *concept* of actuality with absoluteness of the *property* of actuality, and thereby evade the sceptical problem.
6. For a rather different approach not addressed by Lewis, see Theodore Sider, "The Ersatz Pluriverse", *Journal of Philosophy* **99** (2002), 279–315.
7. See especially Robert Stalnaker, "Possible Worlds", *Noûs* **10** (1976), 65–75, and Alvin Plantinga, *The Nature of Necessity* (Oxford: Clarendon Press, 1974). Stalnaker calls his view "moderate realism" to distinguish it from Lewis's view, which he calls "extreme realism".
8. Peter van Inwagen, "Two Concepts of Possible Worlds", *Midwest Studies in Philosophy* **11** (1986), 185–213, notes that Lewis's argument against magical ersatzism applies, with minor adjustments, to Lewis's own acceptance of sets. David Lewis, *Parts of Classes* (Oxford: Blackwell, 1991), 35–8, contains a brief response.
9. See Roderick Chisholm, "Identity Through Possible Worlds: Some Questions", *Noûs* **1** (1967), 1–8, for an early, classic statement of the problem.
10. For example, after an extensive review of the relevant literature, John Divers concludes: "In sum, I have come to think that the objections against [modal] realism, even taken collectively, are not convincing … I here take [modal] realism to be more credible than [ersatzism] and I think that [modal] realism may be credible *tout court*" (*Possible Worlds* (London: Routledge, 2002), xii).
11. Anti-realist approaches to modality were given short shrift in Lewis's book. The two most prominent approaches are *fictionalism* (see David Armstrong, *A Combinatorial Theory of Possibility* (Cambridge: Cambridge University Press, 1989) and Gideon Rosen, "Modal Fictionalism", *Mind* **99** (1990), 327–54, and *modalism* (see Kit Fine, "Postscript: Prior on the Construction of Possible Worlds and Instants", in *Worlds, Times, and Selves*, A. Prior & K. Fine, 116–61 (London: Duckworth, 1977) and Graham Forbes, *The Metaphysics of Modality* (Oxford: Clarendon Press, 1985)).
12. Thanks to Jake Bridge and the editor, John Shand, for helpful comments.

Further reading

For further background in the metaphysics of modality, I recommend Melia (2003) and Divers (2002). Melia (2003) is an introductory survey of approaches to modality; Divers (2002) provides a more comprehensive treatment that focuses on the debate between modal realism and ersatzism. The anthology Loux (1979) contains many of the classic articles to which Lewis is responding in his book. The text Girle (2000) provides an introduction to possible-worlds semantics for modal logic.

Bibliography

Adams, R. 1974. "Theories of Actuality". *Noûs* 8, 211–31. Reprinted in Loux (1979), 190–209.

Armstrong, D. 1989. *A Combinatorial Theory of Possibility*. Cambridge: Cambridge University Press.

Bricker, P. 1991. "Plenitude of Possible Structures". *Journal of Philosophy* 88, 607–19.

Bricker, P. 1996. "Isolation and Unification: The Realist Analysis of Possible Worlds". *Philosophical Studies* 84, 225–38.

Bricker, P. 2001. "Island Universes and the Analysis of Modality". In *Reality and Humean Supervenience: Essays on the Philosophy of David Lewis*, G. Preyer & F. Siebelt (eds), 27–55. Lanham, MD: Rowman & Littlefield.

Bricker, P. forthcoming. "Absolute Actuality and the Plurality of Worlds". In *Philosophical Perspectives 20: Metaphysics*, J. Hawthorne (ed.). Oxford: Blackwell.

Chisholm, R. 1967. "Identity Through Possible Worlds: Some Questions". *Noûs* 1, 1–8. Reprinted in Loux (1979), 80–87.

Divers, J. 2002. *Possible Worlds*. London: Routledge.

Fine, K. 1977. "Postscript: Prior on the Construction of Possible Worlds and Instants". In *Worlds, Times, and Selves*, A. Prior & K. Fine, 116–61. London: Duckworth.

Forbes, G. 1985. *The Metaphysics of Modality*. Oxford: Clarendon Press.

Girle, R. 2000. *Modal Logics and Philosophy*. Chesham: Acumen.

Kripke, S. 1980. *Naming and Necessity*. Cambridge, MA: Harvard University Press.

Lewis, D. 1968. "Counterpart Theory and Quantified Modal Logic". *Journal of Philosophy* 65, 113–26. Reprinted in Loux (1979), 110–28.

Lewis, D. 1973. *Counterfactuals*. Cambridge, MA: Harvard University Press.

Lewis, D. 1986. *On the Plurality of Worlds*. Oxford: Blackwell.

Lewis, D. 1991. *Parts of Classes*. Oxford: Blackwell.

Loux, M. (ed.) 1979. *The Possible and the Actual: Readings in the Metaphysics of Modality*. Ithaca, NY: Cornell University Press.

Melia, J. 2003. *Modality*. Chesham: Acumen.

Nolan, D. 2005. *David Lewis*. Chesham: Acumen.

Plantinga, A. 1974. *The Nature of Necessity*. Oxford: Clarendon Press.

Rosen, G. 1990. "Modal Fictionalism". *Mind* 99, 327–54.

Sider, T. 2002. "The Ersatz Pluriverse". *Journal of Philosophy* 99, 279–315.

Stalnaker, R. 1976. "Possible Worlds". *Noûs* 10, 65–75. Reprinted in Loux (1979), 225–34.

Van Inwagen, P. 1986. "Two Concepts of Possible Worlds". *Midwest Studies in Philosophy* 11, 185–213.

13

Charles Taylor

Sources of the Self:
The Making of the Modern Identity

Ruth Abbey

Introduction

Since its publication in 1989, Charles Taylor's *Sources of the Self* has commanded much attention and generated considerable controversy. It has attracted lavish praise and fierce criticism – sometimes from the same commentator![1] Yet when one considers its scope and ambition, it is not surprising that *Sources of the Self* should have elicited, and should continue to elicit, such a range of reactions. This chapter provides an overview of the book by outlining what Taylor was attempting to do in *Sources of the Self*; what conception of the self it adduces; what the sources of the modern self are and how these are supposed to "source" the self.

The book's aims

In the Preface to *Sources of the Self*, Taylor suggests that his ambition in writing the book is a genealogical one: he hopes to "articulate and write a history of the modern identity" (*Sources*: ix). Shortly afterwards he declares that "This book attempts to define the modern identity in describing its genesis" (*Sources*: x). Looking back on his work several years after its publication, Taylor reiterated and elaborated on this characterization:

> The book is genealogical. I start from the present situation, from formative ideas, from our conflicting forms of self-understanding,

and I try to unearth certain earlier forms from which they arise … it is not a complete historical reconstruction, it is a very selective step backwards to rediscover certain sources.   (Taylor 1998: 362)[2]

This suggests then that *Sources of the Self* aims at nothing less than a genealogy of modern morals.[3] But unlike Friedrich Nietzsche, who coined the phrase genealogy of morals, and Michel Foucault, who styled himself as Nietzsche's legatee (Foucault 1984), Taylor undertakes a genealogy of morals without a hermeneutics of suspicion.[4] By this I do not mean that Taylor takes a naive attitude towards those things that he identifies as the moral sources of the modern self, nor that he accepts their meaning at face value. On the contrary, commentators often observe what subtle, insightful and illuminating interpretations Taylor offers of the sources of the modern self. Rather, claiming that his genealogy of morals proceeds without a hermeneutics of suspicion signals that Taylor does not adopt a mercilessly sceptical or hostile attitude towards the values, self-understandings or moral sources of modern selfhood. His project is not undertaken with primarily critical intent; his aim is not to disabuse people of their ethical illusions nor loosen the hold of their most cherished values. Instead, he focuses on what is attractive and positive in modern values and outlooks. Thus Jeremy Waldron describes *Sources of the Self* as "an optimistic, affirmative work" (1990: 325; cf. Baum 1991), while Martha Nussbaum says that "Taylor's account aims to show how traditional views can justify themselves through careful argument … [he mines] the dominant intellectual tradition for moral insight" (1990: 32).[5] Further evidence that Taylor lacks a hermeneutics of suspicion comes from Judith Shklar's observation that he systematically ignores the darker side of some of the influential philosophies he discusses. As she says:

> Throughout his review of virtually every phase of European literary culture, Taylor only seems to dwell on the sunny side of the street: Montaigne without contempt, Pope without misanthropy, no Swift at all, Rousseau without his curses, Romanticism without violence, Dostoyevsky without gloom and rage, and, finally, modernist authors engaged in epiphanies, among whom Beckett is not to be found. This is a very upbeat book.   (Shklar 1991: 106)

Nor does Taylor accentuate the goods, values, ways of life or worldviews that have been eclipsed or effaced by the arrival of these new values, self-understandings and moral sources: once again, his focus is on the benefits and bonuses of modernity rather than its losses (cf. Calhoun 1991: 240; Skinner 1991: 142–5; Ricoeur 1998: 31).

Some of Taylor's prefatory remarks suggest, however, that he would not be entirely pleased with this depiction of his achievement in *Sources of the Self*. Introducing the book, he reflects that whereas many other attempts to come to grips with modernity have urged either celebration or condemnation, he proposes a more mixed assessment, one that takes the measure of modernity's greatness and its depredations. As he says, "We have yet to capture, I think, the unique combination of greatness and danger, of *grandeur et misère*, which characterizes the modern age" (Taylor *Sources*: ix–x). Readers are left to infer that *Sources of the Self* will, or at least try to, distil the wonders and the weaknesses of the modern era, just as it will help us to "see the full complexity and richness of the modern identity" (*Sources*: x).

Yet Taylor's tacit aspiration to reveal the strengths as well as the shortcomings of modernity through a delineation of the modern self seems to be at odds with his practice as a genealogist. His focus on the attractions and benefits of the values and attitudes that distinguish the modern self is grounded in his method. As he explains two hundred pages into the book, he quite deliberately attends to the appealing, rather than the appalling, dimensions of the sources of the modern self. He tries to give:

> an account of the new identity which makes clear what its appeal was. What drew people to it? Indeed, what draws them to day? What gave it its spiritual power?[6] We articulate the visions of the good involved in it … [we try to] show why people found [or find] it convincing/ inspiring/moving, which will identify what can be called the "idées-forces" it contains. … We can say: in this and this consists the power of the idea/identity/moral vision, however it was brought into history.
> (*Sources*: 203)

As this indicates, for Taylor the best way to explain the power of any idea or practice is to appreciate the image of the good that it embodies and affirms. For him, seeking the good in a particular morality or way of life is a more useful means of accounting for its power and influence than believing that people are lured by its evil or moved toward it primarily by self-interest.

Taylor's attention to the history of the modern self also has the aim of contributing to self-knowledge. He believes that telling the history of the modern self will illuminate "the modern identity as we live it today" (*Sources*: 319). Recounting or reconstructing the history of the modern self enhances self-knowledge by shedding light on those aspects of the self that are specific and historical rather than universal and ontological, for it shows how certain parts of ourselves that are often taken for granted or seen as natural have come into being over time (*Sources*: 112). An emancipatory intent can also be discerned behind Taylor's historical reconstruction of the modern identity. One of the things his work underlines is what a multiple and complex entity the modern self is, and he hopes that uncovering this complexity will free people from the tendency to deny and stifle the plurality of goods that modern selves effectively, if not always knowingly, affirm (*Sources*: 106–7, 503, 511, 514, 520).

Because Taylor's aim is to explain how various contemporary conceptions of selfhood and value that are prevalent in Western societies came into being, he can avoid any strict demarcation of the modern period. Rather than having any sense of modernity being over, or superseded, he thinks that we are still living the modern features of selfhood focused on in the book. Conversely, by arguing that there are several different strands of modern selfhood, he can trace their "beginnings" to different centuries. Yet because his attention is directed at ideas that gradually filter through culture and society, even identifying the first philosophical expressions of such ideas is not tantamount to saying that this is when a particular conception of selfhood started or took hold. So there are no fixed and firm start and end dates to modernity in Taylor's thinking: rather he takes a more relaxed approach to the question of periodization, and sees himself as trying "to comprehend the momentous transformations of our culture and society over the last three or four centuries" (*Sources*: ix).

It may seem strange that a discussion of the aims of a book with the terms "self" and "identity" in its title should turn so quickly to moral matters. The reason for this is that in this book at least, Taylor's conception of the self is a pre-eminently moral one. As he declares early in the work, "Selfhood and the good, or in another way selfhood and morality, turn out to be inextricably intertwined themes" (*Sources*: 3; cf. x, 33, 41, 105). Taylor construes the term morality broadly to include not only those matters usually considered moral, such as questions about obligation, duty, justice and the right, but also questions about what it is good to be and what it takes to live a meaningful, fulfilled life. In the modern era, this first cluster of questions has typically been seen to be susceptible to universal answers. What it is right to do, what our obligations to others are, are supposed to be answerable in general, abstract and impartial terms (*Sources*: 79, 84), while the second cluster of questions about meaning and fulfilment is more amenable to personal and particular responses. Some call this latter cluster of concerns ethical to distinguish them from the moral in the abstract, universal sense. Yet while Taylor sympathizes with the distinction, he does not deploy it. Rather, when he talks throughout *Sources of the Self* of morality, he means morality to encompass the moral and the ethical. As he says, "To understand our moral world we have to see not only what ideas and pictures underlie our sense of respect for others but also those which underpin our notions of a full life … these are not two quite separate orders of ideas" (*Sources*: 14; cf. 4).[7]

When it comes to the semantics of the term the self, Taylor acknowledges that the idea that one has a self, that selfhood can be talked about as some distinct phenomenon, is a modern development (*Sources*: 112–14). He calls this attention to the self as such "radical reflexivity". Whereas all societies have a notion of reflexivity covering those things and experiences that pertain to oneself, not all have the radical sense of this. Radical reflexivity refers to a focus on the self *qua* self, the turning of attention towards what sort of self it is that has experiences of knowing, feeling and so on. As Taylor says, "Radical reflexivity brings to the fore a kind of presence to oneself which is inseparable from one's being the agent of experience" (*Sources*: 131; cf. 130, 176). The notion of identity is also a historical development, hence Taylor's claim that "Talk about 'identity' in the modern sense would have been incomprehensible to our forebears a couple of centuries ago" (*Sources*: 28; cf. 42). That individuals now talk of identity so freely can be explained by reference to the modern belief that questions about who I am cannot be answered solely in universal terms (*Sources*: 28), which is, in turn, derived from the modern ethic of authenticity, discussed below. Yet notwithstanding his awareness of the historical specificity of some of his terminology, Taylor tends to use the terms self, person, subject and identity, and those of selfhood and personhood, interchangeably and in a way that transcends the different cultural and historical periods traversed in *Sources of the Self*.

What is the self?

For the purposes of understanding Taylor's project, this key question needs to be subdivided into two more precise ones: what is Taylor's conception of the self; and what are the distinctively modern features of selfhood according to Taylor? As this separation suggests, Taylor believes that any conception of selfhood should recognize the permanent or structural features of selfhood as well as those that are shaped by particular cultural, social and historical forces. Part I of *Sources of the Self* delineates primarily the features that Taylor believes are constitutive of human selfhood,[8] while in Parts II–V he traces the distinctively modern aspects of the self.

As indicated above, the conception of the self in *Sources of the Self* is primarily a moral one. Taylor believes that having a moral orientation or framework is a cardinal feature of all human beings. This belief lies behind the phrase "inescapable frameworks", which provides the title of Part I, Section 1. A moral framework is a series of beliefs and judgements that gives shape, meaning and direction to individuals' lives. It provides answers, no matter how implicitly, to the existential questions that all individuals face about the purpose and conduct of their lives (*Sources*: 27). Frameworks thus provide guidance about moral questions in the broad sense outlined above: about what it is right to do with regard to others as well as what it is good to be. While no particular framework is inescapable, especially in modernity where the number of moral frameworks has multiplied, having some framework is inevitable: "living within these frameworks ... [is] not an optional extra, something we might just as well do without, but ... [they provide] a kind of orientation essential to our identity" (*Sources*: 78; cf. 31, 68). Having a moral framework within which to make sense of one's life and the surrounding world is an essential part of being a functioning human being. Thus for Taylor the fact of a framework is necessary, even though the content of any individual's particular framework can vary (*Sources*: 16).

In both these ways – fact and content – one's framework plays an important part in structuring one's identity. As Taylor explains:

> My identity is defined by the commitments and identifications which provide the frame or horizon within which I try to determine from case to case what is good, valuable, or what ought to be done, or what I endorse or oppose. In other words, it is the horizon within which I am capable of taking a stand. (*Sources*: 27)

Frameworks provide, moreover, not just a sense of where an individual stands but also of where they are headed. Taylor maintains that one of the things all human beings care about is how they are placed in relation to the good(s) in their lives. Human beings want a sense of moral progress, to feel that they are moving, or can hope to move, closer to, rather than further from, the good(s) they prize (*Sources*: 44–7). As he sees it:

> one of the most basic aspirations of human beings [is] the need to be connected to, or in contact with, what they see as good, or of crucial importance, or of fundamental value ... The fact that we have to place ourselves in a space which is defined by these qualitative distinctions cannot but mean that where we stand in relation to them must matter to us. (*Sources*: 42)

When Taylor asserts that "doing without frameworks is utterly impossible for us" (*Sources*: 27), part of what he means is that an individual without a framework would be thrown into a crisis of meaning. Her ability to make moral judgements would be crippled, any sense of the meaning and direction of her life destroyed. Given the close connection between identity and morality for Taylor, such a person would correspondingly suffer an acute identity crisis (*Sources*: 18, 27, 31).

The concept of "strong evaluation" is integral to Taylor's account of moral frameworks, because an individual's framework incorporates his or her strong evaluations (*Sources*: 19–20, 27, 29). The idea of strong evaluation refers to the fact that although human beings harbour a range of desires, we do not judge them all equally. Some are seen as higher, more admirable or worthier, than others. Thus individuals see their various desires as being qualitatively different, and in making distinctions of worth among them, we engage in strong evaluation. The goods I value strongly in this way play, in turn, a defining role in my identity. Hence Taylor's claim that "in order to make minimal sense of our lives, in order to have an identity, we need an orientation to the good, which means some sense of qualitative discrimination, of the incomparably higher" (*Sources*: 47).

Yet from Taylor's assertion of the centrality of frameworks that incorporate strong evaluations, it should not be inferred that individuals are always highly cognizant, or even wholly conscious, of the role these play in structuring identity. Our values are often taken for granted; they orient us morally but might do so imperceptibly. Strongly valued goods need not be explicit in order to exercise a powerful influence on a person's actions and sense of purpose: we often proceed unaware of our qualitative discriminations. So while individuals can be conscious of the moral judgements that underpin their strong evaluations, they need not be (*Sources*: 21, 26, 77). As Taylor says, being rightly placed in relation to the good "may not be very obtrusive in our lives if things go well and if by and large we are satisfied with who we are" (*Sources*: 44). It is, conversely, typically in times of challenge, conflict or crisis that one is forced to reflect on and perhaps spell out the underlying assumptions and judgements that inform one's moral positions (*Sources*: 9).

As this suggests, while moral frameworks can remain largely tacit, it is possible for them to be articulated. Taylor describes the function of articulation in this way:

> To articulate a framework is to explicate what makes sense of our moral responses. That is, when we try to spell out what it is that we presuppose when we judge that a certain form of life is truly worthwhile, or place our dignity in a certain achievement or status, or define our moral obligations in a certain manner, we find ourselves articulating inter alia what I have been calling here "frameworks".
>
> (*Sources*: 26; cf. 9, 77, 80)

While this is true of frameworks in general, Taylor also notes that the logic of some frameworks urges articulation while that of others discourages it. Thus a moral framework that prizes the ability to give a rational account of one's values and beliefs, such as that pioneered by Socrates, has an inner bias towards articulation. A framework that prioritizes the life of self-communion, inner peace and contemplation of ineffable realities, probably has an inherent bias against articulation (*Sources*: 20–21, 34, 92). Taylor thinks, however, that on the whole it is better if frameworks are made as explicit as possible. One reason for this preference is his belief that articulating moral frameworks can strengthen their hold on people. Articulation makes the goods inherent in the framework especially vivid, and in doing so can heighten their appeal. This is what he means when he says that articulation empowers: bringing a set of goods to light, raising consciousness of that which often remains tacit, brings its adherents into closer contact with the good and can invigorate their allegiance to it (*Sources:* 96–7, 504). Conversely, the failure to articulate one's moral framework can weaken it: indeed, Taylor even goes so far as to claim that "Without any articulation at all, we would lose all contact with the good, however conceived. We would cease to be human" (*Sources*: 97).

One of the things Taylor sees *Sources of the Self* as supplying is an articulation of some of the most important goods by which modern individuals live, as well as an articulation of the sources of these goods (*Sources*: 3–4, 8, 10). However, before addressing the distinctively modern components of selfhood he identifies, and the moral sources he explicates, it is necessary to consider two more features that he deems to be universally human facets of identity: the centrality of self-interpretation and the self's enmeshment in webs of interlocution.

Taylor has long argued that human beings necessarily operate with an understanding of who they are and what their lives mean.[9] In order to understand a person, we need not just empirical information about race, class, occupation, age, background and so on but also some sense of how he sees himself, what things matter to and motivate him, how he makes sense of the present, where he sees his life heading and so on. If we keep Taylor's broad conception of the moral in mind, it should come as no surprise that he sees morality as playing a central role in structuring self-interpretations. Strong evaluations form the backbone of self-interpretations.

A person's self-interpretation is, moreover, partly constitutive of his identity. According to Taylor, "To ask what a person is, in abstraction from his or her self-interpretations, is to ask a fundamentally misguided question, one to which there couldn't in principle be an answer" (*Sources*: 34). Yet he is not suggesting that self-interpretations have to be respected as incorrigible. Although partly constitutive of identity, thinking about myself in a particular way does not automatically mean that I am like that: I can have a deluded or exaggerated impression of my talents and possibilities. Nonetheless, even when a self-interpretation is erroneous, the way in which that person understands himself is still a crucial feature of his identity. The self-understanding does not have to be valid to be significant. Nor is any self-interpretation fixed and given in perpetuity. Some interpreted aspects of identity, such as religious affiliations or sense of family belonging, might persist for many years, with others being susceptible to more rapid alteration.

One entailment of Taylor's thesis about self-interpretations being partly constitutive of identity is that if and when self-interpretations change, the self also changes. Taylor further believes that any change in self-understanding will be incorporated by the individual into some sort of narrative structure about the shape and direction of his life. In contrast to Rortyean ironists who adopt new vocabularies in a seemingly arbitrary way,[10] Taylorean self-interpreters situate their new self-interpretation within a larger story of personal development. This story will weave together elements of change with those of continuity and offer some account of that change. Taylor draws the issues of morality and narrative self-interpretation together when he summarizes his position in the following way: "I have been arguing that the issue of how we are placed in relation to this good is of crucial and inescapable concern for us, that we cannot but strive to give our lives meaning or substance, and that this means that we understand ourselves inescapably in narrative" (*Sources*: 51).[11]

Thus far we have established that, for Taylor, all selves are moral and all interpret themselves in ways that depend heavily on their moral frameworks. However, the individual's self-interpretations are not forged in isolation: how I see myself is shaped by how I am seen by, and relate to, others. As Taylor remarks pithily, "a self only exists among other selves" (*Sources*: 35).[12] This brings us to the third "transcendental condition" of selfhood identified by Taylor: that selves are constituted through dialogue. He contends that an ongoing real or imagined exchange with others lies at the very core of all individuals' identity:

> ...this question [Who I am] finds its original sense in the interchange of speakers. I define who I am by defining where I speak from, in the family tree, in social space, in the geography of social statuses and functions, in my intimate relations to the ones I love, and also crucially in the space of moral and spiritual orientation within which my most important defining relations are lived out.   (*Sources*: 35)

Individuals are continuously formed through conversation; this is not just a feature of maturation from childhood to adulthood and the acquisition of language, but an inevitable dynamic of identity. Taylor's dialogical perspective on the self accommodates not just actual conversations but also imagined and internalized ones. Our inner life is a polyphony (or cacophony) of exchanges with others – the living, the dead, those yet to be born, those I have met, those I have not yet met, those I will never meet – and with other beings, such as deities. Who I am always points beyond me as an individual to my relations with significant others, to my partners in the dialogues who help to constitute my identity (*Sources*: 35–9).

What is the modern self?

Parts II–V of *Sources of the Self* chart the changing understandings of what it is to be a person that Taylor deems to have been seminal in forging the modern identity. Before enumerating these, it is useful to outline what he takes to be some of the general features of the modern identity. The first to note is the modern self's multiplicity: it comprises several strands and sources. Taylor also describes the modern identity as "complex and many-tiered" (*Sources*: 29), which means something more than simply consisting of several strands. What makes the modern identity complex is the fact that some of its elements are universal, while others are particular. Any modern individual's moral framework is likely to be composed of qualitatively different elements and so we need different ways of talking about and justifying these various components of the self.

Taylor points out though that the very idea of an individual having a moral framework has been thrown into question in the modern era. One important source of doubts about the existence of frameworks has been what he, following Max Weber, calls the disenchantment of the world. From this perspective, the cosmos is devoid of intrinsic moral significance and prescriptions for the conduct of human life (*Sources*: 148–9, 186). This erosion of belief in an inherently meaningful universe raises the spectre of meaninglessness and the loss of moral frameworks (*Sources*: 16–19). The fact that there is no single, naturally ordained moral framework has been taken by some to mean that there is no framework at all (*Sources*: 16–17, 26–7). However, from the previous section we can see that for Taylor this inference is mistaken, for selves cannot function without moral frameworks. He therefore sets about outlining some of the most important frameworks available in the modern era. Because the way in which any individual borrows from these general models in constructing their own frameworks is an open question, no particular individual's identity will correspond exactly to Taylor's profile of the modern self. Rather, he uses this phrase as shorthand for the range of available options for people in interpreting, experiencing and imagining themselves.

A good indication of the content-specific components of the modern identity appears early on in *Sources of the Self*, when Taylor explains that:

> With this term [the modern identity] I want to designate the ensemble of (largely unarticulated) understandings of what it is to be a human agent: the sense of inwardness, freedom, individuality, and being embedded in nature which are at home in the modern West.
>
> (*Sources*: ix)

Starting with the sense of freedom to which the modern self aspires, we find that freedom is defined as the possibility of radical disengagement from the physical and social world, and the ability to re-shape and re-order these environments. Rather than imagining itself as connected to some wider cosmic-cum-moral order, the modern self believes that it can properly understand and define itself in the absence of any attachment to this ambient reality. The disengaged self makes of its world an object, and stands toward it as a subject whose task it is to understand and control this world (*Sources*: 188). The disengagement here is mental or intellectual; the mind tries to prescind from its involvement in ordinary existence and aspires to a more detached, disinterested perspective on the self as on the world (*Sources*: 149, 175).

By the modern self's sense of inwardness, Taylor means that this self sees itself as an entity with inner depths and believes that coming to know and perhaps to express these inner depths is a valuable undertaking (*Sources*: 178). I turn inwards to discover or get in touch with who I am. In expressing what I find within, I both give voice to, and shape, my identity. This is closely connected with the third component of the modern self listed in the passage cited above: its sense of its own individuality or uniqueness, which brings with it an injunction to be true to that individuality. Behind this injunction lies the belief that being a self is ultimately an individual project or undertaking, that each person must decide for himself or herself what being authentic means. With this ethic of authenticity, each is seen as having his or her own mode of being human and is encouraged to realize this rather than conform to a pre-existing model or a pattern imposed from outside. Everyone has to discover an original way of being, to recognize it as a true or faithful expression of who they are, and to adopt and take responsibility for it. Fourthly, by the idea of the human being embedded in nature, Taylor is referring to the belief that there is something profoundly valuable about contact with nature. Modern selves harbour a sense that interaction with the natural world can be a source of moral renewal, and such contact enables them to hearken to the voice of nature within.

Taylor's summary of his work cited above is, however, incomplete. The modern self is also informed by an ethos he calls the affirmation of ordinary life. This captures the belief that a significant part of one's identity discharges itself in the realms of work and family life: that what happens in these domains makes a substantial contribution to one's sense of the value or meaning of life. Another important modern development has been the dissemination of the ethic of benevolence, with its ambition to improve the lot of ordinary individuals and to diminish unnecessary suffering. All six of these strands of the modern identity articulate at some point with the wider modern imputation of dignity and respect to all persons, simply by virtue of their being human. Thus, for example, when the ethic of authenticity is combined with the universalist and egalitarian aspects of modern identity, all selves appear as equally unique, or at least as having the potential for this.

What are the modern self's sources?

To appreciate more fully what Taylor means by each of these aspects of the modern self, it is necessary to explore what he thinks the source of each is. He contends that returning to these sources is valuable as an aid to self-understanding by retrieving what has become eclipsed or, in some cases, actively suppressed, over time. This exercise in retrieval is also valuable because, as indicated in the above discussion of articulation, shedding light on the conceptions of the good that undergird moral frameworks can foster or renew an appreciation of those goods (*Sources*: 104).

The modern self aspires to what Taylor terms "disengaged freedom". He describes this posture of radical disengagement as "a new, unprecedentedly radical form of self-objectification" that finds its fullest articulation in the work of John Locke (*Sources*: 171; cf. 174). The aspiration to disengagement represents a moral as well as an epistemological doctrine because, like all the moral sources of modern selfhood, it encapsulates strong evaluations: it posits one way of being as superior or more admirable than others. Underlying its claims about correct knowledge of the self and the world are ideals about freedom from nature and determinism, a belief in the dignity that comes from human reason and the pursuit of truth, and the appeal of the power and instrumental control it promises. These deeper moral sources of the doctrine must be understood if its power and influence are to be fully appreciated (*Sources*: 152, 163, 168, 174–5, 177).[13] Taylor argues, moreover, that this emphasis on the disengaged, punctual self growing out of the scientific revolution was originally religious. It placed great emphasis on reason, on the possibility of rational control over both nature and the non-rational parts of the self. In exercising reason, the disengaged individual was deploying a capacity conferred by God, one that distinguished human beings from the rest of his creation: "The awesome powers of human reason and will are God-made and part of God's plan; more, they are what constitutes the image of God in us" (*Sources*: 315; cf. 245, 310). This explains why the capacity for, and exercise of, reason were so closely bound up with a sense of human dignity.

The inwardness that Taylor identifies as one of the features of the modern identity is inwardness of a particular sort. The modern emphasis on introspection can be traced to Augustine (*Sources*: 128–9, 140, 177), but its emphasis has shifted. In Augustine's thought, turning inwards was a prelude to moving upwards towards God and his goodness (*Sources*: 132, 134, 136, 390). In the modern version, the individual turning inwards finds a moral source of a different kind: she finds a being whose richness and complexity call for self-exploration. (Taylor's conception of "radical reflexivity", discussed above, is directly linked with this inward turn (*Sources*: 131)). Jean-Jacques Rousseau was one of the major exponents of this idea of the self having inner depths, and of this having a moral dimension. In order to ascertain the right thing to do, be or feel, the self should turn inwards, not outwards to the opinions of others. By turning inwards one can attend to the voice of nature, which guides one to goodness. So Rousseau's variation on the theme of inwardness posits a close connection between inside and out. Contact with the natural world is a source of moral renewal, just as turning attention to this spontaneous flow of life that also runs through the self, attending to the voice of nature within, is a source of moral guidance and of happiness (*Sources*: 357, 359, 362, 461).

Closely connected to the image of the self as a being with inner depths is the idea of unique individuality. While individual differences in taste, temperament, preferences, values, abilities, inclinations and so on have always been recognized, they have not always been invested with the ethical salience they now enjoy. Taylor argues that the late-eighteenth century represents a watershed with regard to the moral significance of individual differences, and cites the work of Johann Gottfried Herder as providing an especially powerful articulation of this new ideal (*Sources*: 375–6). Herder's suggestion that originality is a vocation was taken up and given forceful expression by John Stuart Mill in *On Liberty*. In Chapter 3, "Of Individuality as One of the Elements of Well-Being", Mill writes: "If a person possesses any tolerable amount of common sense, and experience, his own mode of laying out his existence is the best, not because it is best in itself, but because it is his own mode" (Mill 1993: 135).

Taylor traces the first modern articulation of the idea that nature is a source of moral goodness to the theorists of moral sentiments in the eighteenth century, the Earl of Shaftesbury and Francis Hutcheson (*Sources*: 248). Influenced by neo-Platonist thinkers, this doctrine depicted the world as a harmonious whole, which is ordered for the best and whose parts are complementary. Anyone who correctly understood the world would grow to appreciate its goodness and to love its whole and each of its components (*Sources*: 253–4). Because of providential design, nature is a source of goodness and there can be a bond linking self and world: "Our way of contact with the design of nature also lies within us, in the natural sentiments of sympathy and benevolence" (*Sources*: 282). With its picture of nature as a source of goodness and moral guidance rather than a disenchanted, mechanistic realm, the theory of moral sentiments reacted against the scientistic outlook deriving from the seventeenth century and the ethic of disengaged freedom (*Sources*: 254, 265). As the above reference to Rousseau's respect for the inner voice of nature intimates, he furthered this idea of nature as a source of moral goodness (*Sources*: 357–9, 362). A conception of God plays a key role in both of these outlooks too, for God made the world so good in the first place, and the love owed to him should also be conferred upon his creation (*Sources*: 264, 315, 339, 361).

The phrase "the affirmation of ordinary life" refers to an aspect of the modern identity that Taylor portrays as a legacy of Protestantism. He contrasts this with the classical view that judged those activities that formed part of the good life – political participation and philosophical contemplation – as inherently worthier or nobler than those associated with the production and reproduction of quotidian life. Indeed, the latter were seen as largely instrumental to the former. A life devoted to labour, reproduction and bodily needs was a less than fully human one, for in pursuing these activities human beings were not seen as doing anything to distinguish themselves from animals (*Sources*: 13–14, 211). The Protestant affirmation of ordinary life challenged, however, not just the aristocratic ethos but also the traditionally Catholic one. Catholicism had been premised on the belief that certain undertakings were inherently worthier than others; thus the activity of the priest was seen to be higher than that of ordinary people engaged in working and raising families.

Protestantism repudiated the idea that some activities were qualitatively superior to others, proposing instead that all activities are potentially worthy; what mattered was how they were conducted. Even the most menial activity could become sanctified, if carried out worshipfully, to the glory of God. One way of describing this transition is to say that the object of strong evaluation changed. Previously activities had been deemed noble or base, whereas now it was one's way of participating in them that became admirable or degenerate. In the place of a hierarchy of status, rank or activity, comes a hierarchy of attitudes or dispositions (*Sources*: 214–17). Labour, marriage and family life could thus be devoted to God, lending the worlds of production and reproduction a new religious and

ethical significance (*Sources*: 13–14, 218, 221–4, 226–7, 292). With this affirmation of everyday life, family relations and work come to occupy a central place in
people's sense of what makes life worth living in a way that was, Taylor claims,
unprecedented. He is not suggesting by this that before its evolution people did
not love their children or spouses, or gained no satisfaction from their work.
What changed was not the existence of these things but their ethical importance
(*Sources*: 292–3).

The final distinctive aspect of the modern self surveyed here is its commitment to practical universal benevolence. This refers to a belief that people should
do as much as possible to minimize unnecessary suffering. Taylor claims that no
ancient ethical view gave the place to universal benevolence that modern morality
does, and that no civilization has been as concerned with the reduction of suffering as is the modern Western world (*Sources*: 12–13, 316). He is not suggesting
that pre-modern cultures were indifferent to the pain and suffering of strangers:
after all, the Stoics promoted universal moral duties and versions of Christianity
have always advocated the ideal of universal benevolence, of loving one's fellow
human beings because they are God's creatures (*Sources*: 13). Rather, with the rise
of the ethic of practical benevolence, an existing concern with suffering assumed
greater proportions compared to other ethical considerations.

Taylor traces the origins of this outlook to the scientific revolution of the
seventeenth century and its belief that one of the benefits of understanding the
natural world more accurately would be an increased ability to control it. One
of the things that drove this quest for power over nature was the ambition to
improve the condition of everyday life, to relieve suffering and to better man's
natural estate, to paraphrase one of the first philosophers of modern science,
Francis Bacon (*Sources*: 230). This impulse was given further backing by the
Enlightenment and its dedication to improving living conditions (*Sources*: 318,
331, 394). However, it is not just thinkers impressed by the potential of science and the power of reason to improve society who drove this doctrine of
universal benevolence. This outlook was complemented by the theory of moral
sentiments, discussed above. As the reference there to "the natural sentiments
of sympathy and benevolence" (*Sources*: 282) betokens, benevolence towards
oneself and others also emerges as a key good there. Indeed, such self-love and
fellow-feeling emerge spontaneously in those who are rightly disposed toward
the world (*Sources*: 264).

One of the striking things about the moral sources of the modern self as
traced by Taylor is that they all include a religious element (*Sources*: 495). However, over time these moral frameworks lost touch with their theistic foundations and developed a life and rationale of their own. Their goods came to be
seen as goods in their own right, no longer needing reference to a god to vali-

date them. In some cases they even became hostile to Christianity, or at least to organized religion. Taylor conveys the magnitude of this change when he writes:

> something important and irreversible did happen in the latter part of the nineteenth century with the rise of unbelief in Anglo-Saxon countries. It was then that they moved from a horizon in which belief in God in some form was virtually unchallengeable to our present predicament in which theism is one option among others, in which moral sources are ontologically diverse.   (*Sources*: 401; cf. 408)

One consequence of this reduction in religious belief in the modern world is that many individuals live by moral frameworks that are parasitic on theistic sources that they can no longer respect or even acknowledge (*Sources*: 339). Taylor worries in this context about the fate of the ethic of practical benevolence, in particular. By its very nature, this ethic is insatiable, and he wonders whether purely secular formulations of the good involved in this ethic, such as the belief in universal human equality and the dignity of each individual, can motivate people sufficiently to go on trying to meet its demands. Convinced that "High standards need strong sources" (*Sources*: 516), he suspects that the strongest source for this ethic is a religious one. According to the doctrine of divine affirmation, as creatures of an all-loving God all human beings are worthy of respect, and in evincing respect for our fellow human beings we are participating in God's love (*Sources*: 515–18). This has proved to be a very controversial aspect of *Sources of the Self*, with some commentators discerning in the book a veiled ambition to vindicate religious belief and reinstate it in moral life.[14] Taylor is able to respond by reminding such readers that his point about theism's unrivalled power as a moral source is put forward as a "hunch" rather than a fully fledged argument (*Sources*: 517–18).[15]

I have argued elsewhere (Abbey 2000: 50–51), however, that *Sources of the Self* contains another, more tightly argued route to the affirmation of theism. By insisting on the need to return to moral sources in order to understand the contemporary moral condition, Taylor is according considerable power to Christianity, for the study of all modern moral frameworks leads back to it. However, he is not merely constructing a historical narrative according to which Christianity has been an important moral source and explaining that in order to understand the modern self, we need to appreciate this. Rather, as his point about the power of articulation suggests, making contact with the original moral source is supposed to invigorate, and inspire the love of the good in, those who subscribe to these moral frameworks. By his logic, returning to the religious wellsprings of current moral outlooks offers the possibility of reaffirming our moral values and senses of self.

This section has indicated what Taylor takes some of the main sources of the various strands of modern selfhood to be. The next issue for consideration is how exactly these sources are supposed to have shaped the modern self. In this we come upon another of the more controversial aspects of *Sources of the Self*.

How is the self sourced?

In reconstructing his history of the modern self, Taylor's focus is overwhelmingly on the cultural realm. Within the realm of culture itself, the accent tends to fall on canonical works of philosophy, such as those by Plato, Augustine, Montaigne, Locke, Descartes, Rousseau, Bentham and Nietzsche. Some relatively minor figures in Western thought, such as Shaftesbury, Hutcheson and Herder, are also included. When he looks beyond philosophy to other cultural products, Taylor's interest tends to remain in written texts; he refers to writers such as Rilke, Wordsworth, Baudelaire, Proust, Pound and Eliot. Some consideration is afforded to the ways in which forms of cultural creativity such as music and the visual arts have contributed to the modern identity. But overall Taylor pays minimal attention to the part that economic activities and institutions, changes in modes of production, science and technology, or systems of government and law, have played in forging the modern identity.

At the end of Part II, in a short chapter called "A Digression on Historical Explanation", Taylor outlines and justifies his method (*Sources*: 199–207). He concedes that even within the cultural sphere, his focus is selective, dwelling as it does on "certain developments in philosophy and religious outlook, with an odd glance at aspects of popular mentality" (*Sources*: 199). He acknowledges the role that changing material and institutional factors in the economic, administrative, legal, military, technological and political realms have in shaping identity (*Sources*: 199, 202; cf. 306, 316). Some parallel is implied between the multiple character of the modern self and the multiple forces that have brought it into being (*Sources*: 199, 206). Given the wealth of historical material that could be marshalled to explain the modern self, Taylor tries to clarify his project by identifying two types of questions that this material can be called on to answer. The first is a causal or explanatory question: what brought the modern identity into being? He admits that he lacks the capacity to tackle this enormous issue (*Sources*: 306). The second is a more modest interpretive question, which explores the drawing power of these new conceptions of selfhood, examining why so many people found, and continue to find, them appealing (*Sources*: 202–3, 207). Although Taylor declares himself to be pursuing the interpretive problem, these two questions are not wholly distinct because he clearly believes that the drawing power of these ideas is part of the wider causal story (*Sources*: 203).

When addressing the interpretive question, philosophical and other written texts prove invaluable because they can articulate inspiring visions of the good. Those who practise philosophy typically strive for a rational account and defence of particular positions or prescriptions. Even those like Nietzsche who err on the poetic side of philosophy still articulate visions of the good (and assaults on the bad!) Other cultural products, such as music, literature and the visual and performing arts, might embody visions of the good but do not present these in as accessible and articulable a manner as do philosophical texts (*Sources:* 307). However, in order for these new ideas and ideals to take hold, they cannot remain locked in philosophical texts or other expressive sources but must become institutionalized in practices (*Sources*: 204, 206–7). As Taylor declares, the modern identity "arose because changes in the self-understandings connected with a wide range of practices – religious, political, economic, familial, intellectual, artistic – converged and reinforced each other to produce it" (*Sources*: 206). He further contends that philosophical articulations of the good are related in complex ways to the other social forces that produce change. Philosophers and other makers of meaning can reflect, articulate, intensify and expedite the changes that occur in other milieux (*Sources*: 205–6; cf. 285, 306–7).

Taylor hopes that this digression into historical explanation will forestall any charge that his approach is idealist, that he is advancing these texts as the sole, or even most important, engines of social change. Yet several of the commentaries on *Sources of the Self* disappoint this hope: many of its readers remark critically on its preoccupation with philosophical texts as the sources of modern selfhood.[16] Perhaps Taylor is partly responsible for the failure of some of his readers to appreciate the precise role he was assigning to philosophical texts. First, the chapter in which he explains his methodology is strangely placed at the end of that part of the book entitled "Inwardness". A more appropriate location for it would have been at the end of Part I after his outline of the approach to morality and selfhood, or at the start of Part II, before he embarked on the survey of the major landmarks of Western understandings of the self. This crucial chapter is also strangely titled: indeed, it seems misleading to label a discussion that is central to explaining one's method and rationale as "a digression". Thirdly, the chapter is strangely presented: within the so-called digression, there is a genuine digression into Renaissance conceptions of man (*Sources*: 199–202). Given the peculiarities in the way Taylor presents this important element of the book, we might conclude the he could have done more to pre-empt some of the misunderstandings of his method.

Conclusion

While I have tried to bring out several of the most important ideas contained in *Sources of the Self*, many other significant and interesting issues have, of necessity, been overlooked. These include the question of Taylor's moral realism, his notion of hypergoods, his distinction between life goods and constitutive goods, his discussion of modes of practical reasoning and best account principle, his critique of modern approaches to morality, his readings of particular philosophers and his discussions of modernist art forms. But such exclusions are inevitable given the work's size, scope and depth: indeed, in its richness and complexity, *Sources of the Self* mirrors the richness and complexity of the modern identity that it sets out to trace.

Notes

1. Much of the secondary literature on *Sources of the Self* is listed at http://nd.edu/%7Erabbey1/index.htm

2. Although not published until 1998, this interview was conducted in June 1995. This passage appears in the English translation, "From Philosophical Anthropology to the Politics of Recognition: An Interview with Philippe de Lara", *Thesis Eleven* **52** (1998), 103–12, on page 110.

3. Cf. Paul Ricoeur, "Le fundamental et l'historique: note sur *Sources of the Self* de Charles Taylor", in *Charles Taylor et l'interprétation de l'identité moderne*, G. Laforest & P. de Lara (eds), 19–34 (Quebec: Les Presses de l'Université Laval, 1998), 33. As Gilles Deleuze says, "Genealogy means both the value of origin and the origin of values" (*Nietzsche and Philosophy*, H. Tomlinson (trans.) (New York: Columbia University Press, 1983), 2).

4. The idea of a hermeneutics of suspicion was first articulated by Paul Ricoeur, who cast Marx, Nietzsche and Freud as its masters. Of course, some would argue that a genealogy of morals without a hermeneutics of suspicion is a contradiction in terms: that it is of the very essence of a genealogy to be suspicious about the value of origins. This turns, of course, on the meaning of genealogy, which is itself hotly debated. Peter Berkowitz, for example, argues that Foucault was not doing Nietzschean genealogy (*Nietzsche: The Ethics of an Immoralist* (Cambridge, MA: Harvard University Press, 1995), 68–9), while Jacqueline Stevens ("On the Morals of Genealogy", *Political Theory* **31** (2003), 558–88) argues that even Nietzsche was not doing genealogy! Rather than enter this debate here, I take Taylor's own characterization of his work as genealogical at face value.

5. Charles Larmore characterizes Taylor's "genealogy of modernity" as optimistic ("Review of *Sources of the Self*", *Ethics* **102** (1991), 161) because of his belief that clarity about modern moral sources will "enable us ... to affirm more wholeheartedly much of modern culture" (*ibid.*, 158). At times in *Sources of the Self*, Taylor seems to conflate the practice of genealogy with a hermeneutics of suspicion (*Sources of the Self* (Cambridge, MA: Harvard University Press, 1989), 72, 88) but his later remark, quoted above, that

his approach is genealogical suggests that he would acknowledge the distinction being drawn here.

6. Taylor means spiritual here not in a strictly religious sense, but more in the way it is used to refer to the human spirit, the things that people find compelling and worthy of affirmation.

7. He defends and elaborates on the link between morality and the good life in his reply to Kymlicka in "Comments and Replies to Symposium on *Sources of the Self*", *Inquiry* **34** (1991), 243–4.

8. Primarily but not exclusively, for Part I also includes glimpses of distinctively modern goods such as the accent on avoiding suffering (*Sources of the Self*, 12–13), the affirmation of ordinary life (*Sources*: 13–14, 23) and disengaged freedom (*Sources*: 82–3).

9. See, for example, his essay "Self-Interpreting Animals", in *Human Agency and Language: Philosophical Papers 1*, 45–74 (Cambridge: Cambridge University Press, 1985).

10. See, for example, Richard Rorty, "Private Irony and Liberal Hope", in *Contingency, Irony and Solidarity*, 73–95 (Cambridge: Cambridge University Press, 1988).

11. Nicholas Smith argues that Taylor's claim about the inescapability of seeing identity in narrative terms confuses a particular cultural norm with "an anthropological constant" (*Charles Taylor: Meaning, Morals and Modernity* (Cambridge: Polity, 2002), 97–102).

12. Elsewhere in his oeuvre, Taylor emphasizes the embodied nature of the self, particularly with reference to arguments about perception and knowledge more generally. But this is largely absent from *Sources of the Self* (cf. Bernard Dauenhauer, "Taylor and Ricoeur on the Self", *Man and World* **25** (1992), 222), indicating once again that its self is a pre-eminently moral one. Embodiment is discussed at one point, in the context of a person's sense of her own dignity manifesting itself in her comportment (*Sources of the Self*, 15). To see what a relatively minor role the body plays in the conception of the self in *Sources of the Self*, consider how little evidence John Tambornino is able to marshal from it to illustrate the centrality of embodiment in Taylor's work (*The Corporeal Turn: Passion, Necessity, Politics* (Lanham, MD: Rowman & Littlefield, 2002), 45). Moreover, such evidence as he does cite from *Sources of the Self* pages 4–5 exaggerates Taylor's analogy between involuntary physical reactions and deep-seated moral beliefs and correspondingly neglects the disanalogy Taylor points out on pages 6 and 15. Tambornino also overstates the secondary literature's neglect of embodiment in Taylor's thought.

13. Thus Shklar's claim that the self in question in *Sources of the Self* is not "that of a knowing … agent" ("Review of *Sources of the Self*", *Political Theory* **19**(1) (1991), 105) is not wholly correct. Rather, it would be more accurate to say that in the case of disengaged freedom, Taylor drops the level of analysis from epistemology to morality, indicating again that the self in *Sources of the Self* is pre-eminently a moral one.

14. For discussions of whether there is a religious agenda in *Sources of the Self*, see J. B. Schneewind, "Review of *Sources of the Self*", *Journal of Philosophy* **88** (1991), 422–6; Shklar, "Review of *Sources of the Self*"; Quentin Skinner, "Who Are 'We'? Ambiguities of the Modern Self", Symposium on *Sources of the Self*, *Inquiry* **34** (1991), 133–53; Melissa Lane, "God or Orienteering? A Critical Study of Charles Taylor's *Sources of the Self*", *Ratio* **5** (1992), 45–56; Timothy O'Hagan, "Charles Taylor's Hidden God: Aristotle, Rawls and Religion Through Post-Modernist Eyes", *Ratio* **6** (1993), 72–81; David Braybrooke, "Inward and Outward with the Modern Self", *Dialogue* **23** (1994), 101–8; Deane-Peter Baker, "Charles Taylor's *Sources of the Self*: A Transcendental Apologetic?", *International Journal for the Philosophy of Religion* **47** (2000), 155–74; and

William Greenway, "Charles Taylor on Affirmation, Mutilation and Theism: A Retrospective Reading of *Sources of the Self*", *Journal of Religion* **80** (2000), 23–40.

15. See, for example Taylor, "Comments and Replies", 240; "Reply to Braybrooke and de Sousa", *Dialogue* **33** (1994), 125; and "De l'anthropologie philosophique a la politique de la reconnaissance: Interview with Philippe de Lara", in *Charles Taylor et l'interprétation de l'identité moderne*, G. Laforest & P. de Lara (eds), 351–64 (Quebec: Les Presses de l' Université Laval, 1998), 364.

16. See, for example, Shklar, "Review of *Sources of the Self*", 108; Skinner, "Who Are 'We'?", 135; Craig Calhoun, "Morality, Identity, and Historical Explanation: Charles Taylor on the Sources of the Self", *Sociological Theory* **9** (1991), 239, 260. Nussbaum also points out its "top-down" bias, for the cultural creations Taylor discusses tend to be those of the middle and upper classes ("Our Pasts, Ourselves: Review of *Sources of the Self*", *New Republic* (9 April 1990), 32; cf. Calhoun "Morality, Identity, and Historical Explanation", 260.

References

Abbey, R. 2000. *Charles Taylor*. Chesham: Acumen.

Baker, D.-P. 2000. "Charles Taylor's *Sources of the Self*: A Transcendental Apologetic?". *International Journal for Philosophy of Religion* **47**, 155–74.

Baum, G. 1991. "A Humanist Reading of Modernity". *Canadian Forum* **70**, 25–7.

Berkowitz, P. 1995. *Nietzsche: The Ethics of an Immoralist*. Cambridge, MA: Harvard University Press.

Braybrooke, D. 1994. "Inward and Outward with the Modern Self". *Dialogue* **23**, 101–8.

Calhoun, C. 1991. "Morality, Identity, and Historical Explanation: Charles Taylor on the Sources of the Self". *Sociological Theory* **9**, 232–64.

Dauenhauer, B. 1992. "Taylor and Ricoeur on the Self". *Man and World* **25**, 211–25.

Deleuze, G. 1983. *Nietzsche and Philosophy*, H. Tomlinson (trans.). New York: Columbia University Press.

Foucault, M. 1984. "Nietzsche, Genealogy, History". In *The Foucault Reader*, P. Rabinow (ed.), 76–100. New York: Pantheon Books.

Greenway, W. 2000. "Charles Taylor on Affirmation, Mutilation and Theism: A Retrospective Reading of *Sources of the Self*". *Journal of Religion* **80**, 23–40.

Lane, M. 1992. "God or Orienteering? A Critical Study of Charles Taylor's *Sources of the Self*". *Ratio* **5**, 46–56.

Larmore, C. 1991. "Review of *Sources of the Self*". *Ethics* **102**, 158–62.

Mill, J. S. 1993. *On Liberty*, Geraint Williams (ed.). London: Dent.

Nietzsche, F. 1973. *A Genealogy of Morals*, R. J. Hollingdale (trans.). Harmondsworth: Penguin.

Nussbaum, M. 1990. "Our Pasts, Ourselves: Review of *Sources of the Self*". *New Republic* (9 April), 27–34.

O'Hagan, T. 1993. "Charles Taylor's Hidden God: Aristotle, Rawls and Religion Through Post-Modernist Eyes". *Ratio* **6**, 72–81.

Ricoeur, P. 1979. *Freud and Philosophy: An Essay on Interpretation*. New Haven, CT: Yale University Press.

Ricoeur, P. 1998. "Le fondamental et l'historique: note sur *Sources of the Self* de Charles Taylor". In *Charles Taylor et l'interprétation de l'identité moderne*, G. Laforest & P. de Lara (eds), 19–34. Quebec: Les Presses de l'Université Laval.

Rorty, R. 1988. *Contingency, Irony and Solidarity*. Cambridge: Cambridge University Press.

Schneewind, J. B. 1991. "Review of *Sources of the Self*". *Journal of Philosophy* 88, 422–6.

Skhlar, J. 1991. "Review of *Sources of the Self*". *Political Theory* 19(1), 105–9.

Skinner, Q. 1991. "Who Are 'We'? Ambiguities of the Modern Self". Symposium on *Sources of the Self*. *Inquiry* 34, 133–53.

Smith, N. 2002. *Charles Taylor: Meaning, Morals and Modernity*. Cambridge: Polity.

Stevens, J. 2003. "On the Morals of Genealogy". *Political Theory* 31, 558–88.

Tambornino, J. 2002. *The Corporeal Turn: Passion, Necessity, Politics*. Lanham, MD: Rowman & Littlefield.

Taylor, C. 1985. *Human Agency and Language: Philosophical Papers 1*. Cambridge: Cambridge University Press.

Taylor, C. 1989. *Sources of the Self*. Cambridge, MA: Harvard University Press.

Taylor, C. 1991. "Comments and Replies to Symposium on *Sources of the Self*". *Inquiry* 34, 237–54.

Taylor, C. 1994. "Reply to Braybrooke and de Sousa". *Dialogue* 33, 125–31.

Taylor, C. 1998. "De l'anthropologie philosophique a la politique de la reconnaissance: Interview with Philippe de Lara". In *Charles Taylor et l'interprétation de l'identité moderne*, G. Laforest & P. de Lara (eds), 351–64. Quebec: Les Presses de l' Université Laval. Translated as "From Philosophical Anthropology to the Politics of Recognition: An Interview with Philippe de Lara", *Thesis Eleven* 52 (1998), 103–12.

Waldron, J. 1990. "How We Learn to be Good: Review of *Sources of the Self*". *Times Literary Supplement* (23 March), 325–6.

Further reading

Several prominent figures in the fields of moral, social and political philosophy have commented on *Sources of the Self*. These include Quentin Skinner, Will Kymlicka, Michael Rosen, Stephen Clark and Martin Loew-Beer in "Symposium on *Sources of the Self*", *Inquiry* 34 (1991), 133–254, in which there is also a reply to each from Taylor.

Alasdair MacIntyre, Frederick Olafson and Richard Rorty all contribute to the "Symposium on *Sources of the Self*", *Philosophy and Phenomenological Research* 54(1) (1994), 187–213, in which there is also a reply to each from Taylor. See also:

Calhoun, C. 1991. "Morality, Identity, and Historical Explanation: Charles Taylor on the Sources of the Self". *Sociological Theory* 9, 232–64.

Hauerwas, S. 1994. "Killing Compassion". In *Dispatches from the Front: Theological Engagements with the Secular*, 164–77. Durham, NC: Duke University Press.

Hauerwas, S. & D. Matzko 1992. "The Sources of Charles Taylor". *Religious Studies Review* 18(4), 286–89.

Larmore, C. 1991. "Review of *Sources of the Self*". *Ethics* 102, 158–62.

Nussbaum, M. 1990. "Our Pasts, Ourselves: Review of *Sources of the Self*". *New Republic* (9 April), 27–34.

Ricoeur, P. 1998. "Le fondamental et l'historique: note sur *Sources of the Self* de Charles Taylor". In *Charles Taylor et l'interprétation de l'identité moderne*, G. Laforest & P. de Lara (eds), 19–34. Quebec: Les Presses de l'Université Laval.

Schneewind, J. B. 1991. "Review of *Sources of the Self*". *Journal of Philosophy* **88**, 422–6.

Skhlar, J. 1991. "Review of *Sources of the Self*". *Political Theory* **19**(1), 105–9.

Skinner, Q. 1991. "Who Are 'We'? Ambiguities of the Modern Self ". Symposium on *Sources of the Self*, *Inquiry* **34**, 133–53.

Waldron, J. 1990."How We Learn to be Good: Review of *Sources of the Self*". *Times Literary Supplement* (23 March), 325–6.

Williams, B. 1990. "Republican and Galilean: Review of *Sources of the Self*". *New York Review of Books* (8 November), 45–8.

There are four single-author books about Taylor in English. As each is organized thematically, none contains a chapter devoted to *Sources of the Self* as such. However, each explores Taylor's key concepts and so can be useful in amplifying some of the ideas in this chapter and in setting them in the wider context of Taylor's oeuvre. And because *Sources of the Self* has been Taylor's largest work to date, any overview of his thought necessarily makes considerable reference to it. See:

Abbey, R. 2000. *Charles Taylor*. Chesham: Acumen.

Redhead, M. 2002. *Charles Taylor: Thinking and Living Deep Diversity*. Lanham, MD: Rowman & Littlefield.

Smith, N. 2002. *Charles Taylor: Meaning, Morals and Modernity*. Cambridge: Polity.

Spence, K. 2005. *Charles Taylor: Modernity, Freedom and Community*. Cardiff: University of Wales Press.

14
John McDowell
Mind and World

Tim Thornton

John McDowell's *Mind and World* was first published in 1994. Based on his six 1991 John Locke Lectures, it is the most free flowing of his published work. It is also the only book-length account of his philosophy. It is an important, dramatic and challenging work for three reasons.

First, it addresses what is perhaps the central question of modern philosophy since Descartes: what is the relation between mind and world? This large and rather abstract question is raised through a number of more specific, but still central, questions in philosophy. How is it possible for thoughts to be about the world, for *intentionality* to be possible? What must the world be like if it can be "taken in" by subjects in experiences? What role do the natural sciences play in describing the limits of the natural world, of what is really real?

Secondly, the cast of characters is impressive. McDowell's account of the relation between mind and world draws on the work, among others, of Aristotle, Kant, Hegel, Frege, Russell, Wittgenstein, Sellars, Davidson and Evans. A number of other philosophers from the analytic tradition have a role, such as Strawson, Dummett and Kripke, but Weber, Gadamer and even Marx also make appearances. It is breathtaking that a work of contemporary philosophy should borrow so widely from the history of philosophy to attempt to present a coherent picture of our place in nature.

Thirdly, despite the number of influences from the philosophical canon, McDowell's aim is *not* a piece of substantial philosophical theory-building. He aims not to bridge the gulf between mind and world but to show that there is no gulf to be bridged. The dualisms that seem to generate such philosophical difficulty, and to call for speculative philosophical theory to bridge them, are instead dissolved away. This is a "therapeutic" view of philosophy in a Wittgensteinian tradition.

Lecture I:"Concepts and Intuitions"

Mind and World starts with the claim that its main theme is "the way that concepts mediate the relation between minds and the world" (1994: 3). But this narrow and technical-sounding aim is merely one part of a much broader and more dramatic theme. Understanding the role that concepts play in experience and the role that experience plays in underpinning thought helps clarify the relationship of mind and world. It also sheds light on the nature of nature itself.

Lecture I starts with the claim that examining a famous slogan from Kant's *Critique of Pure Reason* can help shed light on the connection between thought and reality. McDowell suggests that Kant should still have a central place in philosophical discussion of the connection between thought and the world. *Mind and World* is thus a Kantian book, in a way that will become clear shortly.

The slogan is: "Thoughts without content are empty, intuitions without concepts are blind" (Kant 1933: 93, A51, B75). It expresses an important insight into how thought is possible by stressing the importance both of concepts and of direct experiential intake or "intuitions". But McDowell also warns that accommodating these two aspects has typically led to an "interminable oscillation" between positions that overemphasize one side or the other. It is an oscillation between, on the one hand, coherence theories in which there is no friction on thought imposed by contact with the world and, on the other, the Myth of the Given, which attempts to ensure such friction but, impossibly, from outside the space of reasons (McDowell 1994: 9). McDowell suggests that a proper understanding of the Kantian idea should be consistent with the US philosopher of mind and language Donald Davidson's rejection of the "scheme–content dualism" and should unite the role of reason and nature.

In a paper called "On the Very Idea of a Conceptual Scheme", Davidson describes and rejects a dualism of, on the one hand, a conceptual scheme or schemes and, on the other, "content". The dualism is supposed to explain how a worldview is the result of the interplay of a set of concepts that organize either our brute experience of the world or the world itself. But Davidson argues that this idea, this dualism, is incoherent. If the dualism is incoherent, what should we make of Kant's slogan and why does it lead to an intolerable oscillation?

Two preliminary points are worth noting. First, as McDowell points out, there is something potentially misleading in the way these familiar ideas are generally transcribed in that in both the Kantian and Davidsonian context the word "content" has a different sense from recent philosophy of thought. In the latter context, it means representational bearing or meaning. (Sentences have meaning; thoughts have content; and these can be the same.) But in both the Kantian phrase and in the dualism of conceptual scheme and content that Davidson rejects, "content" stands for a partial *explanation* of empirical content or meaning and not for that empirical content itself. McDowell suggests that it might be better to talk of the "Given" rather than content in both Kant's and Davidson's slogans.

Secondly, McDowell comments elsewhere that *Mind and World* is primarily addressed to a particular philosophical audience: those who are subject to a particular philosophical discomfort as a result of subscribing to particular philosophical intuitions. "Only someone who feels the pull of the thoughts I uncover will be subject to the philosophical discomfort I aim to deal with" (McDowell 1998c: 404). To that extent, it does not articulate a free-standing context-independent philosophical theory but rather aims to dissolve a particular philosophical tension felt by only some philosophers. The difficulties that arise in understanding the relation of thought and the world result only from adopting understandable but misleading assumptions about the rational structure of thought and the way thought needs a worldly input. Elsewhere he writes:

> I do not present the Myth of the Given and coherentism as two unsatisfying responses to a problem about thought's bearing on reality – as if philosophers came up with those views in order to deal with a problem that was on the philosophical agenda anyway. Rather, I use the uncomfortable oscillation between these two ways of thinking, in a framework in which they have come to seem the only possibilities, as a way to bring out why there might seem to be a problem about thought's bearing on reality in the first place. (2000: 334)

In broad outline, that tension arises from the following line of thought. Empirical content is portrayed by Kant to be the result of the interplay of two faculties. These are the faculties of "receptivity" and "spontaneity" responsible, respectively, for intuitions – brute experiential intake – and concepts. The fact that the faculty that contributes concepts is called "spontaneity" is significant. McDowell suggests that concepts are characterized by rational relations. And, according to Kant, "rational necessitation is not just compatible with freedom but constitutive of it. In a slogan, the space of reasons is the realm of freedom"

(McDowell 1994: 5). But emphasis on the freedom associated with conceptual judgements threatens to cut off empirical content from the world so that it degenerates into a "self-contained game", a "frictionless spinning in the void" (*ibid.*: 11). This is the danger of mere coherentism where the only constraint on judgement is coherence with other judgements.

The Myth of the Given seems an attractive way, in response to this worry, to provide an external constraint on thought. "The idea is that when we have exhausted all the available moves within the space of concepts, all the available moves from one conceptually organised item to another, there is still one more step we can take: namely, pointing to something that is simply received in experience" (*ibid.*: 6). This final step points out of the conceptual realm to something brutely given. McDowell suggests that this amounts to construing the space of reasons as more extensive than the space of concepts because the act of pointing is still to serve as a reason for belief. (McDowell owes the label "Myth of the Given" to Wilfrid Sellars, who uses it to characterize a form of foundationalism based on experiences that ground, but do not themselves depend on, other conceptualized beliefs (Sellars 1997).)

So described, the "Myth of the Given" is an instance of scheme–content, or scheme–Given, dualism. Thus one way of accommodating Kant's insight that thought depends in part on experiences or intuitions is, sadly, an instance of the dualism that Davidson correctly rejects. McDowell's key objection is simple. The only model we have of a reason for a belief is a relation in which both items related are already conceptualized. So if the final step in giving a reason for an empirical judgement is an extra-conceptual act of pointing, it will not sustain a *rational* friction between belief and the world. We will be not be responsible for the outermost impacts of the world on us, but that will not underpin a notion of getting the world *right*. "In effect the idea of the Given offers exculpations where we wanted justifications" (McDowell 1994: 8).

Thus both coherentism and the Myth of the Given achieve partial insights. Rejecting the Myth of the Given, Davidson advocates a coherentist position based on the claim that "nothing can count as a reason for holding a belief except another belief" and thus rejects any notion of an epistemic intermediary between belief and world (Davidson, quoted in McDowell 1994: 14). But the cost of this, according to McDowell, is to give up the notion that thought bears on the world. A subscriber to the Myth of the Given, on the other hand, can address the idea that there must be worldly input to empirical beliefs but fails to respect the argument that only conceptually structured items can play that role.

McDowell's suggestion to resolve this problem is subtly to balance respect for the Kantian slogan and for Davidson's criticism of the dualism of scheme and content. Thus, although he rejects the *dualism* of scheme and content, he does not reject the "duality" (cf. McDowell 1999: 88). That is, he is happy to talk of the faculties of receptivity and spontaneity but he denies that they can be understood in isolation from one another. It is impossible to adopt a stance outside one's conceptual scheme (or the "space of reasons" in McDowell's terminology) to chart the relation between it and the world each separately understood (cf. McDowell 1994: 34–6). In the case at hand, it is possible to understand the role of conceptualized experience in providing friction between beliefs and the world only "if we can achieve a firm grip on this thought: receptivity does not make an even notionally separable contribution to the co-operation" (*ibid*.: 9).

Lecture II:"The Unboundedness of the Conceptual"

Lecture II starts with the following summary of how things stand. For it not to seem mysterious that thought can bear on the world, or, as less therapeutic philosophers might say, for thought or empirical content to be possible in the first place, there must be a rational constraint between it and reality. Robert Brandom calls this condition for intentionality to be intelligible the "rational constraint constraint" (1998: 369). It can be met providing both that "experiences are receptivity in operation" and that "experiences themselves are already equipped with conceptual content" (*ibid*.: 25). This combination of "receptivity" and "spontaneity" meets the rational constraint constraint and thus eases philosophical wonder about how thought can have a bearing on reality. Experience thus plays a transcendental role and McDowell elsewhere accepts the label "transcendental empiricism" (McDowell 1998c: 405).

This suggestion for how to meet the rational constraint constraint turns, however, on a particular philosophical account of experience, which is not set out until Lecture VI of *Mind and World*. McDowell rejects a deep-rooted, Cartesian, view of experiences based on the argument from illusion. An experience can seem the same to a subject who has it whether it is genuine experience of, for example, a small cat or an optical illusion of such a cat. That qualitative similarity is used by Descartes as the basis for an argument for scepticism now called the "argument from illusion". But it also motivates the "highest common factor" account of experience: the content of an experience is what is common between the veridical and the illusory cases – perhaps a representation or image of a cat.

According to the highest common factor account, experiences are internal states of a subject: states of inner space. They cannot be relational states – states constituted by relations to external matters such as a real cat – because these are not shared by both genuine and illusory cases. McDowell, however, rejects this view and puts forward instead a "disjunctive" analysis. Experience is *either* of a mere appearance *or*, when things go well, of an external fact itself. The argument for this preference is not given until Lecture VI in *Mind and World*. On the highest common factor account, experience could never provide a subject with knowledge. But at this point in *Mind and World* the key idea is the idea that experience is a form of direct openness to the world itself and thus provides a rational link between reality and thought.

Thus when McDowell says that the "joint involvement of receptivity and spontaneity allows us to say that in experience one can take in how things are", this gestures towards the disjunctive account of experience. Furthermore, the idea that experience is a form of openness to the world requires that experience is a form of *conceptualized* uptake. One argument for this is the fact that the content of the experience is the same as the content of a judgement that it can prompt. Of course, sometimes a subject will not endorse the relevant judgement. (McDowell discusses the Muller–Lyer lines, which continue to look different even when one knows to distrust the experience (1994: 11).) But if a subject does endorse an experience in the corresponding judgement then the basis for the judgement – the experience – has the same content as the judgement. The judgement is not based on an *inference* from lesser information.

These points are summarized in the following important passage:

> In a particular experience in which one is not misled, what one takes in is *that things are thus and so*. *That things are thus and so* is the content of the experience, and it can also be the content of a judgement: it becomes the content of a judgement if the subject decides to take the experience at face value. So it is conceptual content. But *that things are thus and so* is also, if one is not misled, an aspect of the layout of the world: it is how things are. Thus the idea of conceptually structured operations of receptivity puts us in a position to speak of experience as openness to the layout of reality. Experience enables the layout of reality itself to exert a rational influence on what a subject thinks. (*Ibid*.: 26)

By construing experience as conceptualized, McDowell can identify the content of experience – when nothing has gone awry – with the same sorts of items that constitute the layout of reality. Experience has the kind of content that is characterized using a "that-clause" and that enables a harmony between it and the facts that collectively constitute the world.

Although McDowell claims that experience is conceptualized, and therefore belongs to the faculty of *spontaneity*, it is nonetheless passive. One is presented with visual experience in which concepts are already involved when one opens one's eyes. But the combination of spontaneity and passivity may suggest a tension. How can the same items – concepts – play both passive and active roles? McDowell stresses, however, that it is because the same capacities that are implicated in experience are also involved in active judgements that a subject can be counted a subject of experience. Only so can the subject be capable of genuinely judging, for example, that there is a red-coloured surface before them.

McDowell argues, following Sellars's rejection of the Myth of the Given, that such judgement requires a background of other beliefs about the world. Furthermore, "active empirical thinking takes place under a standing obligation to reflect about the credentials of the putatively rational linkages that govern it" (*ibid.*: 12). Thus the concepts in play in experience are themselves subject to revision, suggesting continuity in their roles in active judgement and passive experience.

To flesh out these claims about the continuity of the roles of concepts, McDowell considers *secondary* qualities because these are the most minimally integrated into our conception of the fabric of the world. If he can make his point for secondary qualities it should be more obvious for primary qualities. But even here it is the connection between the concepts when drawn into experience and when used in evolving active judgements that enables a subject to understand experiences as *glimpses* of an enduring world that exists independently of experience:

> Concepts of colour are only minimally integrated into the active business of accommodating one's thinking to the continuing deliverances of experience, and hence only minimally integrated into possible views of the world. Still, they are so integrated, even if only minimally. No subject could be recognised as having experiences of colour except against a background understanding that makes it possible for judgements endorsing such experiences to fit into her view of the world. She must be equipped with such things as the concept of visible surfaces of objects, and the concept of suitable conditions for telling what something's colour is by looking at it.   (*Ibid.*: 30)

Occasions when these concepts are drawn into merely "inner experience", such as the seeing of colours after a blow to the head, are derivative from their involvement in characterizing an "outer" world. Although McDowell thinks that one can have an understanding of secondary qualities only if one has an understanding of how they are experienced by a subject (e.g. a relation between being red and looking red) he does not construe the latter as an inner experience:

> It is one thing to gloss being red in terms of being such as to look red, and quite another to gloss it in terms of being such as to induce a certain "inner experience" in us. Note that "red" in "looking red" expresses a concept of "outer experience" no less than does "red" in "being red", in fact the very same concept.   (*Ibid.*: 31 n. 7)

If, by contrast, an analysis of colour terms started with "inner experiences", it is hard to see how that could generate a conception of properties, albeit with a phenomenal quality, located in objects in the world.

McDowell devotes a separate treatment to inner sense generally. He argues that judgements of sensations are also fully conceptualized and that these concepts are also, of necessity, used in third-person judgements. Thus to understand the concept of pain in the first person judgement "I am in pain" requires that one also understands that pain is a general type of state of affairs and one in which another subject can be. But, unlike secondary qualities, sensation concepts are not interconnected with other concepts in such a way as to suggest that such states exist independently of the instantiation of sensation concepts in experiences (e.g. pains).

This difference between judgements of inner and outer sense has to be handled with care, however. It is the basis for the following criticism by Michael Friedman:

> [T]he distinction between passive experience (concerning which we are simply "struck" one way or another, as it were) and active judgment (concerning which we have free choice) is not at all the same as the distinction between that which expresses constraint by an independent objective world and that which does not. The crucial question, in this regard, concerns rather how we distinguish between "inner" and "outer" sense. And McDowell's idea here, if I understand him correctly, is that passively received impressions become experiences of an objective world (and thus impressions of outer sense) only by being *taken as such* by the active faculty of understanding: by being subject, that is, to the perpetually revisable procedure through which the understanding integrates such impressions into an evolving world-conception.   (2002: 34–5)

McDowell responds to this by clarifying the connection between glimpses of the world and the standing requirement on a reasonable subject to reflect on his or her worldview:

But this does not fit the conception of experience I recommend. In my picture, actualizations of conceptual capacities in receptivity are already, in conforming to that specification, at least apparently revelatory of an objective world, and, when all goes well, actually so. They do not need to be turned into experiences with objective purport by being so taken. The point of invoking the perpetual obligation to rethink a world-view is to help make it intelligible that these "passively received impressions" already have objective purport - not to indicate a way in which intellectual activity can somehow make experiences of an objective world out of items that are in themselves less than that.   (McDowell 2002: 273)

Friedman argues that McDowell's account is idealist because the difference between inner states and worldly facts depends merely on what subjects do with their experiences. McDowell's reply is to stress that the phenomenology of outer sense shows it to involve glimpses of the world. The further connection to the reflective role of reason is a transcendental condition on such glimpses. But it does not explain how neutrally described experiences gain their worldly content. In other words, if idealism were separately motivated Friedman's point would be significant. But given the starting-point McDowell adopts, there is no reason to go against the everyday construal that some experiences reveal worldly facts while others are merely "inner" states. (McDowell also thinks that this construal of empirical experience is vital for the very idea of mental states having representational bearing. If one were to deny it then it would be mysterious that empirical content was possible at all.)

So far I have described McDowell's claim that experience can directly take in facts. What one can experience can be the case. In fact, half way through Lecture II, McDowell broadens this claim from experiences to thoughts. He comments that he finds it helpful to reflect on Wittgenstein's comment that: "When we say, and *mean*, that such-and-such is the case, we – and our meaning – do not stop anywhere short of the fact; but we mean: *this – is – so*" (Wittgenstein 1953: §95). McDowell glosses this:

in a style Wittgenstein would have been uncomfortable with: there is no ontological gap between the sort of thing one can mean, or generally the sort of thing one can think, and the sort of thing that can be the case. When one thinks truly, what one thinks *is* what is the case. So since the world is everything that is the case (as he himself once wrote), there is no gap between thought, as such, and the world. Of course thought can be distanced from the world by being false, but there is no distance from the world implicit in the very idea of thought. (1994: 27)

The close connection between what can be thought and what makes up the world might suggest a form of idealism. McDowell disarms this worry by distinguishing between acts of thinking and the thinkable contents. In equating facts and thoughts, he equates facts and thinkables, not facts and acts of thinking. Only the latter view would amount to idealism.

There is, however, a related way of expressing the worry that *Mind and World* is idealist. This is that by denying the Myth of the Given McDowell is deleting "an outer boundary that encloses the conceptual sphere" (*ibid*.: 34), beyond which the world of facts lies. McDowell again deploys the distinction between thinking and thinkables to argue that on his account it is possible to point outside the sphere of thinking at features of the world. But this is not a case of pointing outside the conceptual realm: the realm of thinkables. The view rejected here is a "sideways-on" picture (*ibid*.: 35). It is implicit in the idea that interpreting other people or languages is a matter of connecting a conceptual system and the world from outside that conceptual system. McDowell argues, by contrast, that it is only possible to understand a system as a system of concepts if one has already connected it to features of the world picked out in the same system. The ideas of a conceptual scheme and of the world are interdependent. (This point is developed at length in Part 1 of the Afterword to *Mind and World* (*ibid*.: 129–61).)

Talk of interpretation fits a view of the philosophy of language and thought dating back via Davidson to Quine and Wittgenstein. But McDowell also links this picture further back to Kant. He argues that Kant almost articulates his preferred view; almost but not quite because Kant does not keep a firm enough grip on the thought that receptivity and spontaneity do not make separable contributions to experience. While from the standpoint of empirical experience there is no separation, Kant also gives a further "transcendental story" in which there is. (Responding to criticism, McDowell (1998d) subsequently calls this a "transcendent story".) "In the transcendental perspective, receptivity figures as a susceptibility to a supersensible reality, a reality that is supposed to be independent of our conceptual activity in a stronger sense than any that fits the ordinary empirical world" (McDowell 1994: 41).

But this is, in effect, a reiteration of the Myth of the Given. Once the world is outside the conceptual sphere then it cannot play a rational role in constraining belief. But at the same time: "Once the supersensible is in the picture, its radical independence of our thinking tends to present itself as no more than the independence any genuine reality must have" (*ibid*.: 42). With the contrast with the supersensible in place, the empirical world is tainted with idealism because it is the product of an interaction with subjectivity, albeit off-stage. While *Mind and World* is broadly Kantian, McDowell recommends the post-Kantian German Idealists precisely because they remove the supersensible from their accounts while leaving the Kantian account of the conceptual structure of the empirical world.

Lecture III: "Non-conceptual Content"

So far McDowell has examined in detail the idea that experience is made up of both intuitions and concepts, the product of both receptivity and spontaneity. This is his suggestion for stepping off the seesaw of coherentism and the Myth of the Given. Having discussed Davidson's coherentism in Lecture I, Lecture III looks at the work of Gareth Evans, who plays the role of a subscriber to the Myth of the Given.

On Evans's account, experiences are non-conceptual. They are the product of an information system that is more primitive than the ability to make judgements or form beliefs. Because they are primitive, perceptual information systems are also shared by non-linguistic animals. Linguistic creatures can bring concepts to bear on non-conceptual experiences when they make judgements of experience. (In fact Evans restricts the notion of "experience" to creatures so capable. Other creatures merely enjoy perceptual informational states.)

Because experiences are non-conceptual on Evans's account, his account is a version of the Myth of the Given. McDowell argues therefore that it falls prey to the objection set out in Lecture I. The problem is this. Because experiences themselves are not conceptually shaped they lie outside the realm of spontaneity, responsible for concepts. Evans describes experiences as having content of a special non-conceptual variety. But McDowell suggests that because that content lies outside spontaneity it cannot provide a rational link and thus meet what Brandom calls the "rational constraint constraint", even though Evans's talk of non-conceptual *content* blurs that point:

> But the word "content" plays just the role ... to make it seem that we can recognise rational relations between experiences and judgements, so that we can say, as Evans does, that judgements of experience are "based upon" experience, even though these relations are supposed to hold across a boundary that encloses spontaneity... If these relations are to be genuinely recognizable as reason constituting, we cannot confine spontaneity within a boundary across which the relations are supposed to hold. The relations themselves must be able to come under the self-scrutiny of active thinking.   (McDowell 1994: 53)

This recapitulates the general claim that the only model of a rational link is one where both relata are conceptualized and thus that the link itself is subject to rational scrutiny.

McDowell suggests that one motivation for Evans's view of experience is that Evans takes experience to be more fine grained than the concepts that speakers typically possess. Evans offers the example of colour experience. He suggests that our experience can outstrip our conceptual repertoire because even if we master labels such as "red", "green" or even "burnt sienna", our experience can present us with detail as fine as individual lines on the spectrum. Thus it seems that experience can contain more detail than can be linguistically codified.

McDowell's response is to suggest that experience itself can equip a subject with concepts:

> But why should we accept that a person's ability to embrace colour within her conceptual thinking is restricted to concepts expressible by words like "red" or "green" and phrases like "burnt sienna"? It is possible to acquire the concept of a shade of colour, and most of us have done so. Why not say that one is thereby equipped to embrace shades of colour within one's conceptual thinking with the very same determinateness with which they are presented in one's visual experience, so that one's concepts can capture colours no less sharply than one's experience presents them? (*Ibid.*: 56)

When presented with a colour experience, a subject with the general concept of "shade of colour" can acquire a particular concept expressed with the demonstrative phrase "That colour!" or "That shade!". Such a concept is not linguistically codified but that need not preclude its being conceptual.

Some further conditions have to be met for it to count as conceptual. The recognitional capacity on which the concept depends needs to last longer than the experience that gives rise to it itself even if it is short lived:

> It is the conceptual content of such a recognitional capacity that can be made explicit with the help of a sample, something that is guaranteed to be available at the time of the experience with which the capacity sets in. Later in the life of the capacity it can be given linguistic expression again, if the course of experience is favourable; that is, if experience again, or still, presents one with a suitable sample. But even in the absence of a sample, the capacity goes on being exploitable as long as it lasts, in thoughts based on memory: thoughts that

are not necessarily capable of receiving an overt expression that fully
determines their content.   (*Ibid.*: 57–8)

As long as the capacity has some duration it can allow a particular experienced
shade of colour to play a role in reasoning, via inferences for example, and
thus count as genuinely conceptual. While assessing other arguments for non-
conceptual content – such as those based on the explanation of conceptual abilities – is outside the scope of this chapter, the idea of demonstrative concepts
can at least counter the most obvious phenomenological objection to the idea
that experience is conceptual.

A second motivation for Evans's account is that he can suggest continuity
between linguistic and non-linguistic creatures. Both can possess information
systems even though only linguistic creatures can let this feed into conceptual
judgement (and thus have "experiences" according to Evans, even though non-
conceptual). In advance of further discussion in Lecture VI, McDowell here
simply suggests instead that what we share with animals is perceptual sensitivity.
But we have a different form of it. Ours is "taken up into the ambit of the faculty of spontaneity" (*ibid.*: 64). It remains a task for the next lecture to defuse
an objection to this idea.

Lecture IV: "Reason and Nature"

Lectures I–III articulate McDowell's response to Kant's slogan "Thoughts
without content are empty, intuitions without concepts are blind". McDowell
suggests that both Davidson and Evans fail to see its significance in giving an
account of how thought can bear on reality. Evans realizes, unlike Davidson,
that thoughts have to be rationally responsive to experience ("intuitions" in
Kant's phrase), but because he takes experiences to be non-conceptual he cannot himself account for this. Davidson, unlike Evans, realizes that if experiences
are non-conceptual then they cannot stand in rational relations to thoughts, but
mistakenly assumes that a merely causal connection will do. Each has a cogent
argument against the other.

Lecture IV is the heart of *Mind and World*. In it, McDowell attempts to diag-
nose why neither philosopher adopts his own solution by "uncovering the presumably deep-rooted mental block that produces the uncomfortable situation"
(McDowell 1994: 69). His suggestion starts with the claim that the perceptual
sensitivity that animals have, their sentience, is a perfectly natural phenomenon.
But the suggestion that McDowell has so far defended is that, for linguistic
creatures, perceptual sensitivity is conceptually shaped. He now suggests that

this position is difficult to think of because we normally assume that nature and concepts lie on opposite sides of a deep divide.

In the following passage McDowell offers a diagnosis of the source of the perceived difficulty here:

> What is at work here is a conception of nature that can seem sheer common sense, though it was not always so; the conception I mean was made available only by a hard-won achievement of human thought at a specific time, the time of the rise of modern science. Modern science understands its subject matter in a way that threatens, at least, to leave it disenchanted, as Weber put the point in an image that has become a commonplace. The image marks a contrast between two kinds of intelligibility: the kind that is sought by (as we call it) natural science, and the kind we find in something when we place it in relation to other occupations of "the logical space of reasons", to repeat a suggested phrase from Wilfrid Sellars. If we identify nature with what natural science aims to make comprehensible, we threaten, at least, to empty it of meaning. By way of compensation, so to speak, we see it as the home of a perhaps inexhaustible supply of intelligibility of the other kind, the kind we find in a phenomenon when we see it as governed by natural law. *(Ibid.: 70–71)*

McDowell is not here attacking scientific method. Scientific method, and the self-conscious reflection that accompanies it, has been a genuine achievement of the modern era. But at the same time, the assumption that the disenchantment that has successfully underpinned scientific descriptions of the world also exhausts its nature is "not the educated common sense it represents itself as being; it is shallow metaphysics" (McDowell 1995: 164; 1998a: 182; cf. 1994: 82). McDowell uses the phrase "realm of law" to describe the kind of intelligibility found in the natural sciences in which events are explained by subsuming them under laws of nature. He suggests that in the "shallow" and scientistic metaphysical picture nature is simply equated with the realm of law and that this suggests a tension. If the realm of law exhausts nature, the deployment of concepts by the faculty of spontaneity (rooted in the space of reasons) looks unnatural. But this makes our own position in nature, as subjects able to exercise conceptual judgement, mysterious.

McDowell suggests that there are three styles of response to this difficulty:

- Bald naturalism, which aims to show how the space of reasons can be constructed from concepts that belong to the realm of law. Reductionist forms of contemporary naturalism such as Fodor's "representational theory of mind" fall into this category (Fodor 1987; McDowell 1994: 73).

- McDowell's favoured position, which affirms the genuine distinctness of the realm of law and space of reasons and "resists the characteristically modern conception according to which something's way of being natural is its position in the realm of law" (*ibid.*: 74).

- A position that also affirms the genuine distinctness of the realm of law and space of reasons but claims that the very same things satisfy both kinds of concepts. Davidson's non-reductive anomalous monism is such a position (Davidson 1980). Davidson agrees that the categories picked out in space of reasons (reasons, mental states, etc.) cannot be systematically mapped onto the categories of the realm of law (states of the brain or nervous system) because the former but not the latter is bound by the "constitutive principle of rationality". But at the same time, he advocates a token-identity theory of items instantiating both sets of concepts. Thus every mental event just is a physical event.

McDowell's rejection of the third position depends on the following argument:

> According to the ontological thesis, the items that instantiate the *sui generis* spontaneity-related concepts have a location in the realm of law. But the concepts are *sui generis* precisely in that it is not by virtue of their location in the realm of law that things instantiate those concepts. So if we go on equating something's place in nature with its location in the realm of law, we are debarred from holding that an experience has its conceptual content precisely as whatever natural phenomenon it is. (1994: 76)

The crux of the argument is the last sentence. I think that there are two ideas at work here. One is that Davidson's position precludes the idea that experiences have (conceptual) content as an essential feature, as "whatever natural phenomena they are". But a little later in *Mind and World* McDowell suggests that the problem is ideological not ontological (*ibid.*: 78 n. 8). The conceptual content of an experience, construed as an item in the space of reasons, looks supernatural if the natural is taken to be exhausted by the realm of law. That is to say, Davidson can accommodate the physical or neurological properties of experiential states as part of nature (since the states are construed as physical items in his token-identity theory) but not their content-laden or psychological properties.

McDowell thus rejects the third position and assumes that the first position, bald naturalism, should be avoided as simply opting out of this area of philosophy. He suggests that it can seem that the only other available response is a form of "rampant platonism", which is his label for a position that pictures "the space of reasons as an autonomous structure – autonomous in that it is constituted independently of anything specifically human" (*ibid*.: 77). This would involve a "peculiarly bifurcated" account in which human beings had both animal natures but also supernatural capacities to resonate to a structure that is wholly independent of anything human (cf. *ibid*.: 78, 88). But, again, this requires taking for granted that the natural is limited to what can be captured within the realm of law.

That assumption can, however, be rejected providing one can come to construe the role of concepts, both in experience and in active judgement, as "capturing patterns in a way of living" (*ibid*.: 78). McDowell suggests that the best way to accept this alternative to the scientist view that causes the tension is to think about Aristotle's account of ethics and the notion of "second nature" (*ibid*.: 84). This is the idea that human nature contains, in addition to our animal biology (first nature), further capacities and abilities that can be brought out through education and training. Central to this is the ability to respond to reasons. This is natural but requires initiation. Further, reasons are construed in accordance with naturalized platonism as only partially independent of us. Thinking about ethical judgement is a step towards a proper understanding of how the natural realm in general is not completely independent of human subjectivity.

Aristotle takes for granted the idea that moral judgements answer to external constraints that come into view to those who, through suitable education, have attained an ethical standpoint. The features of that standpoint and the judgements made from it do not need to be given an explanation or justification in terms that are understandable without adopting that standpoint. McDowell thus rejects accounts of Aristotle that attempt to explain moral judgement through its contribution to human flourishing, with that latter notion cashed out in non-moral terms. In the terminology above, such attempts are forms of bald naturalism.

McDowell suggests instead that a proper education furnishes a subject with a natural ability to recognize the demands that, for example, kindness makes in a particular circumstance. Education moulds the practical wisdom of a subject and this includes shaping their motivation. But the underlying idea is that education opens the subject's eyes to moral requirements: "The picture is that ethics involves requirements of reason that are there whether we know it or not, and our eyes are opened to them by the acquisition of 'practical wisdom'" (McDowell 1994: 79). Thus education enables a subject to be sensitive to a further area of the space of reasons. Such sensitivity is natural but because it requires education, it is a form of *second nature*.

McDowell concedes that Aristotle's own confidence in the specific ethical outlook he takes for granted might be a form of intellectual smugness (*ibid*.: 81). But, if so, that is not a necessary feature of a broadly Aristotelian form of moral realism. Given that ethical thinking belongs to the space of reasons, it is under a standing injunction to reflect on its own credentials, on what it takes for granted and what counts as a good reason. It is in this sense in the same boat as empirical thinking. While there is no possibility of stepping outside a moral standpoint to validate or justify it in neutral terms, judgements within it can be scrutinized using other judgements. (In Otto Neurath's simile, a sailor "overhauls his ship whilst it is afloat" (*ibid*.: 81).)

A key element of this account of moral judgement is that, once a subject has attained an appropriate second nature, he or she is capable of responding to demands that are independent of the subject even if the moral world is not taken to be understandable independently of subjective responses to it. Moral reasons are thus independent of moral subjects, if not "brutely independent". This calls to mind a form of platonism but if so it is not rampant platonism but naturalized platonism (*ibid*.: 83). It is only semi-autonomous.

McDowell suggests that this Aristotelian picture of moral judgement and second nature can help connect our ability to use concepts and respond to reasons to the natural world. With it in mind, then, it is possible to reject the conflation of the picture of the world that natural science successfully articulates with the totality of what is in nature. The overall argument of *Mind and World* is summarized thus:

> In these lectures so far, I have taken perceptual experience as an object lesson, in order to describe a kind of predicament we tend to fall into when we think about aspects of the human condition. I promised to try to uncover a deep-rooted but, as we can come to realise, non-compulsory influence on our thinking that accounts for the predicament. I have now introduced my candidate for that role: the naturalism that leaves nature disenchanted. We tend to be forgetful of the very idea of second nature. I am suggesting that if we can recapture that idea, we can keep nature as it were partially enchanted, but without lapsing into pre-scientific superstition or a rampant platonism. This makes room for a conception of experience that is immune to the philosophical pitfalls I have described.
>
> We need to recapture the Aristotelian idea that a normal mature human being is a rational animal, but without losing the Kantian idea

that rationality operates freely in its own sphere. The Kantian idea is reflected in the contrast between the organisation of the space of reasons and the structure of the realm of natural law. Modern naturalism is forgetful of second nature; if we try to preserve the Kantian thought that reason is autonomous within the framework of that kind of naturalism, we disconnect our rationality from our animal being, which is what gives us our foothold in nature.   (*Ibid.*: 85)

Lecture V: "Action, Meaning and the Self"

Lecture V gathers together three main themes that I shall sketch only briefly here. The first and third concern Kant. The second, with which I shall start, concerns Wittgenstein.

McDowell suggests that the Aristotelian picture of ethical judgements set out in Lecture IV is a form of "naturalized platonism" because moral judgement is responsive to "dictates of reason [that] are there anyway" (McDowell 1994: 91). The form of platonism is "naturalized" not "rampant" because the rational structure of moral reasons is not thought of as utterly independent of human subjectivity. Rampant platonism is one of Wittgenstein's targets in the *Philosophical Investigations*, and McDowell suggests that "naturalized platonism" is a good label for the position he advocates in its place.

McDowell suggests that Wittgenstein is concerned with a fundamental dualism of norm, or reason, and nature. The problem is to find how norms can be reconciled with, or fit into, nature. Conventional modern philosophy is concerned with dualisms that are derivatives of this one, such as between subject and object, thought and world. But conventional philosophy approaches these in a characterisatically constructive way:

> Ordinary modern philosophy addresses its derivative dualisms in a characteristic way. It takes its stand on one side of a gulf it aims to bridge, accepting without question the way its target dualism conceives the chosen side. Then it constructs something as close as possible to the conception of the other side that figured in the problems, out of materials that are unproblematically available where it has taken its stand. Of course there no longer seems to be a gulf, but the result is bound to look more or less revisionist.   (*Ibid.*: 94)

This passage, reminiscent of Strawson's (1992) account of conventional philosophical method, highlights the kind of objection McDowell has to taking philosophy to confront a dualism of mind and world. The objection turns on the idea of accepting the terms of the dualism and then trying to bridge the gulf opened up. This same approach is taken by those philosophers who interpret Wittgenstein as defending a radical and revisionary view of meaning. Such commentators take for granted a distinction between norms and nature. The norms are construed as requiring a form of "rampant platonism", such that "the rational structure within which meaning comes into view is independent of anything merely human, so that the capacity of our minds to resonate to it looks occult or magical" (McDowell 1994: 92). Nature is construed as "disenchanted": completely describable by resources from the realm of law. Given the terms of this dualism, the normativity of meaning appears to be *supernatural*. Constructive philosophy is then needed to show how, using only resources from the realm of law, something that approximates to our pre-philosophical view of meaning can be rebuilt and thus accommodated within what is taken to be natural.

McDowell, by contrast, argues that Wittgenstein's rejection of substantial philosophy should be respected. What is needed is the rejection of the presuppositions of the dualism. If nature can be expanded beyond the area described by natural science then there will be no need to see the normativity of meaning as supernatural or spooky. This expansion requires abandoning the ungrounded metaphysical assumption that nature is limited to the disenchanted realm of law. Thus the project of *Mind and World* is in part therapeutic: diagnosing resistance to ideas that can otherwise ease philosophical tensions.

The first and last main themes of Lecture V concern Kant. First, although *Mind and World* mainly concerns philosophical difficulties about the place in nature of experience, McDowell suggests that this is merely one instance of a more general phenomenon. The same philosophical difficulties also face an account of action because movements appear to be a part of nature, narrowly interpreted as events in the realm of law, but need to be conceptually shaped to be actions. "Kant says 'Thoughts without content are empty, intuitions without concepts are blind'. Similarly, intentions without overt activity are idle, and movements of limbs without concepts are mere happenings, not expressions of agency" (McDowell 1994: 89). The account of action and its dependence on intentions and movements runs parallel to the account of experience and its dependence on concepts and intuitions. Actions should be thought of as aspects of our second nature: a nature that also involves conceptual abilities. Thus nature should be thought of as itself capable of containing agency without attempting, with bald naturalism, to reduce agency to a mechanism described in natural scientific terms.

The third theme of Lecture V is an account of why the lack of a notion of second nature distorts Kant's otherwise insightful account of mind and world.

Lecture II has already suggested that Kant combines insight about the nature of the empirical world with a "transcendental framework" that distorts that. Lecture V now suggests that this flows from Kant's overly narrow conception of nature, lacking second nature.

Elsewhere McDowell credits Kant with the realization that the world cannot be, as Hume seems to think, "an ineffable lump, devoid of structure" (McDowell 1995: 160). Instead "an acceptable world-picture consists of articulable, conceptually structured representations. Their acceptability resides in their knowably mirroring the world; that is, representing it as it is" (*ibid.*). But if so, McDowell argues, "we cannot suppose [with Hume] that intelligible structure has completely emigrated from the world ... we have to suppose that the world has an intelligible structure matching the structure in the space of *logos*" (*ibid.*). It cannot, after all, be independent of the space of meaningful thought. True judgements can be taken to mirror the world. "But mirroring cannot be *both* faithful, so that it adds nothing in the way of intelligible order, *and* such that in moving from what is mirrored to what does the mirroring, one moves from what is brutely alien to the space of *logos* to what is internal to it" (*ibid.*: 161). Thus McDowell credits Kant with the realization that the world must itself possess the kind of structure picked out by concepts. It must reflect the space of reasons as well as the realm of law: "Kant – to resort to a thumbnail caricature – established that the world ... cannot be constitutively independent of the space of concepts, the space where subjectivity has its being" (McDowell 1991: 156).

But, according to McDowell at least, this correct conclusion is confusingly combined with a transcendent story. Why? The most explicit account McDowell gives is in the following passage:

> Against Hume, Kant aims to regain for nature the intelligibility of law, but not the intelligibility of meaning. For Kant, nature is the realm of law and therefore devoid of meaning. And given such a conception of nature, genuine spontaneity cannot figure in descriptions of actualizations of natural powers as such. (McDowell 1994: 97)

So far this seems to undermine the claim, quoted above, that Kant realized that the world "cannot be constitutively independent of the space of concepts". But that impression is modified as the passage in *Mind and World* continues:

> The point here is one of some delicacy. For Kant, the ordinary empirical world, which includes nature as the realm of law, is not external to the conceptual. In view of the connection between the conceptual and the kind of intelligibility that belongs to meaning, I have

suggested that defending that Kantian thought requires a partial re-enchantment of nature … But it does not require us to rehabilitate the idea that there is meaning in the fall of a sparrow or the movement of the planets, as there is meaning in a text. It is a good teaching of modernity that the realm of law is as such devoid of meaning; its constituent elements are not linked to one another by the relations that constitute the space of reasons. But if our thinking about the natural stops at an appreciation of that point, we cannot properly comprehend the capacity of experience to take in even the meaningless occurrences that constitute the realm of law. We cannot satisfactorily splice spontaneity and receptivity together in our conception of experience, and that means we cannot exploit the Kantian thought that the realm of law, not just the realm of meaningful doings, is not external to the conceptual. The understanding – the very capacity that we bring to bear on texts – must be involved in our taking in of mere meaningless happenings.

Kant's lack of a pregnant notion of second nature explains why the right conception of experience cannot find a firm position in his thinking. *(Ibid.*: 97)

This quotation suggests that the re-enchantment of nature is broader than just the recognition of second nature: our ability as rational subjects to have our eyes opened to normative relations. The suggestion is that extra-human nature is also re-enchanted even if not to the extent of furnishing meaning in the fall of a sparrow. But the fact that nature is constitutively apt for conceptualization suggests again the worry of idealism, which might be put as follows. If experience is always already conceptualized and if experience is – at least when appearances are not misleading – a form of openness to the world, then the world itself is always already conceptualized. This may or may not be a serious worry. McDowell himself presses the idea that the world is a world of facts and thus has conceptual structure unproblematically. But if so, what of the things that make up the facts?

Lecture V also contains a further suggestion that I will simply note. McDowell suggests that the lack of an account of second nature also explains why Kant's account of the self is unsatisfactory. Kant argues that there is an essential connection between consciousness of the world and self-consciousness. Being able to take one's experiences to be glimpses of an outer world requires that one can also self-ascribe the experiences. He says that "I think" must be able to "accompany all my representations". But, rejecting Descartes's objectification of the "I", Kant argues that the "I" in "I think" is merely a formal notion. It does not pick out a substantial mental entity that persists through time and is, at best, merely a disembodied point of view on the world.

McDowell thinks that this is unsatisfactory, not least because it provides no account of what connects a set of glimpses of the world as belonging to one "I" and not another. Why should we not instead think of the "I" as referring to a *person* capable of being in and moving through the world in both space and time? On this more natural view the subjective aspect to which Kant appeals is an abstraction from an embodied state, not the building block from which such a substantial notion can be built. But to take McDowell's more relaxed view requires taking as basic the idea of a "singled out tract of a life" (1994: 103). And this requires seeing a conceptually structured connected set of actions and experiences as part of nature, which is not possible for Kant without a conception of human second nature as both natural and conceptually structured.

Lecture VI: "Rational and Other Animals"

The final lecture has two main topics. The first is brief: the rejection of a Cartesian "highest common factor" model of experience that I discussed above (Lecture II). It will suffice to note that McDowell here presses the idea that with the disjunctive view in play, the motivation for scepticism falls away. A highest common factor model underpins scepticism because what is available in experience is the same whether it is veridical or illusory. So understood, experience cannot equip a subject with perceptual knowledge. But with a disjunctive model available there is no reason to think that experience "cannot constitute ... having a state of affairs directly manifest" (McDowell 1994: 113).

Of course, if scepticism were independently motivated, a sceptic might press questions about how one might know in particular cases whether one had knowledge. But if the argument for scepticism turns on the faulty account of experience then the availability of the alternative should be enough to rule out such scepticism. "[T]he aim here is not to answer sceptical questions, but to begin to see how it might be intellectually respectable to ignore them, to treat them as unreal, in the way that common sense has always wanted" (*ibid*.: 113).

The main business of Lecture VI, however, returns to the second motivation for Evans's account of experience discussed above (Lecture III). It concerns the status of non-linguistic experience. McDowell resists Evans's idea that linguistic and non-linguistic creatures share the same sort of information systems. There is no common ingredient. But if linguistic creatures have perceptual systems that are conceptually structured, what is common between such creatures and non-linguistic animals?

McDowell borrows a distinction from Gadamer to provide an answer to this. According to Gadamer, animals' lives answer to mere biological factors. They do not respond to rational features of the space of reasons. But "a life that is structured only in that way is led not in the world, but only in an environment" (*ibid.*: 115). This is not, however, to deny them perceptual sensitivity. That is displayed by their ability to move within their environment in accordance with biological needs. This suggests that they have a kind of subjectivity: a proto-subjectivity. Just as McDowell denies that animals' perception amounts to awareness of an outer world, so he denies that if animals can experience pain, for example, this constitutes awareness of an inner world. While animals cannot have pains in the way that inhabitants of the space of reasons do, this is not to say that that "the concepts of pain or fear … can get a grip only where there is understanding, and thus full fledged subjectivity" (*ibid.*: 120).

Developing conceptual capacities enables creatures to graduate from responses to biological factors to being able to make decisions in a "free, distanced orientation". This repeats the connection between concepts and freedom made in Lecture I. It enables a world to come into view. But this raises the question of how this new perspective is achieved. In the case of human beings, McDowell suggests that the concept of second nature is enough. It is natural that a human being can be initiated into being at home in the space of reasons and thus living their lives in a world. But he rejects the idea that an account can be given of this process in such a way that the space of reasons is reduced to the mere animal. That would be a matter of bald naturalism, which has already been rejected.

The lectures that make up *Mind and World* end with the following words:

> a natural language, the sort of language into which human beings are first initiated, serves as a repository of tradition, a store of historically accumulated wisdom about what is a reason for what. The tradition is subject to reflective modification that inherits it. Indeed, a standing obligation to engage in critical reflection is itself part of the inheritance. But if an individual human being is to realize her potential of taking her place in that succession, which is the same thing as acquiring a mind, the capacity to think and act intentionally, at all, the first thing that needs to happen is for her to be initiated into a tradition as it stands.   (*Ibid.*: 126)

This may look like a form of conservatism. But as McDowell repeats, there is a standing obligation on reason to scrutinize the rational links that constitute reasons. But that does not mean that everything can be questioned at the same time. Without tradition there is mere babble rather than meaningful utterance.

"Even a thought that transforms a tradition must be rooted in the tradition that it transforms" (*ibid.*: 187). This perhaps explains the philosophical approach taken throughout: couching an innovative philosophical position in the language and ideas of the philosophical canon.

References

Brandom, R. 1998. "Perception and Rational Constraint". *Philosophy and Phenomenological Research* **58**, 369–74.

Davidson, D. 1980. *Essays on Actions and Events*. Oxford: Oxford University Press.

Davidson, D. 1983. "A Coherence Theory of Truth and Knowledge". In *Kant oder Hegel*, D. Heinrich (ed.), 423–38. Stuttgart: Klett-Cotta.

Davidson, D. 1984. "On the Very Idea of a Conceptual Scheme". In *Inquiries into Truth and Interpretation*, 183–98. Oxford: Oxford University Press.

Fodor, J. A. 1987. *Psychosemantics*. Cambridge, MA: MIT Press.

Friedman, M. 2002. "Exorcising the Philosophical Tradition". In *Reading McDowell*, N. Smith (ed.), 25–57. London: Routledge.

Kant, I. 1933. *Critique of Pure Reason*, N. Kemp Smith (trans.). London: Macmillan.

LePore, E. 1986. *Truth and Interpretation: Perspectives on the Philosophy of Donald Davidson*. Oxford: Blackwell.

McDowell, J. 1991. "Intentionality and Interiority in Wittgenstein". In *Meaning Scepticism*, K. Puhl (ed.), 148–69. Berlin: de Gruyter. Reprinted in McDowell (1998a), 297–321.

McDowell, J. 1994. *Mind and World*. Cambridge, MA: Harvard University Press.

McDowell, J. 1995. "Two Sorts of Naturalism". In *Virtues and Reasons: Philippa Foot and Moral Theory, Essays in Honour of Philippa Foot*, R. Hursthouse, G. Lawrence & W. Quinn (eds), 149–79. Oxford: Clarendon Press. Reprinted in McDowell (1998a), 167–97.

McDowell, J. 1998a. *Mind, Value and Reality*. Cambridge, MA: Harvard University Press.

McDowell, J. 1998b. "Précis of *Mind and World*". *Philosophy and Phenomenological Research* **58**, 365–8.

McDowell, J. 1998c. "Reply to Commentators". *Philosophy and Phenomenological Research* **58** (1998), 403–31.

McDowell, J. 1998d. "Having the World in View: Sellars, Kant, and Intentionality" (The Woodbridge Lectures 1997). *Journal of Philosophy* **95**, 431–91.

McDowell, J. 1999. "Scheme–Content Dualism and Empiricism". In *The Philosophy of Donald Davidson*, L. E. Hahn (ed.), 87–104. Chicago, IL: Open Court.

McDowell, J. 2000a. "Comments". *Journal of the British Society for Phenomenology* **31**, 330–43.

McDowell, J. 2002. "Responses". In *Reading McDowell*, N. Smith (ed.), 269–305. London: Routledge.

Sellars, W. 1997. *Empricism and the Philosophy of Mind*. Cambridge, MA: Harvard University Press.

Strawson, P. F. 1992. *Analysis and Metaphysics*. Oxford: Oxford University Press.

Wittgenstein, L. 1953. *Philosophical Investigations*. Oxford: Blackwell.

Further reading

The best way to try to understand *Mind and World* is to look at critical commentaries, especially those with replies by McDowell himself. The journal *Philosophy and Phenomenological Research* **58** (1998) contains a number of critical responses as well as a précis by McDowell of *Mind and World*. Nicholas Smith (ed.), *Reading McDowell* (London: Routledge, 2002) is a substantial edited collection that includes McDowell's responses. Marcus Willaschek (ed.), *John McDowell: Reasons and Nature: Lecture and Colloquium in Münster 1999* (Munster: Lit, 2000) contains an essay by McDowell and responses: "Experiencing the World", in Willaschek, *John McDowell*, 3–17, and "Responses", in Willaschek, *John McDowell*, 93–117.

McDowell's papers

Most of McDowell's free-standing papers were collected into two volumes in 1998:

McDowell, J. 1998. *Meaning, Knowledge and Reality*. Cambridge, MA: Harvard University Press.

McDowell, J. 1998. *Mind, Value and Reality*. Cambridge, MA: Harvard University Press.

Perhaps the most important free-standing papers are:

McDowell, J. 1977. "On the Sense and Reference of a Proper Name". *Mind* **86**, 159–85.

McDowell, J. 1979. "Virtue and Reason". *Monist* **62**, 331–50.

McDowell, J. 1982. "Criteria, Defeasibility and Knowledge". *Proceedings of the British Academy* **68**, 455–79.

McDowell, J. 1984. "Wittgenstein on Following a Rule". *Synthese* **58**, 325–63.

McDowell, J. 1986. "Singular Thought and the Extent of Inner Space". In *Subject Thought and Context*, P. Pettit & J. McDowell (eds), 137–68. Oxford: Clarendon Press.

McDowell, J. 1995. "Knowledge and the Internal". *Philosophy and Phenomenological Research* **55**, 877–93.

McDowell, J. 1998. "Having the World in View: Sellars, Kant, and Intentionality" (The Woodbridge Lectures 1997). *Journal of Philosophy* **95**, 431–91.

McDowell, J. 2000. "Towards Rehabilitating Objectivity". In *Rorty and His Critics*, R. B. Brandom (ed.), 109–23. Oxford: Blackwell.

Secondary texts

There are at present two book-length discussions of McDowell (and others in press): Maximilian de Gaynesford, *John McDowell* (Cambridge: Polity, 2004) focuses mainly on *Mind and World*, and Tim Thornton, *John McDowell* (Chesham: Acumen, 2004) charts the threads of McDowell's philosophy that feed into *Mind and World*.

Index